Reinventing Democrats

Reinventing Democrats

The Politics of Liberalism from Reagan to Clinton

Kenneth S. Baer

UNIVERSITY PRESS OF KANSAS

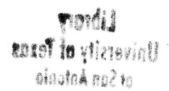

Published by the University Press of Kansas (Lawrence, Kansas 66049), which was organized by the Kansas Board of Regents and is operated and funded by Emporia State University, Fort Hays State University, Kansas State University, Pittsburg State University, the University of Kansas, and Wichita State University

Library of Congress Cataloging-in-Publication Data

Baer, Kenneth S., 1972–

Reinventing democrats : the politics of liberalism from Reagan to Clinton / Kenneth S. Baer.

p.   cm.

Includes bibliographical references and index.

ISBN 0-7006-1009-X (cloth : alk. paper)

1. Democratic Party (U.S.)   2. Liberalism—United States. 3. United States—Politics and government—1981–1989.   4. United States—Politics and government—1989–   I. Title.

JK2316.B28   2000

324.2736'09'048—dc21   99-43434

British Library Cataloguing in Publication Data is available.

Printed in the United States of America

10 9 8 7 6 5 4 3 2 1

The paper used in this publication meets the minimum requirements of the American National Standard for Permanence of Paper for Printed Library Materials Z39.48-1984.

TO MY PARENTS

*For whom no sacrifice is too great
and to whom all credit is due*

Contents

Acknowledgments

Although there is only one name that appears on the cover, there are many people whose help has been invaluable in writing this book. This book grew out of a doctoral dissertation I wrote while a student at Oxford University. For the chance to even embark on this project, I am truly indebted to the Thouron Award—especially Sir John, Tiger, and Jane Thouron—for having enough faith to provide me with the extraordinary opportunity to live and study in England. Once I was there, the Warden and Fellows of Nuffield College not only granted me a funded studentship to continue my work but also provided an ideal setting in which to complete it. Additionally, a Pembroke College Dean of Graduates Research Award helped fund an early research trip to the United States.

At Oxford, the participants in the Graduate Workshop in American Politics offered incisive comments and suggestions during the early stages of the manuscript. Similarly, during the entire life of this project, people on both sides of the Atlantic provided their thoughts on the subject and allowed me to pick their brains. Thanks are due to Nigel Bowles, Gillian Peele, Steve Gillon, Philip Klinkner, Alan Brinkley, Gary Hart, Joel Kotkin, Mary Frances Berry, Jason Duckworth, Andrei Cherny, and Eliza Newlin Carney. Special thanks are due to my two doctoral examiners, Alan Ware and Nelson Polsby, both of whom were generous in offering their advice on how to turn the dissertation into a book and were perhaps equally generous in passing me. Gratitude is also due to Nicol Rae and Hugh Davis Graham, whose comments were critical in guiding me in the writing of this book.

Tom Sugrue continued to offer advice and read drafts, even though no longer bound by the Penn History Department to do so. Fred Siegel was a constant help, plying me with helpful articles, insights, and even edits along the way. Adam Sheingate appeared at the very end of my time at Oxford and gave the manuscript a thorough reading and continued his editing chores as I prepared the manuscript for publication. In addition, all three of these scholars helped me navigate the world of publishing; their help was most appreciated. When presented with the challenge of reshaping the manuscript into a book, I was fortunate to be able to draw on the talents of Josh Tyrangiel and especially Peter Spiegel (my very first editor), two journalists with an ability to rehabilitate just about any sentence plus a healthy understanding of academic discourse.

I have to thank Ken Smukler and Frank Luntz for introducing me to practical politics, and John Saler for taking me to my first Democratic Leadership Council (DLC) meeting, as well as for helping to arrange many of my first interviews. Also, I must thank all those listed in the bibliography who allowed me to interview them; their cooperation was crucial to researching this topic.

As even a cursory read of the text will show, the cooperation of the DLC was central. Foremost, I must thank Al From for providing me with access to his organization's private archives, as well as allowing me to become, at times, a permanent fixture in the DLC offices. The whole staffs of the DLC and the Progressive Policy Institute were equally hospitable, and their hospitality did not go unappreciated. Of this group, I especially have to thank Chuck Alston, Debbie Cox, Debbie Boylan, and Steven Nider, as well as Simon Rosenberg and Jamie Daves, both of whom went above and beyond any call of duty or of friendship in offering assistance too multitudinous to mention in detail.

I thank the Democratic National Committee for allowing me access to its collection, and Steve Boyd for helping me to procure it. Douglas Thurman and his staff at the National Archives, Office of Presidential Libraries; the staff at the Rhodes House Library and Social Studies Faculty Library at Oxford; the staff at the Van Pelt Library of the University of Pennsylvania; and the staff at the Gelman Library at George Washington University all provided appreciated assistance. Finally, I was fortunate to have Michael Baratz as a research assistant who helped me dig for articles and photographs as the deadline approached. I was equally fortunate to have a very understanding boss who gave me time off to complete this book.

I am truly blessed to have an extended family that does not mind offering a bed, desk, car, or hot meal to someone, even if they are not sure exactly what he is doing. Susan and Arnold Baskies lent cars and tape recorders when the occasion demanded it. Randi and Jay Halbert provided accommodation when I ventured to New York. My grandparents kept me stocked with baked goods. But no one matched the sustained generosity of Matthew, Alison, Amy, Fred, and Naomi Glaser, who, by always having a bed—and office—ready for me, made the Washington part of my research logistically possible and thoroughly enjoyable.

It is perhaps not a coincidence that in German, *shafer* means "shepherd," for in his role as my doctoral supervisor, Professor Byron Shafer (without resorting to a crook or the big dog often at his side) ably steered me, by way of pointed comments and detailed advice, from idea to dissertation, from degree to book. I was truly fortunate to find, thousands of miles from the United States, someone with not only a serious scholarly interest in and command of American politics but also an enthusiasm for how it works in practice and for those wishing to study it.

Part of his guidance was steering me to the University Press of Kansas. There, I was in the able hands of Fred Woodward, who never failed to answer my questions or offer support, and Melinda Wirkus, who guided the book through production. Once the book was produced, Susan Schott worked assiduously to promote it, and for that, I thank her.

Finally, there are not enough pages or words to thank my parents. They offered all the kinds of help described above, and more that is simply indescribable.

Abbreviations

ADA	Americans for Democratic Action
AFL-CIO	American Federation of Labor–Congress of Industrial Organizations
AIPAC	American-Israel Public Affairs Committee
CDM	Coalition for a Democratic Majority
CDV	Coalition for Democratic Values
CIA	Central Intelligence Agency
CPE	Committee on Party Effectiveness
DLC	Democratic Leadership Council
DNC	Democratic National Committee
DPC	Democratic Policy Commission
EITC	earned income tax credit
EPA	Environmental Protection Agency
ERA	Equal Rights Amendment
NAFTA	North American Free Trade Agreement
NDC	New Democrat Coalition
NDN	New Democrat Network
NEA	National Education Association
NES	National Election Studies
NHDC	National House Democratic Caucus
OPEC	Organization of Petroleum Exporting Countries
OSHA	Occupational Safety and Health Administration
PAC	political action committee
PF	Progressive Foundation
PPI	Progressive Policy Institute
SALT	Strategic Arms Limitation Talks
SLC	Southern Legislative Conference
STEP	Super Tuesday Education Project

Introduction

EVER SINCE Woodrow Wilson revived the tradition of reporting in person on the state of the Union to Congress, the yearly address has become a celebrated political ritual. Each year, a president makes the trip down Pennsylvania Avenue to deliver a speech on the nation's progress and on the coming year's agenda. Heavy with policy, these speeches are usually unmemorable. Yet at times the words match the ceremony of the event. Who can forget the "four freedoms" outlined by Franklin Roosevelt in 1941? Perhaps it is this potential for history, or perhaps the excitement of the coming policymaking year, that has made this address so eagerly anticipated. During an election year, the stakes are higher, and the anticipation is understandably greater.

On one such occasion, the president of the United States took his position at the rostrum in the House of Representatives chamber. Behind him sat the Republican Speaker of the House, and in one of the first rows in front of him was the Republican Senate majority leader. The president began his speech by, unsurprisingly, affirming that the state of the Union was strong. He celebrated the growth of the economy; the creation of new businesses and new jobs; the decline in the welfare rolls and in the crime, poverty, and teen pregnancy rates; and the prevailing peace. Then, in laying out his thoughts on how the country could best confront its future problems, the president slowly and clearly proclaimed: "The era of big government is over."

One would imagine that at this point, the members of the Republican congressional majority would leap to their feet with applause, relishing the accomplishments of this president, and especially his clear exposition of a belief that, in one form or another, has been central to their party's thinking for at least a century. Yet the Republicans sat sourly in their seats, for there was one problem with this scenario. The president speaking these words in 1996 was a Democrat: Bill Clinton.

He was the man who had led the Democratic Party in capturing the White House for the first time in twelve years. And ten months after this speech, he became the first Democratic president to win reelection to a second full term since Franklin Roosevelt in 1936.

Indeed, this statement, which has received wide attention and analysis, was not simply a rhetorical flourish. It was not some odd historical side note. Nor was it a craven attempt to mimic the GOP. Rather, this sentence, and the entire speech in which it was spoken, marked a profound change in the Democratic Party. A party that for the past thirty years had been seen as profligate "tax-and-spenders," reflexive defenders of federal governmental programs, pacifist isolationists, and advocates of an active social liberalism now had a president who championed the reinvention of government, welfare reform, fiscal restraint, economic growth, free trade, mainstream values, and an internationalist foreign policy. A party that had seen only one of its nominees elected to the presidency during this time now had a leader who had won the White House once and was poised to do it again.

This transformation did not happen overnight. Nor was it the result of a radical change in the condition of the country or in the electorate. Rather, this new public philosophy, and the electoral success apparently tied to it, was the product of a conscious and sustained effort by a group of "New Democrats" and their most important organizational form, the Democratic Leadership Council (DLC). Formed in the aftermath of the 1984 election by a group of elected officials who believed that the Democratic Party was in danger of marginalization and even extinction, the DLC argued that the party had to craft a mainstream public philosophy that had wide electoral appeal.

With the election of Clinton, the DLC's former chairman, to the presidency, the New Democrats have seen many of their ideas become national policy and some of their most prominent members enter the presidential cabinet and staff. As a result, the DLC and New Democrats in and around the organization have become the principal rival to the national party's dominant liberal faction. The appeal of New Democratic policymaking and politics to key parts of the electorate has strengthened the Democratic Party nationally at the expense of the Republicans. In short, over the past decade, the DLC and the New Democrats have become one of the most influential forces in the Democratic Party and in American politics.

Indeed, some pundits and scholars view Clinton's use of the New Democratic public philosophy to reposition the Democratic Party in the eyes of the electorate as his most substantive legacy. "Clinton, I think, will . . . be remembered for reforming the Federal Government and for reshaping his party," judged Jacob Weisberg.[1] The 2000 elections will speak to the accuracy of this statement, but already we know that any Republican standard-bearer will have to challenge the Democratic nominee on an altered political terrain where the Democrats can claim to have balanced the budget, grown the economy, reformed welfare, and reduced crime. No matter what happens in the year 2000, it is safe to assume that the DLC and the New Democrats will be at the center of any debate, or battle, to chart the future of the Democratic Party for the next century.

This book tells the story of the DLC—what it is, where it came from, and what it believes—and how this organization tried to change the public philosophy of the Democratic Party.[2] In doing this, I intend to provide the reader with the first serious account of how the Democratic Party changed during the Reagan-Bush years and how it won back the White House.[3] This assessment, in turn, also enables us to examine the state of the Democratic Party today and what its prospects are in the future.

On a more abstract level, I intend to offer a framework for understanding how modern parties and their public philosophies change. In both scholarly and popular analysis, the dominant paradigm of electoral and ideological change within the party system is realignment theory.[4] In its basic form, this theory holds that only a national crisis, such as a war or an economic depression, can prompt a new line of partisan cleavage in the electorate. This split, in turn, comes to the fore in a "realigning" or "critical" election in which "the basic party attachments" of voters are significantly altered to produce a change in the party in control of the government.[5] If this party effectively handles the crisis and these new partisan loyalties hold and are proved durable, then a realignment is said to have occurred. Most political scientists who subscribe to realignment theory agree that this process occurred, for example, after 1860 (prompted by the Civil War) and after 1932 (prompted by the Great Depression).

Yet as the story of the DLC shows, it is possible for a party faction consciously to change the public philosophy of a party and attract new voters during "normal" political times, without a major national crisis and a precipitating critical election.[6] That is, a group of policy entrepreneurs can facilitate change within a party so that it can adapt to long-term, deeper socioeconomic and political trends.

Of course, different circumstances may require a party to alter a specific policy position. However, on other occasions, the adaptation needed is so fundamental that a party's public philosophy—the "outlook on politics and government [that] . . . serves to give definition to problems and direction to government policies dealing with them"—must change.[7] In this scenario, new problems and conditions require not only new policies but also new guiding principles.

A public philosophy, according to James Ceaser, is composed of four constituent parts. First, there is a "theory of governance," or, to put it simply, an overarching concept of how government should function properly in its given constitutional form. Second are the views on what a society is trying to achieve—so-called consensual values such as liberty, equality, democracy, and progress. Third is the role government (at its many levels) has in achieving those ends. The final component is the role that the country should play in the wider world.[8]

To locate these four components in the political system, we can examine the stances of a party or party faction with respect to three broad issue contexts: economic policy (and the role of government in it), foreign policy (and the role of the United States abroad), and social issues (such as quality of life and moral concerns).[9] Practically, to assess the public philosophy of a party and any changes it has undergone, one must examine official party documents such as the platform, the positions of its activist elite, the attitudes of party identifiers, and how the party is perceived by the electorate at large.

Thus, unlike a political theory, a public philosophy and subsequent reactions to it have a real social and institutional location within the political system. There, they structure political debate, setting the terms for the issue positions that are then submitted to voter approval on election day. These electoral outcomes, in turn, affect the shape of a party's public philosophy, just as the public philosophy itself affects the success of a party at the polls. Sociopolitical, economic, and organizational changes have a similar symbiotic relationship with the set of beliefs affecting a public philosophy and with how it is translated into the electoral arena. So, to examine the New Democratic attempt to change the public philosophy of the Democratic Party, I utilize a general framework of electoral problems and alternatives, issue problems and policy alternatives, and institutional problems and alternatives.

Such a framework, however, will take us only part of the way. It will allow us to examine shallowly the phenomenon of the New Democrats and the beliefs of the DLC, but it will not allow us to understand why the New Democrats came to such prominence and what methods they employed to implement their public philosophy. To accomplish this, we must first view them within the larger theoretical context of political innovation.

Of course, there are inherent difficulties in pinpointing the origin and in judging the impact of a public philosophy—or any new idea, for that matter—in the realm of policymaking and politics. Trying to do so is, in many ways, an endless quest.[10] Nevertheless, some scholars have tried to explain how and why innovations—new thinking with regard to party structure, strategy, and ideology—arise and take center stage for those in and around government.[11] Central to any of these studies is the contention that adverse political events or crises breed innovation. This hypothesis makes intuitive sense, but as others— notably, Nelson Polsby—have argued, innovation is not that neat.[12] Some policy and strategy solutions are not sought out in the wake of a crisis but are devised and then floated by their progenitors into the "subculture of decision-makers."[13]

A more detailed exposition of this view of policy innovation and governmental agenda setting has been offered by John Kingdon. His theory breaks agenda setting in American politics into three streams— problems, policies, and politics—that operate largely independently of one another. Policies, for instance, can be under development; different crises may be brewing; and political events, such as changes in the administration or national mood swings, can be under way. Policy (or political) innovation occurs when a change in the problem stream or political stream forces a "policy window" open—that is, when one of these crises or changes in the political opinions of the electorate comes to the fore. There are some predictable windows of opportunity, such as legislative renewals, budget cycles, and elections. Others are forced open by "focusing events"—precipitating crises or disasters or, even more subtly, deep dissatisfaction with the status quo. It is at these points that new policy and political proposals are sought and policy entrepreneurs push them to center stage. Once a proposal is under consideration, its inherent qualities—such as its technical feasibility, value acceptability, cost, and anticipated response from the public and elected officials—will determine its overall viability.[14]

Kingdon provides a useful set of organizing notions through which to approach the DLC story. Yet in his discussion of how a new policy idea moves from paper to governmental action, Kingdon does not examine what is often a crucial intermediary step: parties. He does not consider how new ideas become planted and take root within a modern American political party and, consequently, does not examine how a party's public philosophy, the outlook that profoundly shapes which policies will progress onto its governing agenda, can or cannot be altered. Proving the validity of Kingdon's theory of policy innovation and governmental agenda setting, however, is not the primary concern here. And despite these drawbacks, his framework can still be used as an entry point to examining these issues.

Indeed, as the DLC chronology shows, the political calendar, with its predictable "windows" of elections, provides "natural" moments for the consideration of alternative political strategies, public philosophies, and institutional arrangements. Thus, the problems and alternatives within these three areas (as structured by the political calendar), the Kingdon framework, and a layer of institutions are used to organize the overall examination of the DLC and the inquiry into how one can consciously change the public philosophy of a party during the postreform era.

But to understand fully why the DLC was established, why it made certain critiques and offered particular alternatives, and why the organization chose certain strategies to change the public philosophy of the Democratic Party, one also must locate the New Democrats and the DLC within the evolution of the modern Democratic Party and, by extension, within the history of American politics since the Great Depression. Only with this historical perspective can one understand the chain of events and trends that created the environment and the potential for the New Democrats to emerge and the DLC to form.

Once this foundation is set, I use each subsequent chapter to examine a different strategy that the DLC employed to change the party at different points over the past fifteen years. In addition to explaining the internal party battles between the New Democrats and liberals during the 1980s and 1990s, I examine how the New Democrats and the DLC tried to effect these changes, thus offering a perspective on how a faction, especially one without grassroots support, can or cannot change the public philosophy of a modern American political party. It is a topic that I believe is of interest to many elected officials and activists in both parties who are dismayed at the tendency of their respective parties to bow to their extreme elements.

The DLC story begins in the aftermath of the election of Ronald Reagan in 1980 with a group of congressmen organized in the House Democratic Caucus. Under the leadership of Caucus Chairman Gillis Long of Louisiana and his top aide, Al From, these young, proto–New Democrats began the task of developing and promoting an alternative public philosophy to rejuvenate the defeated Democrats. When their failure to affect the platform, strategy, makeup, and success of the 1984 Democratic presidential ticket became clear, this group—plus like-minded governors such as Chuck Robb of Virginia and senators such as Sam Nunn of Georgia—formed the DLC in February 1985.

Almost immediately, their plans to use the DLC as a vehicle to develop a new public philosophy and to change the party itself were in jeopardy. Liberals within the party demonized the DLC as "Democrats for the Leisure Class" and even charged that the New Democrats were right-wing and racist. At the same time, wanting to preserve party unity, the Democratic National Committee tried to co-opt the DLC by moving in the rogue organization's direction. Taken together, these reactions threatened the DLC's very existence, prompting the organization to shift its tactics and embrace a "big-tent" strategy of moderating its rhetoric and stances in order to attract a broad array of members and blunt these attacks.

The big tent may have ensured the DLC's short-term survival, but it also undermined the New Democrats' effectiveness. During the 1988 nominating campaign, the DLC hoped that the southern regional primary, "Super Tuesday," would propel a New Democratic candidate, such as Senator Al Gore of Tennessee, to the nomination. Yet once again, the DLC failed to shape the party platform or ticket. Indeed, Super Tuesday did more to increase the influence of the New Democrats' main nemesis, the Reverend Jesse Jackson, than to help the New

Democratic cause. Its effort to work within the party, specifically, tinkering with the nominating process, made the DLC appear ineffective and marginal. Questions of why it should exist at all intensified.

Yet in 1988, another presidential defeat erased these doubts and breathed new life into the DLC. Realizing the failure of its big-tent format, the DLC began to take a more adversarial stance. It presented a lucid and biting critique of the political strategy of the national Democratic Party; established the Progressive Policy Institute (PPI), a think tank to develop fully a New Democratic public philosophy; and embarked on an aggressive presidential strategy. Said differently, the DLC wanted to take over the party by battling for its head.

This plan brought Al From—now executive director of the DLC—to Little Rock, Arkansas, in the spring of 1989 to personally persuade Governor Bill Clinton to take over the DLC, which From promised would be retooled as a springboard for his presidential run. Clinton accepted, and throughout 1990 and 1991, the DLC plied the governor with critical aid during this important "invisible primary" phase of the campaign. The organization unveiled a developed and distinct public philosophy that took controversial stands on a variety of issues, and it established state chapters to give its putative candidate a reason to travel the country and a chance to construct a network of supporters in key states. This work culminated in the DLC's first convention held in Cleveland in May 1991. There, the organization ratified a New Democratic policy platform, highlighted its nationwide strength, and provided a showcase for its chairman, Clinton. Throughout this process, the DLC faced liberal attacks, from broadsides launched by Jackson to picketing by union workers. But this criticism did not derail the DLC, and by October 1991, the New Democrats had their candidate.

Two days after Clinton was elected president, one photograph that ran on the front page of the *Washington Post* and in other newspapers told the political world that the DLC had arrived. There were From and the president-elect, the DLC's former chairman, walking down the steps of the Arkansas state capitol together. If it was not clear already, this picture was a signal that the New Democratic public philosophy, which the DLC had developed and on which Clinton had run, would have a central role in his presidency. From joked that this picture was worth $3 million, as it single-handedly boosted the DLC's take at its gala fund-raiser a month later, where Clinton made his first appearance in Washington after the election.

Yet during the first two years of the Clinton presidency, it seemed that Clinton had abandoned the New Democrats and that the DLC's presidential strategy had failed. Due to a combination of the nature of his victory in both the nominating contest and the general election plus the makeup of Congress, Clinton either proposed "Old" (liberal) Democratic policies or offered New Democratic policies but by way of Old Democratic politics. By 1994, the DLC was demoralized. Its man was in the White House, but nothing seemed to have changed.

In the elections of 1994, everything seemed to change. The Republicans took over Congress, significantly altered the political landscape, and, in the process, reinvigorated the DLC and the New Democratic effort. This outcome convinced Clinton to reembrace the New Democratic public philosophy and created a political situation that practically compelled him to do so. By the time he ran for reelection in 1996, Clinton could point to his balanced budget plan, his signature on a welfare reform bill, and a number of initiatives targeted to the middle class to burnish his New Democratic credentials. With his return to the New Democratic issue agenda and electoral strategy, he handily won reelection.

In claiming victory in 1996, Bill Clinton proclaimed that "the vital American center is alive and well." But as the Clinton era comes to a close and the contest to replace him commences, how vital are the New Democrats? Has the DLC really changed the public philosophy of the Democratic Party? And if so, what does this tell us about how a change in the public philosophy of an American political party can—and cannot—occur? The answer to these questions is in many ways premature, as the New Democratic experiment is still a young one. It is still too soon to tell whether the New Democratic public philosophy will go the way of Dwight Eisenhower's "Modern Republicanism" or endure like Roosevelt's New Deal liberalism.

Time will tell, but even the cautious will grant the significance of the DLC and the New Democrats. They are the most organized and successful challengers to the prevailing liberalism of the post-1968 Democratic Party. They have both restored some of the traditional Democratic values that had been jettisoned over the past thirty years and retooled the party to respond to a world and an economy fundamentally different from those found when the Democrats last dominated presidential politics. In the context of postwar American politics, the DLC and the New Democrats represent a significant development within the Democratic Party and have been a force that has altered the political balance of power between the two major parties.

1 / *Moving from New Dealers to Neoliberals*

AT ONE TIME, all Democrats needed to do to win elections was to ask voters to look in their wallets. In fact, in one of the first television advertisements ever run by the Democratic Party, the party of Roosevelt and Truman made its case in 1952 by asking a man in the street to do exactly that. "You've got more money than you had twenty years ago, haven't you, even after taxes?" the Democratic spokesman noted. "See that Social Security card. It means security for you and your family. The Democrats made it possible," the voice added. After pointing out that the man's savings were now insured and that he had enough money to afford a car and a home, the spokesman made the party's case: "I think the Democrats have given you the chance to do pretty well, Mister. Don't let the Republicans take all those good things away. Vote Democratic."[1]

Although the Democrats lost the presidency that year, the New Deal consensus that this ad encapsulated still dominated American politics. It may have been simple, or even crass, but these pocketbook issues were the keys to the Democratic Party's success and the basis of its electoral appeal for much of the postwar era. By 1972, however, the Democratic Party's presidential candidate was making a pitch to voters that would have seemed as foreign to Democrats in 1952 as an ad for Internet service. In this five-minute spot, George McGovern described an America that was more concerned with foreign affairs than with the millions of people who are "so desperate that they turn to drugs and to crime and to violence." After calling for cuts in defense spending and for peace, the advertisement ended with McGovern stating, "We dedicate ourselves to the eradication of racism, and poverty, and injustice, and to a new assertion of the right of every citizen of this land to the pursuit of justice."[2]

The journey from the liberalism of Truman and Kennedy to that of

McGovern and Mondale, from a liberalism of economic uplift to one of peace and social justice, must be understood to comprehend who the New Democrats are and why they arrived on the political scene when they did. The New Democrats who established the DLC believed that the Democratic Party was losing elections because it embraced a public philosophy that repelled the working-class and middle-class voters who were once at the heart of its coalition. This new variant of liberalism that took root in 1972 and flourished in the decade that followed was seen as the reason for the large Republican victory in 1980 and as a looming problem for Democrats around the country.

The New Deal Consensus: 1932–1964

The Great Depression and then the election of Franklin Delano Roosevelt to the presidency in 1932 marked the beginning of a profound shift in American politics, a shift whose repercussions would reverberate through the rest of the century. Spurred by the economic crisis, FDR undertook a series of political and policy changes that resulted in the creation of a truly unique New Deal or "liberal" public philosophy, one that attracted an electoral coalition that would deliver success to the Democratic Party for years to come. As a result, this period served as an almost mythical benchmark of Democratic electoral and policy success, a mind-set that later served as a crucial foil to the New Democrats.

This liberal public philosophy was based on the principles of federal centralization and of countervailing power for minority groups, or, as Herbert Croly described it, nationality and democracy.[3] Practically, these beliefs meant that the federal government should be used for broad national and democratic purposes. Accordingly, it should take a role in the national economy through the use of macroeconomic planning in order to contain the excesses of industrialism and compensate for capitalism's failures. This management of the economy, in turn, would produce economic growth and full employment. In addition, the New Deal public philosophy advocated using the power of the national state to extend pluralism to previously marginalized groups and integrate them into the national economy and society. Before this time, extension of democracy (and reform efforts in general) was associated with states' rights, limited government, and localism.[4] In sum, as Everett Carll Ladd and Charles Hadley noted, "the New Deal joined the equalitarian and reformist strains which had appeared throughout American political history through governmental nationalism."[5]

It was this question of the use of the federal government in the economy that divided the electorate. FDR initially faced fervent opposition from many (predominantly upper-class foes) centered in the Republican camp.[6] Over time, however, electoral victories began to cement a consensus behind the New Deal public philosophy. By 1940, even the GOP platform supported an extension of Social Security and important labor safeguards, such as the right to collective bargaining.[7] The Republicans could not ignore the consensus forming around the ascendant New Deal public philosophy and grudgingly began to accept the changes it had wrought on American society, differentiating their public philosophy from the Democrats based on their response to it. In Samuel Lubell's memorable formulation, the Democratic Party had become the majority party (the sun) and the Republican Party the minority party (the moon) in the American "political solar system." And in such a universe, Lubell wrote, "it is within the majority party that the issues of any particular period are fought out; while the minority party shines in reflected radiance of the heat thus generated."[8]

The GOP assumed this "lunar" role and had to accept elements of the New Deal public philosophy precisely because it was so electorally popular. By focusing on economic policies and downplaying differences on the U.S. role abroad and racial equality at home, FDR forged diverse groups, including northern blacks, urban ethnics (especially Jews and Catholics), unions, middle-class liberals, and white southerners, into a strong Democratic coalition.[9] The electoral success of this public philosophy was startling: from 1924 to 1932, the Democratic Party went from garnering 29 percent of the popular vote in the presidential election to 57 percent; by 1934, the Democrats held more than 70 percent of House and Senate seats.[10] Even when FDR did not head the ticket, the Democratic Party continued to win, as Truman unexpectedly won a four-way race for reelection in 1948, and the party regained commanding majorities in both houses of Congress.[11]

In practice, this consensus around the New Deal public philosophy was gained by what is now called "interest-group liberalism." At first, with the New Deal's large increase in governmental expenditures and the proliferation of aid programs, the Democrats turned to existing urban machines (and some courthouse rings) for distribution of these monies. This rejuvenated these machines and enhanced their patronage and hence their vote-delivery abilities, firmly wedding them to the New Deal coalition.[12] After World War II and the beginning of an unrivaled period of American economic prosperity, Democrats were able to maintain their diverse collection of interest groups by parceling out targeted programs.[13]

With a consensus on globalism and anticommunism in foreign policy, the gradual Republican acceptance of the New Deal public philosophy, especially on economic matters, and the absence of divisive social issues, this approach was largely adequate to keep the Democratic coalition united. In support of this, the Democratic Party had a group of party leaders, machine bosses, and interest-group spokesmen who brokered differences between the various groups when it came time to settle on national policy goals and a presidential nominee.[14]

Although the Democratic Party lost the presidency to Dwight Eisenhower in 1952 and 1956, the New Deal public philosophy still dominated American politics. "Should any political party attempt to abolish Social Security and eliminate labor laws and farm programs," wrote Eisenhower in a letter to his brother, Edgar, "you would not hear of that party again in our political history."[15] Not wanting to visit this fate on the GOP, Eisenhower joined the Democrats in accepting a role for the government in the economy—for example, supporting an extension of Social Security and establishing the Department of Health, Education, and Welfare—along with embracing a vigorously anticommunist foreign policy.[16]

In office, Eisenhower enjoyed the support of the Democratic congressional leadership, and his successor, John Kennedy, appointed Republicans to important cabinet posts. With a general consensus on the fundamental issues of the day, political campaigns were waged on the basis of a party's ability to implement shared political values. Valence issues and the personal qualities of the candidates thus dominated the presidential campaigns of 1952, 1956, and 1960. Although Eisenhower won significant support among white southerners and Catholics, two key New Deal constituencies, he was not able to solidify them into a lasting coalition, and both returned to the Democratic fold in 1960.[17]

Yet lurking beneath this bipartisan calm were the seeds of polarization. The *Brown v. Board of Education* school desegregation decision in 1954 and the Montgomery bus boycott led by Martin Luther King, Jr., in 1955 marked the beginning of the modern civil rights movement. The emergence of this issue, whose de-emphasis was the key to holding the New Deal coalition together, threatened Democratic Party unity. Moreover, it coincided with the arrival of a whole new set of issue concerns and activists. As postwar American society became more affluent and basic subsistence ceased to be a primary concern, the "crass, but reliable materialism" that undergirded politics up to that point began to yield to a "politics frequently dominated by abstract ideas."[18] Instead of the professional politicians interested in acquiring material benefits for themselves or their client groups, a politics of what James Q. Wilson labeled "amateurs" emerged. Distinguished by their "purposive" goals—which could be realized only in the long term, affected others besides those pursuing them, and were not necessarily related to goods exchanged in economic markets—these activists and politicians began making demands that could not be easily accommodated within the political machines that drove interest-group liberalism.[19]

A ward leader, for example, could easily deliver a patronage job or a government loan but had a harder time answering a demand for open housing or legalized abortion, much less "equality" or "peace." Increasingly, the old political structures could not accommodate the new demands associated with this changing sociopolitical context, and unsurprisingly, they were confronted by rival political organizations formed by many of these "purposive" activists. Notably, on the local level, Democratic reform clubs challenged the old machines and interests within their own party and across the aisle. Nationally, in 1954, liberals in the Democratic Party formed the Democratic Advisory Council under Democratic National Committee (DNC) Chairman Paul Butler in order to develop a more programmatically liberal platform in many areas, including civil rights, and to force the party to draw a sharper line between it and Eisenhower. In the Republican camp, a group of academics, lawyers, and businessmen formed the Ripon Society in 1962, hoping to elaborate a liberal Republican public philosophy; on the Right, conservatives established journals such as the *National Review* and organizations such as Young Americans for Freedom.[20]

At the same time, the rapid development and deployment of television promised to be an increasingly important outlet for those activists and candidates wanting to bypass the traditional party structure. In 1952, Eisenhower ran some of the first political television ads, and in 1960, the live televised debate was firmly established as central to presidential politics.[21] Nevertheless, partisanship was still strong during this period—three-quarters of the electorate still identified themselves as Republican or Democrat—and the control of party bosses over the presidential nominating process had not been seriously diminished.[22] Yet these developments pointed to deeper challenges to the liberal consensus. Underneath all this, the party machine was in critical condition. The foundation of the New Deal coalition was splintering.

The Unraveling: 1964–1968

To a Democrat in 1964, neither the declining health of the party machine nor the breakup of the New Deal coalition would have—or should have—seemed apparent. In the presidential election, Lyndon Johnson crushed the Republican nominee, Senator Barry Goldwater of Arizona, and returned to office with majorities in both houses of Congress. Calling for a "Great Society," LBJ appeared to have the political capital to deliver on lofty promises of eradicating poverty and ensuring equal rights. The Democracy appeared invincible. By 1968, however, it had almost self-destructed. What occurred in the intervening four years is viewed by some as the buildup to a full-fledged partisan realignment of the electorate, and it is recognized by all as the beginning of a period of profound change in American society and politics.

As this period progressed, groups within each party's coalition began challenging the policy assumptions implicit in the consensus of the past decade. Motivated by particular issue and ideological concerns, these factions were fueled by changing socioeconomic conditions and critical events (e.g., the Vietnam War and urban rioting) that independently propelled doubts about the efficacy of the prevailing liberal public philosophy to the fore. The result was polarization within each party and across the political spectrum and an end to the liberal consensus.

The first sign of this change was in the 1964 Republican Party platform, a document that reflected the views of the party's presidential nominee, Barry Goldwater, and the New Right conservatives that supported him. With its explicit theme of protecting individual liberty, the platform's ideological direction is made clear in almost every section. In sharp contrast to the New Deal consensus that Eisenhower and Republicans of his ilk accepted, the platform railed against governmental intrusion in the economy. On the stump, Goldwater reiterated this theme, advocating the establishment of a voluntary Social Security system, the sale of the Tennessee Valley Authority, and right-to-work laws.[23]

In foreign policy, Goldwater and the Republican platform excoriated the Democrats for not sufficiently aiding those resisting communism abroad. Goldwater did this to such a degree that perhaps the most potent charge against him was that he was too extreme to serve as commander in chief of a nuclear nation (this was memorably encapsulated in a television ad that showed a little girl picking flower petals and then segued into a picture of a mushroom cloud). On social issues, the GOP platform condemned society's "moral decline and drift," calling for a constitutional amendment to protect prayer in schools.[24] And on the increasingly salient issue of civil rights, the Republican Party took a strong stance in favor of states' rights, a position that placed it on the side of those in favor of the segregated status quo. In each issue context, the Republican Party staked itself out in stark contrast to the Democratic Party and its liberal public philosophy. As evidenced by its electoral fortunes, it appears that the GOP also positioned itself well to the right of the general electorate.

Yet 1964 was not to be the death of this challenge to the liberal public philosophy or of the Republican Party. Events soon caught up to Goldwater and the New Right. With Lyndon Johnson's expansion of the welfare state through his Great Society programs, his escalation of the U.S. commitment in Vietnam, and his clear commitment to civil rights, he brought the principles of the liberal public philosophy into conflict, leading to practical and political failure. First, trying simultaneously to fund the War on Poverty and the war in Vietnam led to an increase in inflation and higher taxes. For many Americans, the price to be paid for expanding entitlements literally became too high.[25] Moreover, this aid began to be viewed as the government giving people "something for nothing," violating a sense of fairness among the working and middle classes.[26] Dissatisfaction with governmental intervention began to mount. In 1960, for example, 59 percent of the electorate felt that it was the federal government's role to ensure that everyone had a job and a good standard of living; by 1969, that number had dropped to 31 percent.[27]

Second, splits in the foreign policy consensus also began to emerge. In 1964, all but two members of Congress voted for the Gulf of Tonkin resolution, authorizing the president to use force in Vietnam, a reflection of the policy's widespread popular support. By Johnson's midterm, however, a critique of American foreign policy began in earnest. On the Left, scholars such as William Appleman Williams and activists centered in Students for a Democratic Society began to question America's involvement in Vietnam and abroad generally. Instead of seeing the United States as the deliverer of liberty and democracy, they saw it as a country searching for foreign markets and imposing its worldview on indigenous peoples.[28]

By 1965, Senator William Fulbright, chairman of the Senate Foreign Relations Committee, concluded that the United States exhibited an "arrogance of power," signaling the arrival of this critique into mainstream political and, notably, Democratic debate. As American involvement in Vietnam increased, more men were conscripted, and casualties mounted, this viewpoint gained currency among intellectuals, elected officials, and the public at large.[29] Protests against the war that began in earnest in 1965 grew to such a degree that by October 1967, over 100,000 people gathered to march on the Pentagon against the war. The lines were beginning to be drawn on an issue context in which there had once been a large degree of agreement.

The final threat to the liberal consensus was the emergence of cultural or moral concerns as political issues, or what Richard Scammon and Ben Wattenberg came to call the "social issue."[30] Civil rights protesters had already placed the long dormant (or neglected) issue of race back on the national policy agenda, forcing both parties to reckon with it. LBJ chose to handle it by placing the Democratic Party firmly on the side of equal rights for blacks, introducing and advocating passage of the Civil Rights Act of 1964 and Voting Rights Act of 1965. Race, the question that had threatened Democratic unity throughout the century, was now settled on the side of using the federal government to promote and guarantee civil rights.

Complicating this stance were changes in the civil rights movement itself. The appearance of urban rioting in Watts in 1965 and in several northern cities in subsequent years, the movement's embrace of "black power" and rejection of an integrationist ideal, and the extension of the civil rights struggle to the North nationalized the racial issue and entangled it in a web of other growing social concerns. A flamboyant and youthful counterculture characterized by campus unrest, protest of the Vietnam War, a pronounced increase in crime, and the flaunting of conventional standards of behavior—particularly with respect to premarital sex and drug use—aligned with the racial issue and cleaved the electorate into those who supported a wider liberalization of society and those who did not.

On top of this, the Supreme Court issued a series of decisions that seemed to support this revolt against tradition and challenge to the stable status quo. In *Engel v. Vitale* (1962) and *Abington Township v. Schempp* (1963), the Court banned Bible readings and prayer in public schools. In *Griswold v. Connecticut* (1966), the justices overturned any state restrictions on contraception, and in *Mapp v. Ohio* (1965) and *Miranda v. Arizona* (1966), they handed down decisions that gave greater protection to criminal defendants.

The emergence of the social issue only hastened the development of ideological activists in both parties, activists who, despite their clear philosophical differences, shared an animosity toward postwar liberalism. In the Republican camp, Goldwater conservatives battled liberal Republicans such as George Romney and Nelson Rockefeller, but the disputes were muted in comparison to those of the Democrats. After all, the GOP was expected to oppose the dominant public philosophy of the other party. In the Democratic camp, the lines were drawn for a larger battle. The "New Politics" Left—purposive activists found in the New Left, the civil rights movement, peace groups, and other organizations that entered party politics—directly challenged the fundamental tenets of New Deal liberalism by fully accepting new and alternative lifestyles and values (whether feminist, separatist, or homosexual), questioning the merits of economic growth on the grounds that it threatened the quality of life, opposing the U.S. commitment against communism, and espousing the doctrine of equal outcomes over equal opportunities.[31] Notably, the establishment against which they were railing was fundamentally a Democratic and liberal one. The welfare state, which they characterized as a "manipulative bureaucracy" overly concerned with the needs of blue-collar whites, was perhaps the greatest accomplishment of New Deal liberalism in the eyes of traditional liberals, labor, southern Democrats, and working-class ethnics at the heart of the Democratic coalition.[32]

Once proponents of this public philosophy became involved in party politics—an involvement that began in earnest from the start of the 1968 election—this left-wing attack on liberalism had a practical effect on the Democratic Party. Allard Lowenstein, an established New Left figure, initiated the "Dump Johnson" movement that precipitated the candidacy of Minnesota Senator Eugene McCarthy and his stunning showing in the New Hampshire primary, which led to Johnson's eventual withdrawal from the presidential race. As the campaign progressed and more New Politics activists entered Democratic Party politics (in the phrase of the day, becoming "clean for Gene"), they split their support between McCarthy and Robert Kennedy. But after the assassination of Kennedy and the riots and dissent enveloping the Democratic convention that year in Chicago, these purposive activists unsurprisingly turned their backs on the eventual nominee, failing to support enthusiastically the standard-bearer of New Deal liberalism, Hubert Humphrey.[33]

In 1968, the Republican Party was able to unite behind Richard Nixon, who managed to placate both the liberal and conservative camps in his party. The platform was worded nebulously or avoided contentious issues outright, calling for America to come together and advocating a fairly typical postwar economic policy. At the same time, Nixon's vice-presidential nominee, Governor Spiro Agnew of Maryland, served as the point man on divisive social issues. The GOP had apparently learned from its defeat in 1964 and handled its ideological faction more ably. Consequently, it did not experience the internal strife that the Democrats endured publicly at the Chicago convention.[34]

With this lack of public dissent, the Republican Party was able to take advantage of the practical consequences of the challenge to the liberal public philosophy and the conflict within the Democratic Party and try to poach voters from the Democratic camp. Specifically, the white working class—especially white southern Democrats and northern (predominantly Catholic) ethnics—was now in play because, although still attracted to the economic message of the Democrats, it was cross-pressured by the party's increasingly liberal positions on social and racial issues. Yet despite this opening, the GOP hesitated in its stridency during the 1968 presidential campaign—its only mention of civil rights or race in the 1968 platform was a pledge to enforce laws to eliminate discrimination—and did not pursue those voters as blatantly as one might have expected.

That would be left to the true social conservative alternative to the Democratic nominee: the American Independent Party's George Wallace. Wallace, the pugnacious former governor of Alabama, broke out of the New Deal framework and addressed the cross-pressuring concerns of the white, blue-collar voter: economic insecurity and social, predominantly racial, fear.[35] He attacked with gusto federal bureaucrats, federal judges, professors, antiwar protesters, urban rioters, and politicians of both parties. He talked tough against not only the social changes happening in society, from desegregation to the counterculture, but also against the elites—in his words, the "silver-spooned brats," "bleeding-heart sociologists," and "bearded, beatnik bureaucrats"—who rejected America's cultural and religious values and initiated these changes.[36] His conservative populism resonated with voters in the Deep South and in many working-class, ethnic areas in northern cities. In fact, a secret AFL-CIO poll found that one-third of its members backed Wallace, and a *Chicago Sun-Times* survey reported that 44 percent of white steelworkers backed the Alabaman.[37]

With Wallace and Nixon competing for disaffected Democrats, election day became an anti-Democratic landslide, as almost two-thirds of voters rejected Hubert Humphrey. If one considers that Johnson was at the winning end of a similar rout just four years earlier, this result was an incredible turn of events. Unsurprisingly, the defection of southern whites and the working class drove this defeat. Between 1960 and 1970, for example, the number of southern whites who identified themselves as Democrats decreased from 61 percent to 44 percent.[38] Additionally, a combination of voter defection and natural shrinkage in overall numbers dropped the percentage of the Democratic vote comprising white blue-collar workers from about half in 1952 to 35 percent in 1968.[39] At the same time, though, the Democratic Party did well at the subpresidential level, continuing to retain control of both houses of Congress.

In hindsight, 1968 marked the beginning of the modern political era. Divided partisan control of the federal government, the centrality of social issues, the influence of purposive issue activists, and challenges from the Left and Right to the liberal public philosophy that would mark the politics of the next decade emerged in that year's election. More importantly, how these issues were handled by both Republicans and Democrats would set the stage for the development of the New Democrats.

The Transformation: 1968–1980

The battle between the New Politics liberals and the regular Democratic Party continued after the 1968 election. Wanting to make peace with this insurgent faction, the DNC, during the tumult of the 1968 convention, agreed to establish a commission to reform the nominating rules of the party. From one side, New Politics leaders saw the Commission on Party Structure and Delegate Selection (also known as the McGovern-Fraser Commission) as an opportunity to open the party up to their "alternate Democratic coalition" of established liberal interest groups, feminist and reform organizations, and the racial minority leadership.[40] From the other side, some party leaders welcomed these groups, viewing this coalition as the key to future electoral victories.[41] Moreover, in the wake of a divisive national convention, many of these leaders wanted to make peace with the New Politics faction, and if the commission would accomplish that, all the better.

At the commission's first meeting on March 1, 1969, it was clear who would dominate the reform process. The New Politics reformers were in such control that the AFL-CIO pulled its lone commissioner from the body in protest, and the few southern Democrats on the panel remained defiant.[42] With little resistance, the McGovern-Fraser Commission passed a series of changes that emasculated the power held by traditional party bosses and even traditional constituencies. First, in the DNC itself, the McGovern-Fraser reformers replaced ex officio seats used to recognize party service with seats earmarked for members of certain demographic groups.[43] Second, the new nomination process stipulated that delegates must be selected through primaries or caucuses that were easily accessible and open to all voters who claimed membership in the Democratic Party. Third, the commission established delegate quotas for blacks, women, and youth.[44] Finally, the McGovern-Fraser changes institutionalized the field of party reform in the Democratic Party, thus spawning successor commissions to tinker with the rules even further.[45]

The net result of this effort—which, since many of the changes required state legislative action, affected the Republican Party too—was an acceleration and institutionalization of the trend toward candidate-centered elections, featuring campaigns focusing on issues that were of paramount importance to the network of purposive issue activists needed to win. By mandating that caucuses had to be participatory conventions rather than meetings of elite party officials and that primaries had to be elections for delegates pledged to a candidate, the Democratic Party shifted the focus of candidates away from party leaders and toward voters, who were now the key to nomination.[46] Consequently, the media and voters refocused on the individual candidates, abetting the diminishment of party power.[47]

This phenomenon manifested itself in the party system in several ways. For instance, with the party establishment unable to guarantee a candidate's nomination in an increasingly open field, the ability to run and win a party's nomination for congressman or president as an outsider became a reality—Jimmy Carter's journey to the nomination being an archetypal example.[48] However, to take advantage of this, a candidate had to construct his own organization and mobilize his own coalition of voters. Practically, this arrangement appeared to give an advantage to New Politics candidates.

The new nominating process, for example, put intensive participatory demands on party members wishing to exert political influence: one had to have the time to attend caucuses or vote in a primary, along with knowledge about each candidate, in order to make a choice. These circumstances favored better-educated, wealthier, and typically New Politics–oriented activists; the types of voters inclined to participate in the new system were not found in the traditional, working-class Democratic base.[49] To reach these voters, candidates increasingly had to craft messages that resonated with the concerns of this constituency and that appealed to its organized elements—such as political action committees (PACs) that could provide the funds and constituent groups that could supply the necessary volunteers to campaign effectively. Said differently, this created an incentive for candidates to stress their stances on intensely held ideological positions, such as capital punishment, abortion, and racial quotas.

Attracting purposive, New Politics activists to party politics, this new nominating process also created a situation in which the beliefs of a candidate often trumped the organization politician's focus on the political compromise needed to win votes.[50] As a result, the open nominating system limited or removed the brokering role of party leaders in finding a candidate acceptable to all groups in the coalition and in adapting a candidate's positions for public consumption, just as the ideological climate diminished the ability of patronage to cement a coalition.[51] While the party was becoming more fractious, the ability to craft a compromise was being circumscribed.

These institutional changes had an immediate impact on the Democratic Party. The New Politics Left rallied behind Senator George McGovern of South Dakota, an antiwar candidate who embraced its agenda. With the support of these activists, McGovern defeated the regular party's standard-bearer, Hubert Humphrey, and George Wallace, who was running on the same platform he had used as an independent in 1968. More importantly, McGovern—who chaired the commission that reformed the party's rules—understood the new nominating system and translated these wins into delegates, enabling him to win the nomination on the first ballot.[52] With the nomination of McGovern, the New Politics faction was at the zenith of its control of the national Democratic Party and did not fail to execute that power. At the party's nominating convention that year in Miami Beach, they refused to seat the Illinois delegation—led by that master of machine politics, Mayor Richard Daley of Chicago—because of an insufficient number of female and black delegates. Instead, the convention voted to seat an alternative delegation led by Jesse Jackson. There is perhaps no better symbol of the waning influence of the white working class in Democratic Party politics and the transfer of power to the New Politics faction than the ouster of the Daley delegation.

Accordingly, the Democratic platform was a clear exposition of New Politics liberalism. In foreign policy, the platform called for "the immediate and full withdrawal of Americans from Southeast Asia," reductions in military spending to fund domestic programs, and increased cooperation with the communist world.[53] On domestic concerns, the platform began to articulate a "rights-based liberalism" that focused on extending rights and freedoms to individuals and social groups.[54] These commitments translated into an embrace of the liberal positions of the cultural divide. The party, for example, supported amnesty for draft evaders, gun control legislation, busing to achieve school integration, abolition of the electoral college, and ratification of the Equal Rights Amendment (ERA).[55]

In economic policy, this approach led to a rejection of New Deal liberalism's focus on governmental action in the economy to foster economic growth and expand economic opportunity. Instead, the party embraced what British historian Gareth Davies called a liberalism of entitlement, in which the poor were seen as the victims of societal mistreatment and thus had an unconditional right to income and other benefits, a right that could be fulfilled only by the redistribution of wealth.[56] This belief motivated welfare rights advocates, who worked to destigmatize welfare and enroll as many people as possible for it. In New York City alone, the welfare population more than doubled between 1965 and 1971; at over 1 million people, it was larger than the populations of fifteen states.[57] And this belief made its way explicitly into the 1972 platform, which included a plank calling for a guaranteed income for all Americans—the first time a major American political party took such a stance.[58]

With the Democrats far off to the left, and fearing an independent challenge from Wallace on the right, Nixon embarked on a "southern strategy." He hoped not only to pick off southern white Democrats but also to pull in the white working class around the country that had once been the core of the Democratic coalition. He opposed school busing, made conservative appointments to the Supreme Court, supported federal aid for parochial schools, and ran a campaign that did what it could to paint McGovern as an advocate for "acid, amnesty, and abortion."[59]

On election day, this strategy seemed to work. Nixon won in a landslide, garnering 62 percent of the popular vote. He carried every southern state, and his margin of victory there was somewhat greater than it was in the rest of the country.[60] Nixon won the support of 80 percent of those who had supported Wallace four years earlier.[61] Accordingly, he won a majority of the white union vote, the first time that the Democratic nominee did not take this group. In fact, the percentage of the white working class that voted Democratic fell to its lowest level up to that point.[62] Yet despite its large defeat for the presidency, the bottom of the Democratic ticket did not suffer: the party remained in control of the House and Senate, as over half of the 377 congressional districts that gave a majority of their support to Nixon elected Democratic representatives.[63]

The results of the 1972 elections pointed to major shifts occurring in the party system. The Democratic Party's embrace of a New Politics liberalism repelled large parts of its coalition, who saw it "as a set of abstract, even exotic commitments felt strongly by the well-educated members of the upper middle class."[64] The Republican Party, in turn, moved to court these voters with a socially conservative message. What occurred has been described by Ladd and Hadley as a class-ideology inversion in which the party of the Right attracted the working and middle classes and the party of the Left attracted the educated upper class.[65] But this unmooring of party allegiances was neither automatically resolved nor the beginning of an electoral realignment. After all, Democrats still dominated at the subpresidential level. Rather, partisan identification and party loyalty decreased as voters searched for the candidates who best represented their concerns at any given time.

Indeed, as Byron Shafer and William Claggett have argued, it can be said that there were now "two majorities" in American politics. There was the majority that, when economic and social welfare issues are the main concern, will vote for the Democratic Party, and there was the one that, when cultural and national issues are at the fore, will support the Republicans, provided, of course, that both parties are not wildly extremist on their core issues. McGovern lost because he was far to the left on social, national, and economic issues. At the same time, Nixon stressed his positions on social issues and foreign policy, attracting voters who would otherwise be repelled by Republican economic policies. In this system, evangelical Protestant Democrats, high school dropout Democrats, and high school graduate Democrats—the white working-class base of the New Deal coalition—were now the groups under the most "evident (and apparently) sustained cross-pressure" and held the key to national electoral victory.[66] Meanwhile, at the local and state levels, where materialist, pocketbook issues were more important to voters than social or foreign policy concerns, and where local Democrats could stake out positions appropriate for their constituency, the Democrats continued to perform well.[67]

The election of Jimmy Carter in 1976 seemed to be the one great exception to this new state of affairs. With his victory, it was possible to argue that, on the surface, "normal" postwar politics had returned. The majority party, the Democrats, won at both the national and the local level to regain control of both branches of the federal government. However, Carter did not reconstruct the New Deal coalition, which had underpinned previous Democratic victories. In his close victory, the former governor of Georgia failed to win a majority of either the southern or the nonsouthern white vote.[68] In addition, as in the congressional elections of 1974—in which Democratic candidates racked up the second-largest popular vote landslide up to that point—

the Democratic ticket did not perform as well with the lower and working classes as its predecessors had.[69]

Rather, Carter was able to take advantage of a unique situation. First, he was running against Gerald Ford, an appointed incumbent who had pardoned one of the most disgraced presidents in American history and had barely won his party's nomination against a conservative challenger, Ronald Reagan. Second, unlike in 1972, the state of the economy was the most important issue in voters' minds. In fact, in one survey, three-quarters of those polled said that the 7.2 percent inflation rate and the 8.1 percent unemployment rate were their two biggest concerns.[70] With the economy as a central issue and Carter's much-publicized religious devotion, the contentious social issues that plagued the Democrats in 1972 (and, for the most part, were still a part of the Democratic platform in 1976) were off center stage.[71] And the issues that traditionally favored them—which created their "majority"—were on it.[72] Even so, Carter won the election with only 50.1 percent of the popular vote. In sum, Carter was not a party man, nor was he elected as such; he was the alternative to a party and administration tainted by the Watergate scandal.[73] His victory, then, should not have been a cause for celebration in the Democratic camp. There was no sign that Carter had reassembled the pieces of the old Democratic coalition; his victory was his own.[74]

If the election of 1976 showed how a Democrat might win the presidency, the election of 1980 showed how a Democrat might lose it. Under Carter's watch, social and foreign policy concerns returned with a vengeance. On the international front, Carter worked to extend détente with the Soviet Union, only to watch the USSR invade Afghanistan. A fundamentalist Muslim regime in Iran took Americans hostage, and the Organization of Petroleum Exporting Countries (OPEC) wreaked havoc on American energy policy, driving up prices and producing long lines at the gas pumps.[75] On social issues, Carter never fully lived up to the expectations of those who saw him as a social moderate. He appointed younger, New Politics advocates to spots on regulatory commissions and continued the Democratic Party's commitment to liberal positions on civil rights and civil liberties.[76]

At the same time, the economy worsened. Unemployment remained high; between July 1979 and July 1980, 669,000 jobs were lost in the nation's steel mills and automobile plants.[77] Inflation grew to over 13 percent, and by the end of 1979, the prime lending rate reached

16 percent. As inflation increased, so did Americans' tax rates, fueling an already lingering animosity toward the federal government and sparking a full-fledged tax revolt. This revolt kicked off in California in 1978 when voters there passed Proposition 13, a ballot initiative that placed a cap on property taxes. These events set the stage for a Republican resurgence. The issue context that favored them was pushed to the fore (by 1980, 60 percent of those polled felt that the country was spending too little on national defense), and the Carter years represented the first time during the postwar years that a significant economic downturn occurred on the Democratic watch. With unified Democratic control of the federal government, the entire party's credibility on its strongest issue context was undermined. Blue-collar voters, already cross-pressured but remaining loyal to the Democratic Party because of its economic policies, were free to cast their lot with the Republicans and Reagan, the party's thoroughly conservative nominee.

The nomination of Reagan marked the culmination of a rightward shift in the Republican Party that had begun with the nomination of Goldwater in 1964 and signaled the GOP's break with the New Deal consensus. Reagan was able to draw on a conservative movement bolstered by the establishment of an array of think tanks (notably, the Heritage Foundation) and fund-raising bodies (such as the National Conservative PAC) that nurtured and organized the New Right.[78] At the same time, religious conservatives and their church leaders became increasingly involved in American politics, with the *Roe v. Wade* abortion rights decision being the latest catalyst to energize them.[79] Building on this organizational activity as well as on the work of conservative thinkers throughout the 1970s, Reagan cobbled together the three main streams of conservative thought: economic libertarianism, social traditionalism, and militant anticommunism.[80] And in 1980, he forged a Republican Party that was thoroughly conservative on all scores, as evidenced by its platform.

In economic policy, the GOP indicted the whole notion that governmental policy could induce economic growth, along with the belief that the government had a role in the economy at all. Rejecting the Keynesian economics that dominated the postwar world, the Republicans endorsed supply-side economic policies that called for increased incentives for production. Practically, this meant a dramatic reduction in tax rates and in government expenditures in order to stimulate growth.[81] Conservatives argued that the budget deficit that might be created would be offset by the increase in growth and, eventually, tax revenues.[82]

In foreign policy, the Republicans called for a generally more assertive, even aggressive, posture. Devoutly anticommunist, they advocated large increases in military spending and rejected Carter's SALT II missile reduction treaty with the USSR.[83] On social issues, the GOP staked itself clearly on the right side of this divide. Republicans remained opposed to school busing and gun control legislation and in favor of prayer in schools and the death penalty, stands that the party had first adopted in 1972.[84] Furthermore, the Republicans took a hard turn to the right on two important issues affecting the changing status of women. In every platform passed from 1940 to 1976, the GOP had endorsed the ERA. Yet in 1980, the Republicans broke with this stance and refused to endorse this amendment to the Constitution guaranteeing equal rights for women. Also, the platform that year advocated a constitutional amendment to outlaw abortion and backed an antiabortion litmus test for federal judges.[85]

In an environment where the Democratic Party's handling of the economy was discredited and social and foreign policy concerns were paramount, the Republicans' traditionalist and nationalist message resonated with the cross-pressured white working- and middle-class voters. As one conservative leader put it, these citizens were "voting with God instead of voting with the unions."[86] And on election day, they helped give Reagan and the Republicans an impressive victory. On November 4, 1980, the Republican Party won back the presidency, plus thirty-three House seats (including those of four committee chairmen) and twelve Senate seats (including that of Senator George McGovern), giving them control of the latter body for the first time since 1952.[87] Carter received the lowest percentage of the popular vote of any incumbent Democratic president in history.[88] One-third of self-identified Democrats rejected him, and he outpolled Reagan in only a handful of social groups: blacks (where he won by over 80 percent), Hispanics, whites with family incomes below $5,000, whites who did not graduate from high school, Jews, and working-class Catholics.[89] Evidently, the remnants of the New Deal coalition that remained loyal—the poor, racial minorities, and liberals—were insufficient for national victory.

How one viewed the results of the 1980 election and the events of 1968 to 1980 said much about one's opinion of the changes in the

Democratic Party over the previous twelve years and the prospects for its future. To the dominant New Politics liberals, the party had successfully reformed itself. It had altered its institutional arrangements to open the party up to "the people" and had adopted a public philosophy that was truly progressive and liberal. To them, the defeat of Carter was either an aberration or the result of his not being sufficiently liberal; unified Democratic control of government would undoubtedly return.

To other Democrats, the declining electoral fortunes of the party at the national level were a portent of worse things to come, all of which were a direct result of a set of institutional changes that had produced a public philosophy that was electorally unviable. This group included the Democratic activists, thinkers, and elected officials associated with the factions that opposed the changes that the New Politics Left had wrought on the party and on its public philosophy.

Opposition to the New Politics faction had been evident since the tumultuous national convention in 1968 and intensified after the nomination and defeat of McGovern in 1972. The most vocal and well-known group among this opposition were the "neoconservatives," who argued that the Democratic Party had to return to the New Deal liberalism of the immediate postwar era. Tracing their roots to the anticommunist Left (and for some, further back to the anti-Stalinist communists), as well as to those who had ardently backed Truman against the progressive Henry Wallace in 1948, these Democrats fervently opposed any concessions to the Soviet Union. Predominantly a set of intellectuals, neoconservatives—such as Daniel Bell, Daniel Patrick Moynihan, and Irving Kristol—reacted viscerally to the rise of the New Politics faction in the national Democratic Party.

First, they rejected outright this group's conciliatory stance toward the USSR and its flirtations with the international revolutionary Left from Che Guevara to Yasir Arafat. Many of them supported the Vietnam War, a conflict that was escalated by their fellow anticommunist Democrats. Driving both these stances was how the neoconservatives viewed the conflict between the two superpowers. To them, this was a moral conflict, and the United States, as the country of democracy and freedom, had an obligation to counter communism and oppression.[90]

Neoconservatives also differed substantially with New Politics liberals on social issues. They ardently opposed the liberalization of traditional mores that the countercultural movements of the 1960s spearheaded. They argued that it threatened the authority of American institutions, such as universities, and undermined the nation's overall stability, which to them was critical. Although opposed to the unequal treatment of minority groups, the neoconservatives, like many white working-class Democrats, rejected schemes to guarantee equality of results, such as busing and racial quotas in employment and education.[91] Moreover, neoconservatives rejected the New Politics tendency to explain away societal problems (e.g., poverty) or personal behavior (e.g., crime) as the fault of American society or culture, not as the result of personal actions.

Finally, neoconservatives criticized the growth of the welfare state, claiming that it overburdened the federal government and thus threatened its legitimacy. To them, government was trying to do too much, instituting programs that often had the unintended consequence of being a cure far worse than the original problem. Said differently, neoconservatives recognized that there were limits to what the federal government could do. As Moynihan wrote in 1967 in his influential *New Leader* article "The Politics of Stability," "Liberals must divest themselves of the notion that the nation—and especially the cities of this nation—can be run from agencies in Washington."[92]

Neoconservatives had their greatest impact at the level of elite intellectual and policy debate. Based mostly around journals such as *Public Interest* and *Commentary*, their only organizational entity was the Coalition for a Democratic Majority (CDM), formed after the 1972 election, and it never had a mass base.[93] Among Democratic elites, the neoconservatives had allies among many traditional labor leaders (one neoconservative even referred to himself as a "George Meany Democrat") and among the remaining traditional Cold War liberals, the foremost being Senator Henry "Scoop" Jackson of Washington.[94]

In 1976, neoconservatives backed Jackson's failed bid for the Democratic presidential nomination, and although heartened by Moynihan's successful run for a New York Senate seat, they were eventually disappointed with the election of Carter. The only member of the CDM appointed to a foreign policy post was Peter Rosenblatt, who was designated the president's representative to negotiations on the future status of Micronesia. As some neoconservatives sarcastically put it, besides being the only one chosen, Rosenblatt was given neither Polynesia nor Macronesia but Micronesia as an assignment.[95] Opposed to

Carter's warming of relations with the Soviet Union, his emphasis on the Third World in his foreign policy, and the weakness that the United States projected worldwide during that time, many neoconservatives— like many in the Democratic rank and file—supported Ronald Reagan in 1980.

Joining the neoconservatives with similar complaints were white southern Democrats. Once fervently and automatically Democratic, by 1980 they had established a pattern at the grassroots of voting Republican for president and Democratic in subpresidential contests. Yet a strong representation of this group still existed among the elected party leadership. Although rejecting the racism of past southern Democratic politicians, these elected officials still retained many of the traditional values and political views of the South. Reflecting the military tradition and the large defense presence in the region, these elected officials supported a strong military and an aggressive foreign policy. They were generally socially conservative, more partial to business than to organized labor, and, like generations of southern leaders, distrustful of a big federal government.[96]

In all these positions, southern Democrats joined the predominantly northern and urban neoconservatives. Indeed, many prominent southern Democrats—such as Senators Sam Nunn of Georgia and Lawton Chiles of Florida, Governor Charles Robb of Virginia, and Congressman David McCurdy of Oklahoma—allied themselves with the CDM, especially on defense and foreign policy issues.[97] A large ideological gulf existed between southern Democratic elected officials and the New Politics liberals who dominated the national party, a chasm that made them especially sensitive to the worsening electoral fortunes of the party's presidential nominees.

Finally, in the late 1970s and early 1980s, another Democratic faction emerged—the neoliberals. This group of elected officials and other political elites was not so much in opposition to the dominant New Politics faction as a variant of it. Practically, many of those associated with the neoliberals had similar roots as the New Politics liberals. Gary Hart, the senator from Colorado, served as McGovern's campaign manager in 1972, and other major players such as Tim Wirth, Paul Tsongas, Richard Gephardt, Bill Bradley, and Robert Reich were some of the first baby boomers to take prominent roles in public life as elected officials or thinkers.[98] They did not have a formal organizational entity, but they did have a sympathetic periodical, the *Wash-*

ington Monthly, and frequently met early in the morning in a basement apartment in Washington to hear from policy and political experts and debate the future of the party.[99]

Ideologically, neoliberals shared the dominant Democratic Party faction's liberalism on social and foreign policy issues. Moreover, they joined the reformist wing of the party and the New Left, two important components of New Politics liberals, in their skepticism toward interest groups and bureaucracy. Neoliberals, however, believed that despite the prominence of the New Politics liberal public philosophy, government itself had not been reformed. A fealty to bureaucracy, big government, and interest groups—even New Politics interest groups—led the Democratic Party to defend programs that in the end did not help the people they were designed to help. Driving this need to "redefin[e] the role of government" was the belief that changes in the world economy, along with technological advances, presented challenges that, in Bradley's words, "the traditional Democratic responses [that] really had their origins in the Thirties . . . are not going to meet."[100]

In this regard, the neoliberals were pragmatic liberals, holding the same values and goals as other liberals but wanting to view politics realistically and to find solutions that, above all, worked.[101] Also, their futurism and embrace of technology—a stance that earned neoliberals the sobriquet "Atari Democrats," after the popular home video game—ran counter to those in the dominant liberal faction who saw modern technology, development, and economic growth as destructive to the environment and even to society overall.[102] To them, economic policy should emphasize the redistribution of wealth. Neoliberals, in contrast, believed that the central goal of economic policy should be to grow the economy. Accordingly, neoliberals were more open to market-oriented solutions in public policy and had a larger affinity for business, especially entrepreneurs, than did New Politics liberals.[103] Although these differences on economic policy and the organization of government were real, neoliberals were not a vocal opponent to the New Politics faction, with its elected-official adherents voting almost identically with New Politics liberals on most issues.[104]

From these three groups would come the next main rival to the dominant liberal faction in the Democratic Party: the New Democrats. Although some observers viewed the New Democrats as being merely southern Democrats, it needs to be stressed that all the aforementioned groups were partial, but important, practical and ideological antecedents to the New Democrats.[105] Many New Democratic ideas, policies, and proponents can be traced back to each of these earlier groups of critics of the New Politics.

After the 1980 election, the political entrepreneurs behind the New Democratic effort united in the House Democratic Caucus and later in the DLC. They included neoconservatives who had not defected to the GOP, southern Democrats who were witnessing the Republican resurgence in their own backyards, and neoliberals who wanted to modernize the party's approaches to policymaking. Over time, these groups were forged into a distinct New Democratic faction with a distinct public philosophy.

After the elections of 1980, the Democratic Party was not only a defeated party. It was a profoundly different party from the one that had loomed large over the immediate postwar world. Most prominently, its dominant public philosophy had changed. Where it had once embraced an internationalist, anticommunist outlook and the strong defense to support it, the national party was now hesitant in the projection of force abroad, eager to reconcile with the Soviet Union, and willing to divert funding from the military to an array of domestic programs. Although the party still saw the federal government as the primary agent of change in society and the main guarantor of the economic welfare of the citizenry, the goals of economic policy had changed. Instead of embracing growth and the wide provision of basic social insurance and welfare benefits, the national party increasingly saw the redistribution of wealth and the targeted provision of benefits as its main goals.

Where the Democratic Party had once embraced egalitarianism based on the provisions of equal opportunity, it now believed that a whole host of rights mandated the federal government's guarantee of equal outcomes. In this, federal programs were viewed as entitlements, with all the sacrosanctity that this term implies. Finally, changing sociopolitical conditions and critical events forced social concerns to the fore. On a whole host of particular issues, the national Democratic Party advocated positions on the left side of this debate, stances increasingly out of step with the party's traditional base.

These changes in public philosophy point to further changes in the party and in the makeup of its leadership as well. The McGovern-Fraser reforms opened the way for advocates of this new public philosophy to wrest control of the national party from the established party leaders. Whereas party leaders and elected officials once had a large degree of influence on the outcome of the nominating process, now purposive issue activists and their constituent groups organized in open primaries and caucuses had the power. Candidates, in turn, needed their aid in these contests and, unsurprisingly, reflected their issue stances. As this New Politics liberalism took hold, the white working class—especially northern ethnics and southern whites—found themselves alienated from the national party, especially from its social and foreign policies, and attracted to alternatives (mostly Republican) when these issues were of foremost importance.

More importantly, by the early 1980s, voters registered this change. When a survey by the National Election Studies in 1972 asked who composed the Democratic Party, the main responses still reflected the New Deal coalition: the poor, the middle class, blacks, Catholics, and labor unions. When this question was asked in 1984, the answers reflected the New Politics coalition: black militants, the women's liberation movement, civil rights leaders, people on welfare, gays and lesbians, and labor unions. Unfortunately for the Democrats, the New Deal coalition rated an average of sixty-five on a favorability scale of zero to one hundred, and the New Politics coalition scored an average of forty-five.[106]

As Reagan took office, then, many Democrats feared that the once radiant Democratic Party—the sun of the political system—was in danger of being eclipsed by the Republican moon. For them, the process of rebuilding the party and remaking its public philosophy could not come soon enough.

2 / Changing the Rules, 1981–1984

AFTER THE DEFEAT of Jimmy Carter in 1980, Al From returned to Capitol Hill, where he had spent most of the past decade as a senior staffer. For the past year, he had served in the Carter White House as deputy adviser to the president for inflation, a title that belied his years of Washington experience but accurately reflected the times. His return to become the executive director of the House Democratic Caucus was typical of the cadre of professional political staff that is dislocated whenever a branch of government changes hands. And the route that From took to Washington and the political life was typical, at least for his generation of Democrats.

Born into a Jewish family in South Bend, Indiana—who, in From's words, were "Democrats forever" since Harry Truman recognized the State of Israel—From went on to study journalism at Northwestern University in the mid-1960s. Intrigued by the work of the liberal newspaper editor Hodding Carter II, From decided to go to Greenville, Mississippi, to write his master's thesis on how Carter's *Delta Democrat Times* shaped public opinion in a city that in 1964 became the first in the Deep South to voluntarily desegregate its schools. In 1966, while back in Washington, From was introduced to Sargent Shriver, the head of Lyndon Johnson's War on Poverty, who promptly sent From back south to supervise programs in the Southeast region. In this role, he spent a lot of time in Mississippi and Alabama, especially in the civil rights battlegrounds of Wilcox and Lowndes Counties in Alabama. Rural, poor, and black, Lowndes County was where Viola Liuzzo, a Detroit housewife, was gunned down after the march from Selma to Montgomery and where Stokely Carmichael formed the first Black Panther Party.

While working in this hotbed of civil rights activity, From met most of the major players in the movement. But more importantly, he also met his wife, whose stepfather was the only white attorney in Wilcox County who would take the antipoverty program's cases. With the election of Richard Nixon in 1968, the War on Poverty ended, and From moved to Washington to take a job with Senator Joseph Tydings of Maryland. When Tydings was defeated in 1970, From moved to the office of Senator Edmund Muskie of Maine, a presidential hopeful, where From served as staff director of the Intergovernmental Relations Subcommittee for the next eight years.

The events of the 1960s had a profound effect on From, one that went beyond his lingering southern drawl, yet in a way substantially different from those Democrats usually associated with the times. With his short hair and horn-rimmed glasses, From was hardly a countercultural radical. He worked for Muskie, not McGovern, in 1972. On top of this, his proudest achievement from his years in the Senate was his work shepherding the Congressional Budget and Impoundment Act of 1974 to passage.[1] Although a key legislative reform of the era, it was hardly the rallying cry of the young men and women of the Left.

For From, the lessons he drew from the defining events of his generation of Democrats revolved around a disappointment with the party's leftward drift effected by the New Politics faction. His experience in the War on Poverty, especially assessing the community action programs, demonstrated to From the importance of helping the disadvantaged through self-empowerment, not "ossified bureaucracies." His witnessing of the 1972 McGovern candidacy and subsequent defeat served as a warning that the Democratic Party was in danger of abandoning its "working-class, ethnic base." The McGovern defeat also convinced From that the Democratic Party's liberal agenda would never be fulfilled if the party was not "honest about the failings of government programs."[2] To that end, while working for Muskie, From took a lead role in crafting "sunset" legislation that would force federal spending programs to be reauthorized periodically.[3]

Thus, the loss of the White House and Senate in 1980, as well as the loss of thirty-three seats in the House, confirmed his skepticism and resurrected doubts that From and others like him had about the future of the Democratic Party. With Ronald Reagan in the White House and his agenda of tax cuts and increased military spending receiving support from a rejuvenated congressional Republican Party as well as a number of Democrats, they feared that the "Reagan Revolution" might achieve a momentum sufficient to relegate the Democratic Party to the political sidelines in the 1980s.

Into this breach stepped From and his new boss, Representative Gillis Long of Louisiana, the newly elected chairman of the House Democratic Caucus. Like his illustrious political family (Huey "Kingfish" Long and Senator Russell Long were both cousins), Gillis Long was a unique character. A World War II hero, he was first elected to Congress in 1962 from a rural Louisiana district that was in the heart of Kingfish country. Then, in an act of courage for a southern Democrat, Long voted to expand the Rules Committee, a vote that paved the way for the Civil Rights Act of 1964 and similar legislation. As a result, he lost reelection in 1964 to a more conservative opponent, State Senator Speedy O. Long, yet another cousin. In 1972, Gillis Long won back his seat and promptly joined the Rules Committee, where he ascended to the second most senior spot.

A moderate in the House, Long became one of the body's best-liked and most respected members. In fact, when news that he would not run for governor of Louisiana reached the House floor, more than fifty congressmen—conservatives and liberals—rose to praise him for not leaving Congress. Yet what his colleagues did not know on that April day in 1979 was that Long had also suffered a heart attack. Two years later, Long would undergo open-heart surgery just weeks after he won the chairmanship of the House Democratic Caucus.[4]

Long may have been in poor health, but in From, he had an executive director who was able to help him use the caucus—the party's most powerful remaining organized element in government—to accomplish a central goal of his chairmanship: drawing up a blueprint to turn the party around. These analyses and recommendations, along with key personnel, would later turn up explicitly among New Democrats in the Democratic Leadership Council and elsewhere. Therefore, to understand the DLC and the strategies it adopted, an examination of the Long-From efforts within the House Democratic Caucus from 1981 to 1984 is crucial. It is here that the notion of a chronic decline of the Democratic Party reemerged; it is here that the New Democratic public philosophy and political strategy began to be developed; it is here that the players who drove these efforts first came together.

Specifically, key members concluded that the New Deal coalition, which had enabled the party to dominate national politics for the past four decades, was falling apart. As evidenced by the 1980 election results, the public philosophy of the party no longer resonated with the values and needs of many of the (previously Democratic) voters. To revamp the Democratic Party's public philosophy and thus restore its electoral success, these early reformers—these nascent New Democrats—believed that they had to alter institutional arrangements within the party itself, such as its nominating procedures and organization, arrangements that had been transformed by the McGovern-Fraser Commission and subsequent reform bodies.

More generally, they contended that only by reasserting the role of elected officials within the national apparatus of the party would it be possible to replace its New Politics, interest-group liberalism with a more politically advantageous public philosophy. But due in part to this group's own organizational weaknesses and in part to the power of the New Politics liberals within the national party, making these institutional changes would not be easy. Thus, when the Democratic Party lost another presidential election in 1984, these inadequacies would prompt the formation of the DLC itself.

Reform Efforts in the House Democratic Caucus

In the early 1980s, some of the youngest and most promising members of Congress, including Representatives William Gray of Pennsylvania, Tim Wirth of Colorado, Al Gore of Tennessee, and Richard Gephardt of Missouri, could be found meeting every Thursday on the seventh floor of the Longworth House Office Building as part of the House Democratic Caucus's Committee on Party Effectiveness (CPE). Formed by Long and his allies after the 1980 election to develop "policy and a guide to party affairs," the CPE, they hoped, would be the main vehicle for the rejuvenation of the Democratic Party.[5]

The CPE has been called "the first organizational embodiment of the New Democrats."[6] However, it would be misleading to view the thirty-seven members of the CPE and their allies as New Democrats, a recognizable and self-consciously distinct party faction. At this point, the label "New Democrat" had not yet been coined, and the actors involved would not have viewed themselves in that way. Indeed, many of the CPE members were identifiable members of other

groups—such as neoliberals, neoconservatives, and southern Democrats—that opposed elements of the dominant public philosophy of the
party; others still had their political roots deep in the New Politics faction (the prime example being Barney Frank of Massachusetts). Long's
claim, then, that CPE members represented "every philosophy and
region" in the caucus, although an exaggeration, was not a complete
overstatement.[7] Thus, I will not use the term "New Democrat" to describe this group, reserving that label for the next chapter, when this
faction differentiated itself by establishing the DLC.

Nevertheless, from the CPE, Long hoped to forge "general consensus positions on the most important national issues that form the
thread that gives our party meaning."[8] This rethinking of party policy
and ideology was not solely a legislative exercise. It was part of a larger
effort to reassert the role of congressmen, and elected officials in general, in the party. Indeed, although based in the House, the CPE's focus
was on party politics, not congressional politics. The CPE was a place
to develop policy proposals and even a new public philosophy for the
party. But just as importantly, it was an organizational base for efforts
to reform the national Democratic Party so that these policy initiatives could have a chance of being adopted.[9]

ELECTORAL PROBLEMS AND ALTERNATIVES

The strength of the Reagan-Bush ticket among many key Democratic
groups, the party's dramatic loss of the Senate, and the overall good
showing of the Republicans at every level frightened many Democratic
elected officials. Democrats in the House were not immune from these
fears. Although they retained control of the lower chamber, four committee chairmen lost reelection, and the percentage of Republican representatives increased from the low of 40.4 percent in 1974 to 48.7
percent in 1980.[10]

From and Long appeared to be facing a growing problem of electoral viability. They concluded that the 1980 defeat was not a fluke,
nor even a personal repudiation of Carter. Instead, it pointed to a
deeper rejection of the Democratic Party's platform and of its ability
to govern. Yet interestingly, in their own experiences, almost no CPE
members were under any immediate electoral threat. Indeed, mirror-
ing high rates of reelection to the House throughout this period, over
half the CPE members won in 1980 with over 65 percent of the two-

party vote; one-quarter of them did not face any opposition at all in the general election.

Still, underlying even these victories were trends that pointed to political weakness. For instance, all but four of the thirty-seven members of the CPE hailed from states that Reagan had won, and all but one had won a higher percentage of the popular vote in their districts than the Carter-Mondale ticket had received in their states as a whole. In that regard, CPE members, especially the majority who hailed from southern and border states, were overcoming statewide trends—in essence, swimming upstream—in the process of winning. To them, the relatively declining electoral fortunes of the national Democratic Party were becoming an increasingly uncomfortable reality.[11]

Furthermore, even though polling data at the time indicated that voters were more often repudiating Carter than embracing Republicans, there was reason to fear that the Reagan victory might be manipulated to produce a durable Republican majority based in the South and West. Feeding this fear were the results of the 1980 census, which made it clear that seventeen congressional seats would be transferred from the industrial Midwest and Northeast—Democratic strongholds—to the Sun Belt of the South and West, a move that could give a long-term boost to the GOP in the House.[12] This shift might further institutionalize in Congress the ongoing move of white working- and middle-class voters all over the country into the GOP camp. All in all, long-term and short-term factors pointed to a growing, and possibly dominating, Republican presence in American politics.

To Long and From, the answer to this potentially critical problem was not to give up on these constituencies. Instead of focusing on increasing the registration and turnout of more reliable Democratic coalition members, they wanted the party to make efforts to win back the support of Middle America by reworking the Democratic Party's public philosophy into one that addressed the "national interest" as opposed to "special interests." In the view of Long, From, and their allies, their party's positions revolved around the specific demands of narrow special-interest groups—especially the civil rights, peace, environmental, and feminist groups of New Politics liberals—at the expense of the needs (and electoral support) of the majority of the country.

The critique and alternative public philosophy that the CPE offered was thus an answer to what it perceived to be, at its roots, an electoral problem. To win elections, CPE leaders argued, the party had to alter its policy and political positions. In short, at this point of the New Democrats' history, ideology was linked to the perceived realities of electoral politics. It was a link that would reoccur again and again.

ISSUE PROBLEMS AND POLICY ALTERNATIVES

Perhaps the most illuminating example of what From and Long meant when they attacked the party for advocating special interests over national interests, and thus an example of the interconnectedness between electoral politics and policy positions, is their response to drafts of issue papers designated by the national party for approval at the 1982 midterm conference. In a letter to Charles Manatt, chairman of the Democratic National Committee (DNC), Long wrote that he was "becoming increasingly concerned" that these planks did not demonstrate that the Democratic Party "is once again ready to focus on the concerns of Mainstream America—the hard-working men and women who have long supported Democratic candidates."[13]

Specifically, Long felt that the issue papers gave the impression that the party was still beholden to special interests; wanted principally to tax and spend in response; and, "in sum, refuses to heed the lessons of the 1980 election." These draft documents stressed controversial issues that, to him, did not represent the concerns of the nation as a whole and only caused electoral problems for those who had to stand for reelection. As examples, Long pointed to the "Citizen Rights and Personal Security" section, which did not mention fighting crime until the sixteenth page, and the "Making Government Work Better" section, which defended a myriad of programs while suggesting no areas to cut or eliminate.[14] The congressman also did not think it necessary to mention issues such as abortion, gay rights, and gun control, since they were divisive and would "inevitably cause problems for candidates in the fall."[15]

Long wanted the national party to adopt a public philosophy that was not fixated on the concerns of interest groups that embraced beliefs far to the left of the sentiments of the general electorate. In some ways, he wanted the party to return to its pre-1968 roots, to a liberalism that stressed fostering economic growth and providing opportunity by controlling federal spending and investing in high technology and education.[16] In turn, as From argued, this strategy would enable the Democratic Party to recapture the "vital center" and to show that it had "the compassion to care and the toughness to govern."[17] To work out the details of this policy agenda and emerging public philosophy, the CPE published *Rebuilding the Road to Opportunity*, a book of policy papers, in 1982.

In the preface to *Rebuilding the Road to Opportunity*, Long presented this overview: "In these papers, we renew our commitment to the fundamental principles of the Democratic party—to equal opportunity, to economic growth and full employment, and to a strong national defense."[18] These principles, as Long acknowledged, were at the core of New Deal liberalism, largely rejected by the New Politics faction. However, Long wrote that the CPE effort was more than a nostalgic attachment to times past, noting that "our policies must change—because our country and the world have changed."[19] With these changes in mind, the CPE report called for a steadily growing, noninflationary economy that was adapted to the realities of globalization and the growth of high technology, the controlling of federal spending and of growth in government, the elimination of "wasteful or outdated spending," investment in new technology and education, a tough stance on crime, a strong but "strategically constructed" defense, and a fostering of the entrepreneurial spirit in business.[20]

It must be noted that the policy manual did include issues that had been placed on the Democratic agenda by the New Politics faction, such as the protection of the environment and the expansion of opportunities for women. As From admitted, in order to placate both liberals and conservatives on the committee, much of the document was "still at the level of rhetoric."[21] Nevertheless, these policy prescriptions broke from those found in Democratic Party platforms of the 1970s and deviated especially from the agenda of many New Politics groups. For example, the defense paper called for the promotion of American values abroad, advocated an end to subordinating foreign policy objectives to human rights, and opposed a unilateral nuclear disarmament or test ban.[22] Likewise, the environmental policy paper took a strong pro-environmental position but stressed that environmental control measures should not hamper economic growth.[23]

Furthermore, in a more abstract sense, *Rebuilding the Road to Opportunity* challenged the relationship between state and citizen implicit in the dominant public philosophy of the national Democratic

Party: "We believe that the job of government is not to confer happiness, but to give people the opportunity to work out happiness for themselves."[24] For the New Democrats, the egalitarian impulse would be tempered, shifting from a position advocating equality of results to one advocating equality of opportunity. Although at this time they did not champion the specific policy positions that this stance implied, it is clear that these nascent New Democrats were rejecting the entitlement strain of liberalism that New Politics groups had brought into the party in 1972 and had remained a strong influence in Democratic thinking ever since.[25]

The CPE could have asked that its manual be considered at the 1982 midterm party conference, but Chairman Manatt, wanting to avoid the usual public fight among various groups of activists, had moved the meeting to June, reduced the number of attendees, and changed the function of the conference from approving issue resolutions to preparing for the upcoming congressional elections.[26] Although the likelihood that such a national party gathering would adopt *Rebuilding the Road to Opportunity* was slim, Manatt's changes also affected the CPE, in the sense that this move closed a once regularly occurring political window of opportunity, forcing From to develop an alternative strategy to disseminate these ideas.

As a result, Long moved within Congress, asking Democratic members on the relevant standing committees to report back within three months with their reactions to the specific planks of *Rebuilding the Road to Opportunity*. To publicize the plan outside of Capitol Hill, From enlisted Representatives Martin Frost of Texas, Gephardt, and Wirth to sell the policy manual to editorial boards as both a "new underlying philosophy" and a new political approach for the party, one developed by its young leaders.[27] From, in a briefing paper to these congressmen, advised them to stress the new economic strategy, the "commonsense" approach to the environment, the tough stance on crime, and the new defense positions advocated in the document. He and Long wanted to get the message out that there was a group of Democrats advocating positions that were firmly in the mainstream.

Ultimately, *Rebuilding the Road to Opportunity* was well received in Washington and within the party.[28] In Congress, Long, Speaker Thomas "Tip" O'Neill of Massachusetts, and James Jones of Oklahoma, chairman of the House Budget Committee and later a founding DLC member, produced a budget resolution in 1983 that reflected a number of proposals found in the plan.[29] Outside of Congress, the economic planks of the plan were especially noted for their innovative qualities. The Democratic Business Council, a group of approximately one hundred business leaders who contributed at least $10,000 to the national party, voted its approval of the CPE's economic package.[30] But more importantly, the entire policy manual was able to be used by congressional candidates as a campaign resource, and later, *Rebuilding the Road to Opportunity* formed the basis of the DNC's half-hour televised response to President Reagan's 1983 State of the Union Address.[31]

Building on this effort to remake the public philosophy of the Democratic Party, From and Long established the National House Democratic Caucus (NHDC) in July 1983. This spin-off of the CPE was independent of Congress, thus enabling the inclusion of private citizens and the utilization of private funds.[32] In January 1984, the NHDC released *Renewing America's Promise,* a document similar to *Rebuilding the Road to Opportunity* in substance and strategy. Written by the same team that had produced *Rebuilding the Road to Opportunity,* this new set of policies hoped to accomplish the same goals. Again, Long asserted in the paper's preface that the positions in it were intended to "re-establish" the Democratic Party's identity as a party of growth and of national strength, and that it also hoped to provide a new "public philosophy and an action program" on which Democratic candidates could run.[33] But *Renewing America's Promise* went a step further, including some recommendations that were starkly deviant from the positions of the national party. For instance, it called for a reevaluation of an all-volunteer army, citing its cost and contributions to building a national community; for equality for all Americans through a plan "that is not specific to minorities but is designed to broaden the opportunities and assure the rights of all"; and for a review of entitlement spending, including whether wealthy retirees and farmers received too much aid.[34]

To publicize these proposals, the NHDC held regional issue forums in places such as St. Louis and Baltimore, which generated both national and local media coverage, and tried to recruit selected Democratic governors to sign on to its proposals.[35] Yet publicity alone was not enough. With the 1984 election cycle approaching, the organization also hoped that *Renewing America's Promise* could be submitted and eventually passed as the Democratic Party's platform.[36]

Indeed, the political calendar appeared to offer Long and his colleagues a ripe opportunity to insert their policies and the beliefs underpinning them into the official policy statement of the party.

Or at least it seemed that way. At one time, the chairman of the House Democratic Caucus and his allies would have found it relatively easy to become key players in the crafting of such a document. Moreover, their prospects would undoubtedly have been enhanced by the fact that, as the only group of Democrats who controlled a part of the federal government, the caucus was arguably the party's most influential collection of elected officials. Yet in the postreform era, as New Democrats in 1984 and beyond realized, there were institutional barriers preventing them, as elected officials, from exercising influence over the policy formation and political strategy of the national party. Therefore, in order to change the Democratic Party's public philosophy and restore its electoral viability, these Democratic elected officials found that they had to focus on removing these barriers and revamping the party's institutions, specifically its nominating rules and national organization.

INSTITUTIONAL PROBLEMS AND ALTERNATIVES

The root of the CPE's problem lay with the McGovern-Fraser reforms that had gone into effect in 1972. These changes—along with larger trends of the nationalization of politics and the rise of purposive issue activists—had already altered the balance of power within the party, so that elected officials' and traditional party leaders' control over the national party apparatus, including the selection of a presidential nominee, was greatly diminished. In attempting to "open up" the nominating process and the conduct of party affairs, reformers had created a situation that enabled ideological, predominantly white-collar activists to take a more central role in party affairs.

Ironically, instead of "the people" becoming more involved in the nominating process, as reformers had intended, "the next most extensive and next best organized groups and individuals" within the party began to dominate the process.[37] The power of groups such as the National Education Association (NEA), which had white-collar members with intense attachments to the organization and a high likelihood of participating in politics, and of focused issue organizations such as environmental and civil rights groups increased greatly at the expense of the power of elected officials. In the new system of open primaries and caucuses, winning the support of such activists—who not only would take the time to run for and serve as delegates but also could deliver primary votes—became more important than courting the support of elected officials.[38]

Although these congressmen and senators would have been helpful to a presidential hopeful early in the nominating process by organizing an area or putting together a slate of delegates, they had little political incentive to do so. If they committed their support early enough to do these tasks, they ran the risk of backing a losing candidate and forfeiting their chance of having influence with the eventual nominee—or president.[39] All in all, the ability of elected officials to become delegates, as well as their power to control the outcome of the convention, including changes in the rules and party platform, had decreased significantly.[40] Consider that in 1968, 68 percent of Democratic senators and 39 percent of Democratic House members attended the national nominating convention as delegates; by 1980, these numbers dropped to 14 and 15 percent, respectively.[41] With elected officials out of party affairs, alternative groups that were unrepresentative of the party's rank and file began—or so the New Democrats argued—to craft a party platform and message more in line with their wishes, not those of most voters.[42]

This complaint was voiced specifically, repeatedly, and early by the CPE. In a letter to DNC Chairman Manatt, for example, Long complained that, with regard to the development of party policy for the 1982 midterm conference, the drafting and review process did not give members of Congress an opportunity to read and consider the policy papers adequately. Indeed, only one proposal, the national security paper, was sent in time for enough members to review it at all.[43]

In the wake of the 1980 defeat, then, From, Long, and their allies had come to believe that to change the public philosophy of the party and make it more electorally successful in the future, elected officials needed to reenter party affairs. They contended that elected officials were uniquely qualified to rejuvenate the party, since intrinsic to their status as elected officials was the fact that they had been chosen by voters and thus represented a more broad-based constituency (and agenda) than party activists. Consequently, elected officials should be able to craft a more mainstream party platform (and ideology), one that would be attractive to the general electorate. Moreover, Democrats in and around the CPE thought that elected officials were also specially suited to act as brokers between different party interests, another advantage in crafting a more mainstream party.[44]

Reasserting the role of elected officials within party affairs was not a new concern, having been recognized almost immediately after the McGovern-Fraser reforms took effect. In 1973, after assuming chairmanship of the DNC, Bob Strauss—From's acknowledged mentor—formed the Democratic Advisory Council of Elected Officials to focus on rebuilding the party's center and, more importantly, to bring elected officials back into party affairs.[45] Yet, as From notes, Strauss's efforts did little in the way of curbing the New Politics faction's clout, since he and his successor, John White, gave them free rein with rules in exchange for party peace.[46]

By the early 1980s, however, more national party leaders began to realize that the power of purposive activists had to be curtailed. To this end, Manatt altered the size, timing, and mission of the 1982 midterm party conference. Moreover, he asked Harold Kwalwasser, a Los Angeles attorney, to organize a policy council that would unite elected officials and experts to develop the Democratic agenda for 1982. Yet this effort also had little impact. Unwilling to forfeit their monopoly on Democratic policymaking, congressional Democrats, including From and Long, strongly objected to such a body being established by the national party, resulting in a limiting of its scope.[47] Indeed, the National Strategy Council did little work. By the end of 1983, it had met three times, and its four task forces had not met at all.[48]

As had happened in the past, policy councils would not be the center of party reform. Recognizing the realities of the postreform Democratic Party, CPE Democrats knew that to make the changes they desired in the public philosophy of the party, they had to steal a page from the playbook of the New Politics faction and jump into the ongoing process of reform that their rivals had initiated after the 1968 election. In this, they looked to the Commission on Presidential Nomination, formed after the 1980 election and chaired by Governor James B. Hunt, Jr., of North Carolina, for the chance to have their reform plans heard and possibly adopted by the national party. As David Price, the commission's staff director, noted, Carter's defeat in 1980 had made the body and its work "a focal point for those attempting to diagnose the troubles of 1980 and wishing to 'do something' about the party's condition."[49] The Hunt Commission was particularly attractive to the CPE, since Hunt and many of those on the commission saw the opportunity to rewrite the party's nominating rules as a chance to pursue goals similar to those of Long and his CPE allies.

Reflecting the growing belief among senior party leaders that the national party was too beholden to the wishes of a vocal activist fringe, Hunt and DNC Chairman Manatt, who had appointed him, wanted to make the nominating process more representative of the party's rank and file, to increase the likelihood that the party's nominee could campaign and govern effectively, and to accomplish these goals by bringing elected officials back into party affairs.[50] Like those in the CPE, Manatt and Hunt believed that elected officials would be able to exercise a type of peer review, since officeholders were more likely to know the candidates. Furthermore, they hoped that these procedural changes would help heal the rift between the national and congressional wings of the party, which had become apparent during the Carter presidency.[51]

Consequently, the Hunt Commission made the issue of party-leader and elected-official representation at the convention a top priority. It was a concern shared by other Democratic groups as well. The AFL-CIO, the Senate Democratic Conference, state party chairs, and the House Democratic Caucus all joined Hunt's staff in offering proposals that provided for an unpledged "add-on" to the regular delegation— ranging from 20 to 30 percent of the current delegate total—to be reserved for party leaders and elected officials.[52] In the end, a plan providing for these "superdelegates" was drafted by Representative Geraldine Ferraro of New York and Mark Siegel, former DNC executive director, and after two amendments, it was adopted by the commission.

The Ferraro-Siegel plan gave add-on slots to each state for its party chairperson and vice-chairperson and allocated four hundred additional unpledged delegate positions to the states, based on their delegation size. This would accommodate two-thirds of the House and Senate Caucus membership (to be selected by the members), along with governors, big-city mayors, and other elected officials. Finally, the scheme provided for another 10 percent add-on of pledged delegates to be allocated by the states themselves; for those states that still could not accommodate all their major elected officials, it gave them additional "bonus" delegates.[53]

Now with a guaranteed delegation of congressmen at the 1984 convention, the chief aim of From and Long became "leveraging the

164 House delegates to the 1984 convention in a way that influences the Presidential race."[54] The CPE wanted to make it clear to the national party that since members of Congress are ultimately hindered by promises made to party interest groups, it was "dead serious about participating in the nominating process" and ensuring that its national interest agenda would be adopted by the Democratic Party and its presidential nominee.[55]

To this end, From wanted Democratic congressmen to flex their new institutional muscle, challenge the early endorsement strategy of powerful interest groups (e.g., AFL-CIO, NEA), and become prominent players in the nominating process. As the 1984 campaign season approached, From recommended an array of strategies to Long, including inviting presidential candidates to appear before the House Democratic Caucus, publicizing *Renewing America's Promise*, expanding the NHDC to include all elected officials, and organizing the unpledged delegates to the party's nominating convention into a coherent bloc.[56]

All in all, From planned for the NHDC to have a large impact on the 1984 election and beyond. He hoped that its "elected-party official infrastructure" would be able to develop and promote a new public philosophy for the Democratic Party.[57] Yet as the 1984 nominating campaign and election demonstrated, the group was far from having any meaningful influence in these matters. Despite the alterations to its rules, the party proved resistant to the CPE's calls for change. However, the ensuing electoral defeat added credence to the claim that the Democratic Party had a problem that needed remedying and provided momentum for the institutionalization of the New Democrats: the creation of the Democratic Leadership Council.

The CPE and the 1984 Election

The defeat of Walter Mondale and the apparent failure of his traditional interest-group strategy reinforced these incipient New Democrats' analysis that the party had a problem of electoral viability, one inextricably tied to its public philosophy. Just as the 1980 defeat had focused attention on perceived problems within the party and provided an opportunity to act on them, the results of the 1984 elections created an opportunity for disaffected Democrats to take even further action. The case that the Democratic Party had a problem was strengthened, and the political calendar—with the election of a new DNC chairman, for example—again provided openings for evaluation and innovation. Thus, after election day 1984, the pace and scope of the original CPE effort quickened and broadened.

ELECTORAL PROBLEMS AND ALTERNATIVES

After the party convention in July, From made his—and the CPE's—case to the Mondale campaign. He wrote that it had to attract men and whites to the Democratic ticket by adopting a message with broad national appeal, one that would pledge to hold the line on spending. Yet even five months before election day, From was already disenchanted with the Mondale campaign, resigned to the probability that it would not heed his advice, and fearful of what its failure would portend for members of Congress and the Democratic Party.[58] In a memo to Long, he wrote that although people like him would "stay Democrats because of history and personal ties to the party," he feared that a younger generation of potential Democrats—especially white men—would never join the party. The bottom line was stark: From feared that a Mondale loss would mean an electoral realignment.[59]

It is not surprising that From objected to Mondale's electoral strategy, since it ran so strongly counter to the approach of anti–New Politics Democrats. At first, it appeared that Mondale, a leading liberal, would embrace new thinking on Democratic policy and strategy. According to Steven Gillon, Mondale's biographer, the former vice-president recognized in September 1981 that the Democratic Party had to embrace noninflationary growth, question the proper role of the federal government in the economy, and develop positions on social issues that did not repel middle-class voters. Yet in the end, Mondale could not embrace a political strategy that did not recognize that "labor, blacks, and liberal organizations provided the backbone of a successful campaign and the foundation for effective governance."[60]

Partly driving this decision were the results of the 1982 elections, in which immense dissatisfaction with Reagan's handling of the economy, particularly among industrial workers, women, and minorities, had generated large Democratic gains: twenty-six House seats, six governorships, and control of six state legislatures.[61] As Gillon has pointed out, these returns convinced many Democrats, including Mondale, that the "old gospel" would be sufficient to reassemble the New Deal coalition.[62] A few weeks later, on December 1, 1982, Senator Edward Kennedy of Massachusetts, Mondale's most formidable potential opponent, announced that he would not seek the presidential nomination, freeing up constituency group endorsements for the taking.

The other key factors in this equation were Mondale himself and the new realities of the nominating process. He could not follow the strategy, epitomized by Carter in 1976, of courting highly educated and/or highly alienated voters by stressing that he was not a part of the political establishment; Mondale was perhaps the quintessential Democratic insider, intimately involved with national politics since the early 1960s. His only other option in the postreform nominating system was to court organized groups and ideologically committed activists.[63] This tack was reinforced by Mondale's New Deal roots: he saw nothing wrong with crafting an electoral coalition by winning the support of various organizations representing a wide array of interests.

What he could not counteract was that in 1984, with the national media squarely focused on the nominating process and with a highly cynical electorate, these deals were made in plain view of voters, reinforcing the notion that the Democratic Party was beholden to various interests.[64] Furthermore, unlike in the New Deal era, the groups with whom he had to forge a coalition were more steadfast in their beliefs and dedicated to their causes, and thus reluctant to concede a principle in order to ensure victory. But above all, the problem lay with the public philosophy he used to attract the support of these groups. It simply was not sufficient to win a presidential election.

For instance, the Mondale campaign hoped to attract those in the electorate who felt attached to federal largesse, yet this group constituted only about one-third of all voters, not a majority. Additionally, the strategy repelled many swing voters who felt that the government helped only the "undeserving poor" and who felt that the Democratic Party was wedded to a belief that "the whole welfare state apparatus is sacred."[65] This problem was difficult enough in the abstract, but in practice, because of the surprising showing in the early nominating contests of Senator Gary Hart—who pitched his appeal to these swing voters—Mondale increasingly had to rely on the traditional Democratic interest groups to win the nomination. Come November, he found it difficult to move himself to more centrist positions in order to win crucial independent and moderate voters.[66]

In the general election, the Mondale-Ferraro ticket suffered a land-slide defeat. President Reagan swept to reelection with 59 percent of the popular vote and a record 525 electoral college votes as he took every state except Mondale's home state of Minnesota plus the District of Columbia.[67] On many levels, the Democratic Party was also at the losing end of some disturbing trends. First, Mondale forged majorities only among racial or political minorities such as blacks and members of union households—groups that, taken together, still constituted a clear minority of the total population.[68] Beyond that, young voters, especially the baby-boom cohort, which constituted approximately 40 percent of the electorate in 1984, mirrored the national trend: 60 percent backed Reagan, 50 percent voted for GOP congressional candidates, and 39 percent identified themselves as Republican.

More alarming, though, was that only 34 percent of baby boomers identified themselves as Democrats, compared with 47 percent of voters nationwide; and only 41 percent voted for a Democratic congressional candidate, compared with 51 percent nationwide.[69] As Gerald Pomper, the Rutgers political scientist, commented, "These results are a dark portent for the Democratic future. The party might be able to dig out after Mondale's landslide defeat, but it could not easily sustain a continuous hail of rocks."[70] Moreover, the Republicans appeared to have been benefiting from an eight-year drift in the general preferences of "Middle America"—for example, those with moderate incomes or blue-collar workers.[71] Finally, the Republican president did well even among some formerly key members of the New Deal coalition; from 1976 to 1984, for example, the percentage of Catholics supporting the Republican ticket increased by eleven percentage points.[72]

Yet the most massive swing to the Republicans was found in the once solidly Democratic South. The South, whose white residents backed Reagan by a five-to-two margin, was actually his strongest region. Aiding Reagan was the fact that 40 percent of former Carter voters in the South cast their ballot for the Republican.[73] The South moved even more clearly toward the GOP if one considers that between 1980 and 1984, the nation swung 4.2 percent to the Republicans: this movement was twice as large in the outer South and border states, and three times the national number in the Deep South.[74] The Republican Party made advances at the subpresidential level in the South as well. Of the fourteen House seats that they gained in the 1984 election, Republicans won nine in southern and border states.

The Democrats did have some victories. For example, they picked up two seats in the Senate. Yet this was little comfort. On top of the election results, underlying trends pointed to an even more potentially troubling future. Among those who identified themselves as a member of a political party, the National Election Studies found a slight drop (4 percent) among voters considering themselves Democrats and a larger increase (6 percent) among those identifying themselves as Republicans. Although small, the Democratic decrease placed the party below the 50 percent mark for the first time since 1952, when the NES began collecting data on the question.[75]

The 1984 election appeared to confirm the worst fears of From, Long, and their allies: the GOP was making major inroads into the Democrats' ideological and geographical bastions, and the top of the ticket was becoming the weapon for the opposition party to use against subpresidential Democrats.[76] For evidence of this, they only had to look at the defeats of two formidable, moderate Democratic Senate candidates, James Hunt of North Carolina and Walter Huddleston of Kentucky, whose losses were attributed to their being tagged "Mondale liberals" by their opponents.[77] Will Marshall, who had worked with From and Long in the House Democratic Caucus but left to work on Hunt's Senate campaign, reflected, "it helped convince me that the national Democratic Party drag was such that good candidates were carrying an albatross around their necks with the words 'Democratic Party' written on it when they went in to elections."[78] After 1984, Marshall—who was to become a key New Democratic thinker— concluded that such Democrats could no longer "run away" from the party's national candidates.

What really happened on November 6, 1984? Was it just an aberration, or a sign of worse things to come? Among the "snap" analyses of academics and pundits, there was little agreement on the election's meaning. To some, the problem lay with Mondale and his wooden campaign style, especially on television.[79] To others, the situation was direr. Conservatism was taking hold in the electorate; the possibility of a full-scale realignment could not be dismissed.[80] Other analysts were almost optimistic about Democratic prospects. They pointed to the relative stability in party identification beneath the vote, to the fact that Democrats were still very successful at the subpresidential level, and to the way that 1984 represented a continuation of postwar second-term reelection landslides.[81] Even William Galston, Mondale's issues director and an intellectual founding father of the New Democrats, pointed out that "in the special circumstances of 1984, a Democratic ticket headed by Jesus with Moses in the second spot would have gotten about 45 percent of the vote against Reagan and Bush."[82] The recession that generated the victories in 1982 had disappeared. Times were too good, and the incumbent Reagan was too popular for anyone to defeat him. In this view, there was no realignment under way and no crisis that merited the wholesale rethinking of Democratic ideology and strategy.

ISSUE PROBLEMS AND POLICY ALTERNATIVES

From, Long, and their allies, however, had no doubt about any of this. The 1984 Mondale defeat confirmed their belief that the public philosophy and issue positions of the national Democratic Party were an active hindrance to the party's success. They believed, for instance, that Mondale's forthright pledge in his acceptance speech at the Democratic convention to raise taxes in order to shrink the budget deficit and to restore "fairness" to the tax code did not earn him points for candor or courage but backfired, actually repelling the middle-class voters the CPE Democrats felt should be pursued by the party.

Although they did flirt with some of the rhetoric found in *Renewing America's Promise,* mostly as a concession to the Hart camp, Mondale and the national Democratic Party constructed a platform that did not follow the CPE's "national interest" strategy.[83] The platform reflected a belief that the federal government should play a large role in ensuring the redistribution of income to benefit those less well off. Accordingly, Mondale called for a 15 percent minimum corporate tax, a 10 percent surcharge on those making more than $100,000 a year, a deferral of the indexing of tax brackets, and the elimination of many tax loopholes.[84]

At one time, these policies had been the "meat and potatoes" of an economic policy that attracted working-class voters to the Democratic Party. However, in 1984, with taxes cut and high inflation apparently beaten (and, more importantly, with Americans believing this to be true), voters had the Republicans to thank for solving an economic crisis that had reached its zenith under a Democratic administration.[85] Tellingly, 43 percent of Americans in 1984 felt that the condition of the economy had gotten better over the last year, as opposed to 12 percent who felt so in 1982 and 4 percent in 1980.[86] It is no surprise, then, that only 10 percent felt that Mondale's centerpiece issue of "fairness" was salient.[87]

Additionally, the Democratic Party platform was essentially an accurate rendering of postreform, interest-group liberalism, full of policies targeted to win the support of various and narrow constituencies, policies that usually repelled working- and middle-class voters. For example, to shore up labor's support, Mondale embraced many of its core issue stances. Most notably, he shucked the Democrats' free-trade stance, calling for a limit on cheaper imported goods to protect American workers.[88] Moreover, the document was expanded to 45,000 words to accommodate individual concerns of groups such as Japanese Americans, single homemakers, federal employees, illegal aliens, American Indians, and those with sickle-cell anemia.[89] Further reflecting the constituencies of the postreform Democratic Party, the platform was still to the left of the electorate on social and foreign policy concerns. It took a strong stance supporting women's rights, affirmative action, abortion rights, church-state separation, and the immediate negotiation of a nuclear freeze.[90] Finally, corroborating this image of pandering to special interests, Mondale publicly interviewed a group of possible running mates that deliberately included at least one representative from key Democratic constituencies.[91]

In the end, Mondale and his policies were repudiated at the polls. Voters appeared to approve of Reagan's performance, and when they clearly did not—as in the case of the growing federal budget deficit—they disapproved of the Democrats' handling of the problem even more. To committed CPE members, the 1984 election outcome, at its heart, was a product of the institutional barriers that they and other elected officials faced in participating in and having a significant impact on the nominating and platform-drafting processes. Despite the efforts of the CPE and the NHDC, these obstacles remained during the 1984 campaign season, a fact that spurred members of these organizations and like-minded Democrats to attempt more ambitious strategies to reshape the party.

INSTITUTIONAL PROBLEMS AND ALTERNATIVES

By the time of the 1984 Democratic convention in San Francisco, the CPE and sympathizers outside of the House already felt that their overall approach to politics and government had been rejected by the national party and that the resulting Democratic ticket was not going to win the presidency. Adding to this frustration was the fact that although the national party had indeed undertaken institutional changes to include more elected officials in party affairs, the presidential ticket and platform did not reflect CPE and NHDC prescriptions as a result. It appeared that their strategy of pursuing alterations in party rules to increase the role of elected officials was not producing the results they had expected.

Consider, for example, that the most prominent change made by the Hunt Commission to the delegate selection rules was the establishment of superdelegates, a device to give automatic delegate status to a percentage of party leaders and elected officials. Superdelegates were the most direct method of increasing the influence of elected officials in a nominating process that had become dominated by issue activists and, hypothetically, of increasing the likelihood that the party would steer a moderate course. This was not the only change the Hunt Commission had enacted to bolster the chances of the party's mainstream candidates. It had shortened the campaign season by closing the time between the Iowa caucus and the New Hampshire primary to one week, it had allowed states to award a bonus delegate to a candidate who won a congressional district, and it had raised the proportional threshold—the popular-vote total needed to win any delegates—to 20 percent.[92] All such measures were aimed at weakening the intense, activist fringe.

Party officials had hoped that these alterations to the nominating process would decrease the chances of an outsider candidate winning the nomination. The presence of more elected officials in the process was intended to be a moderating influence on the delegate pool, but designers of these rule changes also hoped that shortening the time between the first two nominating contests and raising the threshold would aid better-financed and -organized candidates. Ultimately, this would force the party to "close ranks" early behind a likely nominee, thus avoiding a protracted, divisive nomination fight among candidates with little electoral support but wanting to further a cause.[93]

In the end, these changes probably did just that. That is, they probably succeeded in helping Mondale, the establishment candidate, fend off Hart. Early superdelegate committal, in particular, enabled Mondale to withstand early Hart primary victories. Superdelegates had to commit by the second Tuesday in March, and at that time, it was still too early in the nominating process for a cautious politician to back an insurgent candidate. After all, few elected officials would want to cross their future party leader or, potentially, president.[94]

From the perspective of the CPE, then, the Hunt Commission reforms did not ultimately aid its cause, as the platform and the candidate reflected the liberalism of the New Politics faction. But more importantly, it appears that most available institutional changes in and of themselves would not have mattered. The Democratic Party did nominate its established, mainstream candidate. Yet in 1984, that was not enough to win—or even to be competitive in—the general election. In the CPE's view, the national party had so absorbed the public philosophy and constituent groups of the New Politics—and the transformation of the party's nominating rules and organization had institutionalized both to such a degree—that a presidential candidate would have to court and represent these groups to win the nomination and unite the party.

Simply put, the Democratic Party at the national level had become a New Politics liberal party. The mainstream of the national party was not in the mainstream of the Democratic rank and file or of the general electorate.[95] The constituent groups of this faction (e.g., civil rights, environmental, and peace organizations) had planted themselves in the center of the Democratic Party, reshaped its public philosophy, repelled certain constituencies, and subsumed others. By the mid-1980s, then, the neoconservatives, the southern Democrats, and some of the New Deal liberals had either diminished in sheer numbers, left the party, or joined the minority faction (soon to be the New Democrats). Other New Deal liberals and, notably, labor had adapted themselves to the New Politics, becoming part of the dominant faction that I will now refer to as "liberals."

Facing such an entrenched faction and a changed institutional environment, it thus became clear to the incipient New Democrats that participating in organized party meetings and rules commissions, often at the last minute, was insufficient to reshape the public philosophy of the Democratic Party and to restore electoral success. Therefore, when the defeat of the Mondale-Ferraro ticket seemed likely, CPE Democrats and their fellow travelers began considering an alternative course of action. It was at this point that From, a political entrepreneur, could offer (and implement) a comprehensive strategy that he had developed to change the party. From argued that the group must take advantage of the opportunities provided by the likely defeat of the presidential ticket. Without a winning candidate and with the coming expiration of Manatt's term as DNC chairman, the Democratic Party would be without a titular head. A DNC election was approaching, and From wanted this nascent group of New Democrats to take over that committee.

He wanted them to back a candidate for DNC chairman—specifically, Chuck Robb, a former marine, son-in-law to LBJ, and popular governor of Virginia. From felt that this position might eventually determine the result of the 1988 presidential nomination and thus was critical.[96] In the process, he hoped to expand the NHDC to all elected officials, disseminate the policy manuals developed in the House Caucus, and convert the NHDC into a membership organization that would become "the intellectual force of the party." In turn, From hoped that this would make its endorsement for DNC chairman, and even president, crucial.[97]

As the convention unfolded, it was marked by public posturing and horse trading between Mondale and both Hart and Jackson on platform planks and rule changes, as well as similar maneuvering with various caucuses and constituency groups. Observing all this, Elizabeth Drew of the *New Yorker* remarked that "groups are treating the Convention as a sort of bazaar."[98] Watching this situation develop, a group of elected officials began to sense (like From) that the Democratic ticket would surely be defeated and began to assign blame to the nomination process and the public philosophy of the party. As Representative David McCurdy of Oklahoma, a CPE member, recalled, "there wasn't any commonsense in it [the nomination process] anymore. . . . It had become McGovernized, and at that point, it was out of control."[99] David McCloud, Robb's chief of staff, recounted that the governor felt that "the party was more focused on group politics than on . . . winning elections and . . . governing."[100]

At the San Francisco gathering, then, three sets of elected officials, all sharing the same basic analysis of the party's problems, met in Long's hotel room: senators led by Lawton Chiles of Florida and Sam Nunn of Georgia, governors led by Bruce Babbitt of Arizona and Robb of Virginia, and House members led by Long and Gephardt.[101] These groups had begun to meet and discuss various ways to reshape the party. According to accounts, the discussion focused on a range of options, including influencing the selection of the next DNC chair, forming a think tank (as Nunn advocated), and establishing an unofficial party organization.

By the end of the convention, the consensus was that the party itself was not the best place to develop their new message.[102] Yet despite one effort by Nunn to arrange a meeting with Robb and fourteen of Nunn's Senate colleagues, no course of action was decided on.[103] However, after the election, momentum began to build among these three separate groups of elected officials to join forces and act on From's plan.

On November 28, 1984, a high-level group of Democratic elected officials and party leaders—including Governors Robb (who chaired the meeting) and Babbitt, Senator Chiles, Congressmen Jones and Wirth, former DNC chairmen Bob Strauss and John White, and Carter domestic policy adviser Stuart Eizenstat—met for dinner to plot strategy.[104] From briefed Long on which "Lessons of the Election" he should highlight, or how to define the Democrats' problem. First, he stressed the dire state of the party. On the national level, it could no longer rely on a coalition of minorities and women to win, and on the subpresidential level, candidates could not keep running away from the top of the ticket.[105] Next, From told Long that the cure for the party was to build a winning Democratic coalition based on ideas, not constituency groups.

Furthermore, such a message had to have national appeal and attract moderates, conservatives, and voters in the South and West. Finally, the way to effect such change was through elected officials taking a more active role in party affairs as soon as possible.[106] In sum, From had Long pitch his strategy of organizing outside the national party in order to take it over. Specifically, he wanted to use an expanded NHDC to coordinate elected officials to gain control of the national party apparatus and reshape the party for the 1988 election. And with the election of the next DNC chairman approaching, the group had to act quickly to implement this plan.

Thus, soon after this November dinner, Babbitt and Robb contacted From to seek his assistance in drafting a new DNC chairperson.[107] The two governors were part of a larger effort by southern and western governors and state party chairs, as well as by the neoconservative remnant left in the Coalition for a Democratic Majority, to find a centrist party leader.[108] The leading candidate after the election was

Paul G. Kirk, Jr., a Boston attorney and longtime Kennedy hand—not strong New Democratic credentials. But although he was tied to the liberal senator from Massachusetts, Kirk actually agreed with much of the CPE agenda. In fact, he was an NHDC member.[109]

Specifically, Kirk—along with his main competitors—agreed to abolish the DNC special-interest caucuses. In addition, he wanted to form a national policy body, composed primarily of elected officials and private-sector leaders, that would draw on their ideas to draft a "New Democratic Platform" for the 1986 midterm conference.[110] Kirk stressed that the new policy body would represent the views of a majority of Americans, not just a "narrow fringe." He wrote, "The platform would be sensitive to but insulated from the direct hands-on pressures of narrow groups with single issue agendae [*sic*]."[111]

After meeting with Kirk for an hour and a half, From was "most impressed" with him and reported to Long that "he talks our line."[112] But From still thought that Kirk, with his close ties to Ted Kennedy, presented the wrong image. Therefore, From considered the best option for DNC chairman to be Robb.[113]

The search for a suitable New Democratic candidate came to a head at the meeting of Democratic governors in Kansas City in mid-December. Kirk was vigorously courting the governors and wanted them to approve his plan for a national policy-drafting committee.[114] At the same time, the Babbitt-Robb search for a candidate was not going well: Governors Scott Matheson of Utah and James Hunt of North Carolina both refused to stand, and their final choice—former Secretary of Transportation Neil Goldschmidt—also refused to be drafted, since he wanted to run for governor of Oregon in 1986.[115]

As From recalled, no one wanted to take the job, and "even if we found someone to do it, he probably [wouldn't] be able to get elected because we didn't have any votes on the national committee."[116] Recognizing the reality of the situation, From advised that unless Representative Tony Coelho of California, Gephardt, or a candidate of similar stature agreed to run, they should recommend that the chairperson be selected from the current field.[117] In the end, Kirk—with heavy AFL-CIO support—beat Nancy Pelosi and Terry Sanford to win the chairmanship.[118]

Yet the efforts of the CPE and NHDC to reshape the party would not end with this defeat. As Kirk was sewing up his victory, From recommended that Robb announce the formation of a new "Governing

Council" made up of elected officials from around the country who would "help set the future direction of the party," an idea that mirrored From's earlier suggestion to expand the role of the NHDC. He added that if the DNC would not create it, the group would form such a council outside the party structure "by fiat."[119] Although their attempt to take over the party directly was unsuccessful, From pushed the dissident Democrats who had gathered around Long to continue with his plans to form an extraparty organization of elected officials to influence party affairs. Having decided to go along with this idea, a group of New Democrats would form the Democratic Leadership Council in the beginning of the following year.

In many ways, the proto–New Democrats organized in the House Democratic Caucus were but the latest incarnation of opposition to the New Politics faction that had gained prominence in the national party in the early 1970s. Much like the neoconservatives, and even like the southern Democrats, these disaffected Democrats opposed both the substantive changes to the party's public philosophy and the institutional changes to the nominating process and party organization that this liberal faction had undertaken.

The New Democrats emerged when they did because the 1980 Republican triumph had made clear the decline of Democratic dominance of the presidency, as well as the continuing breakdown of the New Deal coalition. In turn, it produced a window of opportunity that enabled political entrepreneurs such as From and Long to push their plans for change: revamping the Democratic Party's public philosophy in order to woo back defecting voters, specifically, white, middle-class voters.

To bring these disaffected groups back into the party, From and Long advocated policy planks that were significantly different from those of the party's liberal wing. They endorsed a strong military and an interventionist foreign policy, advocated a de-emphasis of the party's stance on many contentious social issues, and made a call—however vague at this point—for an egalitarianism in both social and economic policy based on equality of opportunity, not equality of outcome. Accordingly, these Democrats backed an economic policy that placed growth, not redistribution, at its center. In addition, following on from the neoconservatives and the neoliberals, CPE Democrats were more comfortable with market mechanisms and recognized that the federal government ran programs and performed functions that needed to be eliminated.

Although these policies were popular among the electorate, the CPE Democrats had a difficult time getting themselves heard in the years leading up to the 1984 general election. On an organizational level, these Democrats—first organized in the House as the CPE and briefly outside of it as the NHDC—did not have their own resources, particularly staff, to focus on party activities, a prerequisite for a group of officeholders occupied with governing matters. Said differently, they were not sufficiently institutionalized. The CPE and NHDC entered policy and party debates on an ad hoc basis and often, such as during the reforms of party rules, late in the process.

On an institutional level, their efforts were additionally ineffective, since the New Politics, or liberal, faction had become entrenched in the national party. The changes in the party system that had weakened party leaders' and elected officials' control over the affairs of the national party placed the liberal faction in command of party apparatus and the presidential nomination process, both of which had already been transformed so as to bolster the liberals' hold. Accordingly, the national party would assent only to comparatively minor procedural changes that would not substantially alter the balance of power within the party and would not bring about a transformation of its public philosophy.

The nascent New Democrats' failure to mount a challenge for the vacant DNC chairmanship was the most visible sign of their relative impotence. Indeed, just as they did not have the power to affect the outcome of the nominating contests or the content of the party's platform, they did not have the power within the national party to win this post—or even to find someone credible who was willing to run for it. With this option closed off, there was only one other choice: to work outside of the national party structure. Following the strategy mapped out by From, they began to form an organization that would continue the push for rules changes, to develop an alternative public philosophy, and, ultimately, to shape the results of the 1988 presidential election.

3 / "Saving the Democratic Party," 1985–1986

ON FEBRUARY 28, 1985, at a small Capitol Hill press conference, a group of elected officials announced the formation of the Democratic Leadership Council. Since the defeat of the Democratic ticket in November 1984, members of the CPE, who had begun party reform efforts in the House Democratic Caucus, along with like-minded senators and governors, had been working on establishing an organization that could reform the Democratic Party. As the new year began, this activity intensified. Governor Chuck Robb of Virginia regularly helicoptered to Washington from Richmond to help organize this effort. And From remembers one Capitol Hill meeting where he sat across the table from the newly elected senator from Tennessee, Al Gore, as the two of them drafted the press release announcing the formation of the DLC.[1]

By establishing this extraparty organization, these "New Democrats" hoped to remake the public philosophy of the Democratic Party by pressuring the national party from outside its official apparatus. In their view, they were loyal Democrats who wanted to convince wavering Democrats to "change the party rather than changing parties."[2]

To national party leaders and activists, however, this new institutional manifestation was interpreted as a break with, if not a direct threat to, the party. Liberal rivals saw the DLC and its outlook on politics as unacceptable even for consideration within the Democratic Party and immediately attacked the credibility of New Democratic motives, analyses, and proposals. As a result, the viability of the DLC and of the New Democratic project itself was threatened at the outset. If the New Democratic alternative embodied values unacceptable to the party elites, then it was unlikely that that they would adopt it as a legitimate course for the Democratic Party to take.

To remain a credible voice in Democratic and wider political circles, as well as to keep their alternative plan alive among the competing remedies proposed in the wake of the Democrats' 1984 presidential defeat, the New Democrats would have to alter their own immediate goals and strategies. In short, the DLC had to become more like the national party in order to remain a force that could potentially change it. The organization had to broaden its tent, welcoming liberal Democrats to join the DLC and avoiding any strident policy stands in order to attract them.

At the same time, the national party leadership—in particular, Paul Kirk, the DNC chairman—was coming to many of the same conclusions about the state of the party and had begun to take steps to address these problems, including the formation of a commission of elected officials to craft a more moderate policy platform. In that light, Kirk and others in the national party viewed the establishment of the DLC as even more of a direct challenge to the party and a threat to its unity. This, in turn, gave added impetus to Kirk's moderating moves, as they also served his aims of bridging this gap and keeping the party unified.

Thus, in order to blunt liberal attacks, the DLC began to become more like the national party. And in order to preserve party unity, the national party began to follow some of the DLC's advice. By the end of 1986, this blurring of lines began to lead many to ask why the DLC was needed at all. Yet to those who had established the DLC, there was no question that the organization was necessary. But even the strength of their commitment could not overcome the intense intraparty conflict, a conflict that profoundly affected the development of the DLC and its short-term success.

Establishment of the DLC

In the aftermath of the Democrats' crushing defeat in 1984, the search for remedies to their electoral problems began in earnest, and the competition to provide a solution and have it implemented by the national party was strong. In this fluid political environment, the New Democrats found that to exploit this opportunity, they needed an organizational structure independent from the national party. But, as they quickly discovered, this independence was illusory, as the sharp reactions of the DNC and the liberal faction to the formation of the DLC forced it to change its tactics and structure.

ELECTORAL PROBLEMS AND ALTERNATIVES

Their failure to elect a New Democrat to the DNC chairmanship convinced New Democrats that an extraparty organization of elected officials, as From had suggested earlier, was necessary to change the party's public philosophy. Logically, they turned to From to coordinate the effort. He had extensive political experience, plus direct involvement in the CPE and the NHDC. And on January 20, 1985, Long died of a heart attack while watching TV in his Washington apartment, making From one of the sole links to the earlier House efforts.[3]

In the beginning of 1985, From laid out what would become the core New Democratic analysis of the party's problems, along with its proposed alternatives. Sent to a group of New Democratic elected officials, potential funders, and other interested persons, the memorandum drew mainly on the analysis developed over the previous four years in the CPE and the NHDC. But as seen in its title, "Saving the Democratic Party," it also reflected the New Democrats' sense of urgency.

"The National Democratic Party is in grave jeopardy of losing its majority status," wrote From at the beginning of the memo.[4] In 1984, the Republicans had won whites, independents, and youth, groups that From argued were the keys to winning the presidency, presently and in the future. Democrats on the national level, conversely, had forged their coalition from demographic groups—labor, liberals, residents of northeastern states, and the poor—that were in political decline and from constituency groups that represented them.

Such a strategy, as Gephardt, the DLC's first chairman, explained in a press statement upon its founding, had resulted in losing four of the last five presidential elections, winning more than 42 percent of the popular vote only once during that time, and witnessing Democratic identification among the electorate plummet.[5] From and the New Democrats feared that if the inadequacy seen in 1984 on the national level persisted, "the lack of competitiveness would ramify throughout the rest of the party, [and] would have an effect down the ticket and bring down good candidates."[6] It is interesting to note, though, that as with the original members of the CPE, the initial members of the DLC were not themselves in any immediate electoral danger.

Of the forty-three acknowledged DLC members as of March 18,

1985, only three congressmen—Tim Wirth of Colorado, Les Aspin of Wisconsin, and Martin Frost of Texas—had won by less than 60 percent of the vote in 1984, and only three members who had last stood for election in 1982—Governors Jim Blanchard of Michigan, William O'Neill of Connecticut, and Robb—had fared similarly in statewide races.[7] However, all but four original members came from states that the Reagan-Bush ticket had carried in both 1980 and 1984. Overwhelmingly hailing from southern, western, and border states, then, these electoral officials could see firsthand the political shift occurring across the country.

The proposed solution to this electoral problem was to forge a new electoral coalition among moderate and "populist" southerners and westerners, plus the "so-called neo-liberals" in other parts of the country, around "ideas, not constituency groups."[8] From argued that such an alliance had already surfaced in the House Democratic Caucus when it produced the two policy manuals *Renewing America's Promise* and *Rebuilding the Road to Opportunity.*[9] In short, From and the New Democrats advocated an approach to rebuilding the Democratic Party that broke fundamentally with the political strategy that had dominated Democratic thinking for the past sixteen years. They believed that minorities, New Politics issue activists, and labor should no longer be at the center of the party's national coalition. The DLC was prepared to challenge the political strategy that had dominated Democratic thinking in the postreform era.

Although a bold vision, it was not one held exclusively by the DLC's founders. At the time From began organizing the DLC and developing its political strategy, the national party, under the leadership of its new chairman, seemed to be heading in the same direction. Although much of the DLC leadership had opposed his election due to his ties to liberal standard-bearer Ted Kennedy, Kirk's vision for the future of the party actually appeared to be very similar to theirs. Indeed, Kirk ran for the position advocating a major reappraisal of the public philosophy of the Democratic Party.

As he later recalled, Kirk believed that the party needed a "national message to a national audience," not individual pitches to specific interest groups.[10] Therefore, he supported the establishment of a policy council that would not only develop this agenda but also serve as a conduit for the voices of moderates and elected officials.[11] In fact, when Kirk and the DNC announced the formation of the Democratic Policy Commission (DPC) on May 15, 1985, it became clear that the group's political analysis, goals, and even membership were strikingly similar to those of the DLC.

ISSUE PROBLEMS AND POLICY ALTERNATIVES

Those instrumental in the founding of the DLC felt that, like the Democrats' electoral coalition, its platform was an amalgam of special-interest concerns and was too far to the left of "mainstream" America on many issues. As Bruce Babbitt, then governor of Arizona and a DLC founder, warned the DNC in his capacity as head of the Democratic Governors Association, the party must move "to reconcile fiscal reality with the social progressive tradition of the Democratic Party."[12]

Therefore, during the planning stages of the DLC, From stressed that "our agenda will be moderate in traditional political terms, far different than the liberal agenda with which the party is identified today."[13] Specifically, the DLC would advocate sustained economic growth, equal and expanding opportunity, and the aggressive defense of freedom with the promotion of democratic values abroad.[14]

At approximately the same time, Kirk and his staff were entertaining analyses similar to those of the DLC. In early 1985, Stanley Greenberg, a Democratic pollster, presented a report to the Association of State Democratic Party Chairs and to the DNC, arguing that the party was in danger of losing traditional Democratic voters, especially white blue-collar voters, because they viewed the party as too extreme on social issues and too tied to the concerns of blacks and other minorities.[15] As Greenberg recounted it, he argued that "the Democratic Party was seen as contemptuous of working-class culture."[16] The party needed to realize the importance of family to voters, as well as the sense of middle-class Americans that the rich were paying no taxes, the poor were receiving all the benefits and giving nothing in return, and they were left footing the bill.[17]

Overall, the initial DLC policy agenda was not particularly new, as these positions had all been developed in the House Democratic Caucus. What had changed was the means by which these ideas were to be placed into Democratic Party thinking. In light of their previous lack of success in affecting the national Democratic Party—a result that reflected, in turn, the institutional realities of the national party— and considering their own resources, the New Democrats decided to form the DLC as an extraparty organization.

INSTITUTIONAL PROBLEMS AND ALTERNATIVES

To grasp why the New Democrats chose to form the type of organization they did, one must understand their perception of the state of the national party and how it operated. As they had for at least the past four years, many New Democrats believed that the Democratic Party was offering unpopular policy positions and following a flawed electoral strategy because of changes in the party's rules and organization. These, in turn, effectively shut elected officials out of party affairs, opening the way for narrowly focused ideological activists, who, in From's estimation, "seem much more concerned about their own roles in the party structure and about their own agendas than about helping the party win elections."[18]

In the view of the New Democrats, these interest groups used their power to impose litmus tests on policy statements and on candidates, disregarding the electoral consequences such demands might have. According to Robb, this led to a situation in which elected officials "didn't even feel welcome in strictly partisan settings anymore."[19] To From, the arrangement created a conflict between the "institutional party," centered in the DNC and congressional committees, and the "governing party," consisting of elected officials who were more moderate and who "often win elections by actually running *against* the national party."[20]

Therefore, the DLC began operating on the premise that it had to revamp the institutional arrangements of the Democratic Party so as to reassert the role of elected officials in party affairs and, in turn, change the party's public philosophy. This argument was made from the earliest planning stages of the DLC and led it to seek fundamental changes in the party's organization and operating procedures. For example, the group wanted to eliminate provisions of the DNC charter that catered to special-interest concerns, such as those that provided for self-consciously created caucuses, and to pressure the Fairness Commission—the Hunt Commission's successor, charged with reviewing the presidential nominating process—to write nominating rules that gave a nominee the best chance of winning the general election.[21]

To accomplish these alterations, New Democrats could have proceeded through "normal" channels—lobbying DNC members, electing their own to the national committee, and cooperating with Kirk and his DPC. But their failed effort to elect a New Democrat to the DNC chairmanship—their sheer marginality to that process—and their failure to affect the outcome of the 1984 nominating campaign had soured them on working within established party channels. These setbacks, along with their intense antipathy to interest groups and to the perceived hold of these groups on the Democratic Party, led the DLC founders to fear that any reform effort undertaken within the party would, in the end, be constrained by the party's need to placate every interest in the coalition.

As Babbitt explained, "It [the DLC] needs to be financially independent so it is not subjected to all of what I call the Noah's Ark approach—all the requirements that every interest group has to be represented."[22] Another DLC member referred to the formation of an extraparty organization as an "insurance policy" in the event that Kirk and his group (the DPC) were unable to make the changes they saw as necessary to revamping the party. This assessment undoubtedly was born out of many DLC members' suspicion of Kirk, who had decided not to appoint a New Democrat–backed candidate to the post of DNC finance chairman and had refused to join the DLC itself.[23]

Personal slights and doubts aside, there were more substantial reasons for the formation of an extraparty organization. Even though Kirk said that he was going to alter the party's structure, rules, and platform to make it more mainstream, the DLC would have substantially greater freedom to push this agenda from outside the party, in comparison with Kirk and reformers within the party apparatus. As party chairman, Kirk's priority was maintaining party cohesion, which forces party leaders to focus on "introverted" tasks such as party building, raising money, recruiting candidates, affirming party symbols, and developing the party's program, instead of on the "extroverted" tasks of adapting the party's strategy and message to appeal to increasingly uncommitted voters.[24]

As a result, Kirk's incentive to "diminish conflict, bring unity and harmony, and be able to convey a message" made him more inclined to err on the side of maintaining the cohesion of the existing Democratic base than on the side of remaking the party in order to build a new Democratic coalition, as the DLC advocated.[25] In fact, according to Greenberg, these motivations led Kirk to quash a study on Reagan Democrats in Macomb County, Michigan, that Greenberg did for the DNC because of its explosive findings about racial attitudes and voters' views on government and the Democratic Party, findings that Kirk feared would fracture the party.[26] This is not to say that Kirk did not take risks in reorganizing the party apparatus and in beginning an effort to draft a new type of platform, nor that his actions were not often met with heated protest. But Kirk, as with party chairmen generally, would not be able to indulge in the iconoclasm of the DLC, since he was tempered by one overriding concern: maintaining party cohesion.

Although the difference between the internal and external party reformers—in this case, the DNC and the DLC—was a "matter of degree, not kind," it provided enough incentive for New Democrats not to join Kirk in his similar efforts to remake the party.[27] Deciding not to cooperate with, much less incorporate their efforts into, the national party apparatus, the New Democrats next had to determine what type of organization they should develop. In principle, they could have formed a PAC to fund like-minded candidates. But in practice, that would not have addressed the issue of a party whose policies and image were a hindrance to candidate fortunes. At the opposite extreme, these New Democrats could have formed a grassroots organization, one that would have recruited activists to "take over" the party apparatus. However, New Democrats were ostensibly an elite group of officeholders, not leaders of a well-organized and far-reaching "movement," so this was never a realistic option.

Finally, the New Democrats could have founded a policy research institute in which to develop the agenda they thought necessary for electoral victory. Again, in principle, there was a niche in Washington for their thinking, as the early 1980s saw the founding of no fewer than four Democratic-leaning think tanks, none of which represented the New Democrat point of view.[28] But the New Democrats did not yet have sufficient resources to launch such an organization, and a think tank would not have been a natural organization from which to lobby directly for changes, especially institutional ones, within the party.[29]

Unwilling or unable to follow one of these more conventional options, the New Democrats sought to establish an organization that could develop new policy prescriptions and pressure the party to change its procedures and structure. Such an organization also needed, fundamentally, to serve the interests of its elected-official members, especially their career goals of reelection, policymaking, and political influence, in order to provide the incentives necessary to establish the organization and then to attract new members.[30] Therefore, the DLC was established as an extraparty organization with membership open to all Democratic federal elected officials plus governors. As Jon Hale described it, the DLC "bore a strong resemblance of [*sic*] an intra-party congressional caucus, but was organized as an unofficial party group."[31] In many ways, the DLC replicated the structure of the NHDC, the immediate past incarnation of the New Democrats, but with a membership expanded beyond House members.

The consensus among those elected officials most active in the DLC's formation was that Gephardt should chair the organization. A rising star in Congress (he had just been elected chairman of the House Democratic Caucus), Gephardt had been one of the young House members actively involved in the CPE and had looked to Long as a mentor. More than that, From recalled that the Missouri congressman got the nod since he was regarded in Democratic circles as a "team player." Robb was seen as a "renegade," Nunn was perceived as "way outside the mainstream of Democratic politics," Senator Lawton Chiles of Florida had just led the challenge against Senator Robert Byrd for the minority leader post, and Babbitt was viewed as a "maverick."[32] Although not chosen as chairman, these men plus a handful of other elected officials became the DLC governing board and were intimately involved in the organization's early activities.

Yet the most crucial organizational move was the hiring of From to run the DLC and of Will Marshall to develop the New Democratic message. Marshall, who had worked for From and Long on *Rebuilding the Road to Opportunity*, had just returned to Washington after the unsuccessful Hunt Senate campaign in North Carolina. Frustrated with the state of the party, the intense Virginian saw the DLC not only as a reentry into Washington but also as a vehicle for reform. Turning down more stable opportunities on Capitol Hill, Marshall joined the effort.[33] From, who was concerned about making enough money to send his children to college, agreed to take the job, according to Robb, only after the governor "personally guarantee[d] his [From's] salary for the first year because he wasn't sure that this organization had any chance of lasting at all."[34] It was important to ensure that From and, to a lesser degree, Marshall took the DLC jobs. They were key links to the New Democratic efforts in the House and at the vanguard of promoting the New Democrat public philosophy, and the DLC was an organization in which the role of staff would be crucial. The busy schedules of elected officials meant that DLC staff members would have a large influence over the direction and activities of the organization.[35]

The other key element in the DLC's successful establishment was funding. Organized as a 501(c)4 nonprofit organization, the DLC was not subject to campaign finance regulations and was able to raise money in large amounts. This presented further opportunities for its elected-official members, since such money was not counted against the overall contributory limits of their donors. As From reminded Gephardt, he should look for fund-raising opportunities while traveling, even among those donors who had "maxed out" for his own PAC.[36]

By March 1985, the DLC was already active in its pursuit of funds from individual contributors to supplement the $1,000 membership fee it charged.[37] By September of the same year, the DLC had half of its $400,000 annual budget in hand, most of which was raised in a series of fund-raisers held when DLC members went on issue trips to different states.[38] Held all over the country, these early events—as well as the DLC fund-raising effort generally—featured the involvement of prominent Democratic Party leaders. In Florida, for example, William Crotty, a man who had raised hundreds of thousands of dollars for Mondale in 1984, held a DLC fund-raiser.[39] In New York, Charles Manatt and Peter Kelly, the former DNC chairman and DNC finance chairman, respectively, participated in an event that raised $100,000 for the DLC.[40] In Atlanta, former president Carter attended a reception at which the DLC grossed $60,000.[41] And in Washington, Bob Strauss, former DNC chairman and U.S. trade representative, was an early and active fund-raiser for the DLC.[42]

The lure for most donors was the association with an individual elected official or the desire to cultivate relationships with a handful of the party's rising stars.[43] Robb's appeal as a potential national candidate in 1988, for example, undoubtedly helped the DLC raise $325,000 at a dinner held in 1986 at the estate of soft-drink bottler Ed Brideforth in Robb's home state of Virginia.[44] Likewise, the DLC consciously used this cachet to attract wealthy benefactors, offering, for instance, private retreats with DLC leaders for its most generous donors.[45]

Indeed, from the beginning, just as the DLC's membership was limited to elected officials, its base of support was similarly select. Although the DLC did have an option for supporters to contribute $50, it primarily pursued givers who could donate at least $1,000, which is also the legal maximum for a personal donation to a candidate for federal office.[46] In that sense, the DLC was an elite organization in every regard.

Although it had the funding and the staff in place, there was no guarantee that the DLC would survive. Forming any advocacy organization arguing the New Democratic line would have provoked a strong reaction from other party factions and organizations, but establishing such a group outside of party control especially incensed other Democrats. In light of the stated goals, organization, and timing of the formation of the DPC and of the similarities between the two organizations, it appeared that the DLC was established to challenge at least Kirk and perhaps the whole national party leadership. As a result, an icy relationship surfaced between the DLC and DNC, one that persisted throughout the next decade.

From the outset, though, the DLC founders stressed that they were not in competition with, much less in opposition to, the DNC, Kirk, or his policy commission. Gephardt argued, "We view the council not as a rival to any other party entity but as a way-station or bridge back into the party for elected Democrats."[47] Democratic partisans and the media, however, saw things differently.[48]

The California Democratic House delegation, for example, "virtually ordered" Congressman Tony Coelho to quit the organization when it was announced that he was a member. Of the forty members that the DLC claimed, only twenty-three allowed their names to be used on the initial formal list of members.[49] According to one report, AFL-CIO officials warned that they might decrease support of Democratic congressional candidates in the 1986 midterm election if the DLC was formed. Other Democrats questioned the true motives of the New Democrats, wondering whether the organization had more to do with presidential politics or "parochial politics."[50] Finally, undergirding most criticisms was the fear that the organization would create a schism in the party, or at least be perceived as such, thus adding to the Democratic Party's fractious image.[51] It was with these conflicts with the DNC and party liberals as a backdrop that the DLC set out to remake the public philosophy of the Democratic Party.

Factionalization and Adaptation

The dynamics of intraparty politics touched everything the DLC did during its first year of operation. On the one side, the DLC faced the organized national party in the form of the DNC, which undertook moves that mirrored DLC suggestions. On its own, this independent but parallel movement would have taken some of the wind from the DLC's sails. Mixed with the imperative of party chairmen to preserve party unity, this tack also became an effort to co-opt the rogue organization. On the other side, liberals from the dominant Democratic Party faction attacked the New Democratic public philosophy with vigor, as could be expected. If they threatened the overall viability of the DLC in the process, so much the better from their point of view. To adapt to these pressures from both directions, the DLC reshaped its own organization, as well as how and what it championed, moves that had a significant effect on the DLC.

ELECTORAL PROBLEMS AND ALTERNATIVES

In the electoral arena, the DLC did little to provoke its opponents, as its activities stood to benefit the entire party. By focusing on the South and West, two areas where liberal influence was markedly less powerful and that were recognized as tough for Democrats, the DLC did not exacerbate tensions with its factional rivals. Even if they did not agree with the analysis that led to its actions, liberals could not deny that the DLC was trying to help the party overall.

Driving the New Democrats was their belief that the 1984 election had been the beginning of a full-scale electoral realignment that would benefit the GOP—an analysis shared by Republican leaders.[52] Adding urgency to the DLC's efforts was that the GOP began to take steps to hasten the realignment's arrival. Specifically, in the spring of 1985, the Republicans launched the "Operation Open Door Campaign," a 100-day effort to convince 100,000 Democratic voters and elected officials—especially Reagan Democrats, predominantly in the South—to switch affiliations.

The Republicans focused on Florida, where they hoped to attract 45,000 party switchers, and Texas, where, since 1980, forty-one Democratic officeholders had already crossed over to the GOP.[53] In the end, the GOP would secure no more than 50,000 switchers, including a handful of current and former Democratic elected officials.[54] Nevertheless, to counter this Republican assault—or, in the DLC's words, to "stall realignment"—as well as to establish its image and message around the country, the DLC undertook an early series of trips to battleground states.[55]

The central mission of this effort was best summed up by Robb: "We intend to challenge disaffected Democrats to join us in a movement to change the party rather than changing parties."[56] Accordingly, From and Marshall advised the officeholders making these visits to stress that the DLC was a "counterweight" to the special interests in the party and comprised "New Democrats, different from the Old Guard Democrats and from the Republicans," who were "the legitimate heirs to the Democratic heritage as the party of progress and opportunity, as the agent of change and hope."[57]

So, beginning in the summer of 1985, the DLC sent some of its best-known members to Georgia, Texas, North Carolina, Florida, and California. Typically, the DLC visited the state's major media markets, tried to recruit local political leaders, made their pitch for a new policy agenda and electoral strategy for the Democratic Party to interested business and civic leaders, and met with the press. These trips were intended not only to raise the profile of the DLC and the New Democratic message but also to boost Democratic candidates in the 1986 midterm election.

Indeed, the 1986 contest offered a political window of opportunity for the DLC to help elect allies and to prove the efficacy of its electoral strategy and accompanying issue agenda. Therefore, to help Democratic candidates, the DLC launched an "Issues Blitz" from October 14 to 16, 1986, which entailed flying to four states in three days and holding issue forums "to spur debate on national defense and economic policies."[58] A chartered plane brought the DLC's high-powered political talent, wealthy backers, and fifteen members of the national media to help with the Senate campaigns of Wirth, Harriet Woods of Missouri, Bob Edgar of Pennsylvania, and Bob Graham of Florida.[59] These visits focused media attention on the candidates and helped counteract GOP efforts to link them with what Robb called their "favorite strawmen, like Tip O'Neill, Jimmy Carter, or Ted Kennedy," thus providing "some cover for the charge that they are nothing but a knee-jerk, radical, national Democrat."[60]

Despite the occasional incendiary remark, such as Robb's, the DLC did not undertake the most confrontational of potential strategies. The organization wanted to promote itself and its proposals, but it did not want to provoke unnecessarily the ire of its intraparty opponents. Therefore, the organization did not work to help New Democratic candidates during primary contests and rejected calls to form a PAC.[61] Rather, it sought to help the party retake the Senate in 1986 by aiding nominees in tough races, even if they were hardly New Democrats, such as Woods and Edgar.

Determining the effect these visits had on individual races is impossible, but what is clear is that after the 1986 election, the DLC claimed immense electoral victories. First, every DLC member in the House who ran for reelection won—not such an amazing feat, considering the astronomically high rate of reelection for House members during this period. Second, the DLC acquired impressive representation in the Senate, newly retaken by the Democrats: seven of the eleven freshman Democratic senators were DLC members who hailed from the South and West, and three incumbent DLC senators also won reelection. Moreover, half of all standing committee chairmen were DLC members.[62] Ostensibly, the DLC now had influential allies who could help implement its public philosophy.

ISSUE PROBLEMS AND POLICY ALTERNATIVES

Intraparty considerations also affected the development of the New Democratic public philosophy and issue agenda. From the beginning, the DLC leadership had a clear vision of what had gone wrong with the party and its public philosophy. Because of its close ties to liberal interest groups, the party had become "hesitant and ambivalent" about asserting the country's role abroad, had embraced an "adversarial stance toward mainstream values," and had become "wedded to a redistributionist agenda" that took tax dollars from the middle class to pay for programs for the poor and the unemployed.[63] Only a distancing from this perceived liberal orthodoxy could make Democrats immune, or at least resistant, to GOP attacks that they were fiscally irresponsible, weak on defense, beholden to special interests, and bereft of any economic policies that could address the country's problems.[64]

But the development of the New Democratic public philosophy was stunted during the DLC's first years of operation as the organization tried to accommodate its liberal critics and the party leadership tried to accommodate the DLC. Consequently, the DLC chose to employ rhetoric and highlight policies that would not antagonize its liberal rivals. Thus, during its first two years of operation, the DLC focused most of its attention on economic growth and competitiveness as well as on national military strength, issues that did not have the accompanying passion of many social concerns.[65]

To develop these proposals, the DLC established three working groups of elected officials to study the economy, national security, and party rules and considered a proposal to begin a New Democratic policy journal.[66] The first results of this effort were seen on October 2, 1985, when the DLC released its first policy proposal entitled "Winning in the World Economy." This paper called for a cut in the budget deficit, an increase in American productivity, and a change in monetary and tax policies to make the U.S. economy more globally competitive. In addition, contrary to the views of many in the Democratic Party—including the official party stance as spelled out in the 1984 party platform—the DLC remained committed to free trade, dismissing protectionist measures as "a quick fix." This was, of course, the traditional stance of southern Democrats, who accounted for a large number of DLC members.[67]

After this initial policy proposal, the DLC did not release any major policy statements until the middle of 1986. By then, From and others in the DLC had become keenly aware of the opportunity that the 1988 election presented, and they hoped to shift the policy debate onto the DLC's "turf" as the presidential race heated up throughout 1987.[68] They wanted to establish their "national-purpose" approach as a viable alternative to interest-group liberalism. As From explained to Robb, who replaced Gephardt as DLC chairman in 1986, "the measure of our success in changing the party's message and shifting its center of gravity will be in how and on what issues the 1988 candidates campaign."[69]

However, the DLC was neither going to launch a full assault on the prevailing public philosophy of the party nor offer a detailed elucidation of a New Democratic alternative. As before, the organization had to consider intraparty politics and the reaction of its liberal rivals. Consider that the DLC now had Robb as its chairman. As the first Democratic governor of Virginia in sixteen years, Robb embraced moderate positions on social issues and fiscal conservatism and became extremely popular. After his term was up in 1985, he was widely touted as a Senate candidate in 1988, and even as a potential national candidate. Yet, despite having Robb—one of the most attractive potential presidential candidates—as its chairman, the DLC could use him only to deliver a series of speeches that highlighted the general position of the group on a variety of issues.[70]

Similarly, the DLC attracted enough political talent to hold its first annual conference in Williamsburg, Virginia, from December 10 to 12, 1986. It was attended by some of the most important Democratic elected officials, covered by the national press, and televised in full on the C-SPAN cable network.[71] However, here too the DLC did not harshly criticize the liberal public philosophy or offer a distinct alternative out of fear of instigating factional opponents.

Furthermore, although the Williamsburg meeting provided a public forum for the advocacy of spending cuts, mainstream values, and a stronger defense, these stances had already become less novel. The DNC, in the form of Kirk's policy commission, had begun to draw similar conclusions about the public philosophy of the national party and had, at least officially, moved toward these positions. In turn, these positions also served the purpose of accommodating the DLC, a task that was made easier since the organization had already muted its policy demands in order not to provoke party liberals.

The similarities between the DPC and the DLC were clear enough. Those in charge of the policy commission, for example, desired a final document that would stress "basic beliefs," not specific policies and programs, and thus "make it easier to be a Democrat again" for those in the South and West and in the middle class who were leaving the Democratic Party.[72] Like the DLC, the DPC believed that the Democratic Party had emphasized the agenda of special interests at the expense of a more national perspective. As Kirk, commenting on the DPC's work, proudly proclaimed during one drafting session, "The larger interests and broader agenda of the Democratic Party and the nation have superseded the singular agenda of elite groups."[73]

In addition, the DPC, which comprised mainly elected officials, wanted the party's platform transformed from a "liability" to an "asset" in order to aid those running for office.[74] To that end, the DPC agreed that the substance of this change had to emphasize fiscal discipline, progressive leadership, "change," and the belief in a strong national defense.[75] As one Democratic official explained to the *New York Times*, the DPC was an effort "to get out from under the false image that Democrats are weak on defense, have weird lifestyles, and are big taxers and spenders."[76]

When the DPC's final proposal was issued in September 1986, it became clear that the commission had realized its goals. The DPC report, entitled "New Choices in a Changing America," made a "commitment to stronger families" a top Democratic goal, stressed the importance of private investment and "entrepreneurship in growing the economy," and offered a tough criticism of the Soviet Union while endorsing the principles behind the Reagan arms buildup.[77] The document made no mention of abortion and gay rights, two controversial topics that epitomized the type of issues that, in the DLC view, strained the Democratic coalition and repelled many in the general electorate.

But perhaps the best proof of the similarities between the DLC and DPC positions was that the DPC proposals sustained a blast of liberal criticism. At the time of the DPC's unveiling, 1,000 liberal Democrats representing peace activists, labor leaders, minorities, and feminists rallied to denounce the party's perceived move to the right.[78] Then, once the commission had issued its report, Michael Harrington—head of Democratic Alternatives, a coalition of liberal and labor groups— strongly criticized the economic policy proposals because they did not call for full employment or support Great Society programs that he considered successful. In truth, dissent had already appeared during the drafting of the document in the form of intense debate over military spending and the U.S. role abroad, an argument that had delayed the document's release for months.[79]

Against the backdrop of these parallel moves undertaken by the DPC, the policies offered by the DLC seemed even more benign. Yet From greeted the DPC proposals by claiming that the similarities between them and the stances of the DLC were proof that his organization was succeeding at shifting the party's "center of gravity."[80] Although the DLC was very vocal and surprisingly influential for a young organization, it surely overstated any case that it was the main force behind national party moderation. Rather, much of the perceived tilt derived directly from Kirk and from his desire for an elected-official policy council, a plan he had proposed the year before the DLC was founded. Moreover, the DNC's moves were influenced by its desire to keep the party unified.[81] The formation of the DLC, which represented a cleavage within the party, in effect institutionalized that cleavage and provoked the ire of other Democratic factions.

INSTITUTIONAL PROBLEMS AND ALTERNATIVES

From the day of its opening press conference, the DLC, much to its chagrin, was tagged by the press as an organization of southern and western conservative Democrats who wanted the party to lurch to the right. The timing of the founding's announcement, right after Kirk's election to the DNC chair and before the anticipated unveiling of his policy council, contributed to this perception, in that it caused many analysts to see the DLC as an anti-Kirk movement. As From noted, it appeared that the DLC was "just a bunch of soreheads out to get Paul Kirk."[82]

Yet the strongest reaction came from liberals within the Democratic Party. Arthur Schlesinger, Jr., for example, in a *New York Times* column, called the DLC a "quasi-Reaganite formation" and criticized it for "worshipping at the shrine of the free market."[83] Ann Lewis, national director of the liberal Americans for Democratic Action (ADA), charged the DLC with bashing the party in front of "business-oriented audiences," a strategy that she felt would fail with the Democratic and general electorates.[84] And Jim Hightower, the populist Texan politician, quipped about the DLC that "if the meek shall inherit the Earth, these timid voices will be land barons."[85] But perhaps the most famous barb along these lines was uttered by Jesse Jackson, who mockingly called the organization "Democrats for the Leisure Class."

Along the way, the party's left wing also took steps to counter the DLC's electoral and ideological strategies. From May 2 to 4, 1986, for example, the Left held a "New Directions" conference in Washington that had as its slogan an implicit attack on the DLC (and even on Kirk's own moves at the DNC): "Because one Republican party is more than enough." With speakers including Gloria Steinem, Michael Harrington, Representative Ronald Dellums of California, and Jackson, there was no denying that the conference represented the very organized Left that the DLC hoped to counter.[86]

Although being tagged as "me-too Republicans" or "conservative Democrats" was not to the DLC's liking, the most biting and potentially harmful criticism was that the DLC was at least implicitly racist—and possibly overtly so. Jackson, for example, said that the DLC was "sending a clear signal" by "traveling around the country as a group of all whites."[87] In 1986, Douglas Wilder argued that the DLC was making a "demeaning appeal to white Southern males."[88] In the same vein, it became common in active political circles to refer to the DLC as the "southern white boys' caucus."

The fact that the DLC had a minuscule number of minority members, especially for a Democratic organization, was indisputable. At its establishment, the DLC had exactly two black members and a mere handful of Hispanics and women. The charge of racism—along with the larger claim that the DLC was a group of reactionary, southern white men—placed the organization in a precarious position, since this image virtually precluded the DLC's meaningful participation in Democratic Party politics. Although southern whites—even overtly racist southern whites—had been a reliable and key component of the Democratic Party up to and through its winning New Deal days, by 1980, the party (and indeed national politics) had been transformed.

The Democratic Party, not the GOP, had become the party of civil rights and the political home of black Americans. By 1982, according to the National Election Studies, 91 percent of blacks identified themselves as Democrats, making them by far the most Democratic demographic group.[89] A combination of the relative proximity of these civil rights battles, the strength of civil rights activists within the national Democratic Party, and a genuine shift of party attitudes regarding this issue—no doubt abetted by the exodus of southern Democrats and others opposed to a liberal civil rights stance—had made race a true litmus issue in Democratic Party politics. Viewpoints deviating from the liberal stance of the national party simply would not be tolerated, and such positions would preclude anyone from being taken seriously in this arena.[90]

Yet the DLC, despite having a number of white Democrats from the South among its leadership core, was not an organizational embodiment of the "southern Democrats." The southerners involved in the DLC—such as Robb and Chiles—were products of the "New

South"; they counted blacks among their electoral coalitions and did not share the animus to civil rights and blacks that marked the southern Democrats of the past. Furthermore, southerners were not the only ones attracted to the DLC; elected officials such as Babbitt from Arizona and Gephardt from St. Louis, Missouri (both associated with the neoliberals), also played central roles in the establishment of the organization.

However, in this case, perception ran the risk of becoming reality. The values of the DLC's innovations, as understood by other political elites, were in danger of becoming unacceptable—unworthy of even consideration by this audience—if charges of racism could be made to stick. Although the DLC had been organized outside the aegis of the party, condemnation of the New Democratic option by the majority faction could ensure the New Democrats' marginalization in party debates, precluding the consideration of any of their policy and political recommendations.

Therefore, after only a few months in operation, the DLC began to move toward a "big-tent" strategy with regard to both the changes it advocated for the party and the arrangement of the organization itself. In this, the DLC refashioned itself more along the lines of a forum where differing ideologies and opinions could be debated and discussed, rather than fashioning itself as an advocate of one ideological stance, as originally planned. Practically, this meant that the organization would actively recruit elected officials from a wide array of ideologies and, more importantly, backgrounds.

As an organization of elected officials whose greatest asset was its membership list, the DLC was left with no other effective way—except broadening its membership—to convince political elites inside and outside of the Democratic Party that the organization was not the southern, white, male, conservative caucus. "We had some representation outside, but it wasn't enough really to be credible," Robb explained.[91]

Therefore, the DLC actively pursued minority and female federal elected officials. But since these groups were not well represented at this level, the DLC agreed to accept state and local officials as members, with the intent of actively recruiting women, blacks, and Hispanics.[92] By the end of 1986, the DLC could claim as members black officeholders such as Mayor Tom Bradley of Los Angeles, Hispanic officials such as Mayor Henry Cisneros of San Antonio, women such as former representative Barbara Jordan of Texas and Representative Barbara Kennelly of Connecticut, and liberals such as Representative Sander Levin of Michigan.[93] Its biggest coup, though, was the agreement of Congressman William Gray III of Pennsylvania, one of the most powerful black politicians in the country, to serve as a DLC vice-chairman. As Marshall advised Robb to put it, the DLC was now a "philosophically diverse group—liberals, moderates, and conservatives whose common aim is to infuse the party with a new sense of national purpose."[94]

Why did these seemingly non–New Democratic elected officials join the DLC? Robb opined that liberal elected officials and those with strong ties to labor joined the DLC because they viewed it as a "matter of self-preservation" to reassert the role of elected officials in the party and as a way of "covering all their bets" in case the DLC was correct in its diagnosis and solutions.[95] From averred that some of these politicians hoped to use the DLC as a "beard" to hide the fact that they supported national Democratic policies.[96]

To these claims, one must add that by supporting the DLC, many elected officials (especially House members) were able to show their support for Gephardt, who was chairman of both the DLC and the House Democratic Caucus, thus helping their own political standing in Congress. Others joined because it enabled them to build bridges to a wing of the party with which they did not have close ties, thus helping them to build legislative and political coalitions.[97] Finally, many officeholders came to see DLC membership as a way to be involved with "intellectual innovation" and "new ideas" in the party, an association that presumably served them electorally.[98]

The fact that such a broad sample of politicians could embrace the "new ideas" being developed by the DLC testifies to how much the DLC had to alter the substance of the changes it wanted in the party's public philosophy in order to establish the organization's credibility. Indeed, the DLC in effect abandoned its original goal of promoting "cutting-edge" issues, to which the rest of the party would eventually move, and instead embraced and practiced a kind of "consensus politics."[99] In this mode, the New Democrats deliberately avoided certain "fights" within the party.

As noted, the first policy paper that the DLC released was a proposal dealing with the economy and global economic competitiveness, relatively uncontentious topics. In addition, From recalled that in its initial push for party reforms, the DLC did not bring up the issue of racial or gender-based quotas, since that would have "killed" any chance the DLC had of surviving, once many in the party had questioned the organization's motives as racist or sexist.[100] Also, the DLC began to link itself and the New Democratic public philosophy to Democratic Party icons and ideologies of the past in order to make the argument that they were the true standard-bearers of Democratic tradition.

In a letter to the *New York Times,* for example, From made the case that the DLC's support for aid to the contra rebels in Nicaragua— a position at odds with that of Democratic liberals—was true to John Kennedy's commitment to keep communism out of the Western Hemisphere.[101] Similarly, Marshall advised Robb to explain the DLC as "an effort to revive the Democratic party's progressive tradition."[102] In planning the DLC's 1986 Williamsburg conference, From wrote to Robb that he hoped that the meeting would make the case that the New Democrats were "the trustees of the real tradition of the Democratic Party."[103]

While the DLC was dealing with these liberal attacks, its formation had also provoked the organizational embodiment of the national party, the DNC. Yet the DNC and its chairman, Kirk, did not want to confront and destroy the DLC: that would have been too damaging to party unity, the paramount concern of a party chairman. Instead, Kirk wanted to accommodate the DLC and bring it and the New Democrats back under party control. Since Kirk was coming to many of the same conclusions about the public philosophy and rules of the national party as the New Democrats were, and since the DLC was moderating its own positions to preserve its big-tent format, accommodating the demands of the DLC was not exceedingly difficult.

Consider, for example, the area of party organization and nominating rules. The DLC wanted to serve both as a "counterweight" to the liberal wing of the party and as a "vehicle" by which elected officials could reassert their role within party affairs.[104] One of the DLC's outlets for this effort was the debate over the party's presidential nominating process. Just as in 1982, when the CPE utilized the opportunity presented by the Hunt Commission, the DLC took advantage of the creation of the Fairness Commission after the 1984 convention— another party council established to examine and recommend changes to the nominating rules. Overall, the DLC wanted the commission to make the primary season as much like the general election as possible and thus produce a nominee who was not beholden to any interest or interests, who was seasoned, and who reflected the views of the (more centrist) general electorate.[105]

To that end, the New Democrats advocated a series of changes to the rules that they hoped would limit the influence of special interests, aid front-runners, and contribute to a moderate candidate being nominated. The DLC's Task Force on Party Renewal thus recommended instituting a system of winner-take-all primaries that were based on the returns in individual congressional districts and were open to independent voters; allowing states to determine when they wanted to hold their primaries; eliminating a candidate's right to approve delegate slates; and granting automatic delegate status for the national convention to all senators, congressmen, and governors.[106]

In the end, the Fairness Commission did not accede to the DLC's somewhat radical demands, but it did institute a series of changes that were agreeable to the organization. Again, the DLC, with its testimony in front of the commission and its own lobbying, may have made a contribution toward these changes. But once more, Kirk and the party were coming to similar conclusions that the "party had lost because it was the captive of special interests" and therefore needed to amend its nominating procedures in order to produce a more electorally viable nominee.[107]

Thus, in the composition of the Fairness Commission, the DNC resisted efforts to load the process in favor of liberal forces. For instance, even though the establishment of the commission itself was a concession to the losing 1984 presidential candidates, Kirk appointed Don Fowler, a white southern Democrat, to head the commission, not Jesse Jackson's choice, Maynard Jackson, the mayor of Atlanta.[108]

More importantly, the final decisions of the commission did not accede to Jackson's wishes on substantive issues. He had advocated the allocation of delegates based on pure proportional representation, but the commission decided to decrease the threshold only from 20 percent to 15 percent, a far cry from Jackson's demand.[109] Also, the commission ignored the objections that Gary Hart and Jackson had to ex officio delegates and decided to include all 372 DNC members as convention delegates and to increase the number of congressional Democrats appointed as superdelegates from 60 percent to 80 percent of the House and Senate delegations.[110]

The DLC saw these Fairness Commission recommendations as a victory for its efforts, and in a handwritten note, From congratulated Kirk on them.[111] From claimed that lobbying by Chiles and Frost had ensured that the delegate threshold was decreased only to 15 percent, and he praised Kirk's resistance to Jackson's demands as "his single most important instance of turning down a powerful interest group in the party."[112] But the DLC's lobbying clearly was not the primary motivator behind the moves undertaken by the DNC. In light of other steps taken by Kirk, it becomes apparent that the DNC chairman himself was resolved to reorganize the party and decrease the influence (or perceived influence) of interest groups.

First, Kirk did not endorse the black caucus's candidate for party vice-chairman, Richard Hatcher, a move that particularly strained Kirk's relations with the Congressional Black Caucus.[113] Second, in May 1985, he had removed formal recognition from all party caucuses, allowing the black, Hispanic, and women's caucus representatives to the DNC Executive Committee to keep their seats as a consolation. Third, he asked the AFL-CIO to refrain from endorsing a presidential candidate prior to the nominating convention as it had done in 1984 by backing Walter Mondale. Finally, Kirk eliminated the midterm party convention, which, with its infighting and parade of issue groups pushing their own agendas, had become in his words "an exercise in damage control."[114]

As with the results of the Fairness Commission, the DLC welcomed these moves and boasted—at least privately—that it had provided "cover" for Kirk to make such changes by placing these institutions into debate.[115] It is highly debatable whether the DLC's existence enabled Kirk to make drastic alterations in party organization and procedure. In recounting these years, Kirk explicitly denied that the DLC had provided him with any help or cover at all.[116] Nevertheless, these moves did have the additional benefit of minimizing the New Democrats' objections to the national party, thus forestalling the DLC effort and helping to bring these dissidents back under party control.

Said differently, having a vocal and increasingly powerful party faction competing for membership and press attention not only undermined the national party but also reflected poorly on Kirk, for it made it appear that he was unable to prevent divisiveness, the one condition the Democrats had feared most since the tumultuous convention in 1968. With the DLC outside the aegis of the party, factional fighting was also beyond his control, a dangerous situation for a chairman in charge of a fragile coalition. Therefore, Kirk and his successors continued the facade of amicability while trying to co-opt the DLC and make amends with its members in order to draw the organization within the orbit of the DNC.

Thus, beneath the surface, there was an intense rivalry between the DLC and the DNC.[117] At one end, From acknowledged that relations between the two organizations could never be completely harmonious, since they were "involved in a power struggle (though covert) over who determines the direction and the perception of the national party."[118] At the other end, the DNC saw the DLC as a threat to party unity and to the power of the national party that had to be contained. As Wally Chalmers, Kirk's chief of staff, wrote to his boss, "[the DLC] presumes to compete with the DNC as the sole disseminator of the Democratic Party's point of view. Daily, people who would otherwise count on the DNC to fill that role join the DLC's ranks."[119]

Kirk too believed that the DLC was attempting "to claim [that] it, and not the DNC, was the 'true' voice of the party." Accordingly, he hoped that the Democratic Policy Commission would "undercut the efforts of the DLC."[120] Yet the competition persisted. For example, the two bodies jockeyed for members and supporters. Robb recalled that Kirk tried to convince Governor Bill Clinton of Arkansas not to join the DLC, and Chalmers wrote to Kirk complaining about two DNC members joining the DLC.[121] Furthermore, the DLC's ability to attract prominent Democratic donors to its cause provoked the ire of DNC officials, even though this did not represent a large sum of money.[122] In an advance copy of the agenda for the DLC's Williamsburg conference in 1986, one DNC staff member highlighted the name of Bob Strauss among a list of benefactors and wrote, "Call—put in a plug for Kirk or the party."[123]

Kirk and his staff were so vexed by the DLC, despite its comparatively tiny size, because they feared that it would reinforce the Democratic Party's fractious image.[124] Keenly aware of the danger factionalization posed to the party, the DNC staff monitored the activities of the DLC and of its leadership, paying particular attention to any DLC slights against the DNC.[125] For instance, Don Sweitzer, a DNC staffer, wrote to Kirk that Maurice Sonnenberg, a big Democratic donor, was "deserving of an outraged phone call" because he had disparaged the DNC and praised the DLC to the press.[126] What irked Sweitzer was that "such a comment does nothing for party unity."[127] Deputy DNC Chairwoman Jean Dunn also asked Kirk to rope in renegade DLC members. Specifically, Dunn was upset over comments that Chiles and Nunn had made at a dinner in Atlanta to honor Nunn. She asked that Kirk place a phone call to the senator from Georgia to remind him of all the national party had done for the Georgia state party and to note "that if we Democrats act independently of each other, how can we expect to go forward and win elections."[128]

Suspicions ran the other way as well. DLC members were concerned about what the DNC was saying about their organization. Representative Buddy MacKay of Florida, for example, wrote to Kirk inquiring about negative comments the DNC chairman had apparently been making about the DLC.[129] From too was sensitive to what the DNC may have been saying about the DLC to other political actors. For instance, he believed that Kirk was leaking to the press—specifically, to syndicated columnist Jack Germond—that the DLC, just months after its establishment, was no longer relevant since the DNC had accomplished the goals to which the DLC aspired and, as a result, the DLC was about to fold.[130]

Nevertheless, the DNC's senior staff was acutely aware of the benefits of cooperating with the DLC and of potentially controlling or coopting it, and it worked toward this end. For example, Phil Burgess, executive director of the DNC's Democratic Policy Commission, placed the development of a "mechanism for cooperation and coordination with other Democratic policy groups," including the DLC, as a priority for the DPC, since "the benefits for the Party and the chairman's leadership are enormous."[131] Thus, Burgess sent copies of the organization's first draft of policy proposals to both From and Marshall for their review and critique.[132]

Kirk too expressed the DNC's desire for cooperation. In his reply to MacKay's letter, Kirk wrote—after first praising the DLC as a "positive force"— that he had worked closely with DLC members and believed that the DLC and DNC were "on a parallel course toward common and important objectives." Summing up, Kirk added, "I look forward to the day when we will be working as one, moving ahead under one banner into the important elections of 1986 and beyond."[133] In short, party unity was a high priority for Kirk. Healing potential rifts within the party was the least that a party chairman could do, and failure to do so could doom his tenure in the post. Therefore, Kirk and the DNC tried to get the DLC back under its tent as soon as possible.

From and the New Democrats responded that the DLC, as an extraparty organization, was necessary for the DNC and in fact complemented Kirk's efforts. The DLC argued that it offered "cover" for Kirk to take action against special interests, such as his elimination of the caucuses.[134] It acted as a "counterforce" to interest groups, keeping the DNC from drifting out of the mainstream.[135] Whereas Kirk, whom From believed was "probably sympathetic" to the New Democratic cause, was placed in between a "party entity heavily influenced by . . . interest groups and liberal activists" and the DLC, the New Democrats organized in the DLC did not, at least in theory, have the constraints of this position.[136]

However, the opposition of the dominant liberal faction of the party did in fact constrain the efforts of the DLC, as the organization had to alter its organization, temper its rhetoric, and develop only certain aspects of its policy agenda and public philosophy in order to remain a credible participant in Democratic politics. Indeed, as the DLC approached its second birthday, this effort to broaden its tent appeared successful. Yet this accomplishment was also a Pyrrhic victory.

Basically, the more that the DLC's membership began to approximate the ideological and factional makeup of the party as a whole, the less relevant the DLC and its accomplishments seemed to be. The DLC, for example, could claim as members the chairmen of several Senate committees. Yet because they were not necessarily committed New Democrats—and even if they were, the DLC lacked a clearly defined agenda for them to advocate—this feat meant very little. As one political commentator wrote at the end of 1986, "In its two years, the DLC has changed the national Democratic establishment and been absorbed by it."[137]

On one level, this observation was accurate. Chairman Kirk had made many of the procedural and organizational changes that the DLC advocated. In particular, he had established the DPC—counting among its membership prominent DLC members such as Senators Al Gore of Tennessee and Dale Bumpers of Arkansas and Governor Richard Riley of South Carolina—which eventually issued policy prescriptions that toed the New Democratic line.[138] He had also made the changes to the nominating rules and organization of the party that the DLC desired. Although these did not satisfy the demands of ardent New Democrats, Kirk's moves did satisfy the more modest changes that the institutional environment forced the DLC to advocate. Thus, the mix of condemnation from liberal rivals, which pushed the DLC to moderate its stances, and the co-optation of the organization by the DNC, which satisfied these tempered demands, led, at the very least, to a dilution of the DLC's own raison d'être.

When the New Democrats founded the DLC, they hoped that the establishment of a permanent extraparty organization would be an effective way by which to change the Democratic Party. By using the political prominence of its elected-official members, the DLC hoped to open the party up to them and alter its public philosophy. If one looks at the substance of the changes made in the Democratic Party during the DLC's first year of operation, it appears that the organization was quite successful.

Electorally, the Senate was once again under Democratic control, and many of that body's key committees were actually headed by DLC members. In the area of issue development, the DLC had offered, to much acclaim, a proposal to make the economy more competitive, and the DPC had issued a policy statement in line with New Democratic sentiments. Institutionally, changes recommended by the party's Fairness Commission followed many of the DLC's suggestions, and Kirk, the party chairman, even eliminated the midterm convention and special-interest caucuses.

However, if one focuses on the efficacy of the methods and strategies that the New Democrats employed, a different story emerges. By establishing an extraparty organization, the New Democrats provoked intraparty hostility that threatened the viability of the DLC itself. True, with their criticism of the national party, the New Democrats should have expected a reaction by other Democratic factions. Yet by forming a separate organization and thus giving the appearance that the party was fracturing, the New Democrats ensured an even more hostile response from the DNC and party liberals.

As a result, the DLC became an organization significantly different from the one originally planned. By rearranging the organization as a forum for a wide array of Democrats, it dulled its critical edge. Instead of offering a sharp critique of the Democratic Party and a pointed alternative public philosophy, the DLC could only rally its members around a nebulous commitment to "new ideas" and its most benign policy recommendations. In turn, the DLC actually made it easier for the DNC to accommodate its demands, as the demands themselves were considerably tempered.

Consequently, by the end of 1986, the DLC, to many, seemed redundant. Nevertheless, the organization endured. This was possible because the DLC was able to retain its elite political and monetary support. The organization's needs were not that great—its operating budget was only a fraction of the amount spent on a competitive statewide campaign—and the DLC possessed an impressive pool of political talent, which attracted these wealthy benefactors as well as media attention. Moreover, this lineup of prominent national figures was especially valuable with the 1988 elections looming on the horizon. Both money and media followed the moves of potential Democratic nominees, including DLC founders Robb and Nunn.

As the 1988 presidential nominating campaign neared, it appeared that this campaign would be especially attractive to a DLC candidate. Changes in the nominating process—specifically, the creation of a large southern regional primary—gave the DLC a unique opportunity to affect that process and, possibly, Democratic Party politics. Thus, although the DLC was induced by factional rivalries to become an organization different from the one that was first conceived, the 1988 election provided it with an opening to push its alternatives onto the party agenda.

4 / Selling Super Tuesday,
1987–1988

As ELECTION DAY 1988 approached, the Democrats were anxious. After two decisive defeats, they appeared to be facing an extremely promising opportunity to recapture the White House. Two years earlier, the Democrats had in fact regained control of the Senate. In the interim, the Iran-contra scandal had arisen, and the stock market had crashed. In addition, the nomination of Robert Bork to the Supreme Court reenergized a coalition of liberal interest groups, and his subsequent defeat seemed to validate their apparent strength. On top of this, and unlike 1984, the Democratic nominee would not be facing an incumbent president; for the first time since 1968, the presidency was truly "open."

For Democratic policy entrepreneurs like the DLC, the 1988 election also presented them with an attractive prospect. First, a large number of presidential hopefuls would reliably be searching for causes to make their own, for policy solutions to the problems of the day, and for fresh electoral strategies with which to win the White House. Second, a change in the presidential nominating process appeared to have made the party more institutionally open to the New Democrats. The establishment of a southern regional primary—"Super Tuesday"—by southern Democrats, many of whom were involved in the DLC, promised to give a special boost to a candidate espousing the New Democratic public philosophy and courting the region's moderate voters. DLC leaders believed that they had a key they could use to pick the liberals' lock on the nominating process. Thus, the DLC focused its attention on ensuring that the dynamics of the nominating campaign would, in fact, help a New Democrat win the party's nomination.

However, when Super Tuesday did not turn out as the DLC had planned, its leadership came to recognize the limits of tinkering with the nominating system as a way to affect the outcome of the presidential nominating campaign, much less to reshape their party's public philosophy. Perhaps more importantly, failure in this endeavor illustrated to the DLC leadership the limits of its present organizational form, the big-tent format it had assumed to placate its factional critics. In fact, the blurring of the DLC's distinctiveness from the rest of the party, while the party itself was correcting some of its most egregious policy and institutional excesses, resurrected calls for termination of the DLC. By the end of the 1988 Democratic National Convention, at which the changed tone of the party and its nominee was evident, there seemed to be few convincing answers to the question why the DLC should continue to exist at all.

Super Tuesday and the Politics of Presidential Nomination

As 1987 began and the attention of the political world shifted to the coming nomination campaigns, New Democrats felt that their prescriptions for reshaping the party were as urgently needed as when the organization had first been formed two years earlier. Although the party leadership was relatively responsive to—indeed, generally in concurrence with—their critique of party process, organization, and strategy, the DLC leadership felt that the New Democratic line was neither widely accepted by national party elites and their allies in Congress nor seen by the general public as the dominant message and image of the Democratic Party. With the advent of the southern regional primary, the New Democrats saw an opportunity to take advantage of a nominating process that, for the first time in sixteen years, had apparently been altered in their favor and to further their cause. Accordingly, the DLC immediately took steps to ensure that the dynamics of the nominating campaign would benefit New Democratic candidates.

ELECTORAL PROBLEMS AND ALTERNATIVES

Although the DLC had seen the elimination of such institutions as the midterm convention and special-interest caucuses, as well as the drafting of a more moderate policy statement by the DPC, its leadership continued to believe that the partisan situation had not fundamentally changed: liberals continued to control the national party, to advocate their agenda, and to constrain the electoral viability of the

Democrats.[1] With the approach of the 1988 presidential nominating campaign, however, New Democrats were presented with yet another regularly occurring opportunity to challenge this arrangement and push their alternative public philosophy, an opportunity that they seized.

At one level of involvement, the DLC gathered data to make the argument for a New Democratic electoral strategy. In October 1987, Stanley Greenberg conducted a poll for the DLC of 500 "swing voters"—southern Democrats who had voted for Reagan twice but for a Democratic Senate candidate in 1986—in the metropolitan areas of Jacksonville, Florida; Charlotte, North Carolina; and Atlanta, Georgia. He found that these swing voters were not unlike those in the rest of the country; they were mostly young baby boomers who categorized themselves as independents or Republicans.

The data showed that only about one-third of these voters intended to vote Democratic in the 1988 presidential election, and that most of this group were women.[2] As the DLC and Greenberg argued, the Democrats could not concede this large bloc of voters to the GOP and expect to win in November.[3] Additionally, the DLC data showed that this constituency was disenchanted with the national Democratic message. Sixty-one percent of those polled felt that the Democrats were "too eager to satisfy special interest groups," and over half agreed that the Democrats had "lost touch with the needs of middle-class and working people" and could not "be trusted to spend our tax dollars wisely."[4]

Further confirming this analysis were the responses to a DLC-sponsored presidential debate on national security held in Miami. The DLC's analysis found that Gore and Gephardt, two DLC members, were the biggest winners with voters; substantial numbers reported that their opinions of these two candidates rose after hearing their positions on defense issues.[5] In sum, this poll was used to further the DLC argument that southern white voters were crucial to Democratic success, that the Democratic Party was losing these swing voters because they did not see the party as representing the national interest or as possessing the competency to lead, and that the national-purpose message of the New Democrats—with its emphasis on a strong national defense—resonated with this key demographic group.

On another level, the DLC tried to influence the contest for the Democratic presidential nomination directly. First, the organization moved to become a player during the "invisible primary"—the time from the day after the most recent presidential election to the day of the first primary, when presidential hopefuls jockey for support among political elites.[6] From argued that it was "very important" for the New Democrats to keep the threat of a late southern candidacy alive, since that would enable them "to exert maximum influence on the way all the candidates campaign."[7]

Aware of the DLC's precarious existence within Democratic Party politics, From added that the threat of such a run—by Robb or Nunn—would be more effective than an actual candidacy, since the DLC would avoid criticism for not adhering to party orthodoxy yet still be able, in theory, to affect the outcome of the nominating campaign.[8] At a DLC forum in Atlanta in June 1987, Robb made this threat public when he suggested that if no announced presidential hopeful took hold with southern voters, the South should adopt a series of favorite-son candidates in the hopes of forcing a brokered convention.[9]

Both Robb and Nunn remained highly touted as late entries to the presidential race or as vice-presidential picks. Both were white southerners who had won election in increasingly Republican territory by being social moderates and fiscal conservatives who also had strong defense credentials. It also would be difficult for a Republican candidate to label Robb, a former marine, or Nunn, a senior Democrat on the Senate Armed Services Committee, as weak on defense or foreign policy issues, a usual vulnerability of national Democrats. As the election approached, Robb decided to run for the Senate, and talk about a Nunn candidacy intensified. In response, From sent a confidential memo to Nunn entitled "Should You or Shouldn't You?" "The bottom line is this," wrote From, "if we don't have a candidate who raises the stakes of the nominating battle and sweeps through the primary process, our efforts in the DLC will largely be for naught and we'll have to start all over again in 1989. We're at the point where the revolution we've started requires a leader to take it over the top."[10]

It is possible that From's strong rhetoric was born out of a personal desire to see Nunn run. However, since the organization's inception, From and the DLC had been keenly aware of the presidential nominee's central role in shaping the party's electoral strategy and issue agenda, and they had explored this strategy thoroughly. As we shall see, after the 1988 election, the DLC became more attached to this analysis and actively pursued the presidential option.

For the impending 1988 contest, however, the DLC could claim four hopefuls as members: Bruce Babbitt, former governor of Arizona; Senator Joe Biden of Delaware; Gephardt; and Gore. Among this group, Gore seemed the most viable of those committed to the New Democratic public philosophy. Consequently, in addition to informally counseling Robb and Nunn on their possibilities, From and Marshall offered advice to the senator from Tennessee. There is little way of judging how much Gore heeded the counsel of these two DLC organizers, but that does not detract from its significance. What they told him certainly reflected the New Democratic public philosophy, as well as what one would expect if the DLC were ever to launch one of its own into the race.

From and Marshall advised Gore to draw a sharp line between himself, as a New Democrat, and the rest of the pack. Gore needed to strike a populist note, decry the special-interest groups that controlled the early nominating contests in Iowa and New Hampshire, and claim to be the candidate of the "forgotten Democrats." Along these lines, they also advised him to be strongly independent and name specific governmental programs that needed to be eliminated. Finally, they wanted Gore to frame the nominating campaign as one that would determine the future of the party: Democrats could choose Gore, who represented a continuation of the tradition of Roosevelt, Truman, and Kennedy—what the DLC saw as a mixture of populism and fiscal responsibility—or they could choose a candidate from the rest of the pack, who reflected the McGovern-Mondale tradition of using high spending to win the support of organized constituencies.[11]

In sum, they advised an electoral strategy that flowed from the central New Democratic analyses yet reflected the reality of the DLC's first years of operation. New Democrats could criticize the party's dominant public philosophy, but to defend themselves against the charge of political apostasy, they had to link their proposed campaign message to the Democratic icons of Roosevelt, Truman, and Kennedy.

ISSUE PROBLEMS AND POLICY ALTERNATIVES

The tempered rhetoric of the DLC's first two years also lived on in the New Democratic critique of the national party's issue stances and in the issue agenda the DLC offered as a replacement. The organization continued to frame its policy alternatives within the larger history of the Democratic Party, arguing that the party had strayed from its true "progressive tradition" and had instead embraced "ideas, causes, and values foreign to most Americans."[12] Similarly, the DLC continued to develop those stances that were the least objectionable to its broad membership and to the party at large.

Consequently, the main policy paper the DLC released in 1987, hoping to influence the presidential nominating contests, focused on relatively uncontroversial topics. In "New Directions, Enduring Values," an issue paper released on April 29, 1987, the DLC argued that the Democratic Party had to commit itself to reversing the country's competitive decline in the world economy, to breaking the cycle of poverty and dependency so that the poor could enter the social and economic mainstream, and to building a strong national defense.[13] Moreover, in the preface to this paper, DLC Chairman Robb took pains not to offend either the party leadership or members of the dominant liberal faction inside and outside of the DLC. "Like the party we represent, the DLC is broad and inclusive," he wrote. "Our recommendations do not constitute official party policy; nor is each proposal likely to command unanimous support from the more than 170 DLC members. Taken together, however, they point our party in a promising new direction—a direction we believe that most Democrats can and will embrace."[14]

This emphasis on consensus and uncontroversial positions, plus the use of tempered rhetoric, may have placated the DLC's diverse membership and, to a lesser degree, liberals outside of the organization, but it simultaneously hampered its maneuverability as the 1988 nominating season approached. Consider that From and Marshall counseled Gore on strategy and message, yet From advised the DLC leadership—specifically, Robb and Nunn—to endorse both Gore and Gephardt. His reasoning was that if the organization's leadership supported only Gore, it would reinforce the perception that the DLC was merely a group of southern conservatives and would alienate the 45 of its 106 House members who had already endorsed Gephardt.[15] Moreover, even if the DLC had a candidate eager to carry the New Democratic banner, it did not have a fully developed public philosophy with which he could differentiate himself and rally supporters. In sum, the DLC's organizational commitment to a big-tent form profoundly hampered its effort to influence the 1988 presidential race.

INSTITUTIONAL PROBLEMS AND ALTERNATIVES

Perhaps as importantly, this commitment to the big tent fed the argument that the DLC merely replicated the national party and should fold.[16] Interestingly, the DLC was financially sound. It was able to announce that, beginning in 1989, the $1,000 dues for elected-official members would no longer be required, as the organization had been able to raise enough money for an operating budget of $600,000 in 1987 and $800,000 in 1988.[17] Nevertheless, questioning among political elites persisted, and From had to respond.

In a long memo to Robb, he set out his views on why the organization should continue to exist. First, he argued that even hinting that the DLC was not an "on-going entity" would undermine the credibility of it and its members. Second, even though the DLC had experienced success in gaining members, exerting influence, and developing ideas, the organization had "not yet reached institutional status." Furthermore, From argued that even though, at its founding, most had envisioned the DLC as folding by 1986 or 1988 "at the latest," success for the New Democrats had not really been achieved.

Success, wrote From, would come when the DLC and the New Democrats took over the party and helped elect one of its own to the presidency (he offered Nunn as a candidate). Until the White House was won, there would still be a role for the DLC in Democratic politics.[18] From also argued that the organization had to become a full-fledged "political movement" and therefore had "to develop an ideology, rally political leadership around the country, build grassroots support, and raise enough money to do the job."[19] How the organization was going to accomplish these goals and achieve its self-imposed standards of victory—electing a New Democrat to the presidency and taking over the party—became the central strategic concerns of the DLC.

Organizationally, the DLC leadership had toyed with establishing a federal PAC or an organization like the American-Israel Public Affairs Committee (AIPAC) that would not directly donate money to candidates but would "inform" the contributing practices of affiliated and like-minded PACs, in order to expand its grassroots and fund-raising operations.[20] Strategically, the DLC had actively looked to expand its influence within Congress. The leadership of the organization hoped to work the New Democratic message into the congressional process by having its ideas introduced as legislation and championed on the House floor by DLC members.[21] Additionally, the DLC wanted to help the congressional leadership with its "informal message co-ordination" in order to frame legislation emanating from both the House and the Senate in New Democratic terms.[22] But with its sanitized program and big-tent structure, the DLC was almost destined to be just a supporting element in the activities on Capitol Hill and in the affairs of the party. The impending presidential nominating campaign, however, provided the DLC with a ripe opportunity to push its public philosophy onto the party's agenda.

Interestingly, despite the DLC's long interest and involvement in reforming the presidential nominating process, the Super Tuesday regional primary—a delegate-rich day of presidential primaries encompassing fourteen southern states—was not a DLC invention. The movement to form a southern regional primary had begun in the early 1970s, as part of larger efforts to restructure the whole nominating process around a series of regional presidential primaries. Although New England and the western states had considered forming respective regional primaries for 1976, the first regional primary was ultimately to be a southeastern one, formed by legislative leaders in Alabama, Georgia, and Florida to give President Carter a boost in his 1980 renomination campaign.[23] By 1984, the term "Super Tuesday" began to be used to describe this day of primaries, as five nonsouthern states joined the three states from the 1980 southeastern primary to select their delegates to the national nominating convention.[24]

It was not until after the Democrats' defeat in the 1984 election that southern Democratic leaders—through the Southern Legislative Conference (SLC)—began in earnest the drive to create a truly all-encompassing "super" regional primary. Like their federal counterparts in the DLC, these state officials were motivated by the routing of the national ticket in the country and, specifically, in the South. They were disgusted with liberal presidential nominees who did not reflect the region's more moderate stance, thus making the head of the ticket a hindrance to elected officials who had to run with them.[25]

In this regard, Super Tuesday can be seen as coming out of the same outlook on politics and government as the New Democrats. Formed by southern Democrats, many of whom were also active in the DLC, Super Tuesday was an attempt by a minority faction to decrease the influence of the dominant liberal faction on the national party. These southern Democrats wished to use the postreform nominating rules—the very ones that had facilitated the ascent of New Politics candidates—to force presidential hopefuls to address southern concerns, adopt stances acceptable to the region's voters, and craft campaigns that would fare better with the mainstream voters who participated in the general election.

These leaders hoped that by creating a delegate-rich primary day, presidential aspirants would be forced to focus attention on the South at the expense of the Iowa caucuses and the New Hampshire primary— the two earliest and arguably most influential nominating contests— which appeared to both southern and New Democrats to be controlled by liberals.[26] As Robert Slagle, chairman of the Texas State Democratic Party, explained at the time, "Texas is damn tired of Iowa and New Hampshire exercising a disproportionate impact on the [nomination's] outcome."[27]

Additionally, Super Tuesday proponents hoped that, in the end, a spirited contest involving quality candidates would emerge, thus convincing Reagan Democrats—those traditionally Democratic voters who had supported the Republicans in 1980 and 1984—to return to the Democratic Party.[28] The DNC, in turn, gave the move its tacit approval. Kirk, the DNC chairman, saw it as a way for the party to shed its special-interest image, and by not opposing it, the party was able to build a bridge to southern white moderates.[29]

The SLC, whose members created Super Tuesday by enacting the appropriate legislation in their home states, and the DLC, which supported the efforts and had many members who were instrumental in the primary's establishment, hoped to alter the whole way the nominating process had been run since 1972. From the time the McGovern-Fraser rule changes first took effect that year, the winning of presidential primaries and their accompanying delegates had taken on central importance in the dynamics of winning the party's nomination. No longer could the support of party leaders ensure a candidate's victory at the nominating convention, as it had for Hubert Humphrey in 1968.

In such a world, primaries, which had been in existence since 1912, were no longer used solely to prove to party leaders that a candidate had electoral appeal in different segments of the country—as they had shown for John Kennedy in 1960. In 1988, thirty-three states were to hold primaries for Democratic hopefuls, in which two-thirds of all Democratic delegates would be at stake.[30] As primaries became more prevalent, the party organization's power over delegate selection disappeared.

To replace these vehicles for the winning of delegates, presidential hopefuls had to create their own organizations in each state and raise large sums of money to buy television advertising. To appeal to Democratic activists, candidates found that special-interest organizations, such as teachers unions and civil rights groups, had adherents who not only voted but also could prove crucial in organizing a state.[31] Therefore, candidates crafted their messages to appeal to these specialized interest groups; consequently, interest groups had enormous power in primaries, especially those in small states such as New Hampshire.

This situation was intensified in caucus states, such as Iowa, where the more formidable barriers to participation resulted in even greater influence for organized special-interest groups. As a result, the policies being espoused by Democratic hopefuls were clearly to the left of the party rank and file as well as of the general electorate. Indeed, according to John Kessel's study of Democratic Party activists in 1988, four distinct issue groups existed, with the dominant one— comprising 43 percent of these activists—clearly to the left of all other activists as well as of the party's rank and file.[32] Worse yet, the dominant coalition among activists not only excluded Democratic moderates and conservatives but also had become slightly more liberal than it was even in 1972.[33]

Similarly, the DLC and southern Democratic leaders believed that the two early contests in New Hampshire and Iowa were "easily manipulated" by special interests, which at the very least did not represent New Democratic beliefs and, in turn, produced nominees who were popular only with Democratic activists and thus too extreme for the general electorate.[34] To them, this situation was clearly illustrated by the fact that Democrats running for president spent so much time in these states but lost them in the general election.[35] As From colorfully described the retail politics that future presidents had to play, "With all due respect, I don't think someone who lives in Dubuque should force a candidate to come flip pancakes in their kitchen four or five times in order to judge who should be president."[36]

The establishment of Super Tuesday provided the DLC with an alternative electoral strategy to advocate to political candidates, to party operatives, and to the media. Accordingly, the DLC's central goal during the 1988 nominating campaign became to move the emphasis in the primaries from the early New Hampshire and Iowa contests, where the candidates were forced to address unrepresentative electorates and pander to narrow special interests, to the South and to the Super Tuesday primaries, where the political environment would force candidates to craft platforms that would better reflect the general electorate.[37]

Simultaneously, they wanted to convince the national political press to view the nominating process as the Democratic candidates' attempt "to win back traditional Democratic voters who have deserted . . . [the] party in four of the last five Presidential elections," rather than focusing on the candidates who were doing the best with "the activists in Iowa and New Hampshire."[38] Moreover, they urged the media to consider the winning back of "whites, males, Southerners, ethnics, young voters, and moderates" with a "national purpose" agenda as the key to the race.[39]

To promote Super Tuesday and become a central player in the 1988 Democratic presidential nominating race, the DLC launched the Super Tuesday Education Project (STEP), a series of forums, issue breakfasts, press briefings, candidate debates, and policy papers. Chaired by Senators Bob Graham of Florida and John Breaux of Louisiana, this was a comprehensive effort to boost attention to the regional primary, increase voter turnout, and establish a "national purpose litmus test" that would, in effect, force the candidates to debate the DLC agenda.[40]

STEP was a multifaceted and relatively large endeavor on which the DLC focused its activities for much of 1987 and the beginning of 1988. Because it cost approximately $150,000, From recalled that the DLC "almost lost [its] shirt" financing STEP.[41] This money, though small in comparison to other monies spent during the primaries, enabled the DLC to undertake a wide range of STEP-related activities. In addition to the aforementioned Greenberg poll of southern swing voters and its policy manual "New Directions, Enduring Values," the DLC held a forum in May 1987 at the Kennedy School of Government at Harvard to examine the impact of the media on the presidential race and hosted a "Super Tuesday Summit" on June 21 and 22 in Atlanta to gather southern state party leaders to discuss the regional primary as well as to hear from the presidential candidates who attended.[42]

As the primary season approached, the DLC also hosted three Democratic candidate debates—one in October 1987 in Miami, a second in New Orleans in November, and a final one in Houston in March 1988, right before Super Tuesday itself. Finally, throughout this whole time, the DLC sent out "SWAT" teams of elected officials to Super Tuesday states "to encourage state and local elected Democrats to drum up grassroots interest in the nominating race."[43]

On March 8, 1988, Democrats in twenty states went to the polls to select delegates to represent them, as well as a preferred candidate, at the Democratic National Convention later that year in Atlanta. As the votes were tabulated, it became clear that the results were not what the DLC or southern Democrats expected or wanted. Jesse Jackson, the most liberal of the Democratic field and the nemesis of the New Democrats, took the key southern portion of Super Tuesday. The civil rights leader won five states and 355 delegates; Gore won four states and 328 delegates; Governor Michael Dukakis of Massachusetts won three states—Maryland, Florida, and Texas, with their large non-southern elements—and 288 delegates; and Gephardt won only his home state of Missouri and a total of 94 delegates.[44]

On a theoretical level, Gore's results corroborated the DLC's arguments about the efficacy of its "national-purpose," southern-oriented strategy. Whether coincidentally or purposefully, he had followed the DLC's advice and focused primarily on Super Tuesday at the expense of New Hampshire and Iowa.[45] Indeed, in his speech to 8,000 Iowa Democrats at their party's Jefferson-Jackson Day dinner in November 1987, Gore argued that the nominating process was skewed, since it gave a disproportionate amount of power to one state. Despite this fact, Gore bravely proclaimed, "I will not do what the pundits say it takes to win in Iowa—flatter you with promises, change my tune, and back down from my convictions. I will not play that game or abide by those rules."[46] Committed to going after the Super Tuesday vote, Gore—who referred to himself as a "raging moderate"—thus embraced free trade and attacked those who wanted to limit the role of the United States abroad.[47]

Per the logic of this strategy, Gore succeeded on Super Tuesday in attracting white moderate voters to his candidacy. The senator from Tennessee ran impressively well with white voters, winning (according to CBS News/*New York Times* exit polling) 40 percent of this group's vote. He also won back Reagan Democrats, carrying the most congressional districts that had Democratic representatives but had voted for Reagan in 1980 and 1984.[48] Despite their support, it was not enough for Gore to sweep the South and ride the momentum to front-runner status.

On a practical level, then, the strategy failed, and the reasons were many and fundamental. First and foremost, the electoral dynamics in the South had changed profoundly. No longer was the region's politics dominated by a white, conservative Democratic Party. The rise of race and social issues, along with general demographic changes, had strengthened the Republican Party in the region, leading to the emergence of "normal" two-party American politics. Simply, the South's political peculiarity had waned. Consequently, a contested Republican nomination attracted many formerly Democratic, conservative voters to participate in that contest. At the same time, black voters, now at the heart of the southern state Democratic parties, participated fully in the Democratic primaries and overwhelmingly backed Jackson.

This black support was immense. According to ABC News exit polling, 96 percent of black Democratic voters cast their ballots for Jackson.[49] There were no longer enough conservatives within the party to offset the large numbers of loyal, liberal black voters.[50] In truth, Gore's own conservative credentials were not as impeccable as those of other southern leaders, such as Nunn.[51] Therefore, his appeal to many white voters was based on regional pride—a draw that was not strong enough to pull conservative white voters out of the Republican primary or to the voting booth itself.[52]

Second, Super Tuesday, as constructed, was unable to affect the dynamics of the overall nominating campaign in the way its creators had planned. The primary became so geographically large—covering over 150 media markets—and attracted so much national press attention that the candidates' messages could not be significantly altered to appeal to some stereotypically "southern" voter.[53] Instead, presidential hopefuls found voters throughout the region with whom they apparently resonated.[54] Dukakis chased Hispanic voters in Texas and transplanted northerners in Florida; Jackson pursued the black vote throughout the region. As Charles Hadley and Harold Stanley observed, "For Democrats, the size of Super Tuesday fuzzed its focus."[55]

Ironically, the size of the primary actually increased the importance of the two early contests, as any "bounce" from wins there risked producing an unstoppable momentum that, with the accompanying attention by the media and donors, could help a candidate overcome the enormous task of campaigning in so many states. Indeed, reflecting on the 1988 race, Kirk argued that Dukakis won the nomination because the other candidates were "flat-ass broke."[56] With his large war chest—no doubt itself enriched by his New Hampshire primary win—he was able to afford to campaign effectively in the run-up to Super Tuesday and to continue relatively strongly afterward.[57]

Realizing the continued, if not heightened, prominence of New Hampshire and Iowa, Democratic hopefuls had acted accordingly. Except for Gore and Jackson, all Democratic presidential candidates spent at least as much time in Iowa and New Hampshire as they did in all fourteen southern Super Tuesday states. And despite his avowed Dixie strategy, Gore too hedged his southern bet, spending more money in the New Hampshire primary than he did in any single Super Tuesday state except Texas.[58]

Yet the prominence of the New Hampshire and Iowa contests had its greatest effect on Gephardt, the other viable candidate with New Democratic ties and the DLC's first chairman. Indeed, his journey from New Democratic leader to liberal presidential candidate offers the clearest possible example of the institutional realities of the Democratic presidential nomination process—especially the salience of the early contests and the importance of liberal activists in them—and thus of the failure of Super Tuesday (much less STEP) to alter them.

Hailing from St. Louis's Fourteenth Ward, Gephardt followed a familiar American route on his rise to prominence. Well-mannered and popular in school, he was a strong student who went on to Northwestern University, where he became student body president (notably, a member of this body was Al From). Returning to St. Louis, he worked his way through the political system from precinct captain to congressman, a post to which he was first elected in 1976. In his freshman term, Gephardt won a seat on the Ways and Means Committee, a first step toward distinguishing himself in the House.[59] He represented a German-Catholic working-class neighborhood, and his non-liberal credentials were impeccable. As a protégé of Gillis Long, he was an active participant in the nascent New Democratic efforts undertaken in the House Democratic Caucus from 1981 to 1984. In the first two years of Reagan's first term, he voted with the "conservative coalition"—a majority of southern Democrats voting with a majority of

Republicans in support of Reagan's legislative agenda—on 69 percent of all key votes.[60] In 1985, Gephardt became chairman of the DLC.

However, during this same period, Gephardt—ascending the ranks of the House leadership and, no doubt, harboring presidential aspirations—began to move to the left. His positions on abortion, trade, contra aid, and defense spending came more into line with those of liberal activists, as reflected in his rating by the ADA (a common scale of a politician's liberalism), which went from a relatively conservative forty-five in 1981 to eighty-five in 1983.[61] Likewise, in 1986, Gephardt joined the conservative coalition on only 18 percent of key votes, a sharp turnaround from his 1981 level.[62]

Dave McCurdy, Gephardt's House and DLC colleague, remembered that Gephardt had been frank about why he changed his positions on certain issues. McCurdy recalled Gephardt telling him on a campaign flight to Iowa in 1988, "I'm going to take some positions in this campaign that you are not going to like because I have to win Iowa."[63] Strategically, Gephardt felt that since his national base was relatively small—despite his leadership in the House, he still represented only a congressional district in St. Louis—he had to engage in the personal politics appropriate to New Hampshire and Iowa and espouse the liberal views of their primary electorates.[64]

Unsurprisingly, when Gephardt officially announced his candidacy, he disappointed From and the New Democrats. In a confidential memorandum to the congressman, From criticized an advance draft of his announcement speech—the address that sets the tone for the entire campaign—for embracing protectionism, for mentioning only arms control when discussing defense policy, and for focusing on special interests at the expense of the national interest.[65] "First, the draft you sent me was mush," From wrote. "You ought to throw it out."[66] When Gephardt finally gave this speech, it may have been sharper, but its substance did not change. Summing up the New Democratic reaction to the announcement was Durwood McAlister, a columnist for the *Atlanta Journal:* "[It is] a divisive piece of protectionist demagoguery, setting blue-collar workers against their white-collar counterparts in language that could have been written for him by the AFL-CIO."[67] As From told a reporter, "Dick is still my friend . . . but it's very clear that I'm less enamored with the direction of Dick's campaign than I am with Dick Gephardt himself."[68]

Gephardt has defended this apparent paradox of his involvement with the New Democrats and the DLC, on the one hand, and the positions he took as a presidential candidate, on the other, by asserting that "I never believed that what the DLC was for was to move the party ideologically."[69] In his defense at the time, From and other DLC organizers also noted that Gephardt's commitment to the New Democrats' endeavor was, compared with that of other principal organizers, "lukewarm."[70] From even commented to one reporter that Robb, Gephardt's successor, was the DLC's "first real chairman."[71]

Yet what was clear to both DLC strategists and political commentators, and apparently to Gephardt himself, was that institutional realities forced him to make this turnaround. David Broder of the *Washington Post* explained that the dilemma for a Democratic presidential hopeful was that he had to "satisfy 'litmus-test' liberal constituencies in the early contests and still [be able to] to compete effectively for votes in the more conservative states of the Old Confederacy."[72]

From agreed with this assessment. He commented that as a "longshot" candidate, Gephardt had to court the liberal interest groups that had the capacity to organize delegates and voters in the early contests.[73] Although From recalled that his friend "went off the deep end" once he began to run actively for president, he clearly realized that it was an institutional reality that forced Gephardt to follow this strategy and alter his issue stances.[74] As From explained to Robb and Nunn, Gephardt is the "perfect example of how the system influences a candidate to play within the limits of the orthodoxies."[75]

Indeed, these "orthodoxies" pointed to a substantial and long-range problem for the New Democrats. How could a New Democrat win the presidential nomination if the process governing it was dominated by liberal activists in the early nominating contests? Gephardt's transformation illuminated one possible answer: shed the New Democratic public philosophy. Meanwhile, the failure of the Gore candidacy appeared to highlight the inadequacy of another answer: procedural tinkering with the system in the face of a transformed political world where even southern Democratic state parties were dominated by liberals.

The results of the Super Tuesday effort were destined to weigh heavily on DLC leaders, for they raised fundamental questions about the New Democratic strategy and the overall viability of the organization. At the same time, liberal Democrats relished the irony of Super Tuesday, which the New Democrats had pushed so hard, benefiting a "foreign policy liberal," Dukakis, and "an old-style liberal," Jackson.[76] In the estimation of one longtime liberal activist, the whole project "failed on their [the DLC's] terms," since "the Southern strategy led to Jesse Jackson's victory."[77]

Unsurprisingly, in the face of this factional gloating, the DLC immediately began to contend that although the evidence pointed against a New Democratic victory, the Super Tuesday project had worked, since, as From put it, the DLC had been able to "remind candidates that there was a life, and a real constituency," outside of the Iowa caucuses.[78] However, the DLC could not deny that the results of Super Tuesday were neither to its liking nor consistent with its plans. As Robb's longtime chief of staff observed, Robb had tried to "paper over" the fact that Super Tuesday "somewhat backfired."[79] Also, although it is true that the DLC did not advocate the actual formation of the contest, many of its members were intimately involved with its genesis; the resulting structure played into the DLC strategy; and, as one senior DLC staffer wrote at the time, "if anyone is associated with Super Tuesday, and its ultimate success or failure, we are."[80]

With the failure of their Super Tuesday strategy, then, the DLC and New Democrats did not have a presidential contender or nominee to champion their cause and thus lacked an effective means by which to change the party's public philosophy. Said differently, the DLC's inability to shape the outcome of the nominating contests put it on the sidelines while others determined the future of the party and resurrected nagging questions about the mission and viability of the DLC. Nevertheless, the organization persisted in trying to influence the presidential ticket, the main deliberative committees at the nominating convention, and the wider policy debate of the party.

The DLC and the 1988 Presidential Nomination

Without a contender in the final stages of the nominating campaign, the New Democrats had to fall back on other methods to influence the composition, platform, and strategy of the presidential ticket. These efforts, however, would once again be relatively ineffective, suggesting that the DLC did not have any significant power within the national party. At the same time, many in the national party felt that the New Democrats had been adequately accommodated and thus could not understand why the DLC continued to operate. All in all, the rest of the 1988 nominating campaign played out much like the DLC's institutional efforts during the preceding three years. Yet again, the New Democrats found themselves unable to influence party affairs and policy decisions. Once more, the DLC would look impotent.

ELECTORAL PROBLEMS AND ALTERNATIVES

After Gore's withdrawal from the presidential campaign following the New York primary, it became inescapable to the DLC that its strategy of promoting Super Tuesday as an alternative springboard to the nomination had failed. The field had narrowed to the neoliberal Dukakis and the liberal Jackson, with the latter consistently trailing yet irritating the former. Once Dukakis had the nomination in hand, however, the DLC did not relent in trying to influence the Democratic ticket. Just as it had during the invisible primary phase of the 1988 campaign, the organization used its store of political talent to affect Democratic presidential strategy at the end of the nominating campaign.

Both Robb and Nunn had been highlighted by the press as possible vice-presidential picks, especially as the nominating convention neared. From and Marshall recognized the attractions of having a staunch New Democrat on the presidential ticket. So when it became evident that Nunn would remove his name from consideration, the two DLC organizers appealed to him to leave his hat in the ring in order to retain the DLC's credibility within the national party. They felt that if Nunn abandoned the contest for the vice-presidency at this point, while those on the left opposed his nomination, it would "bolster the myth that you—and the broader movement you represent within the party—are too conservative to merit a place on the national ticket."[81]

In the end, Dukakis chose Senator Lloyd Bentsen of Texas to be his running mate. The selection of Bentsen, a DLC member and southern conservative, met with the DLC's approval, yet his impact on the strategy of the ticket and the ideology of the party was minimal. This stopgap attempt to influence national party strategy by winning the number-two position on the presidential ticket ultimately was unsuccessful. The result of this effort, along with that of the Super Tuesday strategy, presented the DLC with the now-recurring problem of how it would get the national party to follow the New Democratic electoral strategy. In the meantime, the DLC worked on the other element of its public philosophy, the New Democratic policy proposals, and on pushing these onto the issue agenda of the party.

ISSUE PROBLEMS AND POLICY ALTERNATIVES

Criticism of the DLC and the New Democratic public philosophy had continued through 1987 and into the 1988 presidential campaign season. As before, members of the liberal faction attacked the DLC's issue positions and the values underlying them as antithetical to the Democratic Party. Jackson, for one, even resurrected the charge that the DLC was racist, claiming that the organization drummed up support for Gore during Super Tuesday by arguing that "a vote for anybody but Gore is a vote for Jackson." He explained sarcastically that this was "real subtle stuff."[82] In response, the DLC continued its effort to attract a more demographically and ideologically diverse membership, a move that necessitated its other reaction, a moderation of its rhetoric. Consequently, the DLC continued to link its policy prescriptions to those of past Democratic administrations and to focus its attention on introducing measures that were relatively uncontroversial. In this light, after Super Tuesday had passed, the DLC concentrated its energies on promoting its voluntary national service plan.

The idea of requiring or creating incentives for young people to serve their country had begun to regain currency with neoliberals in the late 1970s and early 1980s. In fact, in 1980, Representative Leon Panetta of California and Senator Paul Tsongas of Massachusetts had introduced a bill to establish a Presidential Commission on National Service.[83] By November 1987, it appeared that the idea of national service was gaining popularity, as nearly a dozen bills on the topic had been introduced in the House and Senate, offering plans ranging from compulsory community or military service to voluntary programs providing public jobs for the unemployed.[84]

On May 11, 1988, the DLC entered this debate, unveiling "Citizenship and National Service: A Blueprint for Civic Enterprise," a policy paper written for the DLC by Charles Moskos, a professor of sociology at Northwestern University. The plan called for the establishment of a "Citizens Corps" in which students would receive, for each year of voluntary national service, a voucher worth $10,000 (or $12,000 if the service was in the military) to be used for college, job training, or housing.[85] The DLC argued that this scheme would not only provide a way for young Americans to earn the money needed for education and job training but also foster a sense of "civic activism." Linking the Citizens Corps to the Democratic Party of the past, From wrote that the plan "is rooted in the Democratic Party's progressive tradition of equal sacrifice for the common good"; it was an update of Kennedy's call to "ask not what your country can do for you, but what you can do for your country."[86]

The DLC also stressed that the Citizens Corps differed from past Democratic education and job-training programs in significant ways. First, the plan was premised on a public philosophy in which the relationship between citizens and government was based on reciprocal obligation, not entitlement. In this approach, the government provided benefits to people not because they possessed a certain right to those funds or services but because citizens provided the government and society with something in return. Manifested fully for the first time in this policy, this notion became a core belief of the New Democratic public philosophy, one that differentiated the New Democrats from the liberals. Furthermore, New Democrats hoped grandly that this emphasis on mutual responsibility would foster good citizenship and build a sense of community.

Politically, New Democrats hoped that the national service plan and its underlying rationale would lead to a Democratic social policy more in line with middle-class concerns. They argued that instead of emphasizing the national party's strong stances in favor of abortion rights, gay rights, affirmative action, and other contentious social issues, Democrats could point to the national service proposal, with its emphasis on good citizenship and mutual responsibility. Additionally, by tying benefits to work, this plan addressed the belief among many white working- and middle-class voters that Democratic social policies funded the "undeserving poor," thus giving them "something for nothing."[87] As Moskos explained, "national service moves us beyond the sort of something-for-nothing, every-man-for-himself, me-first philosophy that has been prevalent in the American ruling groups."[88] In sum, the DLC hoped that embracing national service could help blunt the Democrats' extreme image with the public on social issues.

Second, the way in which the program was to be administered represented a shift away from the primacy of the federal government, another aspect of the New Democratic public philosophy. New Democrats believed that the federal government had grown too large and was inefficient in delivering services and unresponsive to local needs in many areas. The DLC wanted the Citizens Corps to be administered by state, local, and private nonprofit agencies, which would receive matching grants to cover three-quarters of their costs from a new public agency, the Corporation for National Service, which would set broad policy for the program.[89]

As opposed to prevailing Democratic thinking on public administration, which focused on "statist policies" and "more bureaucratic direction of our lives," according to From and Marshall, "national service [would] build . . . from the grass roots up and seek . . . to engage the American people in volunteer efforts to solve society's problems."[90] At its maximum extension, the DLC was offering an alternative theory of governance from that found in New Deal liberalism. At the least, it was building on the neoliberal call to reform governmental functions in the interest of efficiency.

From believed that the national service plan, with its emphasis on civic obligation and citizenship, possessed qualities that could make it "the galvanizing idea of the year."[91] However, like much of what the DLC undertook, even this proposal, which had a wide range of support, was not immune from attack. Organized labor opposed it, fearing that volunteers would take jobs away from unionized employees. Some liberals also objected to the plan, since it would force the poor to work to earn money to attend college, while the rich could avoid any service and pay tuition themselves.[92] Despite these rumblings, the idea of national service was already popular among an array of elites in the national party. Therefore, the DLC proposal was much more acceptable to the national party than, for example, its stance on military spending and thus had a greater chance of being accepted by it. Furthermore, the national party, as evidenced by its moderating moves under Kirk, seemed to be searching for new social policies.[93]

Accordingly, the DLC did not necessarily have to sell the national party on the concept of national service. Instead, it had to convince the party that its Citizens Corps program was the best way to embrace this idea. Therefore, during the last two weeks of October 1988, the DLC launched "National Service '88," a series of six public forums held around the country on the issue.[94] The highlight of this effort was a speech by Democratic vice-presidential nominee Bentsen to 2,000 students at UCLA in which he endorsed the DLC national service proposal.[95]

National service became one of the issues most identified with the DLC, one that the organization has continued to champion throughout its existence. Not only did the concept exemplify New Democratic beliefs regarding the proper relationship between state and citizen and in the organization of public administration, but it also appealed across factional lines. In this, national service was an important way for the DLC to soften its controversial image to other Democrats, retain its now diverse membership, and remain a credible participant in Democratic policy and political debate. Yet as the DLC's positions became more palatable to the national party, and as the national party took steps to accommodate New Democratic criticisms, questions about the continued existence of the DLC resurfaced, especially after the 1988 Democratic National Convention.

INSTITUTIONAL PROBLEMS AND ALTERNATIVES

With the addition of superdelegates and the traditional role of elected officials on the convention's powerful rules and platform committees, the nominating convention offered a superficially good opportunity for the DLC, with its surfeit of elected-official members, to effect change within the party. Yet undertaken in the aftermath of the failure of STEP to help a New Democrat win the presidential nomination, this endeavor became an ad hoc move that, because of this failure to control the top of the ticket, was largely ineffective.

Nevertheless, the New Democrats began to push to have one of their own appointed chairperson of the platform committee, as well as to have others selected to serve on this and other key convention bodies.[96] In the end, many DLC members occupied key posts in the convention hierarchy. Governor James Blanchard of Michigan, a DLC founding member, was appointed to chair the platform committee, and Bill Gray, DLC vice-chairman, oversaw the drafting of the actual document. Representative Barbara Kennelly of Connecticut cochaired the Rules Committee with Representative Martin Frost of Texas, an original DLC member, and Ann Richards, the state treasurer of Texas, gave the keynote speech.[97] In addition, Governor Bill Clinton of Arkansas, in an infamously long speech, nominated Dukakis.

Although many DLC members found their way into some of the most important roles at the convention, it did not mean that the New Democrats had the upper hand. Because of the DLC's big-tent membership policy during its first few years, membership did not equal a fervent commitment to the New Democratic agenda, much less an adversarial position toward the national party. Moreover, this strategy stunted the development of that agenda, making it less clear what the New Democratic alternative actually was. Therefore, the occupancy of these key convention posts by DLC members did not necessarily mean that they had been selected to placate the DLC or that they would use their positions to sway the party to the favor of the New Democrats.

Additionally, it was not clear that such an effort was needed. As part of the DNC's—especially Kirk's—effort to co-opt the DLC, and because of Kirk's recognition that the party, after the 1984 loss, had to steer itself toward the center, the national party was moving away from many of the most controversial elements of the previous convention anyway.[98] For example, the platform adopted at the 1988 convention was less than 5,000 words, compared with 45,000 words four years earlier; specific interests and programs were not highlighted but—in the words of the DNC Press Office—were "incorporated in the broader principles that are defined in the document" instead.[99] By addressing values and principles, not specific programs, the Democrats avoided appearing beholden to special-interest groups. As Gerald Pomper observed, "The party platform demonstrated that electoral victory was the predominant consideration."[100] In many ways, it was the "thematic, non-damaging platform" that the New Democrats desired.[101]

Although its ambiguity made the platform palatable to all Democrats, as no programs were singled out for elimination and no interests were specifically rejected, it did not advocate a New Democratic line. The document did not stray from the party's commitment to an activist federal government for addressing social concerns, nor did it reject the pacifism of the dominant liberal faction.[102] Moreover, although the Dukakis camp rejected many specific policy demands made by Jackson, it made other concessions to the runner-up and his issue stances. The document was even entitled "The Restoration of Competence and the Revival of Hope," an embrace of the campaign themes of both Dukakis and Jackson.[103] In sum, although the document was not as objectionable as the 1984 platform, it still did not represent a clean break from the liberalism of the national party.

On party rules, the DLC tried to use the window of opportunity presented by the nominating convention to push for alterations to the nominating system that it had failed to achieve with its Super Tuesday strategy. Generally, the DLC wanted to reform the nominating rules and organization for 1992 so that more rank-and-file Democrats would participate in the primaries and the role of elected officials and party leaders would simultaneously be strengthened, thus jointly offsetting what it saw as the dominance of the process by elite activists.[104]

Specifically, the DLC suggested that the national party use a lottery to choose the state where the first primary or caucus would be held, to de-emphasize the importance of one small state—such as Iowa—while still giving a long-shot candidate the chance to win a contest through the retail politics of shaking hands and ringing doorbells.[105] Other proposals included holding all state and presidential primaries on the same day in order to encourage greater participation by local officials, the extension of superdelegate status to all members of Congress, and the total deregulation of almost all national party rules in order to "invigorate state parties" and remove rules reform as an issue from Democratic politics altogether.[106]

As in the past, these suggestions provoked a firm reaction from Kirk and his DNC staff, who feared that the DLC's proposal would prompt a rules fight at the convention, inflame factional rivalries, and make the party appear divided during its most prominent national activity. As Wally Chalmers, Kirk's chief of staff, wrote, the aforementioned rules changes suggested that "Al From has not abandoned hope for that final donnybrook."[107] Further exasperating the DNC was the fact that, before the nominating campaign began in earnest, Kirk had issued eight "resolves" in order to "keep [the] 1988 nominating process focused on victory in November." The most prominent had been that there would be no rules debate.[108]

Consequently, when it became known that the DLC was mulling suggested changes to the rules on nomination and delegate selection, Kirk fired off a letter to Nunn, who had recently taken over as DLC chairman, asking the DLC staff to work with the DNC and the Rules Committee "so as not to garble a positive message of substance with an arcane rules debate."[109] Fearing that such a discussion would deteriorate quickly into factional fighting and only confirm voters' instincts about the fractiousness of the Democratic Party, Kirk wanted to convince the DLC that working with, not against, the national party would be an equally productive course of action. In the end, the DLC neither made a strong play to alter the nominating rules nor had much say in the eventual changes—as these were part of a private deal between Dukakis and Jackson.

Indeed, in this area as well as in the construction of the party platform, the DLC appeared to be a marginal player. As a result of the limitations placed on the DLC by its big-tent format, the organization was in no position to change the party or construct the platform, or even to participate meaningfully in either activity. This strategy may have inoculated the DLC from potentially fatal charges, but it also compromised its uniqueness, making it easier for the DNC to accommodate the DLC and prompting claims that the organization was unnecessary since it merely replicated the national party itself.

As Robert Kuttner, a liberal journalist, observed, "In effect, to create the unity it espoused, the DLC had to sacrifice its own parochialism."[110] Ann Lewis, executive director of the ADA, publicly asked what the purpose of the DLC was if most of its members had high liberal rankings from her organization.[111] All in all, by becoming more associated with the main Democratic Party message, the DLC risked its own relevance. Moreover, with Dukakis, the neoliberal, and Bentsen, the southern Democrat, leading the Democrats out of Atlanta and apparently on to victory—at least in July 1988—the case for the DLC's existence seemed harder and harder to make.

By the end of the 1988 Democratic National Convention, Democrats were buoyant about the prospects of the Dukakis-Bentsen ticket. From the view of the DNC and others in the national party, the party had successfully corrected many of its excesses: the platform was shorter and less ideological, special interests were less conspicuous not just in the platform but in the convention overall, and a fractious rules debate had been avoided. It appeared that Kirk had successfully accommodated the party's Left and Right. In the process, having taken many of the steps advocated by the DLC and seemingly on the verge of recapturing the presidency, the DNC began to make the DLC look increasingly irrelevant.

From the view of the DLC, conversely, Super Tuesday had not

gone as planned; the national party had not accepted the New Democratic public philosophy; and the organization was needed more than ever. If the DLC, and its fellow travelers in several southern statehouses, had failed to refocus presidential candidates away from the Iowa caucuses and the New Hampshire primary and toward the South and a more moderate or mainstream platform, the causes of this failure were important, for they pointed to the possibility of success or failure of the New Democratic effort in general. At its essence, failure in 1988 was rooted in the fact that the key premises of the New Democratic strategy simply no longer held true.

First, with the extension of voting rights to blacks, southern Democrats were no longer uniquely white and conservative. In effect, this—along with other demographic trends, such as internal migration—made the South more like the country at large. Second, the sheer size of Super Tuesday (twenty states and over one hundred media markets) had actually increased the importance of the two early contests, as the reward of their historic "bounce" became even richer. In turn, the regional primary's size meant that each candidate could find his own niche in the region. The candidates thus divided up the South, but no one conquered it. More importantly, though, the results of the Super Tuesday effort demonstrated to the DLC that if the success of the organization meant taking over the party by electing one of its own president, then just tinkering with the nominating process or latching on to a like-minded candidate would never produce that outcome.

Said differently, by the summer of 1988, it became clear to the DLC leadership that the strategies they had employed up to that point had failed. To remake the national party, the DLC recognized that it had to have a top-tier candidate to call its own, plus a developed and detailed New Democratic alternative for him to champion. Although in its national service plan the DLC did elucidate part of its New Democratic public philosophy, laying out an alternative theory of governance and approach to public administration, the DLC was hampered institutionally in the development of its public philosophy. At a basic level, the organization had limited resources to devote to this endeavor. It had neither the staff nor the financial wherewithal to develop and promote a full-fledged public philosophy.

Yet this underdevelopment was a product of a more serious situation. The DLC had to ensure that the values underpinning its alternative public philosophy were acceptable to those who might adopt it in order for it even to be considered as a possible path for the party to take. This ongoing fight for credibility within Democratic circles meant that the DLC had to structure itself as a forum for all elected officials, regardless of their beliefs, and thus choose carefully what issues it would address and what policy alternatives it would propose.

This organizational arrangement enabled the DLC to continue operating and, at best, to gain some credibility within the party. However, the New Democrats realized that the existing form was severely limiting. By moderating the organization's rhetoric and attracting a broad-based membership, the DLC was unable to develop and promote a comprehensive New Democratic public philosophy and policy agenda. In addition, the national party could readily accommodate such minimalist demands, especially since many of these were changes it planned to make anyway. Similarly, the national party could easily include many DLC members in party affairs. However, this access was doubly insignificant; not only did these adherents not have a truly distinctive public philosophy to advocate, but they were not necessarily committed New Democrats anyway. They were disproportionately those who had joined the DLC precisely because it had tempered its tone.

Ironically, by trying to gain legitimacy in order to participate in Democratic policy debate, the DLC undermined its reason for remaining as a participant. Until the DLC was able to establish itself financially and politically, so that it could ignore intraparty rivals, its hands would be tied and its own relevance would, consequently, be in question. Moreover, if the Dukakis-Bentsen ticket were successful, the central problem that the DLC had identified—that the Democratic Party was unable to win national office because of its public philosophy—as well as its fundamental reason for being, would have been nullified. At this point, the DLC would have seemed truly unnecessary.

But the Dukakis defeat would turn the Democratic political world upside down. It emphasized to DLC skeptics and allies alike the necessity for a major overhaul of the Democratic Party's strategy and ideology. It opened a window of opportunity for alternatives. Ironically, this loss made the ongoing crisis of electoral viability for the Democratic Party in the postreform era a fresh reality and produced opportunities for innovation that the DLC could seize.

5 / Folding the Big Tent, 1988–1990

THE 1988 PRESIDENTIAL ELECTION was a turning point for the DLC. Going into the general election season, it appeared that, in line with the advice of the New Democrats, the national party had shed its most objectionable liberal trappings. At the same time, more and more Democrats found the DLC less objectionable and had joined the organization. Consequently and ironically, however, the role and continued existence of the DLC were in question. If the party had adopted many of its views, on one side, and if the DLC had come to resemble the party, on the other, it was increasingly unclear what the DLC's real purpose should be.

The defeat of the Dukakis-Bentsen ticket put an end to these doubts. To committed New Democrats, it confirmed that the party and its public philosophy had to be remade. To others, it demonstrated that at least something had to be done. The Dukakis defeat focused attention on the problems of the Democratic Party, thus opening a window of opportunity for the DLC and other political entrepreneurs. Moreover, the defeat had a similar effect within the DLC itself. Another presidential defeat, especially one attributed to the nominee's being identified as too liberal, reinforced the severity of the Democratic Party's problem, as well as the inability of the DLC to solve it. In this way, the election brought to the fore the inadequacies of the organization, prompting it to find new ways to transform the public philosophy of the Democratic Party. This, in turn, led to a reorganization of the DLC, culminating in the establishment of its own think tank, the Progressive Policy Institute (PPI).

Driving this change was a realization of the limits of the organization's big-tent format. By trying to keep a wide range of elected officials in its membership, the DLC had avoided speaking out on controversial issues, mostly social issues, and had generally moderated its rhetoric. Consequently, the New Democratic public philosophy and the case for its implementation had not been fully developed. Therefore, in the two years after the 1988 presidential loss, the DLC focused its efforts on honing its critique of the electoral strategy and issue agenda of the national Democratic Party and on developing a replacement. Representing a shift in the overall strategy of the organization, these moves signaled the end of the DLC's quest for consensus and the beginning of a more adversarial posture.

The Election of 1988

The election of 1988 presented the Democrats with a ripe opportunity. On the presidential level, they did not have to face a popular incumbent; rather, their opponent was his (decidedly less attractive) vice-president. Furthermore, the party's nominating process and convention were less confrontational and purposely less ideological than those of four years earlier. Afterward, the party seemed more unified and poised for victory. The prospects of retaking the presidency, along with the continued dominance of Congress, further buoyed the spirits of many Democrats as unified government seemed possible.

Clearly, however, the 1988 election did not herald a new era of Democratic dominance. Instead, it once again presented the party with the crisis of continued electoral defeat and an apparently eroding base. Additionally, the presidential election proved the ease and efficacy of characterizing the Democratic Party and its nominee as too liberal, especially on social and foreign policy issues. Almost overnight, the DLC went from the brink of irrelevance to the center of a debate on how to rejuvenate the Democratic Party.

ELECTORAL PROBLEMS AND ALTERNATIVES

Leaving Atlanta, the site of the 1988 Democratic convention, Democrats of all kinds felt confident. The CBS News/*New York Times* poll showed Dukakis holding a commanding seventeen-point lead over George Bush.[1] As the summer waned, it became increasingly plausible that the Democrats, after two bruising defeats, could reclaim the White House.

Dukakis's general election strategy followed the contours of the story the Massachusetts governor had laid out during his acceptance speech. "The election is about competence, not ideology," he proclaimed. And throughout almost the entire race, Dukakis would stress that he, not Bush, was the man more able to run the machinery of the U.S. government. As one journalist put it, Dukakis appeared to be running on the platform of being the "smartest clerk in the world."[2]

In some ways, this nonideological strategy underpinned the consensus that had emerged from the Atlanta convention. By producing a smaller, more thematic platform and by not championing many specific policy prescriptions, Dukakis was able to keep the increasingly fragile Democratic coalition together. This cause was helped by the success of the Dukakis camp in placating, by way of nominating rules changes for 1992 and without a public fight, an irascible runner-up, Jackson. In turn, the impression of many observers was that the Democratic Party had learned the many lessons of 1984. It appeared united and ready to govern.

Yet the Republicans countered with a general election strategy that tried to link Bush to the accomplishments of the popular president with whom he had served and that tried to draw a stark line between himself and Dukakis. Accordingly, Bush worked to paint Dukakis as a "liberal," fundamentally out of step with mainstream American values on a variety of social issues.[3] Said differently, he hoped to make the election revolve around social and foreign policy concerns, the issue contexts that had advantaged the Republican Party since 1968.

As summer turned to fall, this strategy was put into place, and by early September, Bush led Dukakis in every major poll. The Democratic nominee was unable to score a knockout punch in either of the two presidential debates and never recovered.[4] In the final tally, Bush handily beat Dukakis: the Republican won 53.4 percent of the vote, forty states, and 426 electoral college votes, while Dukakis garnered 45.6 percent, ten states plus the District of Columbia, and 111 electoral votes. Bush's victory was not a landslide on the magnitude of Reagan's 1984 triumph, but it was, in the words of veteran election observers, a "broad-based win."[5]

The 1988 results followed many of the same trends that had alarmed New Democrats in 1984. Simply put, the 1988 election confirmed the progressive weakening—even the slow death—of the New Deal coalition. Dukakis handily won the Democratic base of downscale voters, union households, and racial minorities and solidified his support among Democratic identifiers, garnering 82 percent of their support—an amount greater than LBJ had secured in victory in 1964.[6] The difference was that in 1988, this was not sufficient to win.

With the atrophying of organized labor and the increasing liberalism in social and foreign policy on the part of the national party, the Democratic Party lost what had once been a reliable and significant component of its coalition. Thus, between 1944 and 1960, one in three Democratic presidential votes came from white union members or people in their households; between 1964 and 1984, that number dropped to one in four; in 1988, only one in five Democratic votes came from this group.[7] Similarly, two key components of the New Deal coalition, Catholics and white southerners, had deserted the party in recent presidential contests, and 1988 was no exception. Bush actually won over half of the Catholic vote and two-thirds of the white southern vote.[8] Finally, the Republican also handily won crucial swing voters, as Bush garnered 55 percent support among independents and self-described moderates.[9]

Not all was misery for Democrats in 1988. Following the trend of the entire postwar era, Democrats still did exceptionally well on the subpresidential level. Indeed, in the face of the Bush victory, the Democrats won an additional Senate seat, bringing their total in that body to fifty-five, and picked up three more House seats, expanding their total there to 260, leaving the Republicans with only 40 percent of that body—the smallest share of the House ever won by a party winning the presidency.[10] In the states, the Democrats also fared well, holding twenty-eight of the country's governorships and leaving only eight states where the GOP controlled both houses of the state legislature.[11] Reflecting the general trend since 1968, then, the Democrats were successful in races at all levels except the presidency.

Despite these positive results, analysts and partisans, including the DLC, began to dissect the most salient outcome of election day 1988 as soon as it was over. Why did the Democrats lose the presidency, and was this seemingly ongoing trend a problem for the party? Among those scholars making judgments right after the election, the reaction was mixed. Among the most pessimistic, Walter Dean Burnham concluded that Bush's victory corroborated that "indeed the majority/presidential party is now Republican."[12] Gerald Pomper and Paul Abramson found instead that the 1988 results were not a repudiation of Dukakis or his party but rather the product of retrospective evaluations of the Reagan presidency.[13] As Pomper wrote, "Michael Dukakis was the loser, but not the cause of the loss. The election was an endorsement of the status quo, not a mandate for policy change."[14] Although this analysis offered some solace to Democrats, even Pomper had to stress that a shrunken Democratic base, defections from once-loyal Democratic groups, and a low turnout also hurt the Dukakis campaign.[15] Furthermore, analysts found that even an improvement in the most easily remedied of these three party woes, low turnout, would not have significantly affected the outcome. If voter turnout among nonvoters, especially blacks and Hispanics, had been higher, Bush still would have won handily.[16]

New Democrats too felt that the 1988 results portended a serious problem for the Democratic Party and could not be dismissed as a product of either the residual popularity of Reagan or the campaign techniques of Dukakis.[17] William Galston, who worked for Gore in 1988, recalled that the Dukakis defeat was even more shocking than Mondale's, since the former had high poll numbers in the spring, ran against a weaker candidate, and was thought to have united the party.[18] As such, the results confirmed the diagnosis the DLC had made after the 1984 election: Democrats needed to win back the voters it had increasingly alienated since 1968.

The defeat also led more people to the DLC's perspective on the Democrats' electoral strategy. Democratic pollster Peter Hart, for example, argued to the DNC Executive Committee that the Democratic Party needed to court white Protestant voters, who, as he pointed out, were not an "aggravated minority" and thus were not attracted to the Democrats' interest-based liberalism.[19] In his quadrennial review of the election, Pomper too posited that the Democrats needed to win back white southerners and Protestants as well as voters in the West in order to be competitive again.[20]

Although the DLC's postmortem of the Democratic electoral defeat would be developed and honed in the months following election day, it was clear to the organization's leadership that what lay at the root of this defeat was how Dukakis had tried to handle the unpopularity of the party's dominant public philosophy. Instead of changing it, he tried to make the election revolve around his own competence and to ignore ideology. But once Bush was able to convince the electorate that Dukakis's political beliefs were out of step with their own, ideology nevertheless became a decisive factor in the Democrat's defeat.

ISSUE PROBLEMS AND POLICY ALTERNATIVES

Bush was able to turn a seventeen-point July deficit in the polls to an almost eight-point victory by focusing on a set of issues that clearly differentiated him from Dukakis. With the moderation of both candidates and Dukakis's nonideological strategy, this seemed, at first glance, more difficult to do than with past Democratic candidates. However, the Republicans found a salient difference in the realm of social issues and turned the election into a contest about the values and the characters of the candidates. In this, Bush charged that Dukakis was a "liberal," a label intended to imply not that the Democrat was far off to the left on economics but that he was soft on crime and weak on defense and held values that were out of touch with those of mainstream America.[21] Accordingly, the Republicans made an effort (most famously in the Willie Horton advertisement) to demonstrate to voters that on a wide array of social concerns—crime and punishment, affirmative action, patriotism, and abortion—Bush was more in line with their beliefs than Dukakis was, and he was better able to protect the United States from enemies within and abroad.[22]

The efficacy of the Republican strategy to demonize Dukakis as a liberal was remarkable. In May 1988, 27 percent of voters believed that Dukakis was a liberal, and among that group, Bush had 50 percent of the vote to the Democrat's 39 percent. In the days before election day, 56 percent of voters believed that Dukakis was a liberal, and they backed Bush by a ratio of two to one.[23] Breaking this trend down, it appears that most voters believed that a Dukakis administration would imperil them and the country. Two weeks before the election, 41 percent of voters felt that Dukakis would weaken the national defense, and over half felt that Bush would strengthen it. Around the same time, 62 percent of voters felt that Bush was tough on crime, and only 37 percent thought Dukakis was.[24] By the end of the campaign, Dukakis seemed unable to shake these perceptions that his values were "at odds with the majority of Americans."[25]

Liberal Democrats fundamentally disagreed with this assessment. The problem with Dukakis, according to Jeff Faux—president of the Economic Policy Institute, a liberal think tank—was that he, like

Mondale and Carter before him, was not a liberal but a centrist. In this view, Dukakis lost not because of his progressive stance but because he was not liberal enough and thus could not rally a populist, interracial, class-based coalition.[26]

New Democrats rejected this evaluation and accepted the analysis that Dukakis had lost because his values and programs were out of step with Middle America. Bill Clinton, then an active DLC member, offered this explanation: "No matter how popular your programs may be, you must be considered in the mainstream on the shared values of the American people, the ability to defend the nation and the strength to enforce its laws."[27] John Baker, chairman of the Alabama State Democratic Party, voiced his concern over the values issue to Kirk before election day. He wrote that by ceding the issues of the flag and family values to the GOP, the Democrats stood to lose his state, which they later did.[28]

Other Democrats also began to share the New Democratic assessment of the 1988 race, agreeing that the central problem of the party was its issue agenda and the public philosophy undergirding it. In his analysis of the election results for the DNC, for example, Peter Hart argued that the Republicans had run on values while the Democrats had run on programs, which was why the former had won.[29] Joseph Califano, the former Carter cabinet official, argued in a lengthy article in the *New York Times* that the Democrats had to rethink their positions on crime and criminal rights, race and affirmative action, and neoisolationism in foreign policy. "With foreign policy, as with crime, we have met the enemy and they are us—not the Republicans," he wrote.[30]

All in all, the most overriding and universal suggestion was that the party needed to "step over a values threshold" and advocate the enforcement of some standards of civil conduct.[31] Said differently, the Democratic Party had to embrace—or at least convince the electorate that it was embracing—the basic, widely held values of the country. If the party did not change its public philosophy, the New Democrats feared that ongoing trends in the party system could relegate the Democratic Party to permanent minority status, or even extinction.

INSTITUTIONAL PROBLEMS AND ALTERNATIVES

After an examination of the data available after the 1988 election, the basis of this fear becomes apparent. The results showed the continuation of the trends of increased independent voting, of ticket splitting, and of the shifting of large parts of the New Deal coalition away from its Democratic home to either independent or Republican status. According to some polls, 1988 found the GOP pulling even with the Democratic Party in party identification; even more cautious calculations showed that the Democrats had their lowest advantage in party identification since 1952.[32] Driving this trend was the movement of whites and youth to the Republican camp. In fact, between 1982 and 1986, there was a ten-point movement of whites toward the GOP. Thus, by 1988, only 40 percent of whites identified themselves as Democrats, and 46 percent identified themselves as Republicans. Among eighteen- to twenty-five-year-olds, the Democrats fared worse: 53 percent of this cohort considered themselves Republicans.[33]

To the DLC, these trends, taken on top of the election defeat, pointed to the need for swift action to remake the party. Therefore, the organization's leadership turned to the next immediate opening for the New Democrats to gain power within the national party: the campaign for party chairman. As they had immediately after the Mondale defeat in 1984, From and Marshall believed that without a president from the party in the White House, the party chairmanship was the key to "gaining control of the party apparatus" and influencing alterations in the party's procedures, electoral strategy, and message.[34] In late June and early July 1988, they had already advised Nunn to tell Dukakis that during the general campaign, he could not turn over the party apparatus, including the chairmanship, to Jackson and his allies. Additionally, the two staff leaders cautioned that if the Democrats lost the presidential election, they would then have to join in the fight for the party chairmanship "if we are ever to be able to make the claim of legitimacy in the party."[35]

Once the campaign for DNC chairman began, the DLC's candidate of choice was Bruce Babbitt, who was coming off an unsuccessful presidential run; truly conservative Democrats backed former congressman Jim Jones of Oklahoma, who was also a DLC founder.[36] The candidate who emerged as the front-runner, though, was Ronald Brown: Washington lawyer, former DNC deputy chairman, deputy campaign manager for Edward Kennedy in his 1980 run for the presidential nomination, and, most recently, convention manager for Jackson. With his ties to Kennedy and Jackson, Brown represented the wing of the party that the DLC vilified. Accordingly, the DLC and its members opposed Brown's nomination. As Breaux told *Time* magazine, Brown was the "wrong person at the wrong time."[37]

But Brown—trading on his skills as a consensus builder, which had been proven in his negotiations at the Democratic convention between the Dukakis and Jackson camps, and spending more than $250,000 on the chairmanship race—gained momentum and support. Babbitt decided not to enter the contest. By February 10, 1989, the date of the vote for DNC chair, Brown's other rivals for the post—former representative James V. Stanton of Ohio, former representative Michael Barnes of Maryland, Michigan State Party Chairman Richard Wiener, and Jones—had all dropped out of the race, and even the southern state party chairmen endorsed Brown.[38] In the end, Brown faced no opposition and became the first black chairman of either party.

After his election, the pattern of the relationship between the DLC and the DNC that had emerged under Kirk continued, perhaps inevitably. On one side, From commented that the DLC was willing to work with Brown. On the other side, the new chairman made overtures to the DLC, stating that he wanted to reach out to voters in the center, as well as retain the party's core constituencies. Additionally, Brown said that it was not his role to "determine the ideological thrust of the party" and that he wanted to see the Democrats follow a "pragmatic and commonsense approach" in order to appeal "to those voters in the middle of the political spectrum."[39]

Like all party chairmen, Brown wanted to smooth factional divisions and, specific to his post, work to co-opt the DLC. Nevertheless, tensions between the two organizations persisted. For instance, in an apparent slap at his New Democratic rivals, Brown stated that Democrats had to "differentiate [them]selves. The last thing we need in this country is two Republican parties. One is plenty."[40]

Once again, the DLC could not beat the institutional party at its own game. Because of the history of rules and organizational changes in the party, this group of dissident elected officials and partisans could not gain control of the party's chairmanship and of its national apparatus by the traditional means of working through its established mechanisms. Therefore, the DLC continued its work outside of the national party structure.

However, before the organization could even move to plant its public philosophy onto the party agenda, it had to develop this alternative philosophy further and address the issue of its own organization. Basically, a comprehensive, viable New Democratic public philosophy had not yet been developed due to the DLC's moderation of rhetoric and its shying away from controversial issues as part of its big-tent strategy. Thus, in the two years after the Dukakis defeat, the DLC committed itself to honing its critique of the national party—the reasons for adopting the New Democratic public philosophy—and establishing its own structure so as to be able to develop these policy alternatives.

"The Politics of Evasion" and the Creation of PPI

The two most significant steps the DLC took in the aftermath of the 1988 election were the development of a biting analysis of the national Democratic Party's electoral strategy and the creation of its own think tank. The latter move was in response to the former, as the leadership believed that they had to reorganize the DLC in order to develop fully an alternative Democratic public philosophy. Together, these developments represented a shift away from the DLC's big-tent strategy and the beginning of its more confrontational stance toward the rest of the party.

ELECTORAL PROBLEMS AND ALTERNATIVES

In the wake of the 1988 election, a competition emerged over defining the central problem (if any) of the Democratic Party and offering solutions to it. In this, the DLC's opening salvo was the unveiling of a sophisticated and trenchant critique of the Democratic Party's public philosophy and strategic analysis. Developed by William Galston—a political theorist by training, a campaign aide to both John Anderson in 1980 and Al Gore in 1988, and the issues director for Mondale in 1984—this analysis was first presented as a speech to the DLC's annual gathering in March 1989. Then it was elaborated further with Elaine Kamarck—longtime Democratic operative, political scientist, and campaign adviser to Babbitt in 1988—and published as a short monograph entitled "The Politics of Evasion: Democrats and the Presidency." Both Galston and Kamarck were shaped profoundly by the Mondale defeat, a defeat that prompted them—like other New Democrats—to believe that the Democratic Party had to embrace a fundamentally different public philosophy. "It was no accident that both Bill [Galston] and I were deeply into the Mondale campaign," noted Kamarck.[41]

These two brought their academic training and long involvement in Democratic politics to bear in "The Politics of Evasion." The resulting analysis and suggestions in this piece encapsulated the New Democratic critique of the electoral strategy and public philosophy of the national party. But more than that, "The Politics of Evasion" represented a new, more adversarial stance by the DLC toward the national party. Accordingly, it quickly became part of the New Democratic canon, guiding alternatives that the DLC would follow for the next four years.

Galston and Kamarck recognized the interconnectedness between ideas, institutions, and electoral outcomes. Said differently, they approached the problem of declining Democratic Party electoral fortunes in a holistic way, one that took into account trends and strategies in all three of these areas. Mistaken perceptions and strategies in those spheres produced what they called "the politics of evasion." The national Democratic Party had refused to recognize that a crisis existed and had explained away past defeats as a function of bad candidates, bad campaign techniques, or a misguided media. Galston and Kamarck argued that the result was that those who dominated the national party clung to three "myths"—the Myth of Mobilization, the Myth of Liberal Fundamentalism, and the Myth of the Congressional Bastion—which precluded them from recognizing that the party had a serious electoral problem that had to be addressed.[42]

The first of these myths, the Myth of Mobilization, dealt with what the DLC saw as a misguided electoral strategy on behalf of the liberal, national party. By examining party identification and voting patterns, Galston and Kamarck countered the idea that low overall voter turnout, as well as depressed voter turnout among blacks, Hispanics, and/or women, was the reason that Democrats lost nationally.[43] Even if black and Hispanic turnout had exceeded white turnout by 10 percent, they noted, Dukakis still would have lost by 2.5 million votes.[44] Thus, they argued that rectifying this problem would not result in a presidential victory.

Instead, Galston and Kamarck pointed out that the Democrats lost because they were not winning the electorate's "heart," that is, northern ethnics and southern Protestants. Furthermore, the two argued that the gender gap—the disparity between voting patterns of men and women—was not exclusively the result of women flocking to the Democrats, but was also due to a loss of male voters to the Republicans. This gap, they wrote, should be viewed neither as a problem for the GOP nor as the salvation of the Democratic Party. Therefore, Democrats had to fight for the support of these social groups, and they could not write off the South (an area still close to the hearts of many DLC members), especially since it was helping to produce a huge electoral college advantage for the Republicans.[45]

To win over these voters, Galston and Kamarck contended that the Democrats had to revamp the policy agenda and ideology they were offering the electorate. In their words, they had to shed the "Myth of Liberal Fundamentalism," the idea that Democratic candidates had to be more authentically liberal in order to win. To Galston and Kamarck, it was incorrect to claim that Carter (in 1980), Mondale, and Dukakis had lost because they were not sufficiently pure liberals.[46]

Rather, they argued that a combination of demographic trends and presidential nominating reforms had resulted in the takeover of the national party by New Politics activists committed to a "liberal fundamentalism," one rigid with litmus tests and out of touch with the electorate.[47] This had produced Democratic presidential nominees far to the left of the Democratic rank and file and of the general electorate. As voters saw more and more liberal presidential nominees—the most visible embodiment of the Democratic Party—they came to see "the party as inattentive to their economic interests, indifferent if not hostile to their moral sentiments, and ineffective in defense of their national security."[48]

The final myth the two authors wanted to dispel was that Democrats did not need to worry about losing the presidency. Many Democrats believed that since the party still controlled Congress, as well as many state and local offices, there was no danger of electoral realignment. Galston and Kamarck referred to this belief as the "Myth of the Congressional Bastion." They argued that losses on the national level had hurt Democrats running for other offices and would continue to do so. "We are witnessing instead a slow-motion, trickledown realignment in which, over time, Republican presidential strength is inexorably eroding Democratic congressional, state, and local strength," they wrote.[49] To corroborate this claim, the authors noted trends in youth voting and party switching, along with the postreform trend of the nationalizing of politics, including congressional races. When the latter occurred fully, they wrote, a realignment would ensue.[50]

In the final analysis, Galston and Kamarck advocated an overhaul of the Democratic issue agenda and its underlying public philosophy, including an effort to address noneconomic social issues in a way consistent with mainstream America. Additionally, they called for the active involvement of elected officials from all levels of government in the affairs and procedures of the party itself, a core concern of New Democrats. These two moves would enable the Democrats to focus on recapturing the center of the American electorate.[51]

After Galston finished laying out these arguments at the DLC conference, "a huge melee broke out."[52] Heated reaction and debate occurred among the invited respondents: Robb, Gephardt, Jackson, and Governor James Blanchard of Michigan. The discussion became so intense that, after the panel was officially over, Robb and Jackson stood up and continued arguing. The television cameras and klieg lights swarmed around the two politicians as they sharply voiced their fundamental disagreement with each other's position.

Robb defended Galston's New Democratic argument, suggesting that Jackson encouraged "the public perception that we [Democrats] are bringing all who have a greater need and putting them in some ways against those who are currently successful," an image that produced national electoral defeat.[53] Jackson countered that the party had to devise a strategy to maintain its support of the poor and minorities while reaching out to the white middle class. The party had to make a decision on what and whom it represented. "We cannot be all things to all people. We have to determine which side of history we are on. If we are all things to all people, we become rather ill-defined, indecisive—kind of like warm spit."[54]

To outside observers, this scene appeared to be only the latest manifestation of infighting within the Democratic Party, which, since 1984, meant mainly a battle between the New Democrats and the dominant liberal faction.[55] Indeed, the argument at the conference was a clear example of the differences of opinion between the two camps. In a sign that it was slowly losing its big tent, the DLC was hardly upset at this tumult. In fact, the whole spat had been largely scripted at least a month before the actual event. In a memo to Nunn, From explained how some DLC funders and elected officials objected to the DLC's inviting Jackson to speak at the organization's gathering.

Breaux, in particular, was concerned that no one would challenge Jackson's arguments. The senator from Louisiana no doubt had in mind Jackson's previous (and first) appearance before the DLC at its Super Tuesday Summit held in Atlanta in June 1987. There, Jackson had asserted that the Democratic Party had to embrace "special interests" as "members of our family." Calling for Democratic unity, he added that "the party has a progressive wing. It has a conservative wing. But it takes two wings to fly."[56] From assuaged Breaux's fear by assuring the senator that the panel was purposely constructed "to challenge Jackson's assertions" and that Galston's paper would "discredit Jackson's political approach." From wrote to Nunn, "I didn't tell him [Breaux] that I've talked to Harry McPherson [a former LBJ aide and a DLC backer] who will be ready to take Jackson on—if our elected officials are not."[57]

From and the DLC used the conference not only to present their alternative analysis and electoral strategy but also to highlight the differences between New Democrats and their rivals. Apparently, the witnessing of yet another Democratic presidential defeat made it clear to the New Democrats that they had to shift away from a conciliatory big-tent strategy and be more aggressive in making their case. From, for example, advised that the time might be at hand to take a strong stance on the future of the party and the positions it should espouse, even if it meant "sacrific[ing] some of our congressional support."[58]

Thus, "The Politics of Evasion" marked the beginning of a four-year change in the overall strategy of the DLC. After failing to change the public philosophy of the Democratic Party by lobbying for procedural changes through established party bodies, by winning the chairmanship of the party, by pressuring the national party from the outside, and by trying to alter the dynamics of the presidential nominating campaign, plus after witnessing a general election in which the Democratic nominee was demonized as a "liberal," the DLC leadership decided to concentrate their efforts outside of the party and work actively to nominate and elect a New Democrat to the presidency.

As argued in "The Politics of Evasion," the DLC believed that only by setting the top of the ticket straight could it remain competitive at the subpresidential level. In a big-picture, strategy memorandum to Nunn, From wrote that he and the DLC had learned "an

important lesson" since its founding in 1985: no matter how successful the New Democrats were in setting the agenda and defining
the direction and image of the party during the first three years of a
presidential cycle, it could all be for naught in the fourth year "if we
nominate a liberal candidate for President in a nominating process
dominated by liberals."[59]

Therefore, From argued that the DLC should do what it could to
prevent being overwhelmed in the fourth year. The two largest steps
in this strategy would be the establishment of a network of local af-
filiates as "a new source of political talent ready made for a centrist
candidate" and the development of new policy agenda.[60] As From
explained to James Barnes of the *National Journal*, the DLC had to
establish a platform on which its candidates could run. He added that
in 1988, "We saw what happened when [we] didn't have an agenda."[61]

In the first two years after the Dukakis defeat, the DLC would
focus much of its attention on the development of this new set of
ideas and issue positions, as well as on establishing the organization
in such a way as to do so effectively. The New Democrats had concluded that the answer to the Democrats' electoral problems lay in the
realm of issue stances and ideology. Said differently, they embarked
on an attempt to remodel the product the party was trying to sell to
voters. They were trying to remake liberalism.

ISSUE PROBLEMS AND POLICY ALTERNATIVES

Before the DLC could begin this effort, it had to possess the organizational resources to develop an alternative public philosophy and issue
agenda, or, as From and Marshall put it, to develop "an *intellectual*
counterforce that can fashion progressive alternatives to special interest policies."[62] Because of the draw of its political talent, the DLC,
despite various defeats, was still able to raise large amounts of money.
Thus, two questions remained: how could they develop a new public
philosophy and policy platform, and how could such an effort be accommodated within the current organizational framework of the DLC?
The establishment of a think tank appeared to be the best answer.

The first to use think tanks successfully as a means to develop and
promote an alternative public philosophy were conservative Republicans, the group most alienated from the New Deal liberal consensus.
As a minority faction of the party out of power, this group found that

many of the other, more common avenues for policy development and dissemination, such as congressional offices and executive agencies, were closed off to it. Therefore, conservative Republicans used already established policy research institutes, such as the American Enterprise Institute; founded new think tanks, such as the Heritage Foundation; and started policy journals, such as the *National Review*, to develop and advocate an alternative to the prevailing liberal consensus that would be viable at the polls, and to prepare a conservative policy elite to govern.[63]

Like conservative Republicans in the 1960s, New Democrats in the 1980s did not have access to areas where they could develop and market policies. Neither group controlled the national apparatus of their respective parties, Congress, or the executive branch. And although both had the support of elected officials, the tasks they wanted to accomplish surpassed the capabilities and desires of any one official and his staff. As the New Democrats discovered upon the death of Gillis Long in 1984, officeholders can leave office unexpectedly, thus placing the whole project in jeopardy.

Therefore, for a dissident party faction without any foothold in other areas of policy development and promotion within government and academia, but with ample funds, the "advocacy" think tank is an attractive organizational form. This new breed of think tank is qualitatively different from other forms that resemble "universities without students" and produce book-length studies by academics (such as the Brookings Institution) and from nonprofit government-research contractors (such as the RAND Institute) that conduct analyses for government agencies, especially the Department of Defense.[64] Specifically, as R. Kent Weaver of Brookings noted, advocacy think tanks "combine a strong policy, partisan or ideological bent with aggressive salesmanship and an effort to influence current policy debates." Advocacy think tanks do not conduct original research, but rather put a "distinctive 'spin' on existing research."[65]

Having seen how conservatives used these types of organizations with an apparent degree of success to advance their cause, it is no surprise that the New Democrats looked to them for guidance and inspiration, as well as adopting a similar strategy in their decision to form a think tank. The DLC especially admired the Heritage Foundation—which its own president has described as a "second-hand dealer of ideas"—for its influence in shaping public debate.[66] From recalled that the DLC respected Heritage's ability to accomplish "effective political work [and] message work" and not only inject its ideas into public debate but reshape it as well.[67] In fact, Ed Feulner, the president of Heritage, met with From and Marshall to offer some advice on raising money and disseminating ideas.[68]

The influence of these meetings and their admiration was clear. In memoranda on the think tank idea, From and Marshall wrote that the DLC's think tank would follow the "Heritage Model" and provide policy proposals, study the political system, brief political elites, contract outside thinkers to draft foreign policy proposals, hold seminars, and form a "high caliber journal of progressive thought."[69] As Marshall envisioned it, the DLC's think tank was to be "an analytic guerrilla group."[70] In sum, the DLC planned to develop an advocacy think tank, one in which proselytizing would be an integral role.

These models, though, only helped shape an idea (the formation of a think tank) that had been under consideration since the inception of the DLC. Nunn had been the first to advocate the idea at the original meeting of disgruntled Democratic elected officials in 1984 and had pushed the idea ever after.[71] When the DLC was first formed, the founding members considered establishing a subsidiary "policy institute" with Governor Scott Matheson of Utah as its head. When Matheson decided to chair the DNC's Democratic Policy Commission instead, the idea was not pursued further. In 1986, From again posited the option to the DLC's governing board, but no action was taken.[72]

INSTITUTIONAL PROBLEMS AND ALTERNATIVES

By the end of 1987, From began to argue that a think tank established outside the DLC structure was necessary to provide substance to the political message of the organization.[73] Only after the floundering of the Dukakis campaign and the ascendancy of Nunn to the DLC chairmanship, however, did plans for a think tank pick up steam.[74] At this point, From was ready to suggest to the DLC Governing Board that the organization's policy of balancing "ideological integrity and broad-based participation" would have to be abandoned, even if defections occurred; the DLC had to cease to be "an organization to provide political cover for Democratic officials in areas where the national Democratic Party is a clear detriment."[75]

When the DLC did form a think tank, however, it was established as a separate entity, thus enabling it to develop and propose more controversial positions while giving the elected-official membership of the organization room for deniability. As Marshall explained to the *Washington Post*, "We wanted to insulate politicians from our proposals and be independent of the constraints."[76] A think tank separate from the DLC enabled committed New Democrats in the organization to develop their alternative public philosophy without immediately sacrificing its broad elected-official support. Nonetheless, it was a significant step in re-forming the DLC as a more adversarial organization.

On December 23, 1988, the DLC filed the papers to officially establish the Progressive Policy Institute (PPI), and on January 11, 1989, its board of trustees held its first meeting.[77] Incorporated as a 501(c)3 corporation, PPI was officially nonpartisan and thus could receive tax-deductible contributions, a large incentive to potential donors.[78] Accordingly, From and Marshall planned to establish a fifteen-member board of trustees who would donate at least $100,000 each and to hire ten staff members.[79] At the first PPI board meeting, From estimated the institute's first-year income at $1.2 million and expenditures at $1.16 million.

Leading the PPI effort financially was Michael Steinhardt, a New York hedge fund manager who was first introduced to the DLC "by pure chance" when a friend invited Steinhardt to a fund-raising dinner at the Virginia home of Robb. As Steinhardt recalled, From courted him for a while, and in the end, he committed to donate $500,000 annually for three years; at the same time, From promised to raise $2 million over the first eighteen months of PPI's existence.[80] In return, Steinhardt was made chairman of PPI's Board of Trustees.

Because PPI had tax-exempt status, it had to be a separate entity from the DLC. Indeed, the formation of PPI raised questions regarding the role of the DLC and the relationship between it and the new think tank. Since PPI was designed to develop and promote ideas that could be embraced by anyone, regardless of party affiliation, From felt that the DLC could then act as a forum for Democratic elected officials, where they could debate policy positions and articulate them as a partisan agenda.[81]

From also considered the possibility of folding the DLC into PPI or keeping it alive only as a corporate shell, activated for specific purposes.

But in the end, he and Marshall concurred that a symbiotic role between the think tank and the DLC should be established, whereby the former "would generate ideas while the DLC would selectively adopt and amplify them."[82] Practically, this changed role meant that the DLC would be scaled back to the level of activity in its first year of operation, 1985. The organization would hold one conference a year, produce a newsletter, host policy forums, and operate a speakers bureau for New Democrats.[83] The DLC's staff would be reduced to three—a fund-raiser, a clerk, and an issues/press officer—and the rest of the staff would be transferred to the think tank.[84] The DLC would be entitled to use PPI publications, as any other entity would be allowed to. But the two organizations would not share office space, and there would be no formal relationship between them except for From, who would serve as executive director of the DLC and vice-chairman and chief executive officer of PPI. With this diminished role for the DLC, From advised the PPI Board of Trustees that the viability of the DLC should be reassessed in each political cycle, since its standing depended on the "political standing of its leaders."[85]

Although PPI was incorporated at the end of 1988 and its board of trustees began meeting early the following year, its formation was not formally announced until the end of June 1989. In the interim, From, Marshall, and the institute's board members worked on establishing it, staffing it, and defining PPI's goals and activities for the coming year. They focused on adding more trustees (with their large contributions); considered adding an advisory board or including prominent academics and political leaders on the board of trustees; and worked on attracting private, corporate, and foundation grants.[86] To staff the institute, Marshall became the president of PPI, and Robert Shapiro—an economist who had been an adviser to the Dukakis campaign, legislative director for Senator Daniel Patrick Moynihan of New York, and a columnist for *U.S. News and World Report*—became its vice-president.[87]

By comparison to the more established think tanks on the Right, PPI was minuscule. Consider that in 1989, the year PPI was founded, Heritage's budget was almost $15 million and it employed 135 people.[88] Nevertheless, the PPI agenda was an ambitious one and mirrored the goals and strategies of its much larger conservative analogs. The New Democrats hoped to sell PPI's ideas to three "target markets." The primary one was the "national public policy community" in the executive and legislative branches (that is, members of Congress, their staffs, policymakers in the White House, and government agencies). The secondary target was the mass media at the national, regional, and local levels. And the tertiary market was the general public, especially the business and civic leaders who influenced the directions of public policy.[89]

In sum, the New Democrats hoped to sell the new policy options of PPI, as well as shape how these and other ideas were evaluated and acted upon by political elites. Therefore, in PPI's first year and a half, DLC leaders planned to hold one or two major conferences, offer a series of half-day seminars on pertinent topics, develop and promote at least one or two major policy innovations, release three or four major studies, hold briefings for the media, and issue a range of publications, including a policy journal.[90]

PPI made its public debut in June 1989 with the issuing of its first policy paper. As its founders had planned, the proposal was a controversial break from Democratic Party orthodoxy, one that would have been difficult for a big-tent DLC to propose. In the plan, Shapiro, its author, argued against raising the minimum wage, a mainstay of Democratic Party thinking. Instead, he suggested that an expansion of the earned income tax credit (EITC) would do more to help the working poor.[91] In the midst of a large public battle on an issue dear to Democratic constituencies, PPI offered a heretical alternative that attracted attention from the media and other political elites.

At the same time, the DLC did not immediately take the diminished form that From and others in the leadership had planned for it once PPI was founded. Indeed, while PPI was being established, the DLC continued much of its policy development and promotion activities, as well as its advocacy for institutional changes within the Democratic Party. In the fall of 1989, the DLC unveiled its new magazine, the *Mainstream Democrat*. In this first issue, the magazine highlighted DLC and PPI initiatives such as national service, the "Politics of Evasion" analysis, their stances on the Democratic Party's presidential nominating process, and features on internal news, such as the formation of PPI.[92]

After this debut, editing of the magazine fell to Bruce Reed, the DLC's new policy director. After spending his youth working on losing Democratic campaigns in his native Idaho, Reed was convinced that the party "had just run out of steam, run out of ideas."[93] So after working in Al Gore's Senate office and on his presidential bid, the boyish-looking Rhodes scholar came to the DLC in January 1990. He was to become a key player in the development of the DLC's political strategy and the elucidation of its public philosophy.

The DLC also undertook a major review of Democratic strategies and policies in the latter half of 1989. On September 25, 1989, the DLC sponsored a seminar on the environment led by Gore and Senator Tim Wirth of Colorado, and the organization held field hearings in Texas, Louisiana, and Mississippi. This process culminated in a one-day conference on November 13, 1989, where panels of elected officials and policy experts reviewed a wide range of topics.

Finally, the DLC made yet another attempt to change the nominating rules of the national party. Specifically, the organization objected to changes in the nominating process that Dukakis had initiated to secure the endorsement of Jackson. These alterations banned winner-take-all primaries, thus making the results more proportional to the actual primary vote, and reduced the number of superdelegates at the next nominating convention.[94]

From the point of view of the New Democrats and their allies, these changes helped Jackson. The latter change cut into support that did not typically go to the civil rights leader, and the former awarded delegates to consistent second- and third-place finishers, thereby empowering liberal activists and interest groups, prolonging the nomination fight, and straining the fragile Democratic coalition.[95] The fact that the Dukakis campaign had made the deal with Jackson without outside consultation upset the New Democrats further.[96]

Brown, the newly elected chairman of the DNC and Jackson's 1988 convention manager, refused to make any changes in the rules. "Any minute we take rehashing rules debates that have been going on for twenty years is a minute we take away from winning elections," he reasoned.[97] In the end, the DLC, no doubt aware of its limited power within party affairs and chastened by its past failures, agreed with Brown's rationale for not changing the rules and chose not to pick a fight. In any event, by then, the organization had already chosen to concentrate on its development of the New Democratic public philosophy and began to look to the next presidential election.[98]

This decision not to challenge the post-1988 changes in nominating rules represented a shift in tactics on the part of the DLC. Up to the

1988 election, the main emphasis of the organization had been on affecting the party's nominating procedures in order to alter the party itself and its public philosophy. This strategy took the form of advocating such changes outright and, once most of them had been made by DNC Chairman Kirk, shaping the dynamics of the nominating campaign itself, especially by championing the Super Tuesday regional primary. At the same time, the DLC moderated its rhetoric, took a more conciliatory stance toward its factional rivals, and broadened its membership in order to blunt potentially fatal criticism from within the party.

At one level, this approach was successful. Kirk made some important changes to the organization of the party that made it appear less beholden to liberal interest groups. Moreover, Dukakis oversaw the crafting of a platform that was distinctly more vague and less particularistic, and he made a conscious decision to stress his own competence rather than the core beliefs he or the party held. Yet despite all this, the Bush campaign was able to convince most of the public that Dukakis held liberal positions on social and foreign policy issues, and it rode these claims to victory.

The defeat of Dukakis focused attention on the woes of the Democratic Party at the national level, opening a window of opportunity for policy entrepreneurs. Additionally, the election results brought to the surface the inadequacies of the DLC's own strategies, prompting it to reexamine these before taking advantage of the larger opportunity to remake the public philosophy of the Democratic Party.

The DLC, then, began to sacrifice the safety of its big tent in return for efficacy. Its leadership decided that the DLC had to deemphasize working within the party, heighten its effort to argue for the adoption of the New Democratic public philosophy by issuing "The Politics of Evasion," and then develop it by establishing a new think tank, PPI. This new bifurcated organization allowed the DLC to offer more controversial policies while still keeping some of its big-tent form and any credibility it had built up over the previous three years as a loyal Democratic organization.

This posture, however, was part of a grander strategy. New Democratic leaders hoped that PPI would produce a comprehensive platform on which a New Democrat could run for president. This effort to develop a coherent New Democratic public philosophy and the programs to embody it, then, was an attempt to provide the fuel a candidate would need to run for the party's nomination, possibly win the general election, and remake the party in the process. Therefore, as the 1990s began, the DLC not only continued to build PPI but also began to search for a possible New Democratic standard-bearer and build an infrastructure to support his run.

Al From, president of the DLC. (DLC photo)

Gillis Long, chairman of the House Democratic Caucus and founding father of what would become the DLC. (Gillis W. Long Collection, Louisiana and Lower Mississippi Valley Collections, LSU Libraries, Louisiana State University, Baton Rouge, LA)

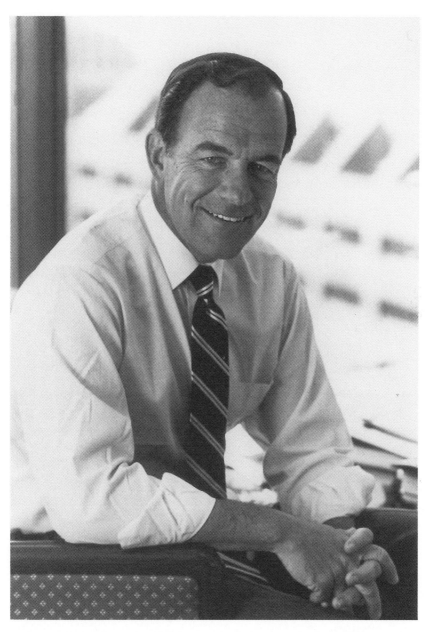

Paul G. Kirk, Jr., chairman of the Democratic National Committee from 1985 to 1989. (Courtesy of Paul G. Kirk, Jr.)

Will Marshall, president of the Progressive Policy Institute (PPI). (Bernard A. Grant)

As part of its Super Tuesday Education Project, the DLC held a series of presidential candidate debates. Pictured at its October 5, 1987, debate on national security in Miami are (clockwise from top), Richard Gephardt, Bruce Babbitt, Al Gore, Michael Dukakis, Paul Simon, Jesse Jackson, and Ted Koppel, the moderator. (DLC photo)

DLC Chairman Sam Nunn (right) and DNC Chairman Ron Brown at the
DLC's annual conference in 1989. (Michael Geissinger)

Immediately after the unveiling of "The Politics of Evasion" critique in March 1989, Chuck Robb and Jesse Jackson get into a heated and public argument on the future of the Democratic Party. (Michael Geissinger)

William Galston and Elaine Kamarck, authors of "The Politics of Evasion." (DLC photo)

Senator John Breaux, DLC chairman from 1991 to 1993, speaks on one of the "New American Choice Resolutions" debated on the floor of the 1991 Cleveland convention. (DLC photo)

Bruce Reed, former DLC policy director, became a key proponent of the New Democratic public philosophy first on the Clinton presidential campaign and later in the White House as domestic policy advisor. (GeorgeLong.com)

Former DLC chairmen (from right to left) Dave McCurdy, Sam Nunn, and Chuck Robb greet Joe Lieberman, the newly installed chairman of the DLC, who took the reins of the organization in its tenth year, 1995. (DLC photo)

A few months before the 1996 elections, Bill Clinton signs into law a key DLC initiative: welfare reform. (Reuters/Steven Jaffe/Archive Photos)

British Prime Minister Tony Blair and President Bill Clinton discuss the "Third Way" at a forum held in September 1998 at New York University. (Lisa Berg/NYU)

Simon Rosenberg, a 1992 Clinton campaign veteran who left the DLC to form the New Democrat Network, a PAC to help elect New Democratic candidates. (GeorgeLong.com)

The founders of the New Democrat Coalition (left to right), Cal Dooley of California, Tim Roemer of Indiana, and Jim Moran of Virginia. (GeorgeLong.com)

Al From, Bill Clinton, and Al Gore in the White House in February 1998. In the background is presidential aide Sidney Blumenthal, the White House's point man on "Third Way" activities. (White House photo)

6 / Pursuing the Presidency, 1990–1992

THE PUBLICATION OF "The Politics of Evasion" and the establishment of the Progressive Policy Institute were each significant steps in the development of the New Democrats. The former was the DLC's most forceful critique of the public philosophy of the national Democratic Party; the latter embodied the commitment of the organization to construct an alternative to it. Together, they were the initial moves away from the big-tent format of the organization. Yet these efforts, in hindsight, have a much greater significance: they were actually the first steps of a conscious effort on the part of New Democratic leaders to participate actively in the 1992 presidential election.

Obviously, this was not the first time the DLC had concerned itself with presidential politics. The organization had already attempted to affect the outcome of the 1988 nominating campaign through its aggressive advocacy of the Super Tuesday regional primary and its lobbying of party officials for changes in nominating rules, platform planks, and vice-presidential picks. The failure of these strategies prompted the DLC to pursue a more ambitious plan in 1992. The New Democrats hoped to take over the party by battling for its head.

In many ways, this was a strategy particular to postreform American politics. In this era of weakening political parties, national party leaders could no longer control who won the presidential nomination of their party. Instead, the candidate himself chose to run for the spot, using his own organization to win delegates in primaries and caucuses. Once a candidate had the nomination in hand, the party machinery— including the party chairmanship—in effect was at his disposal. Moreover, if the candidate was successful in winning the presidency, his ability to mold the platform, rules, and strategies of the party was great. In this sense, even controlling a weakened party was important, as the national party still established an identity for the entire party and, by extension, for those candidates running under its mantle. As a result, he who shaped the party's image framed the national political debate while having an immediate relevancy to individual races. Having the ear or allegiance of a winning presidential candidate, therefore, was one of the most effective means for a policy entrepreneur to get his alternatives onto the agenda of the party and the nation.

Furthermore, such a strategy appeared to mesh with the organizational and institutional resources of the DLC. As it had seen over its first five years of operation, the group lacked the means to work effectively within the national party apparatus. The DLC did not have a grassroots base, either to use as leverage to make demands on the national party or to mobilize behind a bloc of candidates for national and local party offices. What it did have was its network of political elites plus a nascent advocacy think tank. With these, the DLC could provide a New Democratic presidential hopeful with the components he would need to initiate a credible run for the nomination. These included national media exposure, a policy platform and national message, an elite base in key battleground states (and a reason to visit them), a core group of top political contributors, and a staff to focus on the development of all of the above.

To execute this strategy, the DLC leadership had to do two things, at once elementary and complicated: find a candidate, and then deliver on its promises. Regarding the former, the organization was especially lucky. Regarding the latter, the DLC committed itself to revamping its own organizational structure, to heightening its efforts at issue development, and to altering its relationship with other party factions. In the end, the results surpassed even the DLC's own expectations.

The Decision to Play Presidential Politics

The presidency had been an important preoccupation of the DLC since its inception. The ascendance of liberal "amateur" activists into positions of power within the national Democratic Party, the resulting changes to its nominating process and platform, and the argued "drag" of liberal presidential nominees on the electoral prospects of southern and western officeholders had led to the formation of the organization in the first place. Indeed, the whole New Democratic project had been motivated, in large part, by the inability of the Democratic Party to win the White House in the postreform era.

The DLC, in that sense, had always concerned itself with presidential politics, whether by urging its members to testify at DNC hearings on revisions to the nominating rules, trying to draft a candidate for DNC chairman, or actively using its resources to promote the Super Tuesday regional primary. However, it was not until the 1988 defeat of Michael Dukakis that the DLC began to focus on the presidential possibility, specifically and earnestly. It was at this point that the DLC was sufficiently established institutionally to take such a step, and that the crisis of Democratic political viability was acute enough to warrant such action.

Consequently, the DLC, as policy entrepreneur, was able to develop and promote its proposals, and due to heightened sensitivity to the Democrats' problems, the party was more open to consider them. As the 1992 campaign season approached, then, the DLC concentrated on developing the New Democratic public philosophy and on organizing itself in order to benefit a potential New Democratic standard-bearer.

ELECTORAL PROBLEMS AND ALTERNATIVES

The establishment of PPI and the release of "The Politics of Evasion" were the first steps in this presidential effort, an effort that began almost immediately after the ballots had been counted in Dukakis's defeat. As discussed in the previous chapter, the DLC leadership believed that having a think tank in which to formulate policy would enable the New Democrats to "have its ideology and governing agenda form the intellectual and programmatic underpinnings for the Administration of a future president."[1] At the same time, and equally important, many donors and politicians from the New Democratic wing of the party, according to From, began to clamor for an allied candidate for the 1992 or 1996 election.[2]

This commitment to developing a platform on which a New Democrat could run for president, and then finding such a candidate to do so, was part of From's larger vision for turning the DLC into a "political movement." To From, any successful movement required four key assets: political leadership, ideology, grassroots support, and money to fund it all.[3] The money had never been a problem, particularly with such political stars as Robb and Nunn at the helm. In From's view, all that was left, then, was for the DLC to develop a coherent and detailed program in PPI, aggressively promote it, and establish affiliated state chapters in order to build the organization's grassroots support. In sum, From hoped that this strategy would place the DLC at the vanguard of a movement to "challenge the entrenched orthodoxies" in the Democratic Party.[4]

With its establishment of PPI in 1989, along with its subsequent recruitment of a presidential candidate and the formation of state chapters, it might appear that the DLC did indeed go on to implement From's plan. But one must remember that despite his use of the term, the DLC was not a true grassroots organization during this period. The DLC did consider proposals to attract rank-and-file adherents, train New Democrats to run for state party committee and DNC posts (as well as for delegate slots to the national nominating convention), and even challenge liberal Democrats in primaries.[5] Additionally, From and other senior DLC staff were often taken with the idea of launching a "mainstream movement" with thousands of supporters who would "overwhelm . . . the old Democratic party from the grassroots and carry a new Democrat to the White House."[6]

Nevertheless, the organization's "movement" strategy never became an effort to construct a broad-based organization, such as the Christian Coalition or the AFL-CIO, that rank-and-file members would join in order to pursue their views. The DLC was founded as an organization of political elites for political elites, and it remained that way. The New Democrats were instead retooling the DLC to serve its original elected-official clientele, who wanted to see the national party remade so that it would be easier to be a Democrat in their districts; its constituency of political activists and funders, who supported the DLC mainly to be associated with the Democratic Party's rising stars; and, most importantly, the one New Democratic politician willing to make a run for the presidency in 1992.

Said differently, the DLC may have been interested in attracting widespread, grassroots support. Claiming either to have it or to be in the process of acquiring it would, at the very least, attract press attention and increase its influence within the party. Yet it was in no position to generate such a following or provide it to a presidential hopeful. Instead, the DLC concentrated on what it could do: provide the basics that a potential presidential candidate would need to launch a run for the White House. All that was needed was the right candidate.

Perhaps naturally, the DLC leadership looked first to its chairman, since whoever held that position was best able to take advantage of what the DLC had to offer and was probably most committed to carrying the New Democratic banner. Therefore, as Sam Nunn's tenure as DLC chairman was coming to a close, From and the DLC leadership began to search for a replacement, keeping in mind that this person should also be an attractive presidential hopeful. In April 1989, that search took From to Little Rock, Arkansas, to speak to Governor Bill Clinton.

Clinton had been a member of the DLC since its early days, becoming increasingly more involved as the organization grew. As early as January 1987, From realized Clinton's potential, noting to Chuck Robb that the DLC had to make a trip to Arkansas "to get Bill Clinton more active."[7] By 1988, From had begun to speak earnestly with Clinton about taking the DLC chairmanship, a conversation that produced From's 1989 trip to make a personal pitch to the governor. "I said to Clinton, 'have I got a deal for you,'" recounted From. "'If you take the DLC chairmanship, we will give you a national platform, and I think you will be President of the United States. And you will do a lot of good for us because it will make us a national organization.'"[8] As Michael Steinhardt, then chairman of the PPI Board of Trustees, put it, From "perceived that he [Clinton] was the most attractive political animal he had seen in his life," and thus offered to help the governor if Clinton would help the DLC cause.[9]

Within the DLC staff hierarchy, there was widespread support for a Clinton chairmanship. But by the beginning of 1990, From still had not secured a definitive answer from Clinton on whether he would accept the position. In an effort to convince him to take the post, From wrote a personal and confidential memorandum to the Arkansas governor, laying out in clear terms what the DLC could offer a chairman politically, and what the organization asked in return. This memo provides a frank explanation, by the DLC itself, of what it hoped to provide a New Democratic presidential contender and, consequently, of its whole presidential strategy.

What the DLC asked from Clinton could be summed up as allegiance and access. From wanted Clinton to commit himself to raising

$500,000 for the organization from new donors; provide From with timely phone access (apparently, this had been a problem); give the organization the authority to sign his name on correspondence and other documents, as well as to provide input on his political schedule; and be willing to participate in PPI events. Furthermore, From stressed that unlike the days when the DLC had "side-stepped major fights" within the party, it would no longer do that, and he asked that Clinton commit to a "willingness to play political hardball."[10]

For this commitment to the DLC and the New Democratic cause, Clinton would receive a set of political resources especially useful for someone with designs on the White House. Not only was the DLC the "best political forum in the Democratic party," From wrote, but it was also the "best chance" for Clinton to create a political environment "amenable for you or someone like you to run for and win the Presidential nomination—*and* get elected President."[11] Simply, From argued that the New Democratic message was the future of the Democratic Party and the key to its winning the White House. Therefore, whoever was most identified with it would stand to benefit from such an association in a national race.[12] Finally, to make his point perfectly clear, From listed eleven specific political benefits that Clinton could take advantage of if he took the helm of the DLC.

First, From pointed out that the DLC provided Clinton with an ongoing Washington operation, staff backup, funding for travel, substantive support on issues development (courtesy of PPI), a magazine in which Clinton could write a column, and unlimited opportunities to get national press attention. All these were practical aid for a presidential hopeful. A second group of advantages could be seen as crucial benefits to a politician from a small state like Arkansas who was considering a bid for national office. From wrote that the DLC offered access to a growing network of "up and coming political leaders," entree into the Washington and New York fund-raising communities, and admission to a wide array of elected officials in the House and Senate. Finally, From mentioned that he himself could act as a valuable aide, saying things and taking criticism for controversial statements and actions that might otherwise hurt the organization's chairman.[13]

At their essence, these were all advantages that would benefit a presidential hopeful during the campaign's crucial "invisible primary." Indeed, of the seven variables that Arthur Hadley had identified as important for a candidate during this time, the DLC claimed that it could aid Clinton with four of them: staff, strategy, money, and media attention. (The other three were beyond its gift: the candidate's own will, a mobilized constituency, and luck.)[14]

After a courtship of more than a year, Clinton agreed to take the DLC chairmanship, officially replacing Nunn in March 1990. However, although he had almost run in 1988 and was seen as a potential candidate in 1992, at the time, there was no guarantee that Clinton would go on to seek the Democratic nomination for president. From and the DLC tried to keep up the pressure on Clinton to enter the race, making it clear to him that the DLC would have failed if one of its adherents did not win the Democratic Party's nomination in 1992 or 1996.[15] Simultaneously, the DLC kept developing its strategy and working to lay the groundwork for a New Democratic nominee, whoever that might be.

DLC Policy Director Bruce Reed, for example, reminded From that the DLC should not pin all its hopes on Clinton. Instead, it had to focus on "laying the groundwork for a successful 1992 primary campaign" for either one of the DLC's own (Clinton, Nunn, Robb, or Gore) or a candidate the DLC could attach itself to, such as Senator Bill Bradley of New Jersey, Senator Bob Kerrey of Nebraska, or Governor Douglas Wilder of Virginia.[16] To begin this task, the DLC had to continue to develop what it could offer a New Democratic candidate: "an extensive field operation, considerable fundraising resources, a detailed agenda and compelling message, and a persuasive critique of the Bush Administration."[17]

Furthermore, Reed argued that the DLC had to make it appear that the New Democrats were, in fact, taking over the party. It had to heighten its media effort, take credit for any moderate victories in the 1990 midterm elections, and assume control of the state party in a few northern states where the organization was weak in order to show support outside of the South.[18] Reflecting the limits of the organization's capabilities, the last suggestion was never acted upon. However, the DLC, through its think tank, could deepen and elaborate on the New Democratic public philosophy, and the group began to do just that, readying itself for use by a presidential hopeful.

ISSUE PROBLEMS AND POLICY ALTERNATIVES

One of the most critical components of the DLC's grand presidential strategy was developing a detailed, sophisticated program and political message for a New Democratic candidate. To that end, the DLC initiated a policy review process that would culminate with the introduction of a New Democratic credo that included positions on issues on which national Democrats were particularly vulnerable, especially crime, defense, and economic growth.[19]

These were to be unveiled at the DLC's annual conference in New Orleans in 1990. They would then be developed further for the organization's first convention, to be held in Cleveland in 1991, where principles and policy proposals would be voted on by New Democratic delegates—a method intended to show the political world that these ideas had broad-based support. During this two-year process—from the establishment of PPI in 1989 to the ratification of the "New American Choice Resolutions" in 1991 at the Cleveland convention—the DLC honed its critique of the liberalism in the national Democratic Party and offered new policy prescriptions as well as an alternative public philosophy.

From the beginning, the New Democrats had rooted themselves in what they saw as the traditional stances of the Democratic Party. Often as a defense against charges of partisan apostasy, DLC thinkers had linked the organization to a range of Democratic icons from Andrew Jackson to Franklin Roosevelt to John Kennedy and called for the "restoration" of a liberalism in line with their principles.[20] During the early 1990s, the DLC continued to look to the past for inspiration for its policy and philosophical innovations, but it now differed in where it looked and to what end.

While looking to the coming millennium, the New Democrats started to draw parallels between themselves and the Progressive movement active at the beginning of the twentieth century. New Democrats felt that, like the Progressives, they faced the same challenge of applying "basic American political principles to changing circumstances."[21] Will Marshall and others in PPI and in the DLC argued that the Progressives had faced a transition from an agricultural to an industrial economy, from an isolated United States to a global power, and from a relatively homogeneous white, Protestant society to a heterogeneous one. The New Democrats believed that they faced an equally significant change: from a national and industrial to a global and postindustrial—or Information Age—economy, and from a bipolar, Cold War world to an uncertain, multipolar one.

Their challenge, then, was to adapt the public philosophy of the

Democratic Party to these new circumstances while retaining the country's core values of "individual liberty, equal opportunity, and civic enterprise."[22] As the DLC adopted this "futurist" outlook, the organization became increasingly enamored with crafting a public philosophy for the Information Age that "transcend[ed] the limits of the conventional left-right debate" and thus began to focus on attracting those who worked and lived in the "new economy" to the Democratic Party.[23]

This futurist impulse, to craft a public philosophy that went beyond current partisan differences, was found simultaneously within both parties. Despite the end of the Cold War and the collapse of communism, many political elites felt that neither party was addressing what Jean Bethke Elshtain, the political theorist, recognized as the "the need for a reconfiguring of political ideas."[24] President Bush was concerned neither with the "vision thing" nor with domestic policy, and the Democrats seemed tied to simple brokerage and interest-group liberalism. Therefore, in 1990, a group of policy thinkers and elected officials from both parties—including many key New Democrats—organized themselves in order to develop a "new paradigm" for government. Established in February of that year by Elaine Kamarck, a senior fellow at PPI, and James Pinkerton, a domestic policy aide to Bush, the New Paradigm Society held monthly meetings to articulate and elaborate on the view first popularized by Pinkerton in a series of speeches he had given and in one speech he had written for Bush.

This "new paradigm," according to Pinkerton, was based on five principles: a free-market orientation, individual choice, empowerment, decentralization of government functions, and an emphasis on what works in public policy.[25] Pinkerton and New Paradigm fellow travelers—notably, David Osborne, a PPI senior fellow and author of *Reinventing Government*, a DLC favorite—believed that government itself had to be retooled, since technological advances and the rise of a global marketplace were rendering centralized governmental structures ineffective.[26] Therefore, they advocated the privatization of government services, more local control of programs, and the use of vouchers and tax credits to influence economic behavior.

The extent to which Pinkerton and his writings influenced and were influenced by the DLC may be impossible to gauge. But the cross-pollination of ideas between the two was clear enough. PPI and the Heritage Foundation, for instance, held a joint conference on the "new paradigm." Prominent New Democratic elected officials, such as Senator Joseph Lieberman of Connecticut and Congressman Dave McCurdy of Oklahoma, had been linked to the group. And Pinkerton's five principles were evident in future DLC policy statements.[27] However, the DLC's affinity for these beliefs can plausibly be ascribed to the similarities between its own evolving positions and Pinkerton's.

Nevertheless, this parallel and bipartisan effort shows that the DLC was not operating in a vacuum. There were wider intellectual trends that the New Democrats were both following and, to some extent, leading. This effort also points to the DLC's decreased hesitation in being linked to an effort that had some aspect of bipartisanship and was outside the bounds of traditional Democratic thinking. Indeed, an examination of the DLC's policy innovations in the economic, social, and foreign policy contexts shows that the organization was moving gradually but increasingly away from its big-tent strategy, espousing more controversial positions even as it tried to retain the support of its diverse membership.

Consider, for example, the "New Orleans Declaration: A Democratic Agenda for the 1990s," a statement of principles endorsed by the DLC at its conference in that city in March 1990 and the first significant policy statement issued under its new presidential strategy. This document used much of the DLC's futurist rhetoric, discussing, for instance, "the new realities of the post-industrial, global economy."[28] It should be noted, however, that the futurist impulse was still muted in comparison to later statements. As evidenced by the liberals on the DLC board who signed the document and its explicit link to the "fundamental values and principles" of the Democratic Party, the DLC still made efforts to retain its big tent.[29] Nevertheless, the "New Orleans Declaration" is an important policy statement in the history of the New Democrats, one that illustrates the development of its more innovative and controversial stances.

Examining economic policy first, the New Democrats took a position that embraced the free market and was relatively anti-statist. Implicitly criticizing their liberal rivals in the national party, they argued that the "Democratic Party's fundamental mission is to expand opportunity, not government."[30] Instead of focusing on the redistribution of wealth, the party should work to establish a free market, albeit one "regulated in the public interest," which, in turn, would promote economic growth.[31] The DLC renewed its call for a "democratic capitalism," in which government would create the fiscal environment for economic growth by expanding international trade, restructuring the tax code, improving public education and job training, and investing in technology and infrastructure improvements.

At the same time, the DLC called for an easing of the tax burden on "average American families" through a reduction in the Social Security payroll tax and advocated a deficit-reduction strategy that stressed cuts in spending—including a "hard look at federal entitlements and subsidies." Although the DLC wanted, in principle, to restore more progressivity to the tax code, it sought to reduce the deficit primarily through reducing governmental spending.[32] In fact, unlike the liberal wing of the party, the DLC consistently opposed any tax increases, most notably during the 1990 budget negotiations.[33]

Underlying these policies was a belief that the role of government in the economy had to be remade for a new age, while staying true to what the New Democrats saw as basic American values. Accordingly, the role of government on the macro level was to provide a growing economy, and on the micro level to provide the basic tools a person needed to take advantage of it. Besides being the most effective way to produce prosperity in what Nunn called the "new knowledge and information-based global economy," this arrangement also stayed true to New Democratic notions of equality.[34]

Specifically, the New Democrats believed that government should ensure only equality of opportunity, not equality of results. In this, economic opportunity, not economic security, was the priority. As one leading New Democratic thinker explained, whereas a traditional Democrat would advocate guaranteeing a public-sector job to the unemployed, a New Democrat would support giving that person aid to enable him to acquire the training he needed to enter the workforce, if he so chose.[35]

These beliefs about equality and the role of government in the economy also had a large impact on the DLC's responses to social problems. As Marshall explained to PPI's Board of Trustees, the New Democrats envisioned an end to "welfare state paternalism."[36] Or as the "New Orleans Declaration" put it, the DLC wanted to replace the "politics of entitlement with a new politics of reciprocal responsibility."[37] In line with the principles behind its national service proposal, unveiled in 1988, the DLC rejected the idea that citizens had specific rights to a whole host of government benefits.[38] Instead, the government had to provide access to programs and aid, but it could—and, to the DLC's thinking, should—demand that citizens honor obligations to government and society in return.

In this light, the "New Orleans Declaration" called for the establishment of individual development accounts for low-income people to provide for postsecondary education, home ownership, self-employment, or retirement, which the government would contribute to only by matching the individuals' own deposits in these savings accounts.[39] Similarly, the DLC wanted to ensure a guaranteed working wage by expanding the earned income tax credit, a policy that provided aid only to the working poor.[40]

The importance placed on equal opportunity put the DLC in a tough position within the party regarding civil rights issues. Because the organization retained an element of its consensual big-tent strategy, and because of the explosiveness of the race issue, the "New Orleans Declaration" made sure not to take its stance on equality to the seemingly logical conclusion and oppose affirmative action policies. On the one hand, New Democratic leaders were adamantly opposed to any policy that ensured equal outcomes and fostered racial separatism or "neotribalism."[41] This belief was evident in the stand of the "New Orleans Declaration" against set-aside quotas in employment and education for aggrieved minority groups. In addition, civil rights did not receive separate treatment in a section of its own in the declaration, as was common in most post-1968 Democratic policy statements. On the other hand, the DLC made sure to state that it supported "the protection of civil rights," that it championed the cause of outsiders, and, as From said, that the DLC supported affirmative action.[42]

Finally, spurred by Bush's ability in 1988 to paint Dukakis as a liberal who was out of step with mainstream values, the New Democrats emphasized their belief in the traditional American values of "liberty of conscience, individual responsibility, tolerance of difference, the importance of work, the need for faith, and the centrality of family" and the effect these had on the country.[43] Nunn summed it up this way: "It's a circle; the family, the values, the social problems, and the economic problems—a circle."[44]

To remedy the most visible result of this breakdown in values—crime—the New Democrats stressed a tough stance, stating, "We believe in deterring crime and punishing criminals, not excusing behavior."[45] Reflecting the New Democratic emphasis on personal responsibility, this position countered the tendency of liberals in the national party to stress curing the societal ills they saw as causing crime, rather than creating strong penalties and police forces to deter individual criminals. Therefore, the DLC did not advocate additional social programs to prevent crime. Rather, the organization endorsed a Police Corps program to put more officers on the street in exchange for providing them with four years of postsecondary education, as well as a community policing program to have more police walking beats in neighborhoods.[46]

In foreign policy, the DLC continued its commitment to internationalism, supporting an "Emerging Democracy Initiative" to "export democratic capitalism and democratic values to emerging democracies," as well as its commitment to free trade.[47] The DLC also called for a reduction in military spending to adjust to the end of the Cold War. But as with civil rights, military spending was not given a separate treatment in its own section, as it usually was in other Democratic policy papers.[48] Moreover, events around the world were muting the disadvantages that had been associated with this position in the past. As the Soviet empire crumbled, a consensus was beginning to form around reductions of some sort. The parameters of the debate in this issue context were fundamentally changing.

What was not highlighted in the "New Orleans Declaration" also reflected the New Democratic public philosophy. For example, along with civil rights and military spending, abortion and gay rights were not given separate sections. Only by interpreting a statement calling for the government to "stay out of our private lives and personal decisions" could one determine that, like many other Democrats, the DLC was pro-choice and supported equal rights for homosexuals.[49] The DLC did not want to highlight issues on which the Democratic Party's positions were unpopular with the middle-class voters the DLC hoped to attract. Furthermore, on some issues, notably civil rights, the organization did not want to showcase the stances of its leadership and active New Democrats because it had not yet fully committed itself to drawing a clear line between the DLC and other more liberal Democrats within the party.

That move was to come after the New Orleans conference, when the DLC began to focus its intellectual efforts on elaborating these points, in order to craft a more detailed platform to be adopted at its

Cleveland convention. The process of developing and promoting these policies was to have begun with a series of forums in key electoral states, such as Texas, Michigan, and California, commencing on February 25, 1991, and continuing until the spring convention.[50] In the end, however, the DLC modified this schedule, holding a forum in Dallas on families, one in Boston on democratic capitalism, and one in Florida on reinventing government.[51]

These forays into the field were not new to the DLC. The organization had used meetings in different cities to generate local media attention since 1986. However, the burst of state activity in 1990 and 1991 was more than this. In addition to its usual policy forums and recruiting trips, the DLC began to put into place the other piece of its presidential strategy: the establishment of state chapters.

INSTITUTIONAL PROBLEMS AND ALTERNATIVES

To implement an intensive presidential strategy, the DLC had to gauge what internal organizational changes were needed to succeed. After PPI's first year of operation, it became clear to the DLC staff that the think tank, incorporated as a 501(c)3 organization legally separate from the DLC, needed to be recast. As Marshall wrote, "the DLC was frustrated by its inability to freely use PPI products owing to our [PPI's] separate tax status."[52]

Furthermore, the New Democrats realized that the advantages of setting PPI up as a separate organization—such as accepting tax-deductible contributions, raising large blocks of money, and allowing elected officials to distance themselves from controversial ideas—had not materialized. Although PPI did raise almost $700,000 in its first year, it had trouble expanding its fund-raising base.[53] According to From, since many benefactors saw the DLC as the place that would launch the next Democratic presidential nominee, it was easier to raise money for the DLC than for PPI.[54] Therefore, in January 1991, the DLC transferred the special tax status to a new entity, the Progressive Foundation (PF), and merged the operations of the DLC and PPI.[55]

The New Democrats also began to reorganize their activities in the House of Representatives. During the budget negotiations of 1990, a group of moderate and conservative Democratic congressmen came together to prod the Democratic congressional leadership to craft a deal that relied more on spending cuts than on tax increases.[56] After that, under the leadership of Dave McCurdy, a fervent New Democrat, nine charter members of the DLC from the House—including Jim Cooper of Tennessee, Mike Espy of Mississippi, Tim Penny of Minnesota, and David Price of North Carolina—formed the Mainstream Forum in July 1990 to, as McCurdy recalled, "bridge the creation of the ideas and the actual implementation [of them]."[57]

Modeled on the House Republicans' Conservative Opportunity Society, the Mainstream Forum planned to use similar tactics—such as the delivery of special-order speeches on the public-affairs channel C-SPAN, the writing of opinion pieces in newspapers, and the giving of speeches around the country—to generate attention for their ideas.[58] With twenty-five supporters at the outset, McCurdy planned to introduce five or six DLC-generated ideas as legislation called the "Mainstream Agenda."[59] Although the DLC's roots were in the House and it drew a large amount of support from House members, this represented the first time that New Democrats had formally organized themselves in that body.

Yet neither this Capitol Hill development nor the reorganization of PPI was the most significant organizational change the DLC made leading up to the 1992 election. Because the New Democrats' priority was their presidential strategy, the construction of an outside-the-Beltway "movement" was essential to execute it. To that end, the DLC began to establish affiliated state chapters in order to build a network of elite support in key electoral states.

The desire to organize at the state and local level was not completely new to the DLC. On their own, New Democrats had formed state DLCs in Florida in 1986 and in Louisiana in 1987.[60] The national DLC itself, in September 1988, had established the DLC Network program, which organized young professionals into chapters in various metropolitan areas.[61] Furthermore, in late 1987, the DLC considered (and then rejected) a proposal to form affiliated PACs around the country that would donate money to New Democratic candidates based on the recommendations of the DLC in Washington.

Although it had the DLC Network program operating in several cities by 1990, the DLC was now ready to commit itself to establishing true state chapters, which would mirror the national organization in makeup and not be composed solely of affiliated young donors. Publicly, From and company claimed that the organization of state chapters was a way to sell New Democratic ideas to states and to bring innovations taking place in local government back to Washington.[62] Also, the arrival of national Democratic leaders in a state to form a DLC chapter would (and did) generate media attention—free press on which the DLC relied.[63]

But the true impetus behind this initiative was the laying of a groundwork for a New Democratic presidential candidate. Reed wrote that the DLC needed to form chapters in "25 states, including every state with a major primary." In turn, this would "create the illusion of a national movement" and increase the organization's clout for the 1992 race.[64] Moreover, this strategy uniquely aided Clinton, as a governor of a small state. State chapters gave Clinton a reason to travel to key states around the country and the opportunity to generate support for a possible presidential run from local editorial boards, Democratic leaders, and donors who otherwise might not have heard of the governor from Arkansas; and he could do so—as From explained—without having it seem that he was selfishly serving a presidential run.[65]

In April 1990, the DLC officially launched its campaign to charter state chapters. By the end of that summer, the organization could count four new chapters, in South Carolina, Massachusetts, southern California, and Minnesota.[66] With an eye toward the road to the White House, the DLC made sure that its chairman took full advantage of the opportunity to drum up support for or to establish a chapter. Thus, From planned five multicity trips for Clinton during the summer, making sure to include stops in Des Moines, Iowa, and Concord, New Hampshire—the capitals of the states with the two pivotal early nominating contests—along with important Democratic cities such as Philadelphia, Chicago, Detroit, and Los Angeles. Tellingly, in their list of "Midwest target states" to visit, From and the DLC replaced Indianapolis, in Republican Indiana, with Milwaukee, Wisconsin, an important state in any Democratic victory.[67] The DLC also arranged policy forums around the country for Clinton to attend and meetings with the editorial boards of national magazines such as *Time*, which also helped boost his national profile.[68]

At the end of 1990, Clinton made a trip through the South, establishing chapters in at least five more states and bringing the DLC almost halfway to its goal of founding twenty chapters by the Cleveland convention.[69] As the time for that meeting approached, the DLC chartered chapters at a dizzying pace. In March and April 1991, the organization founded chapters in a number of states, including Oregon, Oklahoma, Connecticut, Georgia, and Ohio—the last becoming the twenty-first chapter established. In each state, Clinton's announcement of the new chapter generated local press coverage for him and the wider DLC agenda. Furthermore, Clinton got an opportunity to meet with the leadership of the new chapters, undoubtedly providing him with key contacts in these states.

Usually, the new entity was chaired by a local DLC member along with one other statewide official, sometimes a U.S. senator, but others included state legislative leaders (as in Oregon and Massachusetts) or state attorneys general (as in Ohio). In some states, such as Connecticut, the state Democratic Party chairperson would actually take a leadership role.[70] Regardless of their actual positions, these statewide Democratic political leaders were important guides through the intricacies of their respective state parties and politics and could serve as conduits for later support.

But even more importantly, these chapters were established in states that were crucial to winning the presidential nomination. Thirteen of the original twenty DLC chapters were set up in states whose nominating contests offered 949 delegates and accounted for half the primaries and caucuses held in the first two months of the campaign.[71] Indeed, as Elaine Kamarck recalled, she, From, and Clinton met in Boston's Logan Airport in 1991, where Kamarck, an expert on the mechanics of the nomination process, "walked him [Clinton] through the nomination schedule," and "we mapped Bill Clinton's 1991 travel schedule on the nomination schedule."[72]

The establishment of state chapters was an aggressive organizational move on the part of the DLC, one that exemplified its movement away from a big-tent strategy and consequently antagonized those who disagreed with the DLC's politics or just did not want another Democratic organization in the state. In Minnesota, for example, the sitting Democratic governor, the liberal wing of the state party, the feminist leadership, and most other special-interest groups affiliated with the party did not attend the announcement of that state's DLC chapter.[73]

Clinton's trip to Michigan also met an icy response: one political commentator noted that Clinton's speech on March 11, 1991, in Southfield was "the only big gathering of Michigan Democrats (about

125 showed) in recent memory in which labor's role was zilch."[74] Frank Garrison, the Michigan state AFL-CIO president, bluntly explained the reason for this: "I disagree strongly with most of the right-wing bullshit coming out of [the DLC]."[75] The DLC encountered more labor trouble in Massachusetts when it held one of its policy forums in a nonunionized hotel.[76] And in New Hampshire, that crucial primary state, Chris Spirou, the state party chairman, strongly opposed the formation of an extraparty DLC chapter, apparently out of fear of an alternative power center in New Hampshire Democratic politics.[77]

Nonetheless, by the middle of 1991, the DLC had chartered state chapters throughout the country. The organization entertained the idea of using these entities as the basis of a grassroots movement. For example, with the establishment of state chapters, the organization also formed a "Mainstream Movement," opening up membership in this "movement" to anyone willing to pay a nominal fee; it considered putting together a "Mainstream Academy" to train DLC members to run as delegates to their state or national party conventions; and it discussed proposals to build a large-scale base of donors and supporters through direct mail.[78] The organization even made a brief foray into advertising directly for adherents, running a print advertisement in the *Washington Post Weekly Edition* and in the *New Orleans Times-Picayune* during the New Orleans conference in 1990.[79]

Although Linda Moore, the DLC staff member directly overseeing the chapter effort, claimed that the chapters were to provide "the troops" to elect a New Democratic candidate to the presidency, this help was not to take the form of a large, broad-based popular movement.[80] The DLC established chapters so that its chairman and possible presidential candidate could travel the country, meet like-minded Democratic elected officials and activists, and gain the notice of the local and national media. In many ways, what the DLC planned to do with these chapters once they were founded was not as important as their actual formation. Yet the chapters also served another purpose in the presidential strategy of the DLC. Once established, the chapters would serve as the basis for state delegations to the DLC convention to be held in Cleveland in 1991. That, in turn, would present the appearance of grassroots support for the organization and for its public philosophy.

The Cleveland Convention

The Cleveland convention, held in lieu of the DLC's annual conference, was a seminal event in the history of the New Democrats. Here,
the DLC unveiled its most detailed—and hence most controversial—
policy manifesto; showcased its organizational breadth across the
country; and, arguably, launched the presidential candidacy of its
chairman. With these moves, the DLC broke fully with the big-tent
strategy of its first six years. Accordingly, the Cleveland gathering also
served as a flash point for the anger and animosity of the DLC's factional rivals, resurrecting charges leveled against the DLC since its
founding in 1985 and, in turn, transforming the organization.

ELECTORAL PROBLEMS AND ALTERNATIVES

In planning the Cleveland convention, From and other DLC leaders
hoped that the meeting would shape the 1992 election campaign in
their favor. Specifically, they hoped that by unveiling an issue agenda
more in line with the demands of Middle America than with the
demands of interest groups, by showcasing most of the Democratic
presidential hopefuls for the 1992 race, and by gathering over 1,000
delegates from all fifty states, the New Democrats would "underscore
the strength of our movement" to the over 300 accredited members
of the press in attendance and to the scores of Democratic activists
who would read these accounts.[81] This would then provide momentum for a New Democratic presidential hopeful.

Once under way, the Cleveland convention was seen, as the *New
York Times* put it, as the "first presidential cattle show of 1992."[82]
And if the DLC meeting was a contest of some sort, Bill Clinton
clearly won. He was helped by perennial DLC favorite Sam Nunn's
vote against the use of force in the Persian Gulf and by an abysmal
speech given at the convention by Al Gore, the preferred candidate
of the DLC from 1988.[83] This left a huge window of opportunity for
Clinton, and according to accounts, he did not disappoint.[84] With a
single sheet of paper with only twenty one-word cues written on it,
the Arkansan took the stage and gave one of the best speeches of his
career.[85] He offered a compelling critique of the Republicans, along
with an attractive alternative replete with the New Democratic

themes of opportunity, responsibility, and community.[86] At the end, the crowd gave him a standing ovation. And perhaps more importantly, the reporters, pundits, and political professionals who follow presidential politics and set the "conventional wisdom" took notice of the speech, the vision, and the man delivering it.

The strength of this address and of the whole meeting produced, in Marshall's estimation, "an inexorable movement to a Clinton presidential run."[87] That was, however, hindsight; there was still no guarantee that Clinton would run. In fact, in 1988, Clinton had decided against such a move at the very last minute.[88] The DLC could only set the stage for a New Democrat, and part of that effort was elaborating on its public philosophy by constructing a comprehensive policy platform.

ISSUE PROBLEMS AND POLICY ALTERNATIVES

The policy statement that the DLC ratified at the Cleveland convention was the product of its three-year effort to provide a replacement for the interest-group liberalism of the national party. In many ways, the "New American Choice Resolutions" passed in Cleveland were an extension of the "New Orleans Declaration." However, in providing substantially more programmatic details on a broader range of issues and emphasizing the futurist tone in the "New Orleans Declaration," the "New American Choice Resolutions" took more controversial stances.

The first component of this new posture was a forceful critique of the prevailing public philosophy of the national Democratic Party by some of the most prominent DLC members. In his keynote address, Clinton, for example, argued that despite declining incomes among the middle and working classes, the Democrats were unable to take advantage of these circumstances, since this constituency "has not trusted us in national elections to defend our national interests abroad, to put values into our social policy at home, or to take tax money and spend it with discipline."[89] As McCurdy told the convention, part of the blame for this situation lay with "the forces which took command of the Democratic party in 1972 and . . . have paralyzed many of our government and social institutions."[90]

The alternative the DLC offered was a public philosophy based around the core principles of "opportunity, responsibility, choice, a government that works, a belief in community."[91] These values were not entirely new to the DLC. However, in this new policy statement, there was an increased emphasis on the importance of community and, reflecting its futurist outlook, on the necessity of reinventing government. The emphasis on community was a logical extension of the DLC's beliefs on civic obligation and reciprocal responsibility and, on its own, was relatively uncontroversial.

But by stressing the need to reinvent government, the DLC stepped up its attack on the federal bureaucracy and on the theory of governance implicit in the liberal public philosophy, which called for the federal government to be the primary agent of change. The organization believed that "unneeded layers of bureaucracy" should be eliminated, since "centralized bureaucracies are no longer the best or most effective way to deliver services."[92] The New Democrats wanted to streamline government bureaucracies through the hiving off of some functions to either lower levels of government or private contractors. Both options had significant ramifications; the former implied a change in the federal relationship, and the latter reflected a faith in the free market and private sector that was absent in many national Democrats.

This new commitment to reinventing government manifested itself in a number of policy prescriptions. For example, delegates to the Cleveland convention passed a resolution that not only supported the linking of increases in the growth of federal spending to growth in the economy but also relied on reinventing government to cut government spending. Additionally, the New Democrats called for a review of all government programs to determine their utility and their need to be carried out by the federal government—or indeed, by government at all—along with a 3 percent reduction in the federal government's administrative and personnel expenses.[93]

The anti-statism that informed its emphasis on reinventing government also led the DLC to embrace market-oriented policies in other areas. For instance, the DLC called for health insurance reform—its first real mention of the issue—through market mechanisms, not through the establishment of a single-payer health insurance program, as liberal Democrats had previously demanded.[94] In environmental policy, the "New American Choice Resolutions" called for the replacement of current environmental regulations with market incentives and mechanisms, such as tradable permits, to discourage pollution.[95]

To help the poor, the DLC endorsed the establishment of public-private groups to loan money to poor entrepreneurs, efforts to give public housing tenants more control and even ownership of their residences, and plans to give poor people vouchers by which they could purchase their own social services.[96] Finally, as part of its suggested education reforms, the DLC endorsed a school choice plan within public schools, as well as the establishment of charter schools—two policies eyed with suspicion and derision by the teachers unions, a key Democratic constituency group.[97]

Committed to an active engagement in the world, the DLC had one of its biggest breaks with the national party over trade. The New Democrats endorsed the extension of fast-track negotiating authority for and ultimate passage of the North American Free Trade Agreement (NAFTA), a treaty that organized labor opposed bitterly, fearing the loss of jobs to low-wage foreign workers.[98] Furthermore, the convention delegates rejected an amendment to its pro-NAFTA resolution that called for the strengthening of labor and environmental standards, a concession sought by many Democrats.[99]

Its internationalist beliefs, along with the occurrence of the Persian Gulf War less than six months before the Cleveland convention, profoundly shaped the foreign policy stances of the DLC. Specifically, the decision of many Democrats, including some prominent New Democrats such as Nunn, not to support the use of force in the Gulf—in a war that ended quickly and enjoyed overwhelming support—underscored the Democratic Party's post-Vietnam image of being timid about the use of the military abroad. In response, the DLC moved quickly to assert hawkish positions that it not only believed in but also felt were popular with the groups in the electorate whose support the New Democrats sought. Accordingly, the "New American Choice Resolutions" heaped praise on the "national leadership" and the military for defeating Iraq and endorsed a "robust program" of military research as well as a retooling of the military so that it would remain strong in the face of post–Cold War reductions.[100]

The organization's stance on both trade and defense stood to rankle intraparty rivals, but the positions it laid out in the "New American Choice Resolutions" regarding social issues were its most controversial. Although the organization signaled a commitment to the free market and to individual initiative, its approach to public policy was more than pure libertarianism. In the Cleveland document, the DLC placed the "moral and cultural values that most Americans share" and the family—the heterosexual, two-parent family—at the center of a host of social policies, reflecting a traditional stance that the DLC had not highlighted previously and that liberals did not embrace.[101] Indeed, liberals were uneasy about prioritizing this family arrangement above all others. Recall that in 1980, the Carter White House had held a conference not on "family" but on "families."[102] With its "progressive, child-centered family policy," the DLC sought not only to endorse the traditional two-parent family as the preferred environment for children but also to place the responsibility for raising these children squarely on the parents.[103] As Clinton said in his keynote address, "I will let you in on a secret—governments do not raise children, people do, and it is time they were asked to assume their responsibilities and forced to do it if they refuse."[104] Accordingly, the DLC supported government-mandated family leave, an increase in the tax exemption for children, and the strict enforcement of child-support laws.

Additionally, the New Democrats took a strong law-and-order stance. They backed a seven-day waiting period to buy a handgun, a Police Corps, military-style "boot camps" for young first-time offenders, and stronger mandatory sentences for those who commit crimes with guns.[105] These stances did not mean that the DLC had cast its lot with the social conservatives found mainly in the GOP. In fact, the "New American Choice Resolutions," unlike the statement released in New Orleans the previous year, explicitly supported the right of a woman to have an abortion. Nevertheless, this complex set of positions reflected the DLC's attempt to get the national Democratic Party to recognize middle-class concerns and values and move away from the extreme Left on social issues.

Part of this movement had always stemmed from the New Democratic position that government should provide equal opportunities, not equal outcomes. But in its earlier pronouncements, the DLC had not specified the implications of this tenet for civil rights policy. However, in this iteration of its beliefs, specificity was provided. The DLC affirmed its commitment to the tough enforcement of the nation's civil rights laws and to the use of "affirmative action to ensure that opportunities are in fact equal."[106] But the organization also took an unequivocal stand against quotas: "We oppose discrimination of any kind—including quotas."[107]

This position placed the DLC firmly in opposition to the liberal faction of the Democratic Party on one of the most sensitive issues in American politics. It is not surprising then that this resolution provoked the most debate on the floor of the Cleveland convention.[108] An argument erupted over the phrase "including quotas," and an amendment was offered to strike it from the text. New Democrats had been politically sensitive to this issue, and indeed to this word, ever since 1990, when President Bush vetoed a new Civil Rights Act, charging that it would create quotas for minority groups in employment. In turn, this issue was used effectively in the 1990 elections, contributing to the Senate defeats of Democrats Harvey Gantt in North Carolina and Dianne Feinstein in California. Despite the Democrats' disadvantages on this issue and the efficacy with which it had been used against them, congressional Democrats made the civil rights legislation one of their top priorities for 1991. The New Democrats, however, wanted to avoid a potentially damaging campaign issue for 1992.[109]

On the convention floor, John Breaux argued that if the DLC passed a resolution not including a clear opposition to quotas, it would give the Republican Party "a hammer to beat Democrats over the head with and move us away from the real question of civil rights and equal opportunity."[110] DLC leaders were in a bind. They wanted to seem neither pro-quota nor anti-black. In response, Breaux—upon the urging of Clinton—offered a "perfecting" amendment that called for the end of quotas but stressed the DLC's commitment to providing the legal and economic means to fight discrimination and gain equality.[111] The debate continued as some delegates argued that opposing quotas would alienate others in the party, and some who opposed quotas wanted to reject the Breaux amendment because it smacked of appeasement. In the end, after DLC leaders, including Clinton, spoke in favor of the Breaux amendment, it passed, as did the whole resolution on civil rights, with the stand against quotas intact.

This debate on the floor of the DLC's convention encapsulated the tensions and cleavages that its more strident stance provoked from its own members and supporters, as well as within the Democratic Party at large. The Cleveland convention and the "New American Choice Resolutions" passed by it not only exhibited the organizational and intellectual development of the DLC but also provided a clear drawing of the line between it and other factions in the Democratic Party. In the weeks leading up to the Cleveland convention and at the meeting itself, these stances and the new posture of the DLC provoked a strong reaction from the party's liberal wing, and a vicious and highly publicized fight ensued.

INSTITUTIONAL PROBLEMS AND ALTERNATIVES

The ideological war that erupted around the Cleveland convention had been foreshadowed at the DLC conference the year before in New Orleans. In New Orleans, as in Cleveland, at the center of the controversy was Jesse Jackson, titular head of the liberal wing of the Democratic Party. Jackson, president of the Rainbow Coalition and two-time candidate for the Democratic Party's presidential nomination, had been invited to speak and had spoken at previous DLC conventions. Recall that at the organization's 1989 meeting, Jackson had gained the spotlight as he debated Robb on the merits of the DLC's "Politics of Evasion" paper. Since the founding of the DLC, Jackson had served as a foil for the New Democrats, for he was the most visible embodiment of the liberal policies and strategies they rejected.[112]

Therefore, when Jackson told the New Democrats gathered at the 1990 New Orleans conference that he was "delighted that we are so united," he provoked the ire of the DLC leadership. He argued that the party was united on a wide variety of issues, from cuts in military spending to gay rights. Then, to incite the DLC further, Jackson said that he was pleased that Super Tuesday—which the DLC had backed, hoping to stop a Jackson candidacy—had proved that the Democratic Party was open to all, since it had helped propel his own presidential campaign.[113]

In one speech, Jackson thus appeared to undermine the DLC's entire raison d'être. The DLC held conferences, such as the one in New Orleans, to highlight the differences between the New Democrats and liberals such as Jackson. At a time when observers were noting that the DLC and the national party had become more alike—and thus when the DLC wanted to make clear the distinctions between it and other party factions—Jackson's "delighted that we are so united" speech was precisely the opposite message that the DLC wanted those attending and covering the conference to hear.

The response of the DLC leadership was swift and strong. "We trust that a few people in the press have a brain in their heads," From told reporters at the conference. And Robb said that Jackson's interpretations were "creative."[114] After Jackson's speech itself, Clinton, the next speaker, immediately distanced the DLC from Jackson's remarks, telling the audience, "You know, Jesse Jackson and I are both Southern Baptists and we have a lot of things in common. One is our church is highly decentralized, and it permits a lot of different interpretation of common documents."[115]

As a result of the Jackson speech, From and the DLC leadership, in a meeting held a few months before the 1991 Cleveland convention, decided that the civil rights leader would not be invited to the gathering. "I had to defend [Jackson's appearance] to all of our funders because he came and mocked us in 1990," From recalled. "He was not going to give a major speech."[116]

Also feeding this conflict was the inevitable fact that liberals too were preparing for the 1992 campaign season, developing and promoting their critique of New Democratic policies. The most significant of these efforts began in May 1990, when more than three dozen liberal congressmen and senators, led by Senator Howard Metzenbaum of Ohio, announced the formation of the Coalition for Democratic Values (CDV). The organization, established with $50,000 left over in Metzenbaum's campaign treasury and funded by donations from private individuals and organized labor, was formed in direct response to the efforts of the DLC to, in Metzenbaum's words, "move the party to the right."[117] Committed to "civil rights, human rights, equal rights, concern for minorities, and the economically distressed," the CDV wanted to demonstrate that "the future of the Democratic Party does not lie in the fine-tuning of Reaganism."[118] In January 1991, the organization held its first meeting, attended by 500 people from twenty-seven states, where, among other issues, they debated the Democrats' position on the Gulf War.[119]

But the battle between New Democrats and liberals did not revolve around these two organizations; rather, it centered on Jackson and the DLC's decision not to invite him to the Cleveland convention. Approximately three weeks before the DLC's gathering, which was to begin on May 5, 1991, the *Chicago Sun-Times* reported that the DLC had invited all potential presidential contenders to speak to its convention except for Jackson and former senator George McGovern of South Dakota. When asked why these two leaders were excluded, From told the *Sun-Times* that "Jackson and McGovern represent the old, big government, taxing, keeping America within its shore, not strong defense [wing of the party]. We want to capture the mantle of reform, and they are not reformers."[120]

The decision of the DLC to snub Jackson—and invite other liberals such as Governor Mario Cuomo of New York—was thus made public. Compounding the issue was the implicit New Democratic belief, later made explicit by comments made by Kiki Moore, the DLC's press secretary, that Jackson was a hindrance to the electoral fortunes of the Democratic Party. Not inviting Jackson may have drawn the line that the DLC desired between it and the liberal wing of the party. But doing so as the Cleveland convention, a gathering designed to highlight the strength of the New Democrats, was approaching created a potentially explosive situation.

In response to the DLC slight, Jackson complained in a letter to Clinton about the "personal, provocative, and unprovoked" attack on him by the DLC staff. He also openly challenged the DLC leadership—such as Clinton, Gore, and Nunn, all presidential hopefuls themselves—to state publicly whether they supported From in his decision to exclude Jackson from the convention.[121] Additionally, Jackson—in public comments made the following week—and his allies in the liberal wing of the party resurrected many of the old criticisms leveled against the DLC. The DNC leadership called the DLC's decision "just wrong" and characterized its reasoning for not inviting Jackson as "lame." Willie Brown, Speaker of the California House, attacked the DLC for trying to make itself into a third party.[122]

But the most potentially devastating charge, once again, was that the DLC had not invited Jackson because it was a racist organization. Jackson implied this when he described the New Democrats as modern "Dixiecrats," who were now "organized up North in the same spirit—the Mason-Dixoncrats." He also attacked black members of the DLC—such as Representatives William Gray III of Pennsylvania, a DLC vice-chairman, and John Lewis of Georgia—saying that the organization has "enough blacks to kind of be used as fig leaves."[123] As From recalled, this last comment was part of the "enormous pressure" that Jackson put on every black in the DLC to boycott the convention and to attack From.[124] Others were more explicit in making the racism charge. The *Boston Globe* quoted one party activist who argued that the DLC did not invite Jackson because its leadership thinks that it is "good politics to fight with civil rights activists." The unnamed activist continued that the New Democratic stance in favor of equal opportunity and opposition to equal outcomes was "at best . . . sound-bite demagoguery. At worst, it is old-style, theoretical racism."[125]

Jackson's public attacks on the DLC began to cause cracks within the organization itself, for he implicitly highlighted the shift the DLC was making from a consensus organization to an advocacy one. In turn, more liberal members of the DLC's Governing Board—notably, Gephardt, Gray, and Representative Barbara Kennelly of Connecticut—began to show signs of being unsettled by the increasing militancy of the DLC. Defending their involvement, these elected officials stressed that they always saw the DLC as a "policy forum" open to all Democrats, not an organization advocating a particular ideology.[126] In particular, Gray began publicly to distance himself from the DLC. He criticized the decision not to invite Jackson, saying that the DLC must include Democrats of all types and beliefs.[127] As one of his former congressional aides explained, the decision to exclude Jackson from the DLC convention led to a "major rift" between the congressman and the organization, since not inviting Jackson "had symbolic value much beyond Jesse Jackson. It had racial overtones; it had overtones about who we want to represent and who we don't want to represent, not just racial[ly], but socioeconomically."[128]

Consequently, Gray responded forcefully to a From memorandum in which the DLC head made his usual charge that people view the Democrats as beholden to special interests, calling it a "Republican charge" that "mouth[s] the right-wing Republican attacks on Democrats."[129] Gray stressed that From did not speak for him on policy or political matters. The week of the Cleveland convention, Gray commented that From's and the DLC's critique of civil rights policy "sounds like David Duke," the former Ku Klux Klan leader who was elected to the Louisiana statehouse in 1989 and was running for that state's governorship in 1991.[130] Finally, Gray called for the resignation of From. As one DLC staff member remembered, From and his senior staff met into the night, and From did consider leaving if people believed that he had hurt the organization.[131]

With the beginning of the Cleveland convention, the controversy only persisted. Ron Brown, the DNC chairman, became incensed with the DLC, threatening to cancel his speech to the organization. Only after lobbying by high-ranking DLC members did Brown agree to go ahead with the address.[132] Gray himself still attended and spoke to the gathering. But in his remarks, he stressed that the Democratic coalition must remain "inclusive," and he flatly rejected the notion that those who want to help the poor or disadvantaged are "somehow the captives of special interests."[133] Also inside the meeting, some delegates challenged core DLC positions on issues such as civil rights and trade, and a handful of black attendees voiced their opposition to the direction in which the DLC was heading, since it seemed—especially in light of the Jackson controversy—to be abandoning the concerns of minority voters.[134]

Jackson too made the trip to Cleveland, but he was there to protest the DLC convention. The civil rights leader, along with George Forbes, the former president of the Cleveland City Council, and Representative Louis Stokes of Ohio, made appearances at a local college, at a high school, and at a picket line of striking workers.[135] Outside the DLC convention itself, union members protested the DLC's position in favor of NAFTA.[136] And in Arkansas, the General Assembly's Black Caucus, the Arkansas Fairness Council, and the state AFL-CIO all expressed their unhappiness with the Cleveland resolutions.[137]

In the weeks following the Cleveland convention, criticism of the DLC itself and of its recently ratified resolutions continued. But in addition to the usual charges of being conservative or racist, DLC opponents took another tack, stepping up their criticisms of the source of the organization's funding and support, charges that fed their belief that the New Democrats were merely "me-too Republicans." When the convention was in its planning stages, Metzenbaum—in whose state it was to be held—told the press that it was "absolutely shocking" that James Biggar, the chief executive officer of Nestles Enterprises and a prominent Ohio Republican, gave the DLC $50,000 to help underwrite the Cleveland convention and served as cochairman of the Cleveland Host Committee.[138] At the time of the gathering, journalists too noted that AT&T, RJR Nabisco, and Philip Morris all were corporate backers of the event and that many of the delegates at the convention—the very people who ratified a new "progressive agenda" for the Democratic Party—were corporate lobbyists.

David Broder described the DLC as "barely reflective of the rich diversity that is the Democratic Party."[139] Jackson's reaction was even stronger. In a column in the *Washington Post*, he wrote that he found the role of Republicans in the DLC's convention "vulgar and insulting."[140] Such corporate backing of the DLC, however, was not a new phenomenon. The organization was always an elite organization funded by elite—corporate and private—donors. And similar funding for, say, a Democratic National Convention would not have been "vulgar and insulting." But in a polarized environment where its rivals saw the DLC as trying to assert itself and its public philosophy within the national Democratic Party, this facet of the organization was particularly objectionable to liberals.

Consequently, the source of the DLC's money led other opponents of the organization to accuse the DLC of being "shadow Republicans" who, in Gray's words, were "adopting rhetoric indistinguishable from platform language at Republican conventions."[141] Perhaps most damaging to the DLC and to Clinton in practical terms was the response of Chris Spirou, chairman of the New Hampshire State Democratic Party. He publicly joined these critics, calling the DLC a bunch of "disgruntled Democrats, [and] self-serving lobbyists who were mainly registered Republicans."[142] His opposition to the formation of a DLC chapter in this key primary state continued until August 4, 1991, when Clinton finally opened a chapter there.

Eventually, the frequency and volume of the attacks on the New Democrats subsided. But the repercussions for the DLC and for its relationship with the party were more lasting. With this increased tension with the national party came an end to any hope the DLC had for a rapprochement with labor, much less a continuation of its cordial if cool relationship with Jackson.[143] Already, Jackson had not invited Clinton to a presidential forum that his National Rainbow Coalition held in June 1991.[144]

More importantly, the DLC's strong policy stands at Cleveland and the Jackson brouhaha affected the makeup of the organization itself. As the crisis unfolded, it became clear to many liberal DLC members that the organization had replaced its big-tent posture with a more adversarial and ideological stance, one that they could not support. Consequently, many elected officials who had joined the DLC because they viewed the organization as a center of new ideas and as a forum for all Democrats either stopped being active or dropped out altogether. This group included Gephardt, Gray, and Kennelly, all members of the DLC Governing Board.[145] In response, after the Cleveland convention, From wrote in a memorandum to Clinton that the DLC should move to make sure that "only true believers are on the letterhead [in key leadership roles]."[146]

Driving this concern was From's desire not to face the recurring story of disenchanted DLC leaders quitting the organization, especially during a presidential campaign.[147] Yet the departure of these elected officials from the organization should not have surprised From. Gephardt had clearly broken from the DLC during his 1988 presidential run, and more recently, he had actually addressed the first meeting of Metzenbaum's CDV.[148] Gray too became an original member of that organization.[149] Liberal elected officials had joined the DLC precisely because it had consciously muted its New Democratic rhetoric. Therefore, when this muzzle was lifted at the Cleveland convention, and when the DLC began to highlight its apparent strength, heighten its rhetoric, and stake out more controversial policy stances, they could no longer stay affiliated with the organization.

In many ways, then, the storm that the Jackson snub sparked was inevitable. Unsurprisingly, after the Cleveland convention, the DLC shifted its emphasis slightly, from garnering large numbers of elected-official members to amassing more lay members. It even dreamed of building a true grassroots organization.[150] But in the end, with its success at Cleveland in promoting its agenda and its chairman, plus the window of opportunity presented by the 1992 election, the DLC instead focused on the next phase of its presidential strategy: helping a New Democrat win the nomination of the party and, beyond that, the presidency.

Although the DLC had already done much to lay the groundwork for a New Democratic presidential run, it was by no means certain that the organization would have a candidate to call its own. On one side, President Bush, enjoying almost mythic popularity after the Gulf War, appeared to be a formidable opponent. On the other, liberals called on any Democratic presidential hopeful to abandon moves to the political center and to be—in Jim Hightower's words—"an unabashed, unapologetic, ungentrified, old-time working people's Democrat."[151] Moreover, although the DLC heightened its critique of the party, developed a New Democratic policy agenda, formed state chapters, and held a national convention, all the organization could really do was either wait for a DLC candidate to emerge or follow the less attractive and less effective strategy of trying to shape the message of some announced candidate who was amenable to the New Democrat program.[152]

Thus Reed advised, in a memorandum written a couple of weeks after the Cleveland convention, that the DLC develop its presidential agenda further and "do our best to look like a national movement with clout."[153] Specifically, Reed suggested that the DLC's recently formed state chapters should "invite candidates to come a' courting" and that whoever the New Democratic candidates may be, they should "use them [the chapters] shamelessly as a forum and a source of troops and money" within the limits of the law.[154]

At the same time, the DLC leadership strongly hoped that Clinton would enter the race and made it clear to him that the organization was laying the groundwork for his, or another DLC member's, candidacy.[155] Accordingly, the DLC continued to support Clinton by helping him develop relationships with the Washington press corps and by continuing to provide him with funding and a reason to travel throughout the country, an opportunity that he did not let go to waste.[156] In the fifty-two-day period following the 1991 legislative session in Arkansas, Clinton was in the state only fourteen days, and the expenses for most of this travel were paid by the DLC.[157] For example, in the first week of August 1991 alone, Clinton took a trip to New Hampshire, where he opened the state's DLC chapter, and to Texas, another key presidential battleground state. As one reporter wrote, these and other similar trips found Clinton "wooing big-money types, impressing political junkies, and attracting photo opportunities."[158]

During this time, other Democrats began to announce their candidacy or, for some, their noncandidacy. By October 1, 1991, former senator Paul Tsongas of Massachusetts, former governor Jerry Brown of California, Senator Tom Harkin of Iowa, and Senator Bob Kerrey of Nebraska had each entered the race. But perhaps more importantly, many frequently mentioned possible entrants had decided not to run, mainly due to the high post–Gulf War popularity of Bush. They included Senator Bill Bradley of New Jersey and Senator John Rockefeller IV of West Virginia, as well as Gephardt and Jackson. Likewise notable for their decision not to run were the DLC favorites, Nunn and Gore. The field was generally wide open for a southerner, or indeed for any candidate with an organization and financial backing. After spending the summer consulting with his closest political confidantes and traveling Arkansas to seek supporters' approval to break his pledge to serve out his term as governor, Clinton announced the formation of a presidential exploratory committee on August 15, 1991.[159] He seemed poised to make the run.

On October 3, 1991, Clinton stepped to a podium in front of the Old State House of Arkansas. Against the backdrop of twelve American flags and the building's four white columns, he announced his candidacy for the Democratic presidential nomination.[160] Speaking from a draft labored on into the early morning hours by a three-person writing team that included the DLC's Reed, Clinton delivered a speech very similar to his keynote address in Cleveland, replete with New Democratic themes and language. Clinton stressed that he was fighting for "the forgotten middle class." He said that he would offer the leadership to "provide more opportunity, insist on more responsibility, and create a greater sense of community for this great country." And taking a line right from the DLC's "New American Choice Resolutions," Clinton said, "the change we must make isn't liberal or conservative. It's both and it's different."[161] From the outset, Clinton framed his run in New Democratic terms. According to the *Arkansas Gazette*, Clinton used the phrase "middle class" thirteen times, "responsibility" twelve times, and "opportunity" ten times.[162] It seemed that the DLC finally had found its standard-bearer.

The candidacy of Bill Clinton marked the end of the initial, crucial phase of the DLC's presidential strategy. In light of its failed efforts to remake the public philosophy of the party, the DLC leadership had given up on working within the national party, shed its big-tent format, and reorganized itself to provide aid for a New Democratic presidential hopeful during the important "invisible primary" stage of the presidential campaign. Thus, by elucidating the problems with the public philosophy of the national party ("The Politics of Evasion"), by establishing the means to develop a New Democratic alternative (PPI), by actually crafting it (the "New Orleans Declaration" and the "New American Choice Resolutions"), by providing an infrastructure in key primary states and a reason to travel to them (the chapters), by giving him a national spotlight (the Cleveland convention), and by giving him entree to elected officials and benefactors (the chairmanship), the DLC helped provide Clinton with crucial ideological and institutional support for a presidential campaign.

Central to this strategy was, of course, the assent of a candidate to carry the New Democratic banner, plus the belief that the presidency was the most effective institutional means by which to reshape the public philosophy of a party. Taking the latter first, the candidate-centered nature of presidential politics and the weakening of party influence during the postreform era had created an enlarged opportunity for the DLC to provide an organization and a message for a potential presidential candidate. At the same time, although this phenomenon had resulted in a relative decrease in a president's direct influence on his party, it had not diminished his indirect influence.[163]

As the most visible representative of the party, a president can shape its image through the bully pulpit of his position and by his own policy agenda. By appealing directly to the public, a president can also build popular support for his proposals and put pressure on other elected officials within the party to go along with them. In turn, success in this endeavor could redefine the meaning of the party label to the electorate and even forge new constituencies to the party's coalition.[164] The DLC leadership hoped that this process, along with the direct control that a presidential nominee and president have over the national party machinery, would yield a changed Democratic Party.

With the candidacy of Clinton, the DLC seemed to have the vehicle to put the heart of its presidential strategy into play. The chairman of the organization, chosen for his political promise, and who undoubtedly had chosen to take the DLC post for what it could do for his national aspirations, had decided to enter the race. The DLC now had a potentially powerful champion of its definition of the country's problems and of its solutions. However, as the 1992 nominating campaign, general election, and Clinton administration unfolded, questions began to be raised about Clinton's commitment to implementing the transformation of the Democratic Party that the DLC desired. Just as the DLC appeared to be on the brink of total victory, doubts surfaced about the commitment of its former chairman to the New Democratic public philosophy, about the overall strategy of the organization, and about the DLC's own relevance to Democratic Party politics.

7 / *Counting on Clinton,*
1992–1994

THE ELECTION of a New Democrat to the presidency was to have been the penultimate step to DLC success. The presidency was the key institution for shaping public debate, and the DLC had its program in waiting. By having one of its own win the presidency and become the titular head of the Democratic Party as well, the organization hoped that it would at last be able to change the public philosophy of its party and, in turn, permanently improve its electoral fortunes. Yet the character of Clinton's victory in November 1992, when joined to the ongoing institutional context of the federal government and to the existing balance of forces within the Democratic Party, would have a strange effect on the Clinton administration's ability to stick to the New Democratic line. During the first two years of the Clinton presidency (the 103rd Congress), unified Democratic control of the executive and legislative branches would combine with the character of the perceived mandates from the 1992 presidential election to produce a situation in which either "Old" (liberal) Democratic policies were emphasized at the expense of New Democratic ones or New Democratic policies were pursued, but only within Old Democratic politics.

Thus, while the DLC initially saw a significant increase in its public profile, in its power within the party, and in the consideration of its ideas, it would ultimately be disappointed by the overall performance of the first two years of the Clinton administration. Moreover, since the election of Clinton resulted in his, not the DLC's, setting the bounds of what a New Democrat was, the DLC leadership actually found itself in a quandary. On the one hand, it had helped elect one of its own to the highest office in the land. On the other hand, Clinton's inability to implement the New Democratic agenda caused many to doubt his commitment to the New Democratic cause as well as the utility of the public philosophy generally. Thus, the DLC often found itself at odds with its most famous member and began to reconsider its own strategies and their ability to change the public philosophy of the Democratic Party.

The 1992 Presidential Nominating Campaign

From the moment Clinton announced his candidacy in August 1991, the DLC had the standard-bearer its presidential strategy demanded and was invested heavily in his progress. The DLC not only provided direct help to his candidacy (e.g., staff members) but also saw its labors during the "invisible primary" phase of the campaign bear fruit. Clinton benefited from the financial and political contacts he had made via the DLC, and he left its chairmanship with a refined political message and policy platform. But the dynamics of the actual race were also a significant input in determining the outcome of the election, an outcome that later shaped Clinton's ability to remake the public philosophy of the Democratic Party in the New Democrats' image.

ELECTORAL PROBLEMS AND ALTERNATIVES

By January 1992, the Democratic field was set, and the competition seemed to favor Clinton. First, no prominent liberal, such as Governor Mario Cuomo of New York, had thrown his hat into the ring. Only Senator Tom Harkin of Iowa—whose ADA rating never fell below ninety during his congressional career—could be considered the standard Democratic candidate who appealed to the liberal Democratic primary electorate.[1] Second, Harkin and all the other announced candidates were considered to be from the second tier of Democratic presidential talent. The only one who had run before was Jerry Brown, the former governor of California, whose quirkiness undermined any attempt to be taken seriously. Third, with Jesse Jackson forgoing the race and Douglas Wilder quickly exiting it, there was neither another southerner nor a black candidate running for the nomination, thus freeing up crucial parts of the electorate for Clinton.[2]

With organization, money, and a clear message, Clinton became the early front-runner in this weak field. Also advantaging the former DLC chairman—Clinton had resigned the post as soon as he announced the formation of his presidential exploratory committee and had passed the gavel to Senator John Breaux—were institutional changes to the nominating process itself. For the 1992 election, thirty-one of the fifty states (plus the District of Columbia) scheduled a primary or caucus in the first two months of the delegate selection process. As with Dukakis's victory in 1988, a front-loaded calendar required a large reserve of political and financial resources, and Clinton—largely thanks to the DLC—had the wherewithal to survive this process.[3]

Due in part to his time as DLC chairman, Clinton had a jump start in the formation of his national organization, along with a network of key political and, most importantly, financial support. As Betsey Wright, a longtime Clinton aide, recalled, the help of the DLC in this regard "cannot be underestimated."[4] Indeed, Clinton received early and often critical aid from his fellow DLC members.[5] Financially, Clinton's key Wall Street support was almost exclusively DLC-based and allied with the Arkansan because of his loyalty to a "politics of free trade, free markets and fiscal discipline advocated by the DLC."[6] And these benefactors repaid his loyalty in turn. On February 10, 1992, as the controversy surrounding accusations that Clinton had had an extramarital affair with Gennifer Flowers reached its height, Goldman Sachs partners Kenneth Brody and Barrie Wigmore, a PPI trustee, held a New York fund-raiser that yielded Clinton $750,000 and a clear sign that his elite support was not eroding.[7]

Politically, Clinton drew on the support of many New Democratic governors, former governors, and other state officials. Of these endorsements, the early aid of Governor Zell Miller of Georgia, along with that of Senator Sam Nunn, was especially important, since Miller pushed his legislature to move the state's primary up to March 3, a position that would give an early boost to Clinton as a southern centrist.[8] In fact, Georgia's primary became one of four contests constituting "Junior Tuesday," held a week before Super Tuesday. This, along with the South Carolina primary held on the Saturday in between the two regional primaries, created a schedule that appeared to favor a southerner, especially one running in a field without a black candidate.[9]

Clinton also received important DLC support on the national level. As of February 28, 1992, he led all rivals in House and Senate endorsements—a surprising statistic, since he had never served in either body—winning the backing of eight senators, all DLC members. In fact, over 70 percent of his congressional endorsements came from

DLC members.[10] And in many cases, this support was more than just lip service. For example, once DLC Vice-Chairman Dave McCurdy announced that he would not seek the party's nomination, the congressman—chairman of the House Intelligence Committee and a member of the military reserve—traveled to thirty-six states over eight months, touting Clinton to defense and veterans groups, constituencies that were suspicious both of the Democratic Party and of candidate Clinton.[11]

This combination of a weak field and a front-loaded process helped propel Clinton to the nomination. During the first few weeks of the nominating campaign, the contests primarily went to candidates from the home region (such as Tsongas in New Hampshire) or to those who represented an unusual concentration of sympathetic voters in a particular state (such as Brown in Maine). Nevertheless, even after revelations about improprieties in his personal life and questions about his draft status during the Vietnam War threatened to doom his candidacy, Clinton was able to place a strong second in the New Hampshire primary and thus remain viable until the nominating contest finally became intense—with a large number of primaries and caucuses held over a short period of time—and moved to Clinton's home turf, the South.

On March 3, Clinton won the Georgia primary; four days later, he won the South Carolina contest; and on March 10, Super Tuesday, Clinton won all the contests except those in Massachusetts and Rhode Island. Notably, he defeated Tsongas—the only credible candidate left in the race—in Florida, thus depriving the former Massachusetts senator of a win outside of his region. Clinton also took a commanding lead in delegate totals. Of the fourteen contests held from March 3 to 17, Clinton—with three times the federal matching funds of Tsongas—won ten of them.[12] Included in these victories were Clinton's wins in Illinois and Michigan on March 17, his first big victories outside of the South.

Two days later, Tsongas suspended his campaign. Except for occasional stumbles, such as a close loss in the popular vote to Brown in Connecticut, Clinton cruised through the rest of the delegate selection process. After his win in the Pennsylvania primary on April 28, Clinton seemed to have a lock on the nomination, and more House and Senate superdelegates began to endorse him. Included among those jumping on the bandwagon were liberal Senators Kennedy and

Metzenbaum.[13] All in all, Super Tuesday, which the DLC had championed vigorously in 1988, had finally lived up to its promise. The regional primary provided Clinton with the momentum needed to win further contests in the North and, eventually, the nomination.[14]

This momentum, plus the lack of a credible liberal challenger, helped Clinton win the nomination with heavy support of core Democratic constituencies, such as blacks and downscale voters (i.e., high school dropouts, high school graduates, and those who earn less than $29,999 a year).[15] But that does not mean that Clinton, the former chairman of an organization that was vilified by Jackson and other black leaders and had been accused of being in the pocket of business interests, had totally won over these groups. In no state was black turnout higher than it had been in 1988 or 1984, when Jackson had been in the race; in some states, it was down by as much as 75 percent from four years earlier.[16] In sum, his organizational strength, a favorable calendar, and a weak field of candidates enabled the Clinton team to attract enough of these important, although diminished, groups to win the nomination.

ISSUE PROBLEMS AND POLICY ALTERNATIVES

Nevertheless, from the beginning, some observers argued that Clinton had won the support of the left-leaning Democratic primary electorate because he was not a New Democrat at all. Sidney Blumenthal of the *New Republic* reported that the Clinton campaign had decided to reject the DLC strategy of a "Southern-based campaign of exclusionary strife that would be openly critical of liberalism within the party."[17] Robert Kuttner, the liberal commentator and longtime DLC critic, argued that Clinton's role in the Cleveland convention had been an aberration from his "traditional posture as a progressive" and that the only remaining connection between the DLC and Clinton was the candidate's distinctive drawl.[18]

Others noted a shift in Clinton's message, commenting that it had a more populist tone.[19] Additionally, some prominent liberals associated with the Clinton campaign, such as New York attorney Harold Ickes, and those who came to support him, such as DNC Chairman Ron Brown, stated that they backed the Arkansas governor precisely because he was not a "DLC candidate."[20] There is some evidence that, initially, the DLC leadership itself sometimes doubted the commitment of its chairman to the organization. In separate memoranda in February and March 1991, From queried Clinton as to the strength of his commitment to the DLC and complained about access to, and attention from, the Arkansas governor.[21]

However, this criticism ended quickly, so that it could be explained as nothing more than a clash of working styles or a mismatch in expectations between From and Clinton. Considering his long-standing involvement in the organization, the public stances he took supporting the DLC and its program, and the criticism he received for both, it would be wrong to assume that Clinton was uncommitted to the DLC or its program.[22] Nevertheless, it would also be incorrect to assume that Clinton would sacrifice victory for an ideological stand.

In this light, the primary field shaped the Clinton message. As Bruce Reed—who joined the Clinton campaign as its policy director—explained, the lack of a strong liberal challenger, the strength of the primary campaign of Tsongas, and the entry of H. Ross Perot, the independent, meant that there was not much room in the political center for Clinton. Therefore, the Clinton primary campaign was not "spending as much time competing for votes in the middle as we would have otherwise."[23]

Specifically, with Tsongas winning upscale voters centered in the suburbs and around academic centers, Clinton had an opportunity to win everyone who was not as rich or as socially liberal. Consequently, he stressed the more populist elements of his proposals, such as a middle-class tax cut, and criticized the corporate excesses of the 1980s, such as the savings-and-loan scandal. Still, the populist rhetoric of Clinton did not focus on the problems of the poorest Americans, but rather was geared consciously to the middle.

"What I am trying to be is a middle-class moderate offering radical change," Clinton explained while campaigning at a New Hampshire diner in December 1991.[24] Thus, when he attacked the rich on the campaign trail, he did so not on behalf of the poor but on behalf of the middle class. And what he offered the middle class was not a new entitlement but a tax cut and aid tied to reciprocal obligations. Moreover, his "populism" translated itself into mainstream views on cultural and national concerns, stances firmly in line with New Democratic thinking.

All in all, the dynamics and structure of the nominating campaign played a large role in Clinton's nomination, and in the pursuit of victory, the Clinton team needed to change tack in order to win. But Clinton's bid for the Democratic nomination was fundamentally a New Democratic one. In three speeches at Georgetown University, his alma mater, in the fall of 1991, Clinton outlined his policy positions and vision for the country. Heavily influenced by Galston and written by Reed, these addresses were unmistakably New Democratic.[25]

In his first speech, Clinton embraced the New Democratic public philosophy, stressing the familiar themes of opportunity, responsibility, and community. In this, Clinton criticized the Democratic Party's traditional "tax and spend" economic policies and called for the restructuring of welfare so that it would become a "second chance, not a way of life."[26] Reflecting the New Democratic theory of governance, he cast himself as an adversary of bureaucracy and big government, as well as an opponent to the special interests that seemed to have excessive influence in Washington.[27] Additionally, Clinton called for a new relationship between government and citizens, a "New Covenant" that would "honor middle-class values, restore the public trust, create a new sense of community, and make America work again."[28]

In the two subsequent addresses, Clinton laid out specific policies needed to achieve this goal. On economic matters, he proposed a middle-class tax cut, a national service program, a policy to require companies to provide worker retraining, tax incentives for a wide range of investments in new businesses and research-and-development efforts, and private-public partnerships with low-income entrepreneurs. In essence, Clinton proposed that the government cooperate with the private sector, expand economic opportunity, and invest in the future—values and policies contained in the DLC's "New American Choice Resolutions."

In the area of foreign policy, an issue context that was neither his policy strength nor his intellectual interest, Clinton mainly hoped that his stances would inoculate him against GOP attacks for being weak on defense. To this end, he outlined policies found in the DLC canon. Although the Arkansan recognized that the end of the Cold War necessitated some military cuts, he clearly did not follow the post-1968 liberal line of neoisolationism, of deep cuts in the military budget, and of a unilateral nuclear disarmament.[29] In fact, unlike a majority of Democratic officials, he had supported the use of force in the Persian Gulf.

Clinton also took positions to blunt traditional Republican attacks against Democrats in the area of social issues. For example, he supported the death penalty and dramatized his position by interrupting his campaigning to sign a death warrant in Arkansas. He also took a strong stance on crime, projecting a "law-and-order" image by proposing the use of military-style boot camps for first-time offenders. On other issues, Clinton supported the traditional stances of the party—he was pro-choice and for strong protection of the environment—but as with the DLC generally, these were not the focus of his campaign.[30]

By embracing their values, offering them aid in the form of a tax cut, increasing funding for attending college, and advocating a tough policy on crime, Clinton hoped to win over the voters of Middle America.[31] In all of this, Clinton ran as a New Democrat. That may or may not have been why he won; indeed, he might have won in spite of that fact. Nevertheless, his nomination seemed an enormous victory for the DLC. What remained to be seen was whether this win would translate into a transformation of the Democratic Party.

INSTITUTIONAL PROBLEMS AND ALTERNATIVES

When Clinton clinched the delegates needed for nomination in the spring of 1992, it seemed improbable that he would be able to unite the party and lead it to victory in the fall. Citing the weak field of candidates, the low voter turnout during the primaries, and the various personal problems that had come to light, many within the party questioned the strength and viability of his candidacy.[32] With some polls actually showing him running behind Perot, some prominent Democrats hoped that the convention could be brokered and an alternative nominee found.[33] Overall, the Democratic Party appeared no more unified than it had been immediately after the Cleveland convention the year before.

Within this environment, the DLC leadership made a concerted effort, especially before Clinton's victory was in hand, to have a strong presence at the nominating convention and to have control of the two main committees, Platform and Rules.[34] In the end, for the first time in its history of battling over the party platform and rules, the DLC got all that it wanted—without a shot being fired. The Democratic convention was united, and the platform was a New Democratic one. In the eyes of the press, the nominating convention was seen as a "triumph" and a "stunning victory" for the DLC.[35] Ironically, the person behind these developments was neither From nor Clinton, but DNC Chairman Brown.

Despite never liking From—or, for that matter, Clinton—Brown was determined that the Democrats would win the presidency in 1992.[36] That meant unifying the party if not in reality then at least in front of the American people watching the convention on television. He wanted to avoid the public horse trading over platform planks, rules changes, and even speaking slots that had plagued coverage of the 1984 and 1988 nominating conventions. Thus, once it was clear that Clinton would win the party's nomination, he asked party leaders to rally around Clinton and took steps to ensure that the convention would be the nominee's.[37] In planning the convention, for example, Brown believed that only those who had supported Clinton should be allowed to speak at the gathering. Equally important, the DNC chairman ensured that the Platform Committee and its resulting product would "reflect the positions of the party's nominee, Bill Clinton, which were essentially the positions staked out by the DLC."[38]

First, Brown appointed Governor Roy Romer of Colorado and Representative Mary Rose Oakar of Ohio, recognized as party centrists, to be cochairs of the Platform Committee, and he named Representative Bill Richardson of New Mexico, a DLC member, as chairman of the Drafting Committee, which would produce the document from which the larger committee would work.[39] Second, Brown made these choices early in the campaign season, appointing the rest of the Platform Committee in June 1992 to ensure that the members reflected the nominee's beliefs. To that end, Brown permitted Clinton's staff to dictate roughly half the members of the committee, while the remaining spots went to placate groups that were important to the party but not necessarily in the Clinton camp.[40] At the staff level, John Holum, a Clinton friend, served as the executive director of the Drafting Committee; Reed, Marshall, and Jeremy Rosner (a PPI vice-president) worked on the platform; and From took the role of being Clinton's personal representative to the committee.[41]

At the Drafting Committee's meeting on June 12 and 13 in Santa Fe, New Mexico, far from the media spotlight, the Clinton team controlled the process. No amendments were even offered.[42] At the full committee hearing at the end of June, Clinton delegates possessed—as Brown had intended—a clear majority. Under the floor leadership of Jim Brady, head of the Louisiana State Democratic Party and a DLC member, the Clinton delegation passed the platform along to the convention virtually untouched.[43] Mary Frances Berry, a liberal Democrat and civil rights activist who sat on the Drafting and Platform Committees, recalled that the platform meetings were "scripted" and "planned." In the interest of projecting a favorable image and winning in November, almost all the committee members agreed beforehand not to challenge seriously the New Democratic platform.[44]

Despite some minor changes during the actual drafting process that Berry and others were able to push through, the platform was not significantly altered, and it passed unamended at the full convention.[45] In the end, the document embodied the language and policies of the Clinton campaign and, by extension, of the DLC. It was noticeably more centrist than ever before and was tailored to win back voters who had deserted the Democratic Party in national elections.[46] In addition, it borrowed more from the DLC's "New American Choice Resolutions" than it did from the 1988 Democratic platform.[47] According to the calculations of political scientist Jon Hale, of the fifty-one specific agenda subheadings, thirty-seven were in agreement with the "New American Choice Resolutions," and none were in disagreement; of this second group, none were not in accordance with the New Democratic outlook.[48] The *New York Times* noted the change this way: "The party platform . . . has whole sections that would have been hooted down not too many years ago."[49]

To a New Democratic platform, Clinton added a New Democratic vice-president, Senator Al Gore. This decision not only reinforced Clinton's youth and the aura of "change" around his candidacy but also buttressed the weaknesses of the nominee. Gore was a Vietnam War veteran, a specialist on environmental and defense issues, and a member of the Washington establishment. Also, Gore reinforced the New Democratic message that Clinton hoped to send to the electorate. "By choosing Gore as his running-mate in 1992," wrote Louis Menand in a *New Yorker* profile on the Tennessean, "Clinton was casting himself off from the party of George McGovern, Walter Mondale, and Mario Cuomo."[50] On the day that Clinton accepted the Democratic nomination, Perot—citing this "revitalized" Democratic Party—withdrew from the race. As the Democrats left New York, Clinton enjoyed a large postconvention bounce in the polls. It appeared that the New Democrats' time had come.

The Election of 1992

Pundits and scholars alike have summed up the 1992 election by referring to a sign that hung in the "War Room" of the Clinton campaign headquarters in Little Rock, Arkansas: "It's the economy, stupid."[51] In many ways, this simple phrase encapsulates the strategy and the dynamics of the 1992 race. Yet like any slogan, its simplicity impoverishes analysis. The weak state of the economy heading into the 1992 election provided an amenable political environment for the Democratic challenger and helped him achieve victory. Yet Bill Clinton would not have been able to win the election if he had not run as a New Democrat, addressing the problem of cultural breakdown, the perceived practical failures of government, and public doubts about the welfare state.[52] At the very least, these positions removed impediments to Clinton's capitalizing on a sour economy.

At the same time, although he ran on a New Democratic platform and employed a New Democratic electoral strategy, Clinton did not have a mandate for the implementation of New Democratic policies. Indeed, the unique circumstances of the 1992 election—the lack of a strong liberal challenger in the primaries, plus the presence of a significant independent candidate in the general election—kept Clinton from being able to claim an electoral mandate for New Democratic policies. Nor did they create a situation that would have compelled him to do so. Furthermore, the nature of Clinton's win actually facilitated differing interpretations of it, along with a debate on the suitable agenda to follow for continued electoral success. In sum, the nature of the 1992 election, along with disagreements about its meaning, profoundly affected the fortunes of the Clinton presidency.

ELECTORAL PROBLEMS AND ALTERNATIVES

Although aided by a well-run and well-financed campaign organization, the fortunes of the Democratic ticket were tied to the state of the economy and the strength of the New Democratic alternative to the Republican agenda. By August 17, according to a *Washington Post* poll, this combination had left President Bush with the lowest job approval rating of any president at a similar point in his presidency and the highest disapproval rating of any incumbent president seeking reelection.[53]

Accordingly, Bush's opponents certainly did not allow the state of the economy to disappear as an issue. The Clinton campaign worked to make the election a referendum precisely on Bush's stewardship of the economy. When Ross Perot reentered the race as an independent in the fall, he too focused on this issue, especially the massive budget deficit.[54] But again, Clinton's strategy was more than just hammering on the Bush administration's economic performance. Where and how he targeted his message were different from past, unsuccessful Democratic bids. Taking a page from the New Democratic playbook, Clinton did not focus his efforts on securing the traditional Democratic base. Instead, he decided to reach out for new voters in the suburbs, among Reagan Democrats, and among independents.

The first indication of this approach was in his selection of a running mate who did not balance the Democratic ticket by appealing to core Democratic constituencies, but rather reinforced Clinton's New Democratic image.[55] Beyond that, the Clinton campaign consciously courted these voters by employing New Democratic rhetoric and themes. "They're a new generation of Democrats . . . and they don't think the way the old Democratic Party did," one television advertisement proclaimed. The ad continued that a Clinton administration would work to "end welfare as we know it" and make it "a second chance, not a way of life."[56] Such a message was used, as the DLC had planned, to blunt any counterattacks that the Democratic standard-bearer was a "tax-and-spend liberal" out of touch with the middle class.[57]

On election day, it seemed that this Democratic strategy had worked. Clinton won 43 percent of the popular vote and thirty-two states (including the District of Columbia), for a total of 370 electoral votes. Bush won 37 percent of the vote and eighteen states, for a total of 168 electoral votes. Perot won 19 percent of the vote and no electors. Voters clearly had repudiated Bush: he garnered 9.5 million fewer votes than in his victory in 1988, a drop twice as large as the differential between Jimmy Carter's two elections in 1976 and 1980.[58] However, with the presence of Perot—who garnered the largest aggregate vote of any independent candidate for president in U.S. history—on the ballot, it was not obvious that voters had endorsed Clinton.[59]

In addition, the results of the subpresidential contests offered contradictory results. In line with their decades-long pattern of dominance, the Democrats retained control of both houses of Congress and picked up two more governorships.[60] Yet 1992 was not an unqualified success. The Republicans simultaneously gained nine seats in the House of Representatives, pushing the aggregate Democratic vote in the House to 50.8 percent, its lowest since 1980.[61] As Clinton took office, then, the Democratic Party had 258 members of the House, its smallest delegation since 1944.[62]

Further muddying the message of these results was that there were no great changes in partisan attachments among the electorate, the clearest sign of a critical election and the dawning of a new political era. Yet that should have been expected. The New Democrats were consciously attempting to change the public philosophy and, by extension, the electoral coalition of the Democratic Party, without a precipitating crisis and an immediate realignment. Thus, changes in the party's electoral base would be incremental, and the results of the 1992 election seem to have followed this model.

The Clinton-Gore team made gains (or at least benefited from Republican losses) among key demographic groups that had not backed the Democratic ticket in the recent past and that its strategists—and the DLC—had targeted. For the first time since 1964, the Democratic ticket won a 1 percent plurality of white voters and a plurality of independent voters (39 percent), with support for the GOP among this latter group dropping twenty-four percentage points from four years earlier. Likewise, Clinton won a plurality of the male vote, and among self-described moderates—a group that constituted 50 percent of voters in 1992—the Democrat won 49 percent of the vote. In comparison, Bush garnered just 30 percent of moderates' support, a twenty-five-point drop from his take in 1988.[63] Geographically, in thirty states, Clinton garnered more votes than Dukakis had—even though there was a three-way race. Underlying these impressive results in previously unfriendly territory were the ticket's major inroads in the South and the suburbs, two key components of any successful Republican coalition.[64] In fact, Clinton equaled Dukakis's 44 percent of the suburban vote, but again, in a three-way contest.[65]

However, in the ninety-eight congressional districts where Clinton won an outright majority of the votes, core Democratic groups—minorities, liberals, and the elderly—predominated.[66] All in all, the evidence here had contradictory implications. It confirmed that Clinton had not aggressively courted these blocs of voters and, in consequence, had received commensurably less support from them as a share of his overall total. Indeed, black turnout was down considerably, constituting 2.5 percent less of the total electorate, and of the ten states that Dukakis had carried in 1988, Clinton won them all with fewer votes, even though 10 million more people voted nationwide.[67] Yet these constituencies were also still his bedrock base. The core of the old Democratic coalition had not been replaced. The results of the election, then, did not offer a clear verdict on its meaning. It was possible for anyone to see in them what he or she wanted.

ISSUE PROBLEMS AND POLICY ALTERNATIVES

Immediately after the election, different partisans and analysts weighed in with their thoughts on the key policy positions that had led to Clinton's victory. Some argued that the centrism of Clinton and of the DLC was crucial to his victory.[68] According to this view, Clinton was thus able to "neutralize the Republicans' ideological advantage" and to demonstrate to voters that he could work within the "Reagan-Bush consensus—less government, lower taxes, traditional values," with which a majority of the electorate agreed.[69] Other analysts made the Democratic strategy—New, Old, or neither—nearly irrelevant, stressing that the Democrats had benefited from a "Republican collapse" precipitated by an economic recession.[70] And liberals continued to claim that their agenda and the constituencies wedded to it had produced the Clinton victory.[71]

Although Clinton did keep traditional liberal commitments to, for example, abortion rights and did exhibit a populist strain not clearly evident in the DLC literature, he most assuredly ran in the general election as a New Democrat. Indeed, *Putting People First*, the campaign manifesto published by the Clinton-Gore team, stressed the values of opportunity, responsibility, and community as well as the anti-statist, free-market tendencies of the DLC, and it endorsed many of the suggested programs that emanated from the organization and its think tank. The campaign thus took stances, such as favoring free trade and opposing racial quotas, that were at odds with many in the Democratic Party.[72] And at times, Clinton took highly public steps to distance himself from the liberal image of the national Democratic Party. In a television advertisement during the New Hampshire primary, he attacked members of Congress for voting themselves a pay raise. Later in the year, he repeated his support for NAFTA before the United Auto Workers' convention in San Diego. Also, at a meeting of

Jesse Jackson's Rainbow Coalition in June 1992, Clinton publicly criticized the provocative statements of one of the previous speakers, the
rap music singer Sister Souljah.[73]

As the DLC had hoped, these more mainstream stances were able
to neutralize the advantage that the GOP traditionally held on many
issues. Over half of all voters wanted less government and lower taxes,
and of this group—one that might be expected to back a Republican
overwhelmingly—35 percent voted for Clinton and only 43 percent
backed Bush. Similarly, over two-thirds of the electorate wanted the
government to "encourage traditional family values," and of this
group, 37 percent backed Clinton and 42 percent voted for Bush.[74]

Clinton was aided by three additional dynamics. First, the economy was the most salient issue for voters, and 96 percent of the electorate believed that the economic policies of the federal government
over the past four years had made no difference in the state of the
economy or had made the economy worse, a searing indictment of the
Republican administration.[75] Second, foreign policy concerns—an issue
cluster that also favored the Republicans—"played the smallest role
in any American presidential election since 1936," as only 8 percent
of voters said that it was the most important issue in the election.[76]
Third, voters clamored for "change." Nearly 40 percent of those who
voted said that the quality that mattered most in deciding which candidate to support was the ability to "bring about needed change"; of
this group, 59 percent backed Clinton.[77] For the Republicans who had
been in the White House for twelve years, the national mood was not
running in their favor.

The results, nonetheless, remained mixed and internally contradictory. Despite the success of the presidential ticket and the return
of a united government under the control of the Democratic Party, the
party's overall coalition had not been automatically rebuilt or even
united. In turn, the nature of the 1992 election, especially the strong
showing of an independent contender for the presidency, hurt Clinton's ability to claim an electoral mandate for the New Democratic
public philosophy and to unite his party behind it.

INSTITUTIONAL PROBLEMS AND ALTERNATIVES

The presence of the most successful independent candidate for president made the 1992 election unlike any other up to that point. The

Perot campaign affected relatively stable postreform trends as voter turnout increased, the influence of voters' party identification decreased, and faith in the federal government eroded further.[78] Perhaps more importantly, though, the Perot candidacy also constrained the scope of the Democrats' victory. Bush lost, but the 1992 election was not a wholesale show of support for the Democrats.

Clinton won only a plurality of the total vote. Although the Democratic ticket enjoyed renewed success among certain groups, this did not mean that there was an electoral realignment or the construction of a New Democratic coalition.[79] Instead, this shift could have been "based on discontent with existing conditions and uncertain expectations for the future."[80] Or as Everett Carll Ladd described it, the 1992 contest could have been a "deviating" election in which short-term forces—not significant systemic trends—propelled Clinton to victory.[81]

Uniting the cohorts that did support the Democratic ticket around a new public philosophy, then, would prove difficult for any leader, but perhaps especially for Clinton, whom many party activists viewed as a factional leader of dubious character. Moreover, not only did Clinton lack the political capital of an overwhelming victory, but he also had run on a New Democratic platform—a policy agenda and political outlook not yet shared by the party's activist elite. Compare the delegates who gathered in New York to nominate Clinton and the voters they represented. Fifty-seven percent of the delegates identified themselves as liberals, and just 2.5 percent said they were conservatives. By comparison, only 36 percent of Democratic Party identifiers called themselves liberal, and 26.5 percent said they were conservatives.[82] This gap between rank and file and elites was also significant on the key issues of the day, such as the government's role in the economy, abortion rights, affirmative action, and defense spending.[83] If the voting coalition behind Clinton might be difficult to unite in a governing coalition, this elite-mass division threatened even greater problems.

More immediately, the pressing problem was Clinton's rocky relationship with the Democratic leadership in Congress. He had never served in that body, and he often had not bothered to distinguish between Bush and Congress when attacking Washington on the campaign trail.[84] After the election, however, many Democrats interpreted the return of unified Democratic control of government and the resonance of Perot's anti-Washington message as a sign that voters wanted an end to legislative gridlock. Clinton and the congressional Democrats appeared to have no choice. They had to cooperate.

All in all, as Clinton prepared to take office, major rifts still existed within the Democratic Party. Despite his ability to win the election as a New Democrat and to bring unified Democratic government, these achievements did not necessarily mean that Clinton would be able to bridge these other gaps and govern effectively as a New Democrat.[85] Neither the institutional arrangements nor the distribution of power within the national party had fundamentally changed: it was still dominated by the liberal faction. During the campaign, lacking an alternative, this group had supported Clinton and his New Democratic platform and strategy. Now that the White House was in hand, however, liberals wanted their just desserts.[86]

Unified Government

An interconnectedness among the electoral, ideological, and institutional spheres of politics was clear during the first two years of the Clinton presidency, but of a perverse sort. A New Democrat had been elected president, yet the nature of his victory, plus the institutional and partisan context it created, affected his ability to take the political steps necessary to change the public philosophy of the Democratic Party. In a sense, unified party control of the executive and legislative branches actually impeded Clinton in pursuing the policies and employing the rhetoric to form a lasting New Democratic coalition.

Unified party control created a situation in which, to enact legislation, the Clinton administration sometimes needed to emphasize Old Democratic policies over New Democratic alternatives; at other times, it needed to propose New Democratic programs but pursue them with Old Democratic politics and symbolism. In these instances, Clinton would win the policy battle but lose the political war. And for the DLC and the New Democrats, these defeats had significant repercussions.

Inevitably, once Clinton was inaugurated, he—not the DLC—defined what it meant to be a New Democrat. Consequently, critics began to wonder not only whether Clinton was a committed New Democrat, as once defined by the DLC, but also whether the New Democratic public philosophy was anything more substantial than political posturing. Unsurprisingly, during the first two years of the Clinton administration, the DLC increasingly found itself at odds with Clinton, its former chairman, and lacking a clear sense of its own role and mission. By the end of this period, there seemed very little that was sweet in what the DLC had viewed as its greatest victory.

ELECTORAL PROBLEMS AND ALTERNATIVES

Although its former chairman had won the presidency and stood as the titular head of the Democratic Party, the DLC still perceived immediate electoral challenges. Clinton had not been elected in a realigning election, and his plurality victory had not yielded a New Democratic electoral coalition of any lasting sort. Therefore, the DLC sought to outline a strategy for Clinton to construct such a coalition once he was elected, to create an electoral realignment after the fact.

To "provide a road map to realignment," the organization enlisted the services of Stanley Greenberg, Clinton's pollster in the 1992 race, to conduct a study of Perot voters, the group in the electorate that the DLC believed ripe for Democratic picking.[87] Recalling the prescriptions that Kevin Phillips had offered to Richard Nixon for forming a new Republican majority after the 1968 election, From and Marshall wanted Greenberg to help clarify the muddled mandate of 1992 so that the DLC could make the case to Clinton for using his policy agenda to "realign American politics around a new Democratic governing majority."[88]

To attract Perot voters and accomplish this ex post facto realignment, Clinton had to adhere to the New Democratic agenda, exercise fiscal discipline, embrace mainstream middle-class values, and take a more adversarial stance toward Congress—the one institution that this cohort particularly reviled.[89] Most importantly, Clinton had to follow through on his plans to reform and reinvent government, since this was (in Greenberg's analysis) "virtually a pre-requisite for reassuring and reaching the Perot bloc." Additionally, the Democrats had to address the prevailing sentiment among Perot voters that "hard work goes unrewarded" by reflecting middle-class values in policies such as welfare reform.[90] Of course, liberals disagreed with this advice, arguing either that a new government entitlement was needed to win the political support of the middle class or that accommodating these voters was not necessary at all.

Giving this project particular urgency was a significant drop in Clinton's popularity during his first six months in office, one that the DLC believed was tied to his straying from the New Democratic program. This belief that Clinton was abandoning the New Democratic public philosophy not only heightened the importance of the Perot voter study but also drove the contours of the DLC-Clinton relationship during the first two years of his presidency. Indeed, it was clear even six months into his first term—and more so after two years—that Clinton had strayed from the DLC playbook.

ISSUE PROBLEMS AND POLICY ALTERNATIVES

As the first Democratic president in twelve years prepared to take the oath of office, Democratic policy entrepreneurs faced a uniquely ripe opportunity to place their ideas and policies onto the national agenda. Yet no group, organized or not, was in as privileged a position as the DLC. As the transition began, then, the eyes of political elites turned to the DLC to try to divine what the coming administration would do. With this enlarged audience, the DLC took a page from the conservative Heritage Foundation, which had published *Mandate for Leadership* in 1980 to serve as a guidebook for the incoming Reagan administration, and released *Mandate for Change* in December 1992, a detailed exposition of New Democratic beliefs and programs.[91]

Although the book included sections on federalism and reinventing government that represented the organization's strongest stances on the subject to date, it did not differ considerably from previous New Democratic documents. But *Mandate for Change* garnered a much wider and larger audience than had earlier DLC publications. By July 1993, 137,000 copies of the book were in print.[92] Yet this wide circulation and praise did not mean that the New Democratic agenda would be accepted comprehensively by the Clinton administration. Indeed, as an examination of Clinton's policy stances plus the strategy of policy implementation used during the first two years of his presidency shows, the New Democrats' standard-bearer did not govern as the DLC had hoped a New Democrat would.

That is not to say that the DLC was unable to point to the enactment of some policies that were closely associated with the organization, such as an increase in the earned income tax credit, a national service program, the reinventing government initiative, a tough crime bill, and NAFTA. However, with the exception of NAFTA, which was already in the policy pipeline and came naturally to the front of the policy agenda, none of these New Democratic policies was effectively made a priority on the president's agenda or in his political message.[93]

In this sense, the Clinton administration did not govern by the dictates of the New Democratic public philosophy, since it neither introduced nor explained these initiatives within a New Democratic context. Said differently, by either not highlighting these efforts or not explaining these proposals with the language of the New Democratic public philosophy, Clinton enabled the issue stances of liberal Democrats to dominate and to define him and his presidency during this period. For instance, central to the New Democrats' approach to politics (and presumably to governing) was not that the Democratic Party should abandon its traditional liberal stands on social issues but that they should be moved out of the policy spotlight. Consequently, the DLC, the Clinton campaign, and the 1992 Democratic Party platform did not make these issues their primary focus.

Yet from the first day of the Clinton administration, the president took steps that forced contentious social issues, along with the Democrats' relatively unpopular stances on them, to the fore. His first day on the job, Clinton signed a group of executive orders that lifted restrictions on the federal government regarding the funding, access, and provision of abortion.[94] Later in that same first week in office, Clinton announced that he was going to begin the process of ending the ban on homosexuals serving in the armed forces.

This decision provoked a storm of controversy and, along with the executive orders on abortion and the overt earmarking of cabinet positions for members of specified minority groups, sent the message—by the end of its first month—that social liberalism was central to the governing philosophy of the Clinton administration. This, in turn, could only be expected to irritate the middle-class voters whom he had sought in the 1992 campaign and whom the DLC had courted to forge into a lasting electoral coalition.

One internal poll showed Clinton's popularity dropping twenty points for emphasizing the issue of gays in the military.[95] By the end of the first month of the Clinton administration, it was possible to make the argument that Clinton had restored "the centrality of cultural and social issues" to American politics and was, in truth, an "old Democrat."[96] Soon thereafter, in the spring of 1993, Breaux felt it necessary to meet with Clinton to discuss refocusing his agenda away from "lifestyle and entitlement liberalism" and back toward New Democratic policies.[97]

The nomination of Lani Guinier, a professor of law at the University of Pennsylvania and a civil rights activist, to the post of assistant attorney general for civil rights a few months later only served to bolster this perception of Clinton. Taking into account her views on race in America generally and on guaranteeing minority representation within legislative bodies specifically, both Republicans and the DLC strongly opposed her nomination.[98] Although Clinton eventually withdrew the nomination, the intervening brouhaha over Guinier's views and Clinton's tacit support of them continued to send an Old Democratic, culturally liberal message to the public.

Taken individually and done after his New Democratic credentials had been established, these moves might not have generated as much political heat or inflicted as much damage to Clinton's standing. Yet this combination of early priorities and highly charged symbols painted Clinton in liberal hues and undermined his claim to be a New Democrat. As a result, it became easier for Republicans to portray any of Clinton's initiatives as traditional Democratic policies.

Consider, for example, Clinton's first budget proposal, the crucial initial look at the supposedly new approach to economic policy by Clinton and the Democratic Party. Committed to economic growth, long-term infrastructure investment, deficit reduction, and a middle-class tax cut, the budget plan of candidate Clinton was overall a New Democratic one. In truth, he also advocated an economic stimulus plan to jump-start the economy, a policy dear to Democratic liberals. Yet changing economic numbers, the strong showing of Perot, and the presence of a large cohort of northern Democratic freshmen who had campaigned on deficit reduction forced Clinton to make deficit reduction a priority over an economic stimulus plan.[99] When faced with this situation, however, Clinton dropped his proposal for a middle-class tax cut—a policy that had "anchored his centrist image" during the nominating process—but still introduced an economic stimulus plan, albeit a smaller one.[100]

Without an electoral mandate and with dropping popularity, Clinton could not stop Republicans from opting out of the budgetary process altogether and attacking the plan as "tax-and-spend liberalism." The dynamics were inescapable: Clinton had to rely exclusively on Democrats to pass his budget. In trying to woo this internal party coalition, the Clinton White House did, at times, bungle the process. At other times, in order to win votes within his own party, it engaged in very public horse trading, trying to appease the Left's call for more spending and fewer cuts to social programs and the New Democrats' demands for no tax increases and more spending cuts to reduce the deficit further.[101]

In the process, the New Democratic message got lost. The Democrats appeared fractious, driven by their interest-group liberalism. And the public saw Republicans (and some Democrats) berate the president for increasing taxes and not cutting the deficit enough. In the end, the reconciliation bill passed by a narrow margin in the House (one vote) and in the Senate (a vice-presidential tiebreaker). Neither liberals nor New Democrats, however, were pleased with the plan. Some of the latter, such as Nunn and McCurdy, did not even vote for the budget; others in the House were angry that they had to support controversial tax and spending increases that were later excised in the Senate, and that they had to vote for a stimulus bill that was unpopular in their districts and was later abandoned.

Liberals too felt that Clinton had betrayed their cause. They argued that the president should have pursued more public-sector investment to jump-start the economy, larger cuts to defense spending, and a nationally coordinated industrial policy.[102] Although New Democratic programs may have made it into the final product—and although the bill, in hindsight, did much to reduce the deficit—the drawn-out process of trying to forge a Democratic majority, occurring against the backdrop of contentious social policies, did not lend any credibility to the claim that Clinton, or his budget, reflected New Democratic beliefs.

This phenomenon was also evident with regard to the centerpiece of Clinton's first two years in office: health-care reform. By pursuing a reform of the health-care system before a reform of welfare, Clinton missed an opportunity to burnish his New Democratic credentials at a time when it was not clear that he had ever been a genuine New Democrat. Welfare reform—and the theory of governance that undergirded it—was, quite simply, the most significant policy innovation that differentiated Clinton from liberal Democrats. And the Clinton-Gore team had used the promise that it would "end welfare as we know it" to establish its New Democratic credentials and thus appeal to middle-class voters.

Health-care reform was not ignored by New Democrats, but the issue had been a central concern of liberals in the national party (it had "belonged" to them) for over two decades. Due to the size of the two proposals, it was understood by both sides that the initiatives on health-care and welfare reform were too large for Congress (and the relevant committees) to consider simultaneously. Therefore, priorities had to be set. New Democrats wanted the president to pursue welfare reform first, to prove that he was one of them. Liberals, especially congressional Democrats, argued that it would be impossible to pass welfare reform—of which they were particularly leery—before first enacting health-care reform.[103]

Not wanting to anger the forces on Capitol Hill that would shepherd his legislation through, Clinton decided to pursue health care first. Taken on top of the gays-in-the-military decision, the Guinier brouhaha, and the budget deal, the health-care proposal—regardless of its inherent qualities—was increasingly susceptible to portrayal by Republican opponents as another liberal Democratic program. Moreover, neither the process nor the presentation of the plan was helpful in this respect.

Developed in secret with hundreds of advisers led by First Lady Hillary Rodham Clinton, the Clinton health-care plan was unveiled in a presidential address to both houses of Congress on September 22, 1993. Based on the principles of "security, simplicity, savings, choice, quality, and responsibility," the 1,350-page Health Security Act proposed to provide health-care coverage for all Americans, without compromising on quality, through the use of employer mandates and government-run health alliances that would offer a choice of benefit packages.[104] This plan was not the nationalized Canadian-style health-care system that liberals had advocated in the past, yet the GOP and its affiliated interest groups attacked the proposal as a byzantine, complicated bureaucracy that would place a large and important sector of the economy under government control.

Simultaneously, Clinton managed to please neither camp in the Democratic Party. Liberals, in particular, argued that the plan placed too much faith in the market. By contrast, New Democrats warned that it was too statist and dependent on new bureaucracies. In fact, the DLC publicly opposed the Clinton proposal, especially its mandated price caps and fixed payroll premiums, along with what the organization saw as the political rationale underlying it: namely, that the administration had to provide a large new entitlement to the middle class in order to win its electoral support. Instead, the DLC supported the plan proposed by two of its members—Representative Jim Cooper of Tennessee and Breaux—which did not guarantee universal coverage but, to the New Democrats, was "the least intrusive and most cost-effective path to that goal."[105]

As the debate over health-care reform increased in intensity and began to overwhelm the administration, many New Democrats began to revisit the argument over Clinton's decision to pursue health-care reform over welfare reform. The DLC believed that the eventual choice, plus tackling contentious social issues so early in his tenure, not only showed "questionable strategic judgment" but also "blurred the president's new Democrat image."[106] As William Blount, chairman of the Alabama State Democratic Party, described the situation, in a state filled with voters that the New Democrats desired, "the only message people hear is that he's (Clinton) trying to raise taxes and not cut spending, and put gays in the military."[107]

All in all, as Joel Aberbach, the UCLA political scientist, put it, "the public saw numerous examples of an administration that seemed to stray from the New Democrat themes that dominated much of Clinton's campaign rhetoric."[108] Consequently, by June 1993, a *Los Angeles Times* poll found that only 37 percent of those surveyed would support Clinton for reelection.[109] In response to numbers like these, From began to send memoranda to Clinton arguing that, to regain popularity, he had to return to his New Democrat roots, strike a compromise on health care, and then focus on welfare reform, teenage pregnancy prevention, national service, and a reinventing-government initiative that had been hived off to the vice-president's office.[110]

Clinton did unveil a welfare reform proposal in June 1994, but that too failed to follow the wishes of the New Democrats. Faced with a group of eighty-nine liberal members of Congress who were steadfastly against a time limit on benefits and seventy-seven other Democratic members led by McCurdy in favor of such limits, Clinton bowed to the Left. His welfare reform proposal did not include a time limit on benefits, the crucial provision in the drive to "end welfare as we know it."[111] In any event, by this time, the damage had been done. The health-care proposal never gained public support and never garnered enough congressional backing even to be put to a vote. Moreover, the image of Clinton as an Old Democrat had been set, intensifying any missteps his staff may have taken and obfuscating even ostensibly New Democratic victories.

Both of these dynamics, for instance, were evident in the pursuit and passage of an omnibus crime bill. Arguably the most important initiative offered in the social issues context, the administration ended up having the legislation portrayed in Old Democratic thematics. By the time Congress passed the $30 billion anticrime bill in the last week of August 1994, voters knew more about the controversy surrounding it than about its provisions for almost $9 billion to put more police officers on the street, for $8 billion in state grants for prison construction, for dozens of new federal capital crimes, and for a "three strikes and you're out" rule that automatically gave someone a life sentence after a third felony conviction.[112]

These measures had their political coordinates deep in the New Democratic world. Unlike liberal approaches to crime, the thrust of the bill was on stepped-up law enforcement and tougher penalties. Yet in the process of trying to pass the legislation, the New Democratic thematics were lost. In order to bring a majority of Democrats aboard—notably blacks, who opposed the emphasis on punishment, and conservatives, who opposed new measures for gun control—the House leadership loaded the bill with pork-barrel spending.[113]

Thus the GOP, partly out of retribution for being kept out of conference negotiations on the bill, and partly to prevent the Democrats from stealing this traditionally Republican issue, seized on the pork in the bill, dramatized in such items as funding for midnight basketball leagues. Once again, the Clinton record up to that point made it all too easy for the GOP to portray the president, his program, and his party as soft on criminals, favoring costly programs at the expense of tough penalties and law enforcement, and addicted to wasteful spending on ridiculous-sounding (although at times effective) programs. After failing to hold the Democrats together on the first vote to bring the bill to the House floor, Clinton and the House leadership eventually got the bill passed, but not without acquiescing to GOP demands for cuts in spending for crime-prevention initiatives.[114]

In sum, although it was a New Democratic piece of legislation, the crime bill became bogged down and defined by liberal Democratic politics. It served to reinforce the negative images of the Democratic Party that Clinton and the DLC hoped to counter. Rather than reestablish the Democrats' credentials on crime—New Democratic credentials— it reinforced perceptions of Republican superiority on the issue while simultaneously pleasing neither camp within the Democratic Party.

Interestingly, the DLC was most pleased by and saw the most success in the foreign policy issue context. Specifically, Clinton's advocacy for (and the eventual passage of) NAFTA was a triumph not only for a New Democratic policy but also for New Democratic politics. Opposed by most of the House Democratic Caucus—156 members, including the leader and whip—Clinton had to rely on a "center-out" strategy to pass the accord.[115] In this, he relied on a centrist, bipartisan coalition and opposed many of the old organized constituencies of the Democratic Party, specifically, organized labor. Unsurprisingly, the DLC saw the passage of NAFTA, ultimately, as "the president's finest hour."[116]

Yet NAFTA was the exception to the overall substantive and political focus of the first two years of the Clinton administration. It cannot be denied that Clinton supported free trade and NAFTA, but the fact that the treaty entered the policy arena and was considered when it was (and in the way it was) had little to do with strategic decisions of the Clinton administration. NAFTA was already in the policy pipeline; it was unavoidable. To claim, then, that NAFTA represented a deliberate enactment of the New Democratic agenda seems overdone, especially in light of the Clinton record in other issue clusters.

In sum, Clinton's policy agenda may have included New Democratic proposals, but the priorities of—and the political moves taken by—the White House did not make the case that Clinton was a New Democrat. At times, politics and priorities were actually at odds with the recommendations and beliefs of this group. To understand why Clinton, who had run as a New Democrat, could so easily fail to govern as one, one must consider the institutional environment in which the president operated.

INSTITUTIONAL PROBLEMS AND ALTERNATIVES

By the end of Clinton's first two years in office, the DLC was demoralized. The New Democrats had achieved the difficult goal of electing one of their own to the White House. Once in office, however, he had apparently abandoned both their program and, indeed, their public philosophy. "The DLC themes—social responsibility, anti-crime, pro-business—just got lost," lamented Senator Joe Lieberman.[117] Fred Siegel, a PPI fellow, charged that Clinton was governing on "big government principles," and Representative Rob Andrews of New Jersey, a onetime DLC member and New Democrat fellow traveler, quipped that Clinton "ran like Jack Kennedy and governed like Ted Kennedy."[118]

How did this happen? Some argued that nothing had gone wrong for the New Democrats. Liberals pointed to the withdrawal of the Lani Guinier nomination and, especially, the passage of NAFTA as proof that Clinton was not one of them and never had been. Indeed, one less partisan observer noted at the end of 1993 that, in fact, the DLC did see the implementation of most of its policy program.[119] From this perspective, controlling for the practical necessities of governing, the New Democrats were largely having their way.

Another school of thought explained Clinton's shifting between New Democratic and liberal policies as a function of his personality and personal style. These observers argued that Clinton had inherent tendencies to compromise and had "vacillating desires."[120] Implicit in these and cruder critiques was that Clinton—already perceived as "slick" because of his ability to survive seemingly fatal scandals—lacked a backbone. Indeed, Garry Trudeau, in his nationwide comic strip *Doonesbury*, chose to portray the president as a waffle. In this view, Clinton as president was the champion of no known public philosophy. He was, instead, a total tactician, going this way or that as the situation dictated.

Still another group of analysts put the blame for Clinton's inability to govern at the doorstep of the New Democratic philosophy itself. To them, it was not so much a public philosophy as merely an "electoral strategy" or a "marketing strategy."[121] As such, it was inherently difficult to turn its "often ambiguous, centrist stands" into policy, especially in a polarized political atmosphere.[122] As a result, it might not have mattered if Clinton was a conscious, philosophic strategist. The philosophy itself was an insufficient guide for governance.

But these theories ignore the larger context of the Clinton presidency and hence fail to identify the most potent explanation. Simply put, the larger political context—the partisan institutional environment that Clinton inherited and created for himself—made it difficult to implement the beliefs and programs of the New Democrats. In turn, such a situation made it appear that Clinton had no convictions, or that any beliefs he did hold were incapable of serving as a governing philosophy.

The institutional environment in which the Clinton presidency operated was very much a product of the unique circumstances of his nomination and election. Recall that Clinton won the party's nomination in a weak field and without a significant liberal challenger. Liberal Democrats, who disagreed with some of his policy planks, backed Clinton only because they had no other alternative and they too thirsted for victory. Despite this support, after the votes were counted on election day, Clinton did not garner a majority, much less a clear electoral mandate. As a result, other party factions, which had put aside their differences in order to win the White House for the Democrats, saw no obvious popular endorsement for New Democratic policies and thus had no reason to defer to Clinton once he was elected.

Once in office, therefore, Clinton—ostensibly a factional leader— had to contend with demands from all corners of his coalition. The Democrat had stitched together a coalition whose members' policy wishes were not necessarily in accordance; hence he had "numerous political obligations precisely because each part of his diverse base of support expected him to be unequivocally for them."[123] He had tacked to the center to win the election. But to govern in a unified Democratic government, Clinton had to govern with—even by means of— a liberal Democratic Congress, and thus had to move to the left.[124] With every Democratic member of the House and Senate garnering a higher percentage of the vote than Clinton had received nationwide or in their respective states, he did not possess the political capital that would compel these legislators to follow his policy lead.[125]

Therefore, not only did Clinton appear to be vacillating in his policy choices, but splits within the Democratic Party came to the fore with a vengeance, as they did on health care, welfare reform, and NAFTA.[126] Exacerbating Clinton's problem was the nature of both groups of activists. Although it was ostensibly an organization of elected officials, the staff and donors in and around the DLC shared the intransigence of the issue activists on the left, whose ascendancy in the Democratic Party they deplored.

To former DLC staff members serving in the administration and to other Clinton aides, the DLC had become "100 percenters" who wanted their agenda implemented completely.[127] The organization did not appreciate the demands of other Democratic Party factions or that "governance is an art of incremental change."[128] As Clinton himself tried to tell the DLC at its meeting in December 1993, he had to govern within reality and, consequently, had to compromise in order to build a legislative coalition.[129]

These separate and often conflicting demands on the Clinton team were especially clear in the legislative process. However, these cross-pressures actually first surfaced immediately after the election, during the construction of the administration. Political appointments are the spoils of electoral politics, and factions naturally battle for their fair share. In *Mandate for Change,* however, Galston and Kamarck wrote that Clinton had to assert his leadership over the Democratic Party by defining his mandate and policy agenda and by placing "people loyal to his agenda in the key positions needed to carry out that mandate."[130]

As the outcome of the election started to become clear and political pundits began to hypothesize possible Clinton appointments, it seemed that the DLC would have the major role it desired in the administration. The *Washington Post* opined that Marshall could end up as national security adviser, From as DNC chairman, and Shapiro as director of the Office of Management and Budget or as a member of the Council of Economic Advisors.[131] Moreover, From had a substantial early role in the Clinton presidency; after the election, Clinton named him head of domestic policy transition and appointed Reed as his deputy.

Immediately, lines were drawn over the From appointment. Kamarck said that this made New Democrats such as herself "a lot less nervous," and one journalist hailed the pick as possibly "the single most significant step he (Clinton) has made yet." Conversely, black and Hispanic groups complained to Clinton about From's selection, and Jackson weighed in against the move.[132]

Yet as the appointment process progressed, New Democrats felt that they were being overlooked, even though the DLC claimed seven members of Clinton's original cabinet.[133] On the one hand, DLC leaders knew that prior to 1991, membership in the DLC had not necessarily signaled devotion to the New Democratic cause, since the organization had been arranged to accommodate a wide spectrum of officeholders. On the other hand, five of the seven cabinet members—Bruce Babbitt (Interior), Michael Espy (Agriculture), Richard Riley (Education), Lloyd Bentsen (Treasury), and Les Aspin (Defense)—had been actively involved in the organization, as had Vice-President Gore.[134] Additionally, McCurdy, who had been passed over for secretary of defense, was offered the directorship of the CIA, though he turned down the position.[135]

On the staff and at the subcabinet level, key New Democrats were also tapped for jobs. Galston and Reed were made domestic policy aides (albeit neither in the top job). Linda Moore, the DLC's field director, was made a special assistant for political affairs, and Kiki Moore, the organization's press secretary, was hired as DNC communications director. Kamarck was put in charge of the vice-president's initiative on reinventing government. Also, over the objection of labor unions, Clinton appointed Doug Ross—a New Democratic thinker whose work on the economy and job training had been featured in *Mandate for Change*—to the post of assistant secretary of labor for employment and training.[136]

However, the DLC felt that its allies had been either snubbed for meaningful policy jobs or excluded altogether. Furthermore, some close to the DLC claimed that Marshall and Shapiro were disappointed that they had not been tapped for administration posts, and the organization itself, along with the remnants of Democratic neoconservatives, complained that Clinton had excluded both groups from key defense and foreign affairs jobs.[137]

Contributing to this disappointment was Clinton's pledge to craft a cabinet that "looked like America," a policy that strayed pointedly from the New Democratic commitment to equal opportunity over equal outcomes and painted Clinton as a social liberal. In practice, this commitment to diversity over other criteria such as ideology, internal policy cohesion, and factional loyalty inevitably disadvantaged New Democrats.[138]

Yet even the DLC admitted that some of the problem with appointments was its own fault. "We didn't have enough followers in enough places, and the Old Democrats, they ran the town," Reed recounted.[139] New Democrats may have won the presidency, but liberal Democrats still controlled the national party and the affiliated interest groups to which a president looks when forming a staff. In the final analysis, New Democrats and other observers argued that "a dearth of centrist Democrats on the White House staff . . . contributed to the leftward drift."[140] As Marshall said, "Clinton, like us, is out-numbered in his own administration."[141]

A lack of committed New Democrats within the White House and across the executive agencies contributed to the political and policy moves that helped undermine Clinton's New Democratic credentials, as Clinton himself admitted at times. His aide George Stephanopoulos recounts a note he made to himself on April 14, 1993: "[the President] feels that his appointees aren't committed to his goals."[142] This feeling prompted Clinton in June 1993 to appoint David Gergen, a once-Republican operative who had allied himself with the DLC, to be White House communications director and counselor to the president and steer Clinton back to the New Democratic line.[143] Just how far Clinton had strayed from that line is brought into stark relief when one considers the view from the other side: DLC adversaries admitted, with relief, that there were not as many DLC members appointed as they had originally feared.[144]

In sum, it seemed that the DLC expected Clinton to follow the Reagan model and base his appointments almost solely on ideological purity. Yet Clinton did not have the political capital to appoint more New Democrats—assuming that there were enough suitable adherents to appoint. He had to be attentive to all wings of the Democratic Party and, most importantly, to the Democrats on Capitol Hill. Unlike Reagan, Clinton did not have an electoral mandate and had to deal with a government unified under his own party's control. Ironically, this institutional arrangement had a profound, constricting effect on Clinton's first two years in office.

In a situation of unified government, cooperation is the dominant strategy for the president and his congressional majority. This may not prove cozy, but no other strategy is remotely easier. In such a situation, the minority party has little incentive to cooperate with the majority agenda, since that would only contribute to the political prospects of the majority. Yet the behavior of both parties in Congress also depends on the electoral context. If the president has a clear electoral mandate, it reduces the incentive for an individual congressman from the majority party to defect, since presumably, the president and his program are more popular than the member himself. This situation also affects members of the minority party, since they could suffer in their own districts if they are seen as thwarting the platform of a popular president.[145]

The political context that Clinton partly produced and partly encountered at the start of his presidency was the opposite of this rosy scenario. Elected by a 43 percent plurality in an election that saw his party lose nine seats in the House and remain at par in the Senate, Clinton did not have an electoral mandate by which to convince factional opponents in his own party and foes in the Republican Party to cooperate with his New Democratic agenda. Indeed, the day after Clinton's election, Republican Bob Dole, the Senate minority leader, told reporters that he too had a mandate: to represent the 57 percent of voters who did not support Clinton. "It's not all going to be milk and honey for the Democrats," Dole warned.[146]

As statements like these reveal, the first two years of Clinton's first term saw an increased polarization of political elites and activists, who in turn made "extreme, non-negotiable demands" on policymakers.[147] The House Democratic Caucus itself was more ideologically homogeneous than the last time the Democrats had controlled both the executive and legislative branches. As the old southern Democrats were being replaced either by Republicans or by self-consciously national Democrats, the congressional Democratic Party became more like its northern Democratic majority—more liberal.[148] Across the aisle, the opposite occurred: the GOP became more conservative as liberal Republicans faded into extinction. In this environment, centrist New Democrats were a "minor faction in congressional election politics," with the DLC-affiliated Mainstream Forum claiming no more than forty "hard-core" members.[149] Once again, the New Democrats may have won the presidency, but liberal Democrats controlled the party in Congress.

Another facet of the political context was the nature of policymaking in 1993. The large budget deficit and the Democrats' pledge to reduce it turned much of congressional politics into deciding who had to sacrifice in order to pay for new initiatives and keep the deficit under control. Consequently, as Robert Reischauer—then director of the Congressional Budget Office—has noted, no opposition party would want to accommodate the majority party on budgetary matters, because it would dull the placing of blame. By contrast, allowing the majority party to govern—and decide who had to bear the burdens— would highlight and exacerbate its internal divisions.[150] This logic, along with Clinton's plurality victory, led the GOP to decide to let Clinton and the Democrats go it alone on this and other issues.

Other aspects of the political context that affected Clinton's first two years in office had more to do with the specific players involved. Clinton had never served in Congress and had no other Washington experience. At the same time, congressional leaders had to learn how to work with a president from their own party.[151] Beyond that, Clinton and the Democrats, together, had to deal with the Carter legacy; many in the Democratic Party believed that Carter's lack of success was attributable to his insufficient courting of congressional Democrats. Finally, Democrats interpreted the results of the 1992 election—the return of unified Democratic control of the federal government and the resonance of Perot's anti-Washington message—as a demand to end legislative gridlock. Consequently, there was extra pressure on Congress and the president to cooperate and to pass legislation.[152]

Overall, this institutional context precluded the enactment of the governing strategy—specifically, the reliance on a bipartisan, centrist coalition—that the New Democrats advocated. The DLC believed that, despite his plurality-sized victory, Clinton could claim a "substantial mandate," since "his election embodies as well as symbolizes change."[153] New Democrats called on Clinton to be a "Rooseveltian persuader" and use the "bully pulpit" of the presidency to whip up a groundswell of support that would force centrist Republicans to join in a bipartisan coalition and eventually force liberal congressional Democrats to support Clinton.[154]

In practice, this strategy was unrealistic in light of the aforementioned political and institutional context. In the end, therefore, Clinton made a strategic decision—perhaps the only decision that could have been made—to cast his lot with the congressional leadership. On November 15, 1992, at a dinner in Little Rock with the leadership, House Speaker Tom Foley convinced Clinton not to attack but to work with Congress.[155] According to McCurdy, a few months later he asked Clinton why he would run against a "brain-dead Congress" and then "hook up life support to them." Clinton reportedly responded, "But they're going to determine the outcome of my legislation, my legislative record."[156] Exemplifying the difference in strategy between Clinton and the DLC, McCurdy—then DLC chairman—responded, "You are going to lose if you do that."[157]

By the end of the 103rd Congress, it appeared that both Clinton and McCurdy were correct. On balance, even though Congress did not pass Clinton's two largest initiatives, health-care and welfare reform, it did pass a lot of legislation.[158] Yet success is not always measured in terms of legislative volume. McCurdy was right: by relying on congressional Democrats, Clinton had had to reshape his priorities and, in turn, had lost an opportunity to refashion a new Democratic Party. The role of congressional Democrats in sinking the New Democratic aspirations of Clinton, in turn, became one of the DLC's central explanations for the results of Clinton's first two years in office. As Reed explained, "for the most part, the President had stuck to a New Democratic agenda, but it went through an old Democratic sausage grinder and came out looking diminished in some ways."[159] Even Clinton himself recognized that he had become a "prisoner of Congress."[160]

Although disappointed with Clinton's performance, the DLC was still closely linked with its former chairman. Thus the organization, too, found itself in a bind. On the one hand, with Clinton in the White House, the New Democrats were the toast of Washington. The organization was able to increase its fund-raising efforts substantially by trading on its perceived influence on the new president. For example, in December 1992, the DLC held a black-tie fund-raising event to fete the new administration. Attended by both Clinton and Gore, the event—Clinton's first public appearance in Washington since his election—raised over $3 million for the DLC, more money than the organization had spent in any year up to that point.[161] Indeed, the DLC's fund-raising operation grew considerably once Clinton took office, from two staffers in 1993 to ten in 1995; by 1995, 17 percent of all its expenses were spent on development.[162]

On the other hand, with Clinton in the Oval Office, he now defined what it meant to be a New Democrat. Thus, his apparent deviations from the New Democratic public philosophy and policy agenda undermined the credibility of the New Democratic label.[163] Disillusioned and stunned by this turn of events, the DLC leadership began to examine what had gone wrong with its strategy to remake the Democratic Party and to question what role the organization still had to play in politics generally, plus how it was to relate to the White House.[164] As Richard Berke of the *New York Times* posited, what does an organization that is devoted to electing one of its own president do once it is successful? Moreover, does such an entity, whose cachet is its close relationship with the president, risk antagonizing him when he deviates from its agenda?[165] The principles of the DLC may have favored criticizing the president; its politics prescribed otherwise. Therefore, during Clinton's first two years in office, the DLC wavered between the two courses of actions.

Upon assuming the chairmanship of the DLC, for example, McCurdy vowed publicly to "fight those who would water down our agenda."[166] According to reports, he wanted to exert more pressure in the House and fight the Democratic leadership there when it did not support New Democratic programs.[167] At other times, when Clinton pursued favorite New Democratic policies, the DLC worked to assist him. The clearest example of this role was during the debate over NAFTA. Not only did the DLC vocally support passage of the agreement, but it circulated a memorandum to potential corporate sponsors outlining a strategy to lobby Congress to pass the agreement.[168]

Underlying this lack of a single clear direction was the growing realization by the DLC leadership that its presidential strategy, on which it had worked since 1989, had potentially failed. The New Democrats felt that with the exception of its titular leader—and that too was now in doubt—the Democratic Party had not changed. As From told *Newsweek* in the fall of 1994, "Our great hope was that Bill Clinton, governing as a New Democrat, would stop the realignment [toward the GOP]."[169] But after two years of Democratic rule, recounted Galston, the DLC realized that it had misjudged the transformative effect that a New Democratic presidential candidate and victor could have on the entire party. "Bill Clinton campaigned and won on the basis of ideas that were broadly accepted in the country, but not so broadly accepted within his own party," he recalled.[170] By the midterm elections in 1994, then, the DLC had begun to think that the election of Clinton would not accomplish its goal of remaking the public philosophy of the Democratic Party and restoring it to electoral success, and thus started to consider other vehicles to bring about this change.[171]

The election of Bill Clinton to the presidency was a surprisingly mixed blessing for the DLC. On the one hand, the organization played a key role in preparing Clinton for his race. It provided him with a national stage, access to a network of elected officials and political benefactors, and a honed message (or public philosophy) on which he ran for and won both the party's nomination and the presidency. In other words, the DLC defined the problem, devised the solution, and found the vehicle to take both onto the agenda of the Democratic Party and of the nation.

On the other hand, once Clinton became president, he now defined what it meant to be a New Democrat, and he exposed the public philosophy of the DLC to the harsh realities of Democratic Party politics and policy implementation. Said differently, the fortunes of the New Democratic "movement" were now inextricably tied to those of Clinton. In turn, the success of the DLC's plan was at the mercy of a 43 percent plurality victory and the accompanying limited mandate. It was subject to the realities of a unified Democratic government and a congressional partner that was not enamored with New Democratic thinking. And it had to contend with a liberal national party whose constituent groups also supported Clinton and wanted commensurate political and policy paybacks.

In some ways, this situation was the DLC's own doing. By working outside of the party to prepare a New Democrat to run for president, the DLC did nothing to change the institutional arrangements or distribution of power within the party itself. The DLC may have helped elect a New Democrat to the presidency and to the leadership of the Democratic Party, but it did nothing to diminish the presence of liberal Democrats among party activists and elected officials.

Nevertheless, the DLC wanted Clinton to stick to his New Democratic guns. But considering the partisan and institutional context, as well as the immediate political inputs of the 1992 election, trying to govern purely as a New Democrat seemed risky, especially to a president-elect without any Washington experience. Contrary to those who saw Clinton's deviation from the New Democratic line as either a sign of his true beliefs or a sign of his lack of them, Clinton was almost compelled to vacillate between Old and New Democratic policies and thus muddy the message (and the image) of the New Democrats.

After two years, the DLC had begun to join its critics in questioning whether Clinton was really a New Democrat after all. These feelings of betrayal led to a reexamination of the strategy and mission of the DLC. But as in the past, an upcoming election provided a window of opportunity for the DLC to push its outlook on politics and government. And the shocking results of the 1994 midterm election changed the political situation to such a degree that it resurrected both Clinton and the New Democrats.

8 / Rising from the Ashes, 1994–1996

NINETEEN NINETY-FOUR was supposed to have been the year for Democrats like Dave McCurdy. With a New Democrat in the White House, the stigma of the national Democratic Party as socially liberal, fiscally irresponsible, and weak on defense was to have been finally neutralized. The environment, in theory, was right for McCurdy—a six-term congressman, a national figure on defense issues, and a rising star in his home state of Oklahoma. As a longtime New Democratic leader and now the DLC's chairman, McCurdy seemed poised to grab the Senate seat left vacant by the retiring David Boren, a conservative Democrat.

Yet for McCurdy, and for candidates like him around the country, 1994 was not their year. Bill Clinton was not a help to their candidacies but a hindrance. And for McCurdy, his embrace of the presidential candidate and then president proved fatal for his political ambitions. His association with Clinton, a connection forged by their work together at the DLC, did not help him with the Oklahoman electorate. Rather, it was used to paint McCurdy as being as out of touch with mainstream values as the liberal wing of the national party was. Over and over again, McCurdy was linked with Clinton and the Clinton record. He was attacked for being a "Clinton clone," a social liberal in favor of gun control, against school prayer, for gays in the military, against a constitutional amendment banning flag burning, and for the federal funding of abortions.[1] "I couldn't campaign in Oklahoma as a New Democrat because of Bill Clinton," McCurdy bitterly recounted. "Even though I spent all my career building up to that point to use it and run on it, it had no bite."[2] In the end, Republican Jim Inhofe soundly beat McCurdy, 55 percent to 45 percent.

The defeat of Dave McCurdy was just one of the many losses the New Democrats and the entire Democratic Party suffered in 1994. In a win of truly historic proportions, the Republican Party retook the Senate and the House as well as scores of statewide offices. The GOP's massive triumph, in turn, had a profound effect on President Clinton, his governing philosophy, and his own electoral fortunes. It was interpreted by the White House as a rejection of Clinton for straying from the New Democratic line. This reading of the situation, along with the political opportunities the GOP then created, led Clinton back to the New Democratic fold. By 1996, he was able to run for reelection on just such a program—the original New Democratic program—and win with impressive showings among New Democratic constituencies. For the New Democrats, then, although they lost many races in 1994, in the end, these defeats may have produced their eventual victory.

Divided Government

After a two-year hiatus, divided government returned to Washington in 1994, but of a peculiar sort. This time, a Democratic president would have to contend with a Republican House and Senate. And coming off this massive triumph, the congressional leadership that the White House would have to deal with would be an emboldened one, eager to implement its own agenda.

Ironically, much as political defeat had in the past, the 1994 elections proved beneficial to Clinton and the New Democrats. First, the loss immediately cast doubt on the political strategy and policy agenda of the first two years of the Clinton presidency (one that strayed markedly from the New Democratic line), forcing the administration to search for replacements that might rejuvenate Clinton's personal popularity and his prospects for reelection. Beyond that, the Republican takeover produced an institutional and political environment that virtually compelled Clinton to adopt the DLC diagnosis of the Democratic problem, along with the New Democratic public philosophy it offered as a remedy. And in the end, Clinton did adopt this course of action. This was not, however, an easy and automatic resolution. It took time for this metamorphosis (or return to roots) to become apparent. Meanwhile, the DLC, sadly vindicated by the 1994 election returns, rethought its overall political strategy, especially its relationship with the president and the Democratic Party.

ELECTORAL PROBLEMS AND ALTERNATIVES

Pundits and journalists described election day 1994 as everything from a "meteorite" to an "earthquake" to a "tsunami."[3] Although these characterizations were hyperbolic, there is no denying that the results were shocking and historic. In 1994, the Democratic Party's long-standing dominance of subpresidential government came to an end. For the first time since 1970, there were more Republican governors (thirty) than Democratic ones, and nine of the ten largest states were headed by the GOP. Beyond that, the Republicans gained control of seventeen more state legislative bodies for a total of forty-eight, one more than the Democrats.[4] Although significant in and of themselves, these state results, however, were dwarfed by the change at the national level. For the first time since 1980, the GOP took over the Senate. For the first time since 1954, it took over the House. Losing not one Republican incumbent, the GOP gained fifty-three seats in the House, to create a 231 to 203 majority, and won nine seats in the Senate, a majority increased by another two when a pair of Democrats—Richard Shelby of Alabama and Ben Nighthorse Campbell of Colorado—switched parties, to create a fifty-four to forty-six partisan split. It seemed that the Democrats had suffered a countrywide rout.

Yet in analyzing the vote, it becomes clear that losses among certain key regional and demographic groups, ones with which the Democrats had made great gains in 1992, were what hurt the party most. The Democrats suffered a "collapse" of support among "politically marginal, change-oriented districts," ones that had backed Bush for president in 1988 but Clinton in 1992. The Democrats, according to *Congressional Quarterly*'s Rhodes Cook, lost twenty-one of these congressional districts.[5] Furthermore, in the South, a region that had been moving toward the GOP for the past two decades, but where the Clinton-Gore ticket had assumed that it had stalled that trend, the GOP gained nineteen House seats and three Senate seats, earning the Republicans a majority of the South's congressional delegation for the first time since Reconstruction.[6]

Driving these shifts were trends among key demographic groups. There were massive turnarounds among independents, white men, and middle-class households.[7] From 1992 to 1994, for example, Democratic partisan identification dropped 7 percent among the middle class, twice the rate of decrease among all voters and the largest move-ment of any income group.[8] In the South, exit polls reported that only 40 percent of voters, and only 27 percent of white male voters, approved of Clinton's presidency.[9] These and other voters supported the GOP because they felt that Clinton had not delivered on his promise to govern, in effect, as a New Democrat. Swing voters, espe-cially those who had voted for Perot in 1992, viewed Clinton as an advocate of big-government, tax-and-spend liberalism or of an inter-est-group-driven social liberalism.[10]

Taking advantage of this perception, the Republicans—by way of the "Contract for America," a list of ten items ranging from congres-sional term limits to a capital gains tax cut that they promised to enact if elected—nationalized the election and turned it into a referendum on Clinton and his presidency.[11] Remarkably, despite a feeling among the electorate that the economy had improved since 1992, 51 percent of voters disapproved of Clinton's performance as president, and 83 per-cent of those backed the Republicans.[12] Although there is also some evidence that low turnout among key Democratic constituencies—such as blacks and women—helped the GOP cause, that cannot change the fact that the election was a repudiation of Clinton and his first two years.[13] In fact, it could point to a lack of enthusiasm on the part of Clinton's own Democratic base.

Yet despite the data, in the aftermath of this electoral earthquake, it was hard to say what the election results meant. Were they a repudi-ation of Clinton, of the Democratic Party, or of both? Was the election the resumption (after the strange election of 1992) of Republican ascen-dancy and Democratic decline in national politics? Or was it just a fluke: the two years in every forty that the GOP wins Congress? As ex-pected, partisans and analysts rushed to offer their own interpretations.

Liberals argued that the 1994 election proved that the New Democrats had little mass base—in fact, Mainstream Forum members lost at higher rates than did the rest of the House—and that the whole effort to "re-invent the Democrats as a pro-business, fiscally conserv-ative party was a particular disaster."[14] In 1994, according to this view, voters just chose the real Republican Party, not its New Democratic imitators.[15]

The DLC, along with less partisan analysts, disagreed with this interpretation. The political scientist Harold Stanley, for example, con-tended that Clinton's "moderate, centrist" policies were not many in number and were eclipsed in the minds of voters by issues such as his health-care plan and gays in the military.[16] Clinton's problem was that he had not been a New Democrat on the "big-ticket issues—the politically diciest ones," wrote Burt Solomon in the *National Journal*.[17] This viewpoint was argued forcefully in an analysis by Mark Penn and Doug Schoen, who became Clinton's pollsters for the 1996 election. "The 1994 midterm election was a complete rejection of what the Democratic Party has come to represent—bigger government, more taxes, higher spending, more bureaucracy," they wrote.[18] In sum, this group of analysts believed that the basic problem was that Clinton had failed to define himself adequately as a New Democrat during his first two years in office or during the 1994 campaign season.[19]

Based on this line of reasoning, Al From concluded that the message of 1994 to the Democratic Party was simple: "get with the [DLC] program." In From's view, "This election said the New Deal coalition is Humpty Dumpty and it isn't going to get put back together again."[20] New Deal liberalism, including its New Politics variant, had "run its course." Others took a similar position, noting that the Left had lost touch with the needs of most Americans, and that a liberal Democrat could not conceivably win election to the presidency in the near future.[21] Meanwhile, Republicans heralded the election as the "first real intellectual and ideological realignment since the 1930s."[22]

To face this problem, liberals called for a return to the old-time religion of class politics to rally the old Democratic coalition into a new, grassroots, liberal-labor coalition.[23] The New Democrats had warned in 1989 of the Democratic loss of Congress in the DLC's "Politics of Evasion" paper, and they ostensibly had been working to devise the public philosophy necessary to prevent that from happening. Therefore, when the Democrats did lose Congress, New Democrats—including Vice-President Gore—argued that Clinton had to lead the Democratic Party to the political center by way of their public philosophy.[24] Said differently, the New Democrats did not deviate from their preferred course of action: to face this crisis, the Democratic Party had to remake its public philosophy.

ISSUE PROBLEMS AND POLICY ALTERNATIVES

Although it was not at all clear what Clinton would do in response to the GOP victory, the DLC moved quickly and produced the first

Democratic response to the "Contract." Released a month after the election, the DLC's "Mainstream Contract" called for many of the programs that were outlined in *Mandate for Change*, including a cut in corporate subsidies to pay for infrastructure, technological, and educational investments; a federalism convention; the expansion of NAFTA; vouchers for worker retraining; and the overhaul of welfare and public housing policies.[25]

David Osborne, a former PPI fellow and the coauthor of *Reinventing Government*, also outlined a strategy for a Clinton recovery, one that Osborne noted "comes right out of the Democratic Leadership Council."[26] In an article in the *Washington Post*, Osborne called on the president to construct a "less bureaucratic, more entrepreneurial government" that would create economic opportunity by working with the private sector and would ask for reciprocal obligation from citizens. To implement this plan, Osborne advised that Clinton should correct what many in the DLC saw as one of the biggest problems with his administration and hire more New Democrats to work for him.[27] Clinton noticed this article, and the morning after it ran, From was summoned to the White House. In a three-hour meeting with the president, From reiterated the DLC's argument that Clinton had to return to the New Democratic themes and policies that got him elected.[28]

While the White House began to chart its own course, the New Democrats—emboldened by what they saw as the repudiation of the liberal Democrats—began to elaborate on their public philosophy. The DLC, through the Progressive Foundation, its tax-exempt entity, released *The New Progressive Declaration: A Political Philosophy for the Information Age*, the latest iteration of the New Democratic creed.[29] As the title implies, the New Democrats had become more tied to the notion that they were latter-day Progressives who, like their earlier counterparts, had to adapt the country to the onset of a new type of economy.[30]

Specifically, the DLC believed that the Information Age made the New Deal faith in "an expansive government . . . [as] the means to progressive ends" obsolete, since technology had led to the "emergence of these kinds of decentralized, self-managed or self-organizing organizations which are much more given coherence by vision and common values rather than any command and control structure."[31] This viewpoint informed the recommendations in *Mandate for Change* that called for the devolution of many federal government functions to state and local governments, on the basis that many programs "work best" if carried out at this level and that federally designed programs— even if carried out by state and local governments—"dilute any sense of accountability to the local community."[32]

Yet in the *New Progressive Declaration,* the New Democrats deepened their anti-statist tendencies and rejected outright the theory of governance of New Deal liberalism: "the presumption for democratic action must be reversed. Citizens and local institutions, rather than distant government agencies, should be the public problem-solvers of first recourse."[33] The New Democrats had thus broken from one of the basic tenets of the New Deal public philosophy—that the national government should be the primary agent for progressive change— embracing instead what John Judis has called a "neo-Jeffersonian emphasis on local and state initiative."[34] Fred Siegel, a historian and PPI fellow, and Marshall elaborated on this point in a *New Democrat* cover story, noting that the defeat of the Clinton health-care initiative marked the "end of a half-century effort to create a full-blown American version of the European welfare state."[35] Where progressives should look next for their public philosophy, they argued, was to Woodrow Wilson's "New Freedom," with its "emphasis on citizens rather than clients, markets rather than managers."[36] Programmatically, this belief manifested itself in such recommendations as turning Social Security into a system of private individual savings accounts with supplements for the worse off, and in an unspecified overhaul of Medicare.[37]

This latest version of the New Democratic public philosophy also took on a slightly more socially conservative tone. Emphasizing a belief in individualism, the DLC firmly rejected the governmental consideration of Americans as members of separate ethnic, religious, and linguistic groups. Simultaneously, the organization became more strident in defending the two-parent family, placing more emphasis on its breakdown as the cause of various social ills.[38]

The *New Progressive Declaration* and the "Mainstream Contract" received the usual press coverage, and liberal criticism. In a speech to the ADA, Richard Trumka, the second-highest-ranking official at the AFL-CIO, warned, "The DLC's program isn't just immoral, it isn't just anti-worker—it is a blueprint for a Democratic disaster in 1996."[39] The White House was more tentative in its reaction to the DLC proposals and the Republican victory. Right after the election, in an address at Georgetown University on November 10, 1994, Clinton asserted, "I will work to pursue the New Democrat agenda."[40] Furthermore, one month later, he proposed a "Middle Class Bill of Rights" that would provide a tax cut and other benefits for the middle class.[41]

But as Elizabeth Drew, the Washington journalist, has noted, these pronouncements resembled more a panicky game of catch-up and counterproposal to the Republicans than a serious policy agenda.[42] With their momentum from the election, the congressional Republicans dominated American politics from election day of 1994 to the end of the first hundred days of the 104th Congress in the spring of 1995, initially making Clinton seem irrelevant to national policymaking. However, in the pursuit of its agenda, the congressional Republican Party eventually and unintentionally set the stage for Clinton's New Democrat comeback.

The public philosophy of the congressional Republicans was far to the right of the American political spectrum. Fervently antigovernment, the GOP, under the leadership of House Speaker Newt Gingrich, sought to "destroy the entire force behind the idea of an activist federal government."[43] This "radicalized conservatism" went beyond the boldness of Reaganism, as its devotees added a belief in the elimination of the budget deficit and hence committed themselves to radical cuts in the size and scope of the federal government.[44] As John Kasich of Ohio, chairman of the House Budget Committee, said during the 1994 election season, "In the 1980s, Republicans believed in government [spending programs]. Now they don't."[45]

Although many of the proposals and ideas behind the ten planks of the "Contract for America" had been present in American political debate previously, taken together under the banner of a "Republican revolution" and championed by a group of devoted—and often fanatic—supporters, these proposals and their Republican proponents began to appear extreme. Inflammatory rhetoric, such as when Majority Leader Tom DeLay of Texas called the Environmental Protection Agency (EPA) the "Gestapo of government agencies"; harebrained ideas like the revival of large-scale orphanages; and the simple fervency for cutting the size and scope of government—including popular programs like Medicare—began to worry many Americans.[46]

This situation, in turn, practically compelled Clinton back to the New Democratic public philosophy. To begin with, the election of a radicalized bloc of conservatives to Congress freed Clinton from the obligation to work with a largely liberal Democratic congressional party. If Clinton wanted Congress to pass any of his legislative agenda, he had to propose policies that were palatable to at least some of the Republican majority. And to congressional liberals, these New Democratic policies, although not ideal in their eyes, were more acceptable than Republican proposals. Moreover, as the Republicans pushed the bounds of political debate further right, they created a political incentive for Clinton to embrace the New Democratic public philosophy, since that would give him the chance to woo the support of key groups in the electorate that the GOP had abandoned.

Many observers have described Clinton's strategy for winning over these swing voters as "triangulation," after the ambiguous term used by Dick Morris, the political consultant hired by the White House to oversee this change in course.[47] Yet triangulation was but another, less accurate name for the public philosophy and political strategy the DLC had been advocating over the previous decade. Morris, along with New Democrats in the White House and in the DLC, used the New Democratic public philosophy, with its themes of opportunity, responsibility, and community, plus its own version of anti-statism—an enabling, not mandating, federal government—to counter the strident libertarianism of the congressional Republicans.[48]

Clinton hoped to undercut the GOP on the issues of deficit reduction, welfare reform, and governmental downsizing by reminding the public that he had already proposed initiatives in these areas (though they might not have been highlighted) and that his proposals were not only more humane but also qualitatively and philosophically different. They hoped to improve government, not destroy it altogether. Practically, the president's political team implemented this agenda by linking the changes of 1994 to those in 1992 that had resulted in his election, and by using the powers of the presidency to set out his priorities clearly and establish his credentials as a leader.[49]

Beginning with Clinton's State of the Union Address in 1995, the contours of these changes started to become apparent. At ten o'clock on the day of the speech, Clinton called From to say that he agreed with a memo From had written that argued that the speech had to reembrace the "New Covenant" rhetoric of the 1992 campaign. According to From, Clinton then asked him to rewrite a large part of the speech in this way. With little time left before the address, From contacted Bruce Reed in the White House, and, drawing on the DLC canon, the two of them rewrote two of its sections and sent them to Clinton. "Literally, Clinton put it in on the way up to the speech," From recalled. "It's probably why it was so god-damned long."[50]

The speech was the longest State of the Union Address ever given, but despite its length, the New Democratic public philosophy dominated the speech. Clinton spoke of the challenges the Information Age presented to the country; outlined his previous and continued support for reducing the deficit, reforming welfare, and shrinking the size and scope of the federal government; and differentiated himself from the Republicans by enumerating the areas that government should be involved in, notably, job training, education, and health care for the elderly.[51] Clinton apparently was pleased with this return to the New Democratic line. "Thanks for your help with the State of the Union. It was helpful—at least it was what I really wanted to say—and now for the shorter version," he wrote in a thank-you note to From.[52]

The diverging beliefs on the role of the federal government, or public philosophies, between Clinton and the New Democrats on one side and Gingrich and the Republicans on the other were made especially clear during the budget negotiations in the winter of 1995–1996. Here, Clinton reasserted his New Democratic credentials and succeeded in characterizing the Republicans as extreme, simultaneously reseizing the political center. The showdown began during the 1995 budget process, when the House and Senate budget committees unveiled their respective budget plans on May 9 and 10. Both proposed reducing federal spending by over $1 trillion over the next seven years in order to balance the budget.

The Senate version proposed the elimination of 100 federal programs, along with the Commerce Department. The House version called for the elimination of 280 programs, plus the Departments of Energy, Education, and Commerce. Both plans proposed a reduction in the earned income tax credit, steep cuts in Medicare and Medicaid, and the elimination of Clinton's national service program. To this, the House committee added $353 billion in tax cuts and an increase in defense spending.[53] Although radical in and of itself, the House budget plan's most extreme elements were added during the appropriations process. There, funding for the EPA was cut by one-third, with enforcement funding cut in half, and seventeen legislative riders were attached to the bill prohibiting the enforcement of pending and existing

EPA policies.[54] In other areas, the House appropriations subcommittees cut the enforcement budget of the Occupational Safety and Health Administration (OSHA) in half, abolished the agency that enforces the Endangered Species Act, and eliminated the Council of Economic Advisors.[55]

The House Democratic Caucus first responded to these budget proposals by attacking the cuts, especially those slated for popular social-welfare programs such as Medicare and Social Security. Its members also charged that the proposed tax cut and the overall drive to a balanced budget benefited the well off at the expense of the working class. Yet Clinton did not follow this traditional Democratic approach of class warfare. Instead, on June 13, 1995, he too proposed a balanced budget plan, one that would cut $1.1 trillion in spending over ten years without a tax increase. The plan called for a cut in Medicare that was $100 billion less than the GOP proposal, but a cut nonetheless, as well as a middle-class tax cut.

Unlike liberal Democrats, then, Clinton was calling for a balanced budget and for spending cuts. Unlike Republicans, the president said that he would oppose any cuts in education; that he would support welfare reform, but in a manner calculated to move recipients into jobs; that he would cut taxes on the middle class, not the wealthy; that he would control health-care costs; and that he would not cut the budget so quickly as to hurt the economy.[56]

By matching the House Republican budget plan with his own New Democratic balanced budget, Clinton was able to emphasize his (New Democratic) vision of a retooled, not diminished, federal government. As Garry Wills has explained, Clinton was offering government, though not necessarily big government, as an alternative to no government.[57] With this move, political commentator Joe Klein noted, "The debate changed from left-right to moderate-right, with Clinton commanding the middle."[58] The GOP cooperated with this strategy by refusing to compromise on its balanced budget plan. This impasse forced the federal government to shut down twice during the winter of 1995–1996, with the second closure lasting twenty-one days, the longest in U.S. history.

Unfortunately for the congressional Republicans, the public blamed them for the closures. In the process, they "appeared, by turns, heartless and reckless."[59] And the Democrats made the case, through an aggressive advertising campaign, that they were protecting the values of the American people from Republican extremists.[60] Indeed, during the first government shutdown in November, 68 percent of Americans disapproved of Congress, compared with 40 percent who felt the same way about Clinton.[61]

To his New Democratic stand on the budget, Clinton added New Democratic stands on social issues. Foremost among these was a welfare reform bill, signed by Clinton, that radically restructured the existing system. The DLC praised the legislation but, like Clinton, opposed the bill's harsher elements, such as cutting off benefits to legal immigrants. Nonetheless, the organization felt that, overall, it was a positive step, since it not only "burnishe[d] his [Clinton's] New Democrat credentials," while taking away a potent Republican issue, but also forced structural change.[62]

Liberals were dismayed at Clinton's signing of the legislation. Many of his top advisers, including the secretaries of Housing and Urban Development, Health and Human Services, and Labor, were against the decision.[63] Some junior officials even resigned in protest. With half of the Democratic delegations to the Senate and House voting against the proposal, Clinton could have vetoed the measure easily without a net loss of partisan support. Yet signing welfare reform into law was a highly symbolic act. As Reed and the handful of New Democrats in the White House argued, it kept his 1992 campaign promise to "end welfare as we know it," emphasized to the public that reforming the system was a priority for Clinton, and thus highlighted the New Democratic image that he wanted for the Democratic Party.[64]

In this vein, Clinton took more (socially) conservative positions, too, supporting the "V-chip" so that parents could censor television programs for their children, and announcing his support of a bill that would outlaw gay marriage. By the start of 1996, it was clear that Clinton had reembraced the New Democratic public philosophy. In every policy area discussed in his 1996 State of the Union Address, Clinton offered New Democratic proposals. However, his calls for charter schools, job-training vouchers, community policing, and an internationalist foreign policy were overshadowed by one clear statement made at the beginning of the address: "The era of big government is over."[65]

With this, Clinton rejected both the libertarianism of the Republican Right and the emphasis on federal government action that lay at the heart of the liberal public philosophy. The DLC was ecstatic about Clinton's 1996 State of the Union Address and his embrace of the New Democratic public philosophy and policy program.[66] And as the 1996 election neared, the organization seemed eager to aid his reelection effort. Although this support should have been expected, the relationship between the DLC and Clinton had come full circle. Leading up to the 1992 elections, Clinton and the organization were inextricably bound by policy and political fortune; by the time of his reelection, they were similarly joined at the hip. But in between these two contests came the 1994 midterm elections. And in the aftermath of the stunning Democratic defeats, it was far from clear that Clinton would return to the New Democratic fold, or that the DLC would be standing with him.

INSTITUTIONAL PROBLEMS AND ALTERNATIVES

During the 1994 midterm elections, the GOP had revived a strategy that many Democrats—especially DLC Democrats, who tended not to run in safe districts or states—thought they had seen the last of with the election of Clinton. As they had in 1980, 1984, and 1988, the Republicans tried to link those running for subpresidential offices with an unpopular liberal at the top of the ticket. In 1994, this strategy was particularly successful, since, unlike the situation in the past, many of these more moderate Democrats running in marginally Democratic or traditionally Republican locales had close ties to, and had even fervently supported, the object of vilification: Bill Clinton.

Consequently, New Democrats suffered greatly during 1994. Along with the defeat of DLC Chairman Dave McCurdy, Representative Jim Cooper of Tennessee lost a bid for Gore's former Senate seat by 61 percent to 39 percent, and almost half of the Mainstream Forum's seventy-one members were defeated.[67] After two years of dissatisfaction with Clinton's deviance from the New Democratic public philosophy and policy agenda, and a growing feeling that the DLC's presidential strategy—as well as its larger effort to remake the Democratic Party—had failed, the 1994 defeats fueled New Democratic discontent with Clinton.

These feelings came to a head on December 6, 1994, at the DLC's annual conference. On this day, Clinton was scheduled to address the hundreds of DLC members, supporters, and journalists gathered there.

For the past two years, whenever Clinton returned to the DLC, he was hailed as a conquering hero. But with the wounds of the 1994 elections still fresh, this was not to be the case. McCurdy, who, over the short course of the Clinton era, had gone from reading that he was presidential material to reading his political obituary, took the podium. When he ceased to be an elected official the following month, his tenure as DLC chairman would also end. This would be one of his last opportunities to address the New Democrats as head of the DLC, and McCurdy spoke his mind.

"While Bill Clinton has the mind of a New Democrat, he retains the heart of an Old Democrat," McCurdy charged. "The result is an administration that has pursued elements of a moderate and liberal agenda at the same time, to the great confusion of the American people."[68] Explaining his comments less than a year later, McCurdy said that he had spent his career building up a New Democratic image, but when it came time to run on it, "it was totally discredited" and "it bit me on the tail."[69] As he fumed to one reporter, "Those of us in the center . . . we got screwed."[70]

Embarrassed by this public rift, Clinton immediately called a meeting in the White House with DLC leaders, including McCurdy, From, and Senators Breaux, Lieberman, Robb, and Nunn. In what was described as a "tense, sometimes angry meeting," Clinton accused the DLC of not defending him adequately and expressed his anger at being labeled a "transitional figure" by McCurdy. The Oklahoman countered that to steer the administration off its liberal track, it had to change. Then, looking directly at George Stephanopoulos, the presidential aide perceived as a representative of the party's liberal wing, McCurdy said, "Mr. President, with all due respect to George, you need to have serious personnel changes. The only way the American people are going to believe you've changed is if you show the change."[71]

Speaking to the conference on the same day, Gore tried to soothe the crowd by acknowledging that Clinton might have been better off if he had followed the DLC line and that the organization did provide the "intellectual basis" for the administration's policies.[72] In his own speech that evening, however, Clinton was unapologetic, arguing that the DLC "ought to be proud" and not bitter, since most of its agenda had been enacted. The president called on the DLC to "get out of the peanut gallery and into the arena" to join him in the fight for a host of New Democratic programs.[73] Yet despite this call to arms, many

New Democrats were not assuaged, still smarting from his breach of the DLC faith. Indeed, almost a year after the McCurdy criticisms, From still found them "impolitic, but . . . not inaccurate," and he agreed that Clinton was a "transitional figure."[74] Similarly, Marshall agreed with McCurdy's assessment that Clinton made the distinction between liberal and New Democrat "meaningless" to a lot of voters.[75]

This was a particularly risky situation for the DLC, since the organization was so closely linked to the president. By extension, if Clinton lost his bid for reelection—which at the time seemed likely— liberal Democrats and others would predictably claim that his DLC views were responsible, possibly resulting in the demise of the organization itself.[76] Unsure of what Clinton would do over the next two years, and concerned about protecting the future of the organization (and of other New Democrats), DLC leaders began to rethink their relationship with the president and the Democratic Party. If Clinton would not implement their public philosophy, perhaps they should look for other means of placing it on the party and national agenda.

The day after McCurdy slammed Clinton at the DLC conference, Joel Kotkin, a PPI senior fellow, made the first public call for a break with Clinton. In a *Wall Street Journal* column, Kotkin argued that the New Democrats should sever ties with Clinton, back a primary challenger in 1996, and even consider leaving the Democratic Party altogether.[77] These were only the opinions of one DLC-PPI leader, but the DLC appeared to be making oblique moves that demonstrated the organization's questioning of its allegiance to Clinton and even to the Democratic Party.

The largest such sign was its "Third Way Project," an effort run through the Progressive Foundation that ultimately resulted in the *New Progressive Declaration*. Although never overtly claimed by the DLC leadership, there is some evidence that this project was to be the beginning of a third-party movement. According to Michael Steinhardt, chairman of PPI's Board of Trustees until he resigned at the end of 1995, the Third Way Project was to be a "new approach to separate ourselves from the Democratic Party."[78] He explained that the DLC began to take on a more bipartisan focus, which appealed to a number of contributors, including Steinhardt himself, who advocated the formation of a third party and went so far as to meet with Bill Bradley to try to persuade him to run for president in 1996.[79]

The DLC during this time took on a decidedly less partisan tone.

The organization began to talk not just about changing the Democratic Party but also about revamping the whole of American politics.[80] In the *New Progressive Declaration,* the authors fashioned themselves as the avatars of a movement that welcomed "progressive-minded citizens of all stripes to the discussion: Democrats, Republicans, independents, liberals, conservatives, and moderates."[81] Doug Ross, one of the architects of the Third Way Project, saw the *New Progressive Declaration* as being not just for the use of Democrats but for all those who wanted to embrace it.[82] Indeed, there were some overtly bipartisan moves undertaken by the DLC. From and Jack Kemp, for example, cowrote a column in the *Los Angeles Times* supporting the use of vouchers in job training, and the DLC promoted the latest book by James Pinkerton, the former Bush aide, on restructuring government.[83] Although most in the DLC hoped that the Democratic Party would grab the mantle of change, the organization was no longer relying exclusively on that possibility.

On their own, these actions may not have amounted to much. But they all occurred against a backdrop of the president's apparent repudiation at the midterm election polls and a possible presidential bid by Colin Powell, the immensely popular retired chairman of the Joint Chiefs of Staff. Buoyed by his high profile during the Gulf War and his unknown but seemingly centrist beliefs, Powell became the focus of intense speculation that he might run for president on either major party ticket or as an independent. This excitement over his possible run reached a fever pitch in the fall of 1995, when Powell began a promotional tour for his autobiography. At the first stop, he was greeted by forty camera crews and a line of admirers half a mile long. He appeared on the cover of *Newsweek* twice and of *Time* once, and CNN's polling had him beating Clinton by eight percentage points in a hypothetical matchup.[84] The DLC's actions and rhetoric, then, taken together and in light of these developments, underscored—or may even have fed—the organization's flirtation with a break with Clinton and the Democratic Party.

In the end, however, the DLC was a "little schizophrenic" on the issue of a third party and chose to cast its lot with Clinton.[85] The abandonment of the idea to challenge Clinton in the primaries or even to back the formation of a third party was undoubtedly affected by Clinton's change in direction in 1995 and 1996, by the accompanying end to the hype surrounding a possible independent bid for the presidency by Powell or others, and especially by the risk of losing the main aspect of the organization's cachet—its relationship with the president.[86]

As Clinton rebounded by following the New Democratic public philosophy, the New Democrats too became rejuvenated, but they were chastened by the lessons learned during Clinton's first two years in office. From 1992 to 1994, the DLC had seen liberal Democrats in Congress and within the administration thwart its New Democratic agenda. The organization's leaders realized that the election of a New Democrat to the presidency had not been enough to transform the party immediately. Thus, after the 1994 elections, the DLC focused on recruiting and converting Democratic elected officials at the local and state levels.

As Chuck Alston, then DLC communications director, explained, elected-official membership regained the importance it had once held during the DLC's first years of operation "because what we are realizing is that there have to be deeper and broader changes in the way the people who make up the Democratic Party think."[87] This "new generation of Democratic leaders" would implement New Democratic programs and electoral strategy at the local level, and as their careers progressed, these officeholders would take these beliefs to higher levels of government and party leadership.[88] In this, the DLC was not returning to the days of the "big tent," when it sought members whomever they might be. Rather, the organization was looking to attract like-minded elected officials committed—or at least open to—the New Democratic public philosophy.

To attract this "new generation," the DLC refocused on its chapters. There were thirty of these by 1995, but, according to Simon Rosenberg, then DLC field director, only ten to fifteen were functioning strongly.[89] In many ways, though, the DLC was not really trying to build a grassroots organization by strengthening its chapters. Instead, it was targeting elected officials in the states themselves. The organization hoped to identify potential New Democrats, give them a network of like-minded officeholders, and develop New Democratic proposals for them to implement at the state and local levels. As Rosenberg explained, "if the Democratic Party exists to elect Democrats, the DLC exists to give elected Democrats something to say."[90]

Results of this shift in strategy quickly became apparent. By the spring of 1996, the DLC claimed that nine states had adopted PPI's "work-first" welfare reform initiative, four had passed legislation promoting second-chance homes for teenage mothers, and twenty had passed legislation supporting the creation of charter schools.[91] At the DLC's 1995 annual conference, the theme of the meeting was "building a new generation of Democratic leaders," and the organization held special sessions geared toward "help[ing] Democratic leaders translate the New Democratic philosophy into state and local policy."[92]

Indeed, the 1995 meeting was the largest DLC conference yet, with 1,500 attendees, of whom 300 were elected officials and 100 were state legislators.[93] In fact, by the end of the summer of 1995, the DLC had 505 elected-official members, ranging from the president of the United States to the mayor of Cherry Hill, New Jersey, and the DLC claimed that one in ten Democratic state legislators belonged to the organization.[94] Looking to the 1996 elections, the DLC held four candidate-training sessions that year to school prospective elected officials in New Democratic policies and political strategy.

At the same time, New Democrats working independently of the DLC, but toward the same goal, began to organize. In the House, Representative Jim Moran of Virginia reconvened the Mainstream Forum in January 1995. In November 1996, Moran, Calvin Dooley of California, and Tim Roemer of Indiana reconstituted the caucus into the New Democrat Coalition (NDC). Their pitch was simple: "If your experience on the campaign trail has been anything like ours, you have probably found that advocating traditional Democratic policies did not get you elected," the three cochairmen wrote in a recruitment letter.[95] By the end of November, they had enlisted thirty-two congressmen as members.[96] Working closely with the NDC was the New Democrat Network (NDN), a PAC founded in June 1996 by Lieberman and Breaux along with Rosenberg, the former DLC field director and Clinton "War Room" veteran, to provide monetary support for New Democratic candidates for the House and Senate.[97] Indeed, the PAC helped rejuvenate the organization of New Democrats in the House.[98]

Accordingly, as the 1996 elections approached, New Democrats were both organized and buoyant. They viewed the resurgence of Clinton's popularity as tied to his embrace of New Democratic policies, and his reelection seemed likely. In all these respects, the prospects for remaking the party once again seemed promising.

The Election of 1996

The 1996 elections confirmed the strength of the New Democratic public philosophy to the DLC and its allies. Running on their platform and following their political strategy, Clinton won reelection handily. To the DLC, Clinton had realized the error of his ways in the first two years of his presidency, paid the price for it in 1994, and was now reaping the rewards of returning to the fold in 1996. The DLC now believed that he was poised to remake the Democratic Party and even the whole of American politics.

ELECTORAL PROBLEMS AND ALTERNATIVES

In many ways, the 1996 presidential election was very similar to the one of 1992. First, in 1992, a weak field of candidates had helped ensure Clinton's nomination; in 1996, he ran in the first uncontested Democratic nominating campaign since the McGovern-Fraser reforms went into effect in 1972.[99] Second, it was still "the economy, stupid." In 1992, economic troubles had helped propel Clinton to victory; in 1996, economic successes played that role. Indeed, two-thirds of voters approved of Clinton's handling of the economy, and 79 percent of those who did voted for Clinton.[100]

Third, in 1992, Clinton had run against a Republican who publicly broke his word not to raise taxes. In 1996, Clinton faced Bob Dole, a longtime deficit hawk who shed those feathers and endorsed a 15 percent across-the-board tax cut. With the economy performing well and the deficit shrinking, Dole's new plan backfired with voters. According to a *New York Times* poll taken in the beginning of September 1996, 64 percent of those surveyed believed that Dole would not be able to cut taxes by that much and still honor his promise to balance the budget.[101] Finally, once again, Clinton was able to cast himself as the candidate of the future and of change. Whereas Dole, a World War II veteran, wanted to "build a bridge" to the bucolic past of midcentury America, Clinton campaigned as the candidate who would build "the bridge to the 21st century."[102]

That stark generational contrast, along with the Democrats' aggressive effort to link Dole with Newt Gingrich and the House Republicans—plus Dole's woeful inability to run a smart campaign—

enabled Clinton to build and hold a lead against the Republican. And on election day, Clinton became the first Democrat since Franklin Roosevelt to win a second full term, garnering 49 percent of the popular vote and thirty-one states (plus the District of Columbia), for 379 electoral votes. He dominated in the Northeast, winning every state by at least ten points (except Pennsylvania, which he won by nine), and he at least neutralized Republican domination of the South, matching the share of the regional popular vote for Dole and winning five southern states outright.[103]

Demographically, key constituencies targeted by the New Democrats joined the party's traditional base and supported Clinton in even greater numbers than they had in 1992. Fifty-seven percent of moderates, an eight-point increase from 1992, backed Clinton, as did 53 percent of Catholics, an eleven-point increase.[104] In the traditionally Republican suburbs, Clinton won 47 percent of the vote—slightly less than his overall vote share, but a strong showing nonetheless—and carried twenty-four of the twenty-eight largest suburban counties, six more than he had in 1992.[105] Furthermore, it appeared that driving this support was approval of Clinton's performance as president and approval of his issue stances. Voters were endorsing not Clinton himself—over half felt that he was neither honest nor trustworthy—but "Clintonism."

ISSUE PROBLEMS AND POLICY ALTERNATIVES

These voters were attracted not only to Clinton's able handling of the economy but also to his proposals on the other top concern that year: social issues, specifically, social welfare and public order issues.[106] In this context, Clinton was helped by his signing of welfare reform legislation, his endorsement by the Fraternal Order of Police (a group that had backed Bush in 1992), and his support of initiatives such as family and medical leave and the V-chip, which "signaled empathy with middle-class families who felt embattled in the social rather than economic sense."[107]

This New Democratic approach apparently resonated with voters. According to a postelection survey for the DLC conducted by Mark Penn, Clinton's reelection pollster, the president's most important accomplishment in the eyes of voters was moving 1 million people from welfare into jobs, and 71 percent approved of his position on crime.[108]

Along these same lines, as veteran election-watcher Gerald Pomper has argued, the Democratic Party's moderating of its socially liberal stances and image probably explains the significant shift of Catholics back to the Democratic fold.[109] All in all, one-quarter of all Clinton voters—the largest identifiable group—reported that his vision of the future was the top factor in deciding which candidate to support.[110]

And that vision was now an overwhelmingly New Democratic one. Not only did Clinton begin to govern as a New Democrat after 1994, but he explicitly ran for reelection as one. In the first presidential debate, Clinton stated his belief that the role of the federal government should be to "give people the tools and try to establish the conditions in which they can make the most of their own lives."[111] He struck this chord, for example, while campaigning in Republican strongholds in the South by stressing welfare reform.[112] Clinton's New Democratic outlook also was apparent in his response to Dole's tax-cut plan. Instead of attacking the proposal for being unfair to the poor (much as Mondale had attacked Reagan's economic policies in 1984), Clinton impugned it on fiscal responsibility grounds, calling it a "$550 billion tax scheme that will blow a hole in the deficit."[113]

But the clearest sign of the New Democratic public philosophy's importance to the reelection effort was in the party's platform, a document that from start to finish was a New Democratic document—as it had been in 1992. The Platform Committee was chaired by Governor Zell Miller of Georgia, an active DLC member, and the lead witness at the first committee hearing was Rob Shapiro of PPI. The document itself was written by Elaine Kamarck and Bruce Reed, and the text was structured along four main themes—opportunity; responsibility; community; and security, freedom, and peace—that came straight out of the DLC.[114]

Unsurprisingly, the platform stressed New Democratic achievements of the previous four years: deficit reduction, a strong anticrime bill, welfare reform, an increase in defense spending, and national service. In addition, in its opening pages, it explained New Democratic beliefs about the role of the federal government, calling for a "smaller, more effective, more efficient, less bureaucratic government" that does not "interfere with their [Americans'] lives but enhances their quality of life."[115] Finally, in an implicit break from past platforms, the 1996 document stated that "today's Democratic Party knows that the private sector is the engine of economic growth." In this, the party endorsed an economic agenda that balanced the budget while protecting Medicare, Medicaid, education, and environmental enforcement; cut taxes on the middle class; and expanded trade.[116]

Nevertheless, the interpretive war over all this goes on. Liberal critics have countered that Clinton won reelection because of this defense of Medicare and Medicaid, funding for education, and environmental protection. Moreover, they have contended that the inability of the Democratic Party to retake Congress proves the weakness of the New Democratic public philosophy.[117] The Democrats did have mixed results on the subpresidential level, losing two seats in the Senate and gaining ten in the House, to remain the minority in both. The DLC argued that the Democratic Party did not take back Congress because Democratic candidates were not sufficiently New Democratic.[118] Liberals retorted that allegations late in the race about violations of campaign finance laws by the presidential campaign had hurt the prospects of these congressional Democrats.[119]

What is more likely the case is that incumbency, plus the retirement of some southern Democrats, advantaged the GOP, which now controlled Congress. For example, 95 percent of incumbents won reelection, benefiting from an average financial advantage of three to one over challengers.[120] Thus, open seats played a large role in the election results. Of the nineteen formerly Democratic seats open in the South, seven went Republican, accounting for almost all the open seats the Republicans won.[121] In turn, "Democratic challengers simply picked off the ripest fruit" in other areas of the country, beating Republicans who had won previously by thin margins.[122]

Whether or not Clinton won reelection by running as an Old Democrat, defending Medicare, Medicaid, educational funding, and environmental enforcement, is difficult to assess. From one side, it is true that these stances were an important component of his victory. But from the other, although Clinton was defending popular government programs and functions against the prospect of radical overhaul or elimination by the GOP, he also supported their reform, endorsing, for example, the introduction of charter schools and the use of market-based methods of protecting the environment. Moreover, he launched such a defense after establishing his credentials as a New Democrat, thus framing the moves in the context of this public philosophy. As a result, Clinton's defense of these programs was not simply an embrace of Old Democratic politics, but rather an instance of coinciding priorities between the two factions in the face of a common opponent.

In fact, observers of all stripes commented on how much the Democratic Party had changed under Clinton. In endorsing him for a second term, the *New York Times* noted that Clinton had "refashioned the Democratic Party's approach to government," and the *New Republic* applauded him for "purging the party of activist government of some of its debilitating pathologies."[123] Liberals too recognized this change, bemoaning the apparent betrayal of principles, accusing Clinton of advocating "neo-Republicanism," and warning that the New Democrats were winning the battle over party principles.[124] Some liberals even took public action. The cochairwoman of Clinton's campaign in Washington State, for example, resigned over the candidate's intention to sign a bill that would deny the recognition of gay marriage, and Marian Wright Edelman, head of the Children's Defense Fund and a longtime Clinton friend, organized a march protesting his welfare reform policy and its effect on children.[125]

INSTITUTIONAL PROBLEMS AND ALTERNATIVES

Although Clinton resolved any substantive differences between liberals and New Democrats by siding with the latter, this did not mean the end of factional strife within the party. Despite liberals' complaints about Clinton's platform, the institutional might of their major constituency groups was not diminished by the presence of a New Democrat at the top of the ticket. Indeed, at the grassroots level, environmental, civil rights, and labor groups were still the core of the Democratic base, providing candidates in 1996 with funding, volunteers, and endorsements. The AFL-CIO spent $35 million on an independent campaign to elect Democrats to Congress, and the NEA's PAC donated $5.4 million to federal Democratic candidates during the 1996 elections.[126] Moreover, with the Republican takeover of Congress, business interests now had less of an incentive to donate to Democratic officeholders. As a result, Democratic congressional candidates became increasingly reliant on labor money. In the 1994 election cycle, labor PACs had given Democratic congressional candidates $40 million, and business PACs contributed $67 million; in 1996, labor PACs gave this group $45 million, and business PACs donated only $44 million.[127] Overall, labor PACs accounted for 47 percent of all PAC contributions to Democratic congressional candidates in 1996, up from 34 percent in 1994, and labor PACs provided 71 percent of all PAC backing to Democrats challenging GOP incumbents in 1996.[128]

To counter this, the New Democrats for the first time had their own PAC, the fledgling New Democrat Network. In operation for less than a year, it was able to contribute only $600,000 in the 1996 election cycle to twenty-six congressional challengers. Even so, fifteen of these challengers won, bolstering the ranks of the New Democrat Coalition in the House to forty-one by October 1997.[129] Additionally, after the 1996 elections, the DLC claimed that of the thirteen freshman Republican congressmen who had lost, ten had been defeated by New Democrats. It boasted that of the forty-one new Democratic congressmen, twenty-eight were New Democrats. And the organization saw Jeanne Shaheen, a member of the board of directors of the New Hampshire state DLC chapter, win that state's governorship.[130] Clinton also appointed some well-known New Democrats to key positions. These included Reed as his domestic policy adviser, Erskine Bowles as his chief of staff, Shapiro as the undersecretary of commerce, and Governor Roy Romer of Colorado, vice-chairman of the DLC, as chairman of the DNC.[131]

Still, despite the renewed activity of New Democrats in Congress and these presidential appointments, the House Democratic Caucus was clearly in the liberal camp. This situation, in turn, led to renewed battles between the two Democratic factions. Arguing that Clinton's 1997 budget agreement spent too little on domestic programs and gave too much away in tax cuts, Richard Gephardt, the Democratic leader in the House who was considering a White House run in 2000, characterized the plan as "a deficit of principle, a deficit of fairness, a deficit of tax justice, and, worst of all, a deficit of dollars."[132] Then, in a widely covered speech at the Kennedy School of Government in December 1997, Gephardt attacked the New Democrats directly and Clinton implicitly for lacking core principles. "New Democrats . . . [are those] who set their compass only off the direction of others—who talk about the political center, but fail to understand that if it is only defined by others, it lacks core values. And who too often market a political strategy masquerading as policy," he said.[133]

But the largest conflict between the liberals and New Democrats was over Clinton's request to renew his fast-track negotiating authority for trade agreements. On one side stood the Clinton administration and the DLC in favor of extension, and on the other stood an alliance of liberal groups—including the AFL-CIO, Ralph Nader, the Sierra Club, the National Farmers Union, and the Pure Food Campaign—and the House Democratic Caucus led by Gephardt.[134] In light of the large amount of money that labor had spent in the 1996 elections, the pressure on congressional Democrats was intense.

Meanwhile, the DLC rallied to the administration's cause. "New Democrats should stand squarely with President Clinton. His fight is our fight," From told those gathered at the DLC's 1997 annual conference.[135] Accordingly, the DLC initiated an "Appeal to Congress from the States" to support fast track. With solicitation letters signed by Mayor Ed Rendell of Philadelphia, Mayor Susan Hammer of San Jose, and Governor Lawton Chiles of Florida, the DLC gathered the signatures of more than 100 governors, state legislators, and mayors on a petition urging congressional Democrats to "sustain our economic growth by supporting fast-track authority for this Democratic President," and warning them that "we must not lose tomorrow's jobs because we failed to lead today."[136] To supplement this, the DLC spent about $200,000 on television ads in support of fast track.[137]

In the end, it appeared that only forty-two House Democrats would have supported the extension of fast track, and on November 10, 1997, Clinton aborted the vote, which surely would have gone down in defeat.[138] New Democrats were disheartened as even some of their own—including Tim Roemer, a founder of the NDC—succumbed to the pressure of labor's deep pockets and opposed the extension. Liberals, as expected, reveled in this win. Robert Borosage, the head of a labor-backed effort to counter the DLC called Campaign for America's Future, declared that the fast-track defeat was "the beginning of the progressive struggle for the next decade."[139] Indeed, it seemed that this long-simmering battle was looming ever closer on the horizon.

In many ways, the DLC would have welcomed this fight. Indeed, it had been denied a debate over the future of the party after Clinton's election in 1992 because of his wandering from the New Democratic line. And after the Republican takeover of Congress in 1994, the shock of this loss, along with the abject fright of losing control of the White House, prodded liberals largely to fall in line behind Clinton in the

1996 election. Now, with Clinton back in the New Democratic camp, the DLC happily reconciled with its former chairman, and the New Democratic public philosophy vindicated in another presidential victory, the DLC seemed eager to remake the rest of the party from the top down.

But as before, the precariousness of its presidential strategy profoundly shaped New Democratic fortunes. In the beginning of Clinton's first term, it was his straying from the New Democratic public philosophy. In the beginning of his second term, it was straying of a personal kind. A little more than eight weeks after the fast-track defeat—at a time when the president stood with the New Democrats and the lines for an intraparty battle were being drawn—the *Washington Post* broke the story of Clinton's extramarital relationship with Monica Lewinsky, a White House intern. Over the next year, the specter of scandal overshadowed any Democratic policy and political disputes. Impeachment dominated the political world.

Conclusion:
Securing a Legacy

WHILE WORKING in the White House residence on his 1998 State of the Union Address, Bill Clinton reportedly turned to Michael Waldman, his chief speechwriter, and remarked, "FDR's mission was to save capitalism from its excesses. Our mission has been to save government from its own excesses so it can again be a progressive force."[1] It is perhaps unsurprising that while working on one of his last State of the Union speeches—and doing so as the scandals that had plagued his presidency were about to inflame—that Clinton would be ruminating over his legacy. It is equally unsurprising that when his thoughts turned to how historians would judge him, Clinton would focus on how the Democratic Party's approach to governance and its entire public philosophy had changed during his presidency.

The Clinton legacy and the significance of the New Democratic effort became central concerns of Clinton and the DLC throughout 1998 and into 1999. The interpretation of the achievements of the Clinton presidency not only mattered to his personal reputation but also had a direct relevance to any upcoming struggles to define the Democratic Party once he left office. If his administration was determined to be a success and judged so because of his New Democratic public philosophy, then the argument to stay the course would be strengthened. Thus, the DLC and its allied organizations, the New Democrat Network and New Democrat Coalition, worked to fortify the New Democrats for the 1998 midterm elections, the 2000 presidential contest, and life after Clinton.

They did so confidently. With Clinton's return to the New Democratic fold after 1994, his reelection on that program, and the Democrats' unexpected victories in the 1998 midterm election, the New Democrats felt victorious. To them, not only was the era of big government over, but, in the words of DLC Chairman Joseph Lieberman, "the era of the party of big government is also over."[2] But is it? Has the DLC succeeded in changing the public philosophy of the Democratic Party into a New Democratic one?

There are many measures of success for a political organization, including such mundane but consequential ones as securing the spoils of public office. But for an organization built to change the public philosophy, there is no escaping this second question. In addressing it, a perspective on how one faction can consciously change the public philosophy of an American political party during the postreform era—and do so through the presidency—begins to take shape. From there, one can speculate about the future of the Democratic Party and of the New Democrats within it.

The Third Way

Although of a personal nature, the scandal that engulfed Clinton in 1998 especially affected the DLC and the New Democrats. On one level, it directly threatened the viability of their most powerful supporter and of the DLC's presidential strategy. On another level, it indirectly risked overshadowing Clinton's efforts to remake the Democratic Party in his image. DLC Chairman Lieberman was the first prominent Democrat to chastise Clinton publicly for his behavior, yet his and the DLC's position on the scandal never really wavered from that of the White House. The organization condemned the sin but loved the sinner; it would oppose his impeachment.[3]

With Clinton unable to champion his policy agenda and unwilling to antagonize congressional liberals who would judge him, policy innovation, especially of a New Democratic kind, ground to a halt. Yet the DLC began to look beyond the scandal—and even the Clinton presidency—focusing on ensuring that the New Democratic public policy and the politics and policies implicit in it outlasted Clinton's second term.[4] This was not only a matter of survival for the DLC. It also was a concern of the president's, as the changes he had undertaken in the party stood to be the most substantive alternative to his legacy of impeachment. "The real test of our ideas is whether they outlive this presidency; whether they are bigger than any candidate, any speech, any campaign, and debate," Clinton told the DLC at its annual conference in 1998.[5]

Practically, the New Democrat Network and the New Democrat Coalition intensified their activities to elect New Democrats to Congress. Tapping into many new high-tech businesses for support, NDN in particular grew rapidly. By the time of the 1998 election, the PAC had donated $1.4 million to over thirty Democratic candidates.[6] The DLC began to look to the 2000 elections as well. But instead of focusing on the practical side of electoral politics, the organization began elaborating political strategies and policies for the post-Clinton world, one that was fast approaching.

To accomplish this, the DLC revived an idea that had been considered and dismissed repeatedly throughout its history: the creation of a policy journal. In September 1998, the DLC unveiled *Blueprint: Ideas for a New Century*, a quarterly journal that would be produced until the 2000 elections. Edited by Andrei Cherny, a former speechwriter for Al Gore, *Blueprint* sought to provide an elucidation of core New Democratic beliefs, new policy prescriptions, and political approaches for the next election. In the debut issue, the most prominent contribution was from William Galston and Elaine Kamarck, who wrote an update to their influential "Politics of Evasion," an analysis that had been central to DLC strategy for the preceding decade.

In "Five Realities that Will Shape 21st Century Politics," Galston and Kamarck outlined what they believed to be the five dynamics shaping American politics at the end of the century. The first was that increasing returns on education have propelled more and more Americans out of the middle class, forming a "new learning class" of better-educated, wealthier, more mobile, and more self-reliant Americans. To Galston and Kamarck, this phenomenon explained the decreasing size of the middle class and the increasing gap between rich and poor, two developments bemoaned by liberals. This "new reality" meant that, from a policy perspective, it was crucial to provide a higher quality of education to more people, and from a political perspective, it was a "mistake to believe that Democrats can construct majorities based on a swelling pool of poor and near-poor Americans waiting to be mobilized by an old-fashioned politics of redistribution."[7]

The other realities that Galston and Kamarck outlined included the rise of "wired workers"—those who use computers on the job, work in self-directed groups, and do not need to rely on large mediating institutions (such as labor unions) for information; the passing of the New Deal generation, with its fondness for centralized government, from the electorate; the dominance of suburbia in political life; an increase in the number of children concentrated in fewer households, a situation demanding policies to help them based not on self-interest but on community; and the increasing diversity of the country, which demanded "unifying appeals to shared national values" in place of identity politics.[8] These realities, naturally, pointed to the need to embrace the New Democratic public philosophy. In addition, they became the central arguments for policy prescriptions and political strategies detailed in speeches and articles written by DLC leaders.[9]

In gazing to the future, the DLC also looked beyond the 2000 elections and even beyond the country's shores to add meaning and gravity to the New Democratic public philosophy. Beginning in earnest with the election of Tony Blair and his "New Labour" government in Great Britain in May 1997, the DLC viewed its public philosophy as part of a worldwide revolution in center-left politics. This "Third Way," wrote From, is "the worldwide brand name for progressive politics for the Information Age."[10] In the United States, the DLC argued, this politics took the form of the New Democrats, and in Britain, it took the form of New Labour.

The similarities between the two were clear enough. In defining the Third Way, Blair stressed themes of government reform, equal opportunity, free markets, and reciprocity that are at the heart of the New Democratic public philosophy. His goal of creating a Britain "equipped for the next century where every individual can ascend a ladder of opportunity, and every family has the support of a strong community," was one that could just as easily have been articulated by Clinton.[11] Politically, Blair and New Labour—like Clinton and the New Democrats—wanted to use this public philosophy to attract middle-class voters ("middle England") back to his party. And of course, the term "third way" had been used by the DLC to describe its public philosophy, even being inserted into the 1992 Democratic Party platform by its New Democratic drafters.[12]

The similarities between New Labour and the New Democrats were not a total coincidence. Interaction between the New Democrats and New Labour had gone on before Blair's election, as he and his team sought electoral success for a party long in exile, much as Clinton had done with the Democrats. Once Blair was elected, however, the notion and promotion of the Third Way became a DLC and, to some extent, a White House priority. During Blair's first year in office, he and Clinton met twice to discuss Third Way policies and politics, and Clinton had the same conversation with other apparent champions of this approach. In May 1998, he discussed it with Italian Prime Minister Romano Prodi; a month later, he did the same at Camp David with Brazilian President Fernando Henrique Cardoso; and that September, during the annual opening session of the United Nations General Assembly, Clinton, Blair, Prodi, and Bulgarian Prime Minister Petar Stoyanov held a forum on the Third Way, entitled "Strengthening Democracy in the Global Economy," at New York University.[13] During this same period, Hillary Clinton invited the DLC and New Democrat critics to the White House to discuss the Third Way, and she participated, along with other high-ranking officials and thinkers (including From), in a New Labour–New Democrat retreat at Chequers, the British prime minister's country residence.[14]

Liberals, as expected, dismissed the Third Way as an empty phrase used to describe an electoral tactic. "New Labour's third way is opportunism with a human face," argued New York University's Tony Judt in the *New York Times*.[15] Nevertheless, for the DLC, its Third Way activities boosted its profile and importance as the success of Third Way politicians—especially Blair—plus attention from analysts and admiration from elected officials worldwide, validated the DLC's approach to politics and policy. Also, by casting itself as the pioneer of a worldwide movement, the DLC helped ensure its own legacy. Said differently, the organization was no longer exclusively tied to the fortunes of a president or a party; it was part of something much larger and more durable.

For the White House, the Third Way had a similar effect. Being associated with a revolution in center-left politics, Clinton could claim a legacy wider than his reform of the Democratic Party, and he could begin doing so when his most prominent legacy was becoming scandal and impeachment. This imperative could also explain the intense interest that Hillary Clinton, a prominent liberal, and Sidney Blumenthal, a White House aide who as a journalist had been critical of the DLC, took in the Third Way.

Of course, the plaudits and praise of European policy wonks and intellectuals meant little to the practical success of the New Democrats. The real test of the efficacy of their public philosophy as a governing philosophy and political strategy was a simple one: could it win elections? The DLC argued that it had done just that in 1992 and 1996, and in 1998, to the surprise of many, it was able to make this claim again. For the first time since 1934, the party of the president in power did not lose any seats in Congress. In fact, after the ballots were counted, the Democrats picked up six seats in the House, to give the Republicans the smallest congressional majority since 1953. Democrats also defeated incumbent Republican senators in New York and North Carolina to maintain the fifty-five to forty-five split in the Senate. In the states, they took the governorships of Alabama, South Carolina, and California from the GOP, and won control of five legislative chambers.[16]

In victory, the Democrats not only carried their base of blacks, labor, and Hispanics. They also won strong support from groups targeted by the New Democrats. From 1994, the Democrats gained nine percentage points among moderates to win 54 percent of their support, and they jumped an equal amount among families that made over $75,000 a year to win 47 percent of their vote. Democratic candidates increased their support among Catholics and suburbanites as well.[17] As analyst William Schneider noted, the Democrats also won the support of an emerging constituency that he called the "New Rich." These educated, computer-savvy, suburban, middle-class citizens constituted one-quarter of all voters and were the ones who had benefited from the growing economy under Clinton.[18]

Democrats were able to construct this coalition of the New Rich (the DLC's "wired workers") and the base of blacks and labor unions because many of them copied the New Democratic approach proved successful by Clinton. Consider Lieutenant Governor Gray Davis of California, who won his state's governorship. A longtime liberal who had once served as chief of staff to Jerry Brown, Davis recast himself as a moderate who was tough on crime and dedicated to improving education. With this combination, he won as much as half of his state's moderate Republican vote and cruised to a crushing victory.[19] At the same time, the Republican strategy of stressing the Lewinsky scandal backfired. Only 5 percent of voters polled said that this was the most important issue, and Republican attacks on Clinton rallied liberals, especially blacks, to his and the Democratic cause.[20] Thus, Democratic candidates running as New Democrats were able to attract fervent support from the Democratic base.

For New Democrats themselves, 1998 was a success. All forty-one members of the NDC were reelected, and twenty-six of the thirty-four candidates that the NDN backed won. In this, its biggest victories were in the Senate, where New Democrats Evan Bayh of Indiana and Blanche Lambert Lincoln of Arkansas won open seats.[21] Pointing to the victories in 1998, the DLC claimed that the election was another vindication of the New Democratic public philosophy. "[It's] a victory for moderate, centrist candidates who subscribe to the basic philosophy of our movement," argued Lieberman.[22] As expected, John Sweeney, head of the AFL-CIO, made the case that it was the effort of labor and the turnout of minorities that produced Democratic victories.[23] From countered that these efforts may have helped, but it was the success of the New Democratic public philosophy that inoculated Democrats against charges that they were liberals out of step with mainstream America and enabled Democratic candidates to appeal beyond their base.[24]

In addition to these victories, the DLC reveled in what it saw at its 1998 annual conference. Much like the Cleveland convention had been in 1991, it was the first showcase of Democratic presidential hopefuls for 2000, and not one of the prospective candidates—including Gephardt—deviated much from the New Democratic line. Senator John Kerry of Massachusetts spoke about his proposal to overhaul public education by lambasting its bloated bureaucracy, urging more accountability for results, and calling for an end to value-free schools.[25] Senator Bob Kerrey of Nebraska outlined his strategy to reform Social Security by augmenting it with separate private savings accounts.[26] And Vice-President Gore called for an embrace of "practical idealism," a concept that was not much different from Clinton's Third Way.[27]

To many of the analysts who watch Washington closely, the uniformity of these candidates' New Democratic appeals was not that shocking. Beginning on the eve of the 1996 elections and intensifying after the 1998 elections, a range of pundits observed that the Democratic Party had in fact been transformed into a New Democratic party. For example, Carl Cannon of the *National Journal* opined that Clinton had placed the Democratic Party "on the same page as ordinary Americans on issues such as crime control and welfare reform" and had brought it into the "cultural mainstream."[28] Journalist Jacob Weisberg argued that Clinton's most significant achievement was that "he restored the feeling that domestic government could work," and did so to such a degree that "Clinton's political formula is now almost universally regarded as a winning one for Democrats."[29] Indeed, surveying the state of the DLC, William Schneider wrote that the elected officials who founded the organization "could hardly have imagined, back in those dark days, that 14 years later, the DLC would succeed in changing the country's governing philosophy. But it has."[30] As Frank Watkins, a close political aide of Jesse Jackson, lamented about the Democratic Party, "The DLC has taken it over."[31]

Have the New Democrats really taken over the Democratic Party? Has the public philosophy of the Democratic Party really changed? That is, has a New Democratic alternative become institutionalized as the dominant outlook on politics and government of Democratic office-holders, activists, and identifiers? On one level, it seems that it has. Since 1992, the Democratic Party has ratified two quintessentially New Democratic platforms at its quadrennial national convention. The party's general chairman is also vice-chairman of the DLC, and its national chairman, Joe Andrew, was a founder of the Indiana chapter of the DLC.[32] A Democratic president has signed into law a welfare reform package that places time limits on aid, a free-trade agreement with Mexico and Canada, a balanced-budget agreement, and a crime bill that mandates a life sentence for someone who commits three felonies. He also has cut the number of federal government employees to its lowest level since the Kennedy presidency—and boasts about it. Moreover, the same Democratic president won reelection while garnering impressive support among moderates, Catholics, and suburbanites. In turn, candidates seeking to copy Clinton's success have won elections in swing or traditionally Republican areas by running as New Democrats.[33]

There are signs that the public's perception of the Democratic Party has changed as well. In a *Washington Post*/ABC News poll conducted in March 1999, 47 percent of Americans surveyed said that they wanted to see the country go in the direction that Clinton wanted to lead it (compared with 29 percent who preferred the Republicans); independents preferred the Clinton direction by nearly two to one. Moreover, the Democrats were seen as being more able to handle a wide array of issues. These included their traditional strengths, such as the economy and education, and, surprisingly, more recent weaknesses, such as managing the budget, helping the middle class, and holding down taxes. More surprising, though, was that on traditional

Republican strengths—crime and foreign affairs—the GOP held only a four and eight percentage point advantage, respectively.[34]

On another level, however, it appears that the national party has not changed at all. Environmental, civil rights, and labor groups—who oppose the New Democratic public philosophy—are still the heart of the Democratic base, providing candidates with funding, volunteers, and endorsements crucial at the grassroots. It was the AFL-CIO that once again played a large role in the 1998 elections, spending $20 million on 392 field organizers, 9.5 million pieces of mail, 5.5 million phone calls, and television ads to help Democratic candidates.[35] In comparison, NDN donated only $1.4 million to New Democratic candidates. Looking to 2000, NDN did raise $550,000 in one evening in February 1999.[36] But a week later, at its meeting in Miami Beach, the AFL-CIO approved spending $46 million over the next two years—the first time the group had not dismantled its political operations at the end of an election cycle—in order to help Democrats take back the House.[37]

At the same time, it was the liberal constituency groups that were fervent in their defense of Clinton during his impeachment. Civil rights organizations rallied behind the president, and the AFL-CIO told its state federations to pressure their senators not to convict Clinton. Going even further, the liberal People for the American Way actually ran radio advertisements in four states and in the District of Columbia urging a Senate dismissal of the articles of impeachment.[38] The steadfastness of this support has led many to speculate that Clinton will have to pay back these liberal groups in kind. To some, this was evident in Clinton's 1999 State of the Union Address and in his avoidance of proposing a structural reform of Medicare and Social Security.[39]

Unsurprisingly, the influence of these liberal constituency groups is mirrored in the makeup of the national party itself, as their members, and those sharing their agenda, still constitute the vast bulk of party activists. According to a *New York Times*/CBS News poll of delegates to the 1996 Democratic National Convention, the postreform trend of activists being unrepresentative of the groups and beliefs found among Democratic voters and in the general electorate has continued. Three-quarters of all delegates felt that government should do more to solve the nation's problems, whereas only about half of Democratic voters and one-third of all voters felt this way. Delegates were far more likely to support affirmative action policies than were other Democratic voters. About 33 percent were members of a labor union, compared with 13 percent of Democratic voters; 69 percent were college graduates, compared with 17 percent of Democratic voters.[40] Interestingly, the delegates recognized the differences between themselves and Clinton: 43 percent described themselves as liberal, while only 8 percent described Clinton that way.[41] Clinton's own pollsters found that the electorate also agreed with this assessment, with voters viewing the president as more fiscally responsible, more values-oriented, and generally more favorable than the party as a whole.[42]

Among elected officials, especially in Congress, a similar situation prevails as the liberal faction continues to have a dominating presence. Clinton signed a welfare reform bill and a free-trade agreement over the opposition of most of the Democratic congressional delegation. In 1997, his effort to secure an extension of fast-track negotiating authority was killed by his fellow Democrats as well. Despite having fifty-seven members, making it one of the largest caucuses in the House, the New Democrat Coalition has not made a major impact. Its one attempt to assert its clout—a campaign to elect Cal Dooley, a cochair of the NDC, to be caucus vice-chairman—failed, and the House leadership once again was without a recognized New Democrat in its ranks.

The challenge in interpreting the progress of the DLC is that all this evidence is preliminary. Because the New Democrats are trying to remake the public philosophy of the party without the help of a national crisis to polarize the electorate and without a critical election to realign voters into new partisan attachments, it is too soon— even after six years of a Clinton presidency—to know what eventually will become of the New Democratic public philosophy. But what is clear is that contrary to what critics on both the left and the right have contended, the DLC's positions amount to a coherent New Democratic public philosophy, one whose main components are already recognizable. Moreover, parsing it into the four main components of a public philosophy—a theory of governance, views about the ends of society, the role of government and different levels of government in society, and the role of the country in the world—we see too that the New Democratic public philosophy is distinct from the liberal public philosophy.

In their clearest break from the liberal faction's thinking, the New Democrats believe that the federal government should not be the primary focus for reform efforts. Answers to societal problems and provision of social goods should be sought first in the private sector, then among local and state governments, and only then at the federal level. Underlying this belief, in turn, is a greater reliance on the community and faith in the free market, a faith born out of the belief that the Information Age, with its global, information-based economy, has made centralized bureaucratic structures obsolete. Unlike Republicans, many of whom also want to devolve many governmental functions to the state and local levels, New Democrats want to change the federal relationship to make government more effective, not to destroy it.[43] Furthermore, these tenets do not mean that New Democrats see no role for governmental action, as many on the right do. Rather, if a situation warrants federal involvement, the New Democrats prefer to use market mechanisms, not centralized bureaucracies, to implement policy.

The New Democratic public philosophy also breaks with the liberal interpretation of equality. Hearkening back to pre-1968 liberalism, the New Democrats endorse an equality of opportunity, not of results. They believe that the role of government is to provide equal access to opportunity, not to ensure that resources are distributed more equally. This belief dovetails with the New Democrats' view that the relationship between citizen and state should be one of reciprocal obligation. Simply put, they argue that citizens do not have unconditional rights to certain government benefits. Rather, the provision of many government services is contingent on a reciprocal responsibility on the part of the citizen, either to take the initiative to capitalize on them or to use them to serve society. In this, it can be said that the New Democrats are almost communitarian, placing social responsibilities ahead of individual rights, an inverse of the priorities of New Politics liberalism.[44] To these values—which the DLC and Clinton summarize as "opportunity, responsibility, and community"—the New Democrats add internationalism. Like their neoconservative and southern Democrat forefathers, they ardently support free trade, oppose deep cuts in the military, and believe that the United States should actively promote democracy and market economics throughout the world.

Finally, from the New Democratic public philosophy comes an implicit political strategy. The New Democrats reject the interest-group foundation of postwar liberalism. They do not want to cobble together the demands of particular interests in order to "reach down" to secure the further allegiance of its current base, a base that appears insufficient for electoral victory. Instead, they want to use their public philosophy as a platform from which to "reach out" to constituencies that were once reliably Democratic, as well as to groups—such as the middle class, suburbanites, and "wired workers"—that they believe are key to future electoral victories.[45]

Presently, we cannot know whether the New Democrats will ultimately succeed in replacing the liberal public philosophy as the dominant set of beliefs of the Democratic Party. Putting this uncertainty aside, what has and has not worked for the DLC? Although the ending of the story remains to be written, the rise of the New Democrats and of the DLC already provides us with tentative answers. A group of reformers first needs an institutional base, preferably outside the aegis of the national party. Unlike other groups that opposed the dominant liberal faction, notably the neoliberals and southern Democrats, the New Democrats were organized into a distinct institution. Initially, they were based in the Committee on Party Effectiveness within the House Democratic Caucus, and then briefly in the National House Democratic Caucus, again based in Congress. Yet being part of the House Democratic Caucus and tied to the political standing of its chairman, Gillis Long, these groups were neither sufficiently focused nor independent enough to garner wide attention from other political elites, much less to effect broad changes in the party. As part of the caucus, the CPE had to include and attend to a wide array of concerns and political outlooks, thus muting the distinctiveness and development of its positions.

Consequently, the New Democrats established the DLC outside the party organization. Interestingly, the reaction of the national party leadership to this move underscores the necessity not only of having an institutional base but also of having one outside of party control. A chairman of an American political party has an overriding need to keep the various factions in his coalition unified. His dominant instinct, then, is to co-opt, not to confront, dissenting elements. So although the DLC was formed outside of the party structure, it did not mean that the organization was free of its constraints. The DNC deliberately tried to placate the DLC in order to defuse its challenge.

At the same time, the dominant liberal faction aided in this effort by aggressively condemning the New Democrats as conservative, racist, and sexist. To this group, the New Democratic alternative was not fit even to enter the debate about the future of the party, much less win it. Faced with this potentially fatal criticism, the DLC embarked on a "big-tent" strategy to blunt these criticisms, a tack that also blunted its own efficacy. Thus, contrary to those who bemoan the weakness of American political parties, it appears that they are fairly resilient. Even extraparty organizations can be constrained and co-opted by the party itself. However, if the crisis that warranted the formation of the extraparty organization in the first place should deepen, it can serve as a powerful force of rejuvenation.

For the DLC, the Dukakis defeat played this role. The third consecutive loss by a Democratic presidential nominee, especially in an election that many Democrats thought he could win, underscored the severity of the Democrats' problems and revived the New Democratic effort. It gave the organization the impetus (and courage) to shed its big tent, clearly define the problem with the Democratic Party and its prevalent liberalism, develop a distinct alternative, and search for a means to place it onto the party's agenda. In retrospect, we can see that these basic moves—defining a problem, developing an alternative, and finding a way to plant it in a party—are crucial to changing the public philosophy of a modern American party. They may sound simple, but as the DLC story shows, they are not easy to implement.

First, only when the DLC had a clearly defined critique of the party's public philosophy ("The Politics of Evasion") and evidence to support it (three presidential defeats) was it able to—and perhaps compelled to—mount a credible effort to reform the party. Second, only when the DLC had a fully developed alternative public philosophy was it able to have any real impact on party affairs. After the 1984 election, it became clear to the nascent New Democrats that just tinkering with the party's institutional arrangements, even its nominating rules, would not result in a transformation of the party's public philosophy. Thus, among other things, the New Democrats recognized that they had to define and advocate their alternative. This effort, however, lay dormant from 1985 to 1988, while the DLC leadership continued to maintain a big-tent organizational format.

As a result, when the DLC tried to affect the outcome of the 1988 nominating campaign, it was disadvantaged: it did not have a coherent public philosophy or an accompanying policy agenda for a candidate to champion. In many ways, the New Democrats were still relying on working within the national party and on altering its rules in order to effect a change of public philosophy. Conversely, providing Clinton with this alternative public philosophy helped him develop a message and a program for the "invisible primary," the nominating campaign, and beyond. In sum, one cannot consciously change the public philosophy of a party without a developed substitute to replace the allegedly flawed original.

Once a defined problem and a developed alternative are in hand, the final element needed to change the public philosophy of a party is a means to reset the party agenda. For a minority faction in a modern American political party, this represents a very difficult task. For a faction of elites, it is an even more daunting operation. Theoretically, one can organize a grassroots movement; win seats in the local, state, and national party committees, as well as delegate slots to state and national party conventions; and finally take control of the party machinery itself. This is how, for instance, teachers unions and feminist groups gained a foothold in the Democratic Party in the 1970s, and how religious conservatives did it in the GOP in the 1980s. Such a movement could simultaneously mobilize its members to work on behalf of like-minded candidates, fund them, and vote for them. However, for the DLC, this was never a realistic option. It was an extra-party organization of elected officials and other political elites, and trying to mobilize swing voters—voters who, by definition, have weak partisan ties—to rise to a partisan cause was an impossible task.

Moreover, the New Democrats were particularly disadvantaged because fifteen years of rules changes had shifted power within the party from elected officials to purposive issuè activists and to the organizations to which they belonged. Previously, a group of elected officials and party leaders could have aspired to reform the nominating rules and organization of the party and influence its choice of chairman—and in the past, some did. Now, as the New Democrats learned, they could do neither.

But, as neoconservatives were fond of pointing out, there are unintended consequences of reform. In this case, the new open institutional arrangements that shut elected officials out of party affairs and closed off a traditional avenue of influence created an opportunity for organized elites, like the DLC, to use the presidency to change the party's public philosophy. Of course, this was not apparent in the early days of this system. Then, it clearly advantaged the New Politics liberals, as they had the people willing to participate in party affairs, primaries, and caucuses and in the organizations able to affect them. By currying their support, insurgents such as McGovern and Carter were able to win the party's nomination, and as this faction became the Democratic establishment, it could fend off challenges to its preferred candidate, such as Mondale in 1984.

Beginning in 1988, this system began to change in a subtle but important way. Basically, the nominating process became shorter, with more primaries and caucuses occurring in quick succession and even on the same day, as in the case of Super Tuesday. In 1972, for example, the largest number of delegates to be won on a single day was on the last day of the nominating season in June. Twenty years later, thirty-one of fifty-one primaries and caucuses were held in February or March.[46] With this front-loading, it became more difficult for a candidate relying on retail politics in Iowa and New Hampshire to parlay victories there into viable candidacies. With an accelerated process, there is not enough time in between contests to hone a message, establish numerous state organizations, and raise the money needed to buy the television advertising crucial to reach voters in different states holding primaries on the same day.

Consequently, the invisible primary increased in importance. This period became one of the only times in which a candidate could develop a message and amass a large campaign account. In turn, these tasks became even more critical, as they were signs of viability to elected officials and benefactors seeking to back a winner. Thus, in 1988, Gephardt's assiduous courting of interest groups and activists in Iowa won him that state's caucuses, but Dukakis's money won him the nomination. Likewise, in 1992, Bill Clinton won neither Iowa nor New Hampshire, but he won the nomination; and in 1996, despite early primary wins by insurgents Pat Buchanan and Steve Forbes (in New Hampshire and Arizona, respectively), they were no match for Bob Dole, the establishment candidate.

This is not to claim that organized constituencies have become powerless or that their resources have become meaningless in the presidential nominating system. The front-loaded process could still propel a dark-horse candidate who won an early contest through to the nomination. But even such a candidate would have to possess the resources in reserve to endure such an ascent. Gary Hart, for instance, was hampered by organizational problems in his insurgent campaign in 1984, a year with more widely spaced contests. Thus, the front-loading of the nominating process offers an opportunity for elite organizations of elected officials and benefactors to provide a presidential hopeful with some of the components needed in this "open" system to initiate a credible run for the presidential nomination and to survive it. These components include a developed message and platform, national media exposure, an elite base in key battleground states, and entree to a network of benefactors.

Seizing on this presidential route to party power, the DLC founded a think tank, the Progressive Policy Institute, to develop its public philosophy further; recruited Clinton to be its chairman; formed a network of state chapters; and held a national convention to highlight them all. When Clinton entered the presidential race, he then became a vehicle for the New Democratic message, and his success positioned the New Democratic public philosophy in the spotlight.

Yet what happened next also suggests the precariousness of this strategy. The New Democratic public philosophy and the aid the DLC provided to Bill Clinton were crucial to his win, but so was a set of circumstances beyond the DLC's control. In the nominating campaign, Clinton was helped by an abnormally weak field of candidates, and especially by the absence of a credible liberal or black standard-bearer. Likewise, in the general election, he was aided by the end of the Cold War, which removed an issue context favorable to the GOP from the fore; by a recession that happened on the watch of the Republican incumbent; and even by the presence of a strong independent candidate. In his reelection, Clinton drew an opponent whose campaigning skills paled in comparison to his and who had to contend with a party perceived as too extreme. Finally, the DLC may have been fortunate to find Clinton, who, as a southern governor who had worked for McGovern, may have been uniquely qualified to straddle the divides within the Democratic Party.

If any of these variables did not break the DLC's way, the presidential strategy could have failed, and so too the entire organization. But that did not happen, and Clinton was elected president. Yet the mere election of a president does not transform his party's public philosophy. Indeed, such a sudden change can occur only when there is a major national crisis, a critical election, and a massive voter realignment. However, what the DLC chronology suggests is that the election of a president can initiate a change in a party's public philosophy, provided that the proposed alternative meets two criteria.

First, it must be operationally effective. That is, the public philosophy must adequately address pressing societal problems and do so in a way that is in line with the core values of the country. Second, a public philosophy must be politically effective as well. It must enable a party to win elections and keep political power. Of course, these two criteria are inextricably linked. If a public philosophy fails to deliver on its promises or does so in a way offensive to the electorate, then it and its proponents most likely will be discredited and removed from office. However, a public philosophy can be operationally effective but politically ineffective. The emergence of a new issue concern (especially one that traditionally advantages the other party), a scandal, or just a sense that the other party's standard-bearer would be better at running the country could lead to political defeat no matter how objectively successful a public philosophy may be.

For the New Democrats, the argument can be made that they have met with much operational success. Six years into the Clinton presidency, the country has enjoyed the longest peacetime expansion of the economy in history, more than 18 million new jobs have been created, the unemployment rate is the lowest sustained peacetime jobless rate in forty-one years, the inflation rate is the lowest it has been since the 1950s, and the budget is in surplus.[47] One poll found that 89 percent of those surveyed rated the economic conditions of the country as very or somewhat good.[48] The crime rate is at its lowest in twenty-five years, and the number of welfare recipients has been more than halved.[49] In foreign affairs, America is the lone, undisputed world superpower. Yet despite all this, an electoral defeat sustained for any reason would aid their rivals in arguing that the New Democratic public philosophy must be changed, just as the defeats of the Democratic ticket in 1972, 1980, 1984, and 1988 lent credence to the New Democratic argument that the liberal public philosophy had failed and needed to be replaced.

The DLC and the New Democrats are vulnerable to such a defeat, since they are attempting to change a public philosophy without the benefit of a realigning event and without a mass or activist base. From the makeup of the delegates to the nominating conventions to the main sources of campaign volunteers and funds, it is clear that the liberal faction and its constituent groups continue to predominate within the party. The liberals are still an important, if not vital, component in winning the party's nomination for office from congressman to president, and with their dominance of the congressional party, they are also critical actors in constructing a governing coalition. Lacking this base within the party itself, New Democrats—or an elite faction in either party attempting to change a public philosophy—require a sustained period of political success in order to truly remake the party and wed new groups to their coalition. Said differently, no matter how successful their public philosophy may be, the party still matters. The New Democrats must embark on a "long march through the institutions."

The first step in this process is continuing their hold on the presidency. As the single most influential embodiment of the party, the president can use the "bully pulpit" to champion the new public philosophy, attract new constituencies to the party's coalition, and recast the popular perception of the party.[50] Similarly, the politically ambitious could reasonably be tempted to imitate the successful president and begin to identify themselves with this ascendant point of view. As one commentator explained it, "If Walter Mondale had won, everybody would look like Walter Mondale. But Bill Clinton won, and politicians go with what wins."[51] Moreover, the president, as chief arbiter of the party agenda, dominates the process of defining problems and devising solutions. This control diminishes the market for policy ideas that diverge from the presidential paradigm, and would-be policymakers act accordingly. Even opponents of aspects of the new public philosophy would have to address specific problems within the bounds set by these underlying beliefs.

Yet as already seen in the Clinton presidency, relying on one president or on retaining a hold on one branch of government is a risky proposition. Any number of factors could lead a president to stray from a stated course or could discredit a public philosophy even if he did not. Furthermore, competing power centers held by the opposition faction could hurt the president's effort to redefine the party to voters. On one level, these power centers can make legitimate demands for political appointments and policy concessions. On another level, any disputes over these issues can make the party seem fractious and thus detract from the political, and even operational, effectiveness of the public philosophy.

Thus, a faction interested in changing a party's public philosophy must take the next step and enlist those attracted to the party because of its new public philosophy to run for public office and for positions throughout the state and national parties. Said differently, after winning the head of the party, a faction needs to shift its focus to transforming the parts that make up the "body" of the party, such as the activist base and elected officials. It must combine stable success at the top with mounting advances among the party's grassroots, activists, and elected officials.

It appears that the New Democrats have begun this long march. The DLC has taken on the training of a "new generation" of New Democratic leaders as a primary organizational objective, continuing its efforts to work with and influence up-and-coming state and local officials. The New Democrat Network has grown quickly, increasing its ability to fund New Democratic candidates for federal office, including those running in primary contests. Tied to NDN's success, the New Democrat Coalition in Congress has attracted many new members, turning it into a potential New Democratic beachhead in the House.

The DLC's success in transforming the Democratic Party's public philosophy will be monitored not solely by its liberal rivals. Also watching its progress will be Republicans eager to duplicate the DLC's success in establishing a counterforce to their own purposive activists who are advocating an agenda that is out of touch with the general electorate and even with the Republican rank and file. Indeed, a group of Republican elected officials and benefactors has established the Republican Leadership Council to recapture the GOP's agenda from its right wing and replace it with a more mainstream platform in order to better the Republicans' odds in 2000 and beyond. Like the DLC, these "New Republicans" have impressive elite support among prominent elected officials (such as Governors Christine Todd Whitman of New Jersey and George Pataki of New York) but little representation in the House and virtually none at the party's grassroots. They hope that a New Republican—or a "compassionate conservative"—wins the GOP presidential nomination soon and saves a party that has lost the presidency twice and has seen its newly won hold on Congress weaken.[52]

This parallel and eerily similar development in the Republican Party speaks to the efficacy of the DLC's efforts. It is an unintended endorsement from another faction shut out of party affairs of the New Democrats' attempt to change the public philosophy of the Democratic Party through the presidency. But more than that, it points to a strategy for party factions to reassert and even challenge the hold that purposive issue activists have had on American political parties for the last quarter of the twentieth century. In this, the success of moderate groups in changing the public philosophies of both their parties represents a counterreformation in American politics. After decades in which the parties have been unrepresentative of the views of their rank and file and of the general electorate and in which more and more Americans have ceased to identify with either party, the resurgence of factions eager to place their parties within the mainstream represents a step toward more responsible parties and a healthier democracy. It is an encouraging development in the ongoing American struggle to cure "the mischiefs of faction."

It even can be argued that the party system is settling after the shocks—and arguable realignment—of the 1960s and that the country is headed to some sort of post–Cold War consensus akin to the postwar consensus of Eisenhower and Kennedy. But this is an outcome that hinges on whether either the New Democrats or the New Republicans can attain that ultimate source of vindication: electoral victory. For the New Democrats, at least, even if they are unsuccessful in winning the party's nomination or if a New Democratic candidate should lose the White House, they are far enough along in this rebuilding process that they would not quickly disappear.

After fifteen years, the New Democratic project has succeeded to the degree that one defeat will not destroy it. Capitalizing on political defeat and changing socioeconomic trends, the DLC and the New Democrats have offered the most durable and sustained effort to oppose the dominant liberal faction of their party to date. Establishing themselves outside of the party, guided by able policy entrepreneurs, and following a strategy that played to their faction's strengths, they have united the various groups remaining in the Democratic Party that disagreed with the dominant public philosophy into a potent intraparty force. Outside of the party, the New Democratic public philosophy and policy agenda are now major factors in national debates on issues ranging from entitlement reform to law enforcement to education. Moreover, the DLC's public philosophy can attract swing voters in competitive districts and states, the key to any hope the party has for recapturing the House and Senate. Ultimately, it is success in winning such offices, plus a continuing hold on the presidency, that will institutionalize the New Democratic public philosophy further. And with each victory, it will be harder and harder to return to the liberalism that preceded it.

Notes

Works frequently cited in the notes have been identified by the following abbreviations:

AFPP   Al From Personal Papers
CDF   Communications Director's Files
CQWR *Congressional Quarterly Weekly Report*
DLCP   Democratic Leadership Council Papers
DLCPB   Democratic Leadership Council Press Books
DNCP   Democratic National Committee Papers
NJ   *National Journal*
NYT   *New York Times*
RAP   *Renewing America's Promise: A Democratic Blueprint for Our Nation's Future*
RRO   *Rebuilding the Road to Opportunity: A Democratic Direction for the 1980's*
WP   *Washington Post*

Introduction

1. Jacob Weisberg, "The Governor-President Bill Clinton," *New York Times* (hereafter cited as *NYT*), 17 January 1999, sec. 6, p. 31. Also see Ronald Brownstein, "Clinton's Reversion to Old Tactics Doesn't Bode Well for Democrats," *Los Angeles Times*, 22 March 1999, http://www.latimes.com/HOME/NEWS/ASECTION/t000025585.html; David Shribman, "Past Clinton, on Middle Road," *Boston Globe*, 22 September 1998, sec. A, p. 3; Ross K. Baker, "Presidential Legacy Can't Survive Failure of the President," *Los Angeles Times*, 11 September 1998, sec. B, p. 11; Carl M. Cannon, "What Hath Bill Wrought?" *National Journal* (hereafter cited as *NJ*) 30, no. 45 (7 November 1998), p. 2622; James A. Barnes, "Planting the Seeds," *NJ* 28, no. 45 (9 November 1996), p. 2404; William Schneider, "No Modesty, Please, We're the DLC," *NJ* 30, no. 50 (12 December 1998), p. 2962; and E. J. Dionne, Jr., *They Only Look Dead: Why Progressives Will Dominate the Next Political Era* (New York: Simon and Schuster, 1996), p. 15.

2. Only one chapter in one book and one journal article have been written about the DLC and the New Democrats. See Nicol Rae, *Southern Democrats* (Oxford: Oxford University Press, 1994), chap. 6; and Jon F. Hale, "The Making of the New Democrats," *Political Science Quarterly* 110, no. 2 (1995), pp. 207–32. Jon F. Hale, "A Different Kind of Democrat: Bill Clinton, the DLC, and the

Construction of a New Party Identity," paper presented at the annual meeting of the American Political Science Association, Washington, DC, 1993, is an earlier version of the Hale article.

3. The literature of the Democratic Party during the 1980s and 1990s has been dominated by popular analyses, journalistic accounts, and partisan polemics. For examples, see Thomas Byrne Edsall with Mary D. Edsall, *Chain Reaction: The Impact of Race, Rights, and Taxes on American Politics* (New York: W. W. Norton, 1991); Elizabeth Drew, *Showdown: The Struggle between the Gingrich Congress and the Clinton White House* (New York: Simon and Schuster, 1996); and Jeff Faux, *The Party's Not Over: A New Vision for the Democrats* (New York: Basic Books, 1996).

4. The landmark works are V. O. Key, Jr., "A Theory of Critical Elections," *Journal of Politics* 17 (February 1955), pp. 3–18; Walter Dean Burnham, *The Current Crisis in American Politics* (New York: Oxford University Press, 1982); and James L. Sundquist, *Dynamics of the Party System: Alignment and Realignment of Political Parties in the United States*, rev. ed. (Washington, DC: Brookings Institution, 1983).

5. Sundquist, *Dynamics of the Party System*, p. 5.

6. Walter Dean Burnham, "Realignment Lives: The 1994 Earthquake and Its Implications," in *The Clinton Presidency: Early Appraisals*, Colin Campbell and Bert A. Rockman, eds. (Chatham, NJ: Chatham House Publishers, 1996), pp. 371–72.

7. Samuel Beer, "In Search of a New Public Philosophy," in *The New American Political System*, 1st ed., Anthony S. King, ed. (Washington, DC: American Enterprise Institute for Public Policy Research, 1978), pp. 5, 5n.

8. James Ceaser, "The Theory of Governance of the Reagan Administration," in *The Reagan Presidency and the Governing of America*, Lester M. Salamon and Michael S. Lund, eds. (Washington, DC: Urban Institute Press, 1984), pp. 57–58.

9. To define "issue context," I turn to Byron E. Shafer and William J. M. Claggett, *The Two Majorities: The Issue Context of Modern American Politics* (Baltimore, MD: Johns Hopkins University Press, 1995), p. 1. They define the term as "a grand substantive framework for political conflict. As such, it consists of the more stable, underlying concerns that organize the politics of its era, along with the more changeable, surface concerns that give these underlying influences expression."

10. John W. Kingdon, *Agendas, Alternatives, and Public Policies* (Boston: Little, Brown, 1984), p. 77.

11. Theodore Lowi, "Toward Functionalism in Political Science: The Case of Innovation in Party Systems," *American Political Science Review* 57 (September 1963), pp. 570, 582; and Frank L. Wilson, "The Sources of Party Change: The Social Democratic Parties of Britain, France, Germany, and Spain," in *How Political Parties Work: Perspectives from Within*, Kay Lawson, ed. (Westport, CT: Praeger, 1994), p. 264.

12. Nelson W. Polsby, *Political Innovation in America: The Politics of Policy Initiation* (New Haven, CT: Yale University Press, 1984).

13. Ibid., p. 99.

14. Kingdon, *Agendas, Alternatives, and Public Policies*, pp. 21, 92, 100, 135, 138, 173, 195.

Chapter 1: Moving from New Dealers to Neoliberals

1. Text of Adlai Stevenson for President television commercial from the 1952 general election campaign.

2. Text of George McGovern for President television commercial from the 1972 general election campaign.

3. As quoted in Everett Carll Ladd, Jr., with Charles D. Hadley, *Transformations of the American Party System: Political Coalitions from the New Deal to the 1970's*, 2nd ed. (New York: W. W. Norton, 1978), p. 37. Also see Samuel Beer, "In Search of a New Public Philosophy," in *The New American Political System*, 1st ed., Anthony S. King, ed. (Washington, DC: American Enterprise Institute for Public Policy Research, 1978), pp. 8–11.

4. Ladd and Hadley, *Transformations of the American Party System*, pp. 37–39; and Alan Brinkley, *The End of Reform: New Deal Liberalism in Recession and War* (New York: Random House, 1995), pp. 6–7. Also see Theda Skocpol, "The Legacies of New Deal Liberalism," in *Liberalism Reconsidered*, Douglas Maclean and Claudia Mills, eds. (Totowa, NJ: Rowman and Allanheld, 1983), p. 95.

5. Ladd and Hadley, *Transformations of the American Party System*, p. 39.

6. Robert E. Burke, "Election of 1940," in *History of American Presidential Elections, 1789–1968*, vol. 4, Arthur M. Schlesinger and Fred Israel, eds. (New York: McGraw-Hill, 1971), p. 2928.

7. Ibid., pp. 2960–61.

8. Samuel Lubell, *The Future of American Politics* (New York: Harper and Brothers, 1951), p. 200.

9. James L. Sundquist, *Dynamics of the Party System: Alignment and Realignment of Political Parties in the United States*, rev. ed. (Washington, DC: Brookings Institution, 1983), pp. 217–20; and Benjamin Ginsberg and Martin Shefter, "A Critical Realignment? The New Politics, the Reconstituted Right, and the 1984 Election," in *The Elections of 1984*, Michael Nelson, ed. (Washington, DC: CQ Press, 1985), p. 3.

10. Sundquist, *Dynamics of the Party System*, p. 210; Edgar Eugene Robinson, *They Voted for Roosevelt: The Presidential Vote, 1932–1944* (New York: Octagon Books, 1970), pp. 4, 33.

11. Richard S. Kirkendall, "Election of 1948," in *History of American Presidential Elections, 1789–1968*, vol. 4, Arthur M. Schlesinger and Fred Israel, eds. (New York: McGraw-Hill, 1971), p. 3143.

12. Richard Jensen, "The Last Party System: Decay of Consensus, 1932–1980," in *The Evolution of American Electoral Systems*, Paul Kleppner et al., eds. (Westport, CT: Greenwood Press, 1981), p. 42.

13. Ginsberg and Shefter, "A Critical Realignment?" p. 3.

14. Walter Dean Burnham, "The 1976 Election: Has the Crisis Been Adjourned?" in *The Current Crisis in American Politics* (New York: Oxford University Press, 1982), pp. 230–31.

15. Alonzo L. Hamby, *Liberalism and Its Challengers: From FDR to Bush*, 2nd ed. (Oxford: Oxford University Press, 1992), p. 121.

16. Barton J. Bernstein, "Election of 1952," in *History of American Presidential Elections, 1789–1968*, vol. 4, Arthur M. Schlesinger and Fred Israel, eds. (New York:

McGraw-Hill, 1971), pp. 3290, 3723–26; Malcolm Moos, "Election of 1956," in ibid., pp. 3364, 3391–93.

17. Ibid.

18. William M. Lunch, *The Nationalization of American Politics* (Berkeley, CA: University of California Press, 1987), p. 3.

19. James Q. Wilson, *The Amateur Democrat: Club Politics in Three Cities* (Chicago: University of Chicago Press, 1962); Peter B. Clark and James Q. Wilson, "Incentive Systems: A Theory of Organizations," *Administrative Science Quarterly* 6 (September 1961), pp. 135–36; Alan Ware, *The Breakdown of Democratic Party Organization, 1940–1980* (Oxford: Clarendon Press, 1985), p. 71; Ladd and Hadley, *Transformations of the American Party System*, p. 184.

29. Nicol C. Rae, *The Decline and Fall of the Liberal Republicans: From 1952 to the Present* (Oxford: Oxford University Press, 1989), p. 60.

21. Eisenhower spent $1.5 million on TV and radio advertisements in forty-nine counties in twelve key states three weeks before election day. Barbara G. Salmore and Stephen A. Salmore, *Candidates, Parties, and Campaigns: Electoral Politics in America,* 2nd ed. (Washington, DC: CQ Press, 1989), p. 43.

22. Martin P. Wattenberg, *The Decline of American Political Parties: 1952–1988,* enlarged ed. (Cambridge, MA: Harvard University Press, 1990), pp. 20, 23.

23. John Barlow Martin, "Election of 1964," in *History of American Presidential Elections, 1789–1968,* vol. 4, Arthur M. Schlesinger and Fred Israel, eds. (New York: McGraw-Hill, 1971), pp. 3570–71, 3644.

24. Ibid., pp. 3635, 3645.

25. Ginsberg and Shefter, "A Critical Realignment?" p. 5.

26. Kevin P. Phillips, *The Emerging Republican Majority* (Garden City, NY: Doubleday, 1969), p. 37. Also see William Schneider, "The Suburban Century Begins," *Atlantic* (July 1992), pp. 33–44.

27. Warren E. Miller and Santa A. Traugott, *American National Election Studies Data Sourcebook, 1952–1986* (Cambridge, MA: Harvard University Press, 1989), p.158, table 3.4.

28. John Ehrman, *The Rise of Neoconservatism: Intellectuals and Foreign Affairs, 1945–1994* (New Haven, CT: Yale University Press, 1995), p. 18; also see James Miller, *Democracy Is in the Streets: From Port Huron to the Siege of Chicago* (New York: Simon and Schuster, 1987).

29. Ginsberg and Shefter, "A Critical Realignment?" p. 4.

30. Richard M. Scammon and Ben J. Wattenberg, *The Real Majority* (New York: Coward-McCann, 1970).

31. Everett Carll Ladd, Jr., " The Shifting Party Coalitions—from the 1930's to the 1970's," in *Party Coalitions in the 1980's,* Seymour Martin Lipset, ed. (San Francisco: Institute for Contemporary Studies, 1981), p. 136.
I use the term "New Politics" Left or faction to distinguish those working within the Democratic Party from the many in the New Left who refused to take part in organized, two-party politics and to include those purposive or ideological activists who were not members of the New Left. See Miller, *Democracy Is in the Streets,* for more on the history of the New Left, especially Students for a Democratic Society.

32. Frederick G. Dutton, *Changing Sources of Power: American Politics in the 1970's* (New York: McGraw-Hill, 1971), p. 61.

33. Ginsberg and Shefter, "A Critical Realignment?" p. 10.

34. Or possibly the Republican Party culture itself would make such a convention an impossibility. See Byron E. Shafer, "Republicans and Democrats as Social Types: Or, Notes toward an Ethnography of the Political Parties," *Journal of American Studies* 20, no. 3 (1986), pp. 341–54; and Jo Freeman, "The Political Culture of the Democratic and Republican Parties," *Political Science Quarterly* 101, no. 3 (1986), pp. 327–56.

35. Ginsberg and Shefter, "A Critical Realignment?" p. 19; William Schneider, "Democrats and Republicans, Liberals and Conservatives" in *Party Coalitions in the 1980's*, Seymour Martin Lipset, ed. (San Francisco: Institute for Contemporary Studies, 1981), p. 201.

36. Dan T. Carter, *Politics of Rage: George Wallace, the Origins of the New Conservatism, and the Transformation of American Politics* (New York: Simon and Schuster, 1995), pp. 313, 334, 345.

37. Ibid., pp. 352, 426.

38. Sundquist, *Dynamics of the Party System*, pp. 406–7, table 17-1.

39. Schneider, "Democrats and Republicans," p. 201; Paul R. Abramson, John H. Aldrich, and David W. Rohde, *Change and Continuity in the 1980 Elections*, rev. ed. (Washington, DC: CQ Press, 1983), p. 109.

40. Byron E. Shafer, *Quiet Revolution: The Struggle for the Democratic Party and the Shaping of Post-Reform Politics* (New York: Russell Sage Foundation, 1983), p. 532.

41. On the embrace of the New Politics coalition by elected officials, see Gareth Davies, *From Opportunity to Entitlement: The Transformation and Decline of Great Society Liberalism* (Lawrence, KS: University Press of Kansas, 1996), pp. 157–84. For a contemporary argument favoring the embrace of these groups, see Lanny J. Davis, *The Emerging Democratic Majority: Lessons and Legacies from the New Politics* (New York: Stein and Day, 1974).

42. Shafer, *Quiet Revolution*, pp. 78, 89–90.

43. Ibid., p. 526.

44. Lunch, *Nationalization of American Politics*, p. 37.

45. Shafer, *Quiet Revolution*, p. 526.

46. Ibid.

47. See David E. Price, *Bringing Back the Parties* (Washington, DC: CQ Press, 1984), p. 15.

48. On Carter, see Austin Ranney, "The Carter Administration," in *The American Elections of 1980*, Austin Ranney, ed. (Washington, DC: American Enterprise Institute, 1981), p. 3.

49. Shafer, *Quiet Revolution*, p. 530.

50. Richard Rose and Thomas T. Mackie, "Do Parties Persist or Fail? The Big Trade-Off Facing Organizations," in *When Parties Fail: Emerging Alternative Organizations*, Kay Lawson and Peter H. Merkl, eds. (Princeton, NJ: Princeton University Press, 1988), p. 557.

51. Seymour Martin Lipset, "The American Party System: Concluding Observations," in *Party Coalitions in the 1980's*, Seymour Martin Lipset, ed. (San Francisco: Institute for Contemporary Studies, 1981), p. 430.

52. Sundquist, *Dynamics of the Party System*, p. 393.

53. Ibid., p. 129. Also see Ehrman, *Rise of Neoconservatism*; Miller, *Democracy Is in the Streets*.

54. Brinkley, *End of Reform*, p. 10.

55. Congressional Quarterly, *Guide to US Elections*, 3rd. ed. (Washington, DC: CQ, 1994), p. 130.

56. Davies, *From Opportunity to Entitlement*, pp. 88–89.

57. Fred Siegel, *The Future Once Happened Here: New York, DC, LA, and the Fate of America's Big Cities* (New York: Free Press, 1997), p. 49.

58. Congressional Quarterly, *Guide to US Elections*, pp. 130–32.

59. Ginsberg and Shefter, "A Critical Realignment?" p. 14.

60. Paul R. Abramson, John H. Aldrich, and David W. Rohde, *Change and Continuity in the 1992 Elections*, rev. ed. (Washington, DC: CQ Press, 1995), p. 88.

61. Sundquist, *Dynamics of the Party System*, p. 394.

62. Abramson et al., *1992 Elections*, pp. 150, 152.

63. Price, *Bringing Back the Parties*, p. 14.

64. E. J. Dionne, Jr., *Why Americans Hate Politics* (New York: Simon and Schuster, 1992), p. 79.

65. Ladd and Hadley, *Transformations of the American Party System.*

66. Byron E. Shafer and William J. M. Claggett, *The Two Majorities: The Issue Context of Modern American Politics* (Baltimore, MD: Johns Hopkins University Press, 1995), p. 185.

67. Ladd and Hadley, *Transformations of the American Party System*, p. 263; Gary C. Jacobson, *The Electoral Origins of Divided Government: Competition in US House Elections, 1946–1988* (Boulder, CO: Westview Press, 1990), p. 112.

68. Ladd and Hadley, *Transformations of the American Party System*, pp. 245, 290; Ladd, "Shifting Party Coalitions," p. 140; Abramson et al., *1980 Elections*, p. 106.

69. Walter Dean Burnham, "Insulation and Responsiveness in Congressional Elections," in *The Current Crisis in American Politics* (New York: Oxford University Press, 1982), p. 207; and Burnham, "The 1976 Election," p. 239.

70. Ranney, "The Carter Administration," p. 18; Abramson et al., *1980 Elections*, p. 121, table 6-1.

71. Ranney, "The Carter Administration," p. 28; Congressional Quarterly, *Guide to US Elections*, pp. 135–36; Henry A. Plotkin, "Issues in the Presidential Campaign," in *The Election of 1980: Reports and Interpretations*, Gerald M. Pomper et al. (Chatham, NJ: Chatham House Publishers, 1981), p. 51.

72. Schneider, "Democrats and Republicans," p. 201; Walter Dean Burnham, "American Politics in the 1980's," in *The Current Crisis in American Politics* (New York: Oxford University Press, 1982), p. 253.

73. Burnham, "The 1976 Election," p. 243.

74. For a contrary view, see Ginsberg and Shefter, "A Critical Realignment?" p. 13.

75. Abramson et al., *1980 Elections*, p. 26; Jonathan Moore, ed., *The Campaign for President: 1980 in Retrospect* (Cambridge, MA: Ballinger, 1981), pp. 187, 254; William Schneider, "The November 4 Vote for President: What Did It Mean?" in *The American Elections of 1980*, Austin Ranney, ed. (Washington, DC: American Enterprise Institute, 1981), p. 240.

76. Dionne, *Why Americans Hate Politics*, p. 134.

77. Thomas Byrne Edsall with Mary D. Edsall, *Chain Reaction: The Impact of*

Race, Rights, and Taxes on American Politics (New York: W. W. Norton, 1991), p. 198.

78. David M. Ricci, *The Transformation of American Politics: The New Washington and the Rise of Think Tanks* (New Haven, CT: Yale University Press, 1993), pp. 154–55.

79. Dionne, *Why Americans Hate Politics*, p. 224.

80. Jerome L. Himmelstein, *To the Right: The Transformation of American Conservatism* (Berkeley: University of California Press, 1990), p. 14.

81. Plotkin, "Issues in the Presidential Campaign," p. 49; Abramson et al., *1980 Elections*, p. 31.

82. James Ceaser, "The Theory of Governance of the Reagan Administration," in *The Reagan Presidency and the Governing of America*, Lester M. Salamon and Michael S. Lund, eds. (Washington, DC: Urban Institute Press, 1984), p. 85.

83. Abramson et al., *1980 Elections*, pp. 4–5.

84. Congressional Quarterly, *Guide to US Elections*, pp. 131, 139.

85. Ibid., p. 143; Abramson et al., *1980 Elections*, p. 31.

86. A. James Reichley, "Republican Ideology and the American Future," in *The Politics of Ideas: Intellectual Challenges to the Party after 1992*, John K. White and John C. Green, eds. (Lanham, MD: Rowman and Littlefield, 1995), pp. 72–73.

87. Schneider, "The November 4 Vote," p. 213; Abramson et al., *1980 Elections*, p. 5.

88. Gerald M. Pomper, "The Presidential Election," in *The Election of 1980: Reports and Interpretations*, Gerald M. Pomper et al. (Chatham, NJ: Chatham House Publishers, 1981), p. 65.

89. Ibid., p. 73; and Abramson et al., *1980 Elections*, pp. 96–97.

90. Robert M. Dow, Jr., "Senator Henry M. Jackson and US-Soviet Détente" (D.Phil. diss., University of Oxford, 1995), pp. 3–4; and see Ehrman, *Rise of Neoconservatism*.

91. Peter Steinfels, *The Neoconservatives: The Men Who Are Changing America's Politics* (New York: Simon and Schuster, 1979), pp. 50–51.

92. Daniel P. Moynihan, "The Politics of Stability," *New Leader* 20 (9 October 1967), p. 8.

93. In 1976, neoconservatives formed the Committee on the Present Danger, an organization that advocated a strong posture against the USSR. Since it was a bipartisan group (Ronald Reagan was a member), I do not include it in this discussion of Democratic neoconservatives.

94. Dirk Kirschten, "Here's How Many Democratic Defectors Ended Up Roosting with Bill Clinton," *NJ* 25, no. 8 (20 February 1993), p. 456.

95. David Shribman, "Democrats of 'Mainstream' Regroup to Try Again," *NYT*, 23 May 1983, sec. A, p. 12.

96. See Nicol C. Rae, *Southern Democrats* (Oxford: Oxford University Press, 1994).

97. William E. Farrell, "Democrats Pore Over the Results and Discuss Some New Formulas," *NYT*, 29 November 1984, sec. B, p. 15; Christopher Madison, "Searching for Consensus," *NJ*, 3 May 1986, Democratic Leadership Council Press Books (hereafter referred to as DLCPB), vol. 2, pp. 1043–47; Peter Rosenblatt to Rick Reidy, 16 July 1985, Democratic National Committee Papers (hereafter

referred to as DNCP), Democratic Policy Commission Files, Box 5, Folder: Commission Demographics.

98. Randall Rothenberg, *The Neoliberals: Creating the New American Politics* (New York: Simon and Schuster, 1984), pp. 23–24; Rae, *Southern Democrats*, p. 16; Kenneth M. Dolbeare and Linda J. Metcalf, *American Ideologies Today: Shaping the New Politics of the 1990s*, 2nd ed. (New York: McGraw-Hill, 1993), p. 63. See William Schneider, "JFK's Children: The Class of '74," *Atlantic* (April 1987), pp. 35–58.

99. Gary Hart, conversation with author, Oxford, England, 15 November 1996.

100. Randall Rothenberg, "The Neoliberal Club," *Esquire* (February 1982), p. 38.

101. Rothenberg, *Neoliberals*, pp. 45–46.

102. Ibid., p. 59.

103. Ibid., pp. 51, 68.

104. Ibid., p. 21.

105. For example, see Rae, *Southern Democrats*, chap. 6.

106. William G. Mayer, *The Divided Democrats: Ideological Unity, Party Reform, and Presidential Elections* (Boulder, CO: Westview Press, 1996), pp. 329–30.

Chapter 2: Changing the Rules, 1981–1984

1. Framed on the wall of From's office is a copy of the act signed by its main coauthors, a letter of thanks from Senate Governmental Operations Chairman Sam Ervin, and one of the pens used to sign it, plus a note of thanks from President Richard Nixon.

2. Al From, interview by author, Washington, DC, 7 September 1995. Also see the conversation with From in Bernard Asbell, *The Senate Nobody Knows* (Garden City, NY: Doubleday, 1978), pp. 249–61.

3. See Michael J. Malbin, *Unelected Representatives: Congressional Staff and the Future of Representative Government* (New York: Basic Books, 1980), pp. 46–74.

4. Norman J. Ornstein, "The South Arises Again on Capitol Hill," *Washington Post* (hereafter cited as *WP*), 2 October 1977, sec. C, p. 3; Richard L. Lyons, "On Capitol Hill," *WP*, 7 April 1979, sec. A, p. 5; Richard Pearson, "Rep. Gillis Long, 61, Influential Democrat," *WP*, 22 January 1985, sec. D, p. 4; Jeannine Klein, "Congressman Gillis Long Remembered for Convictions," *United Press International*, 24 January 1985.

5. From interview.

6. Jon F. Hale, "The Making of the New Democrats," *Political Science Quarterly* 110, no. 2 (1995), p. 210.

7. U.S. House Democratic Caucus, Committee on Party Effectiveness, *Rebuilding the Road to Opportunity: A Democratic Direction for the 1980s*, 93rd Cong., 2nd sess., 1982, p. 1. (Hereafter referred to as *RRO*.)

8. Ibid.

9. Hale, "The Making of the New Democrats," p. 210.

10. Seymour Martin Lipset, "Party Coalitions and the 1980 Election," in *Party Coalitions in the 1980s*, Seymour Martin Lipset, ed. (San Francisco: Institute for Contemporary Studies, 1981), p. 20.

11. See *RRO*, p. ii. Analysis of election results in this paragraph is based on data found in *America Votes 14: A Handbook of Contemporary American Election Sta-*

tistics, Richard M. Scammon and Alice V. Gillivray, comps. (Washington, DC: Congressional Quarterly, 1981); and *America Votes 15: A Handbook of Contemporary American Election Statistics,* Richard M. Scammon and Alice V. Gillivray, comps. (Washington, DC: Congressional Quarterly, 1983).

12. Walter Dean Burnham, "Toward Confrontation?" in *Party Coalitions in the 1980's,* Seymour Martin Lipset, ed. (San Francisco: Institute for Contemporary Studies, 1981), p. 380.

13. Gillis Long to Charles T. Manatt, 4 June 1982, Al From Personal Papers (hereafter referred to as AFPP), Democratic Leadership Council Headquarters, Washington, DC, p. 1; see Memorandum from Al From to Gillis Long, 3 June 1982, "Re: Midterm Conference," AFPP.

14. Long to Manatt, 4 June 1982, p. 2.

15. Ibid., p. 3.

16. Memorandum from Al From to Gillis Long, "Subject: A Little Strategic Thought," 21 June 1982, AFPP, p. 2.

17. Memorandum from Al From to Gillis Long, "Meeting with Jim Perry," 2 November 1983, AFPP, p. 2. Perry was a *Wall Street Journal* reporter, and the memo detailed talking points for Long's interview.

18. *RRO,* p. 2.

19. Ibid.

20. Ibid., pp. 2, 10.

21. Quoted in David E. Price, *Bringing Back the Parties* (Washington, DC: CQ Press, 1984), p. 281.

22. *RRO,* p. 120.

23. Ibid., p. 78.

24. Ibid., p. 3.

25. See Gareth Davies, *From Opportunity to Entitlement: The Transformation and Decline of Great Society Liberalism* (Lawrence, KS: University Press of Kansas, 1996), p. 243. Davies contends that after 1972, with the Democratic Party dropping its call for a guaranteed income, this strain of liberalism "disappeared from view." I argue that entitlement liberalism and its proponents were still a strong force within the party, as well as a significant part of its negative image with important parts of the electorate.

26. Price, *Bringing Back the Parties,* p. 277; Dom Bonafede, "Democrats Hope Their Midterm Meeting Will Send a Message of Party Unity," *NJ* 14, no. 25 (19 June 1982), p. 1098. Issue groups within the convention did debate policy stances, and their consensus positions were published in the official proceedings.

27. Memorandum from Al From to Representatives Frost, Gephardt, and Wirth, 12 September 1982, "Subject: Strategy for New York," AFPP, pp. 1–2.

28. Richard E. Cohen, "Gillis Long Presses House Democrats to Establish a New Party Identity," *NJ* 14, no. 49 (4 December 1982), p. 2075; see Edward Cowan, "Democrats Offer New Policy to Sustain National Growth," *NYT,* 19 September 1982, sec. 1, p. 28.

29. Price, *Bringing Back the Parties,* p. 281.

30. "Democratic Council Approves Economic Package," *United Press International,* 20 March 1983.

31. Sidney Blumenthal, "Drafting a Democratic Industrial Plan," *NYT,* 28 August 1983, sec. 6, p. 31.

32. National House Democratic Caucus, *Renewing America's Promise: A Democratic Blueprint for Our Nation's Future* (Washington, DC: 1984), p. vi. (Hereafter referred to as *RAP.*)

33. Ibid., p. v.

34. Ibid., pp. 7, 16, 62.

35. Memorandum from Al From to Gillis Long, "Subject: Some Additional Strategic Thoughts," 10 November 1983, AFPP; Steven Humphreys, "Democrats' Regional Issues Conference Gets Early Start in Election," *United Press International*, 23 January 1984; "Washington News Briefs," *United Press International*, 24 October 1983.

36. See Richard E. Cohen, "A Party Agenda," *NJ* 16, no. 2 (14 January 1984), p. 78; James F. Clarity and William E. Farrell, "Briefing," *NYT*, 28 November 1983, sec. B, p. 6; Memorandum from Al From to Gillis Long, "Caucus Update," 10 July 1983, AFPP, pp. 9, 11; Bill Peterson, "House Democrats Launch Effort to Sell Alternatives to the Public," *WP*, 20 July 1983, sec. A, p. 3.

37. Byron E. Shafer, *Bifurcated Politics: Evolution and Reform in the National Party Convention* (Cambridge, MA: Harvard University Press, 1988), p. 114.

38. Michael J. Malbin, "The Conventions, Platforms, and Issue Activists," in *The American Elections of 1980*, Austin Ranney, ed. (Washington, DC: American Enterprise Institute, 1981), p. 135.

39. Shafer, *Bifurcated Politics*, p. 96.

40. Byron E. Shafer, "Anti-Party Politics," *Public Interest* 63 (spring 1981), pp. 99–100.

41. Malbin, "Conventions, Platforms, and Issue Activists," p. 134, n. 29.

42. On the representativeness of party elites, see Warren E. Miller and M. Kent Jennings, *Parties in Transition: A Longitudinal Study of Party Elites and Party Supporters* (New York: Russell Sage Foundation, 1986), p. 235; Byron E. Shafer and William J. M. Claggett, *The Two Majorities: The Issue Context of American Politics* (Baltimore, MD: Johns Hopkins University Press, 1995), pp. 143, 147; Shafer, *Bifurcated Politics*, pp. 101–7; Price, *Bringing Back the Parties*, p. 198.

43. Long to Manatt, 4 June 1982, p. 1.

44. See Memorandum from Ross K. Baker to Gillis Long and Al From, 5 April 1983, "Restoring the Brokerage Role of the Democratic Party," AFPP, p. 2. Baker was a staffer on the House Rules Committee and is now a professor of political science at Rutgers University.

45. Philip A. Klinkner, *The Losing Parties: Out-Party National Committees 1956–1993* (New Haven, CT: Yale University Press, 1994), pp. 105, 111, 129–31.

46. From interview.

47. For how this was typical of parties out of power, see Klinkner, *Losing Parties*, p. 175. Price, *Bringing Back the Parties*, p. 274; Memorandum from Al From to Gillis Long, "Re: Your Meeting with Chuck Manatt," 11 September 1981, AFPP; Memorandum from Al From to Gillis Long, "Subject: DNC Policy Council," 16 March 1981, AFPP, p. 1.

48. Price, *Bringing Back the Parties*, p. 274.

49. Ibid., p. 159.

50. Ibid., pp. 162–63.

51. Ibid., p. 166; Thomas E. Mann, "Elected Officials and the Politics of Presidential Selection," in *The American Elections of 1984*, Austin Ranney, ed. (Wash-

ington, DC: American Enterprise Institute, 1985), p. 103; see Alan Ehrenhalt, *The United States of Ambition: Politicians, Power, and the Pursuit of Office* (New York: Random House, 1991), p. 267.

52. Price, *Bringing Back the Parties*, pp. 167–68.

53. Ibid., p. 169–70.

54. Memorandum from Al From to Gillis Long, "Subject: Political Strategy," 24 May 1983, AFPP, p. 1.

55. Ibid., pp. 2, 4.

56. Ibid., p. 5.; Memorandum from Al From to [Gillis Long], "Subject: Political Strategy, Eyes Only," 1 March 1984, AFPP, p. 7.

57. From to Long, 1 March 1984, p. 1.

58. Memorandum from Al From to Gillis Long, "Subject: This Campaign," 3 July 1984, AFPP, p. 4.

59. Ibid., pp. 1–2.

60. Steven M. Gillon, *The Democrats' Dilemma: Walter F. Mondale and the Liberal Legacy* (New York: Columbia University Press, 1992), pp. 304–5, 309.

61. Ibid., p. 316.

62. Ibid.

63. Shafer, "Anti-Party Politics," pp. 102–4.

64. Ibid., p. 104; Gillon, *Democrats' Dilemma*, p. 354.

65. Nicholas Lemann, "Implications," in *The Elections of 1984*, Michael Nelson, ed. (Washington, DC: CQ Press, 1985), p. 265.

66. Gillon, *Democrats' Dilemma*, p. 344.

67. Gerald M. Pomper, "The Presidential Election," in *The Election of 1984: Reports and Interpretations*, Gerald M. Pomper, et al. (Chatham, NJ: Chatham House Publishers, 1985), p. 62.

68. Ibid., p. 66; William Schneider, "The November 6 Vote for President: What Did It Mean?" in *The American Elections of 1984*, Austin Ranney, ed. (Washington, DC: American Enterprise Institute, 1985), p. 232.

69. Pomper et al., *The Election of 1984*, p. 69; "Portrait of the Electorate: Who Voted for Whom in the House," *NYT*, 13 November 1994, sec. A, p. 24. These data are from the *New York Times*/CBS News surveys and Warren E. Miller and the National Election Studies, *NES Guide to Public Opinion and Electoral Behavior, 1952–1994* (Ann Arbor: University of Michigan, Center for Political Studies, 1994), http://www.umich.edu/~nes/resources/nesguide/toptables/tab2a_2.htm.

70. Pomper et al., *The Election of 1984*, p. 69.

71. Ibid., p. 69, table 3-3; 70.

72. Ibid., p. 69, table 3-3.

73. Ibid., p. 66; Schneider, "The November 6 Vote for President," pp. 212, 232.

74. Schneider, "The November 6 Vote for President," p. 211.

75. *NES Guide to Public Opinion and Electoral Behavior*, http://www.umich.edu/~nes/resources/nesguide/toptables/tab2a_2.htm.

76. Norman J. Ornstein, "The Elections for Congress," in *The American Elections of 1984*, Austin Ranney, ed. (Washington, DC: American Enterprise Institute, 1985), p. 264.

77. Hale, "The Making of the New Democrats," p. 213. On the Hunt race, see Jerome L. Himmelstein, *To the Right: The Transformation of American Conservatism* (Berkeley: University of California Press, 1990), pp. 181–97.

78. Will Marshall, interview by author, Washington, DC, 19 September 1995.

79. Albert R. Hunt, "The Campaign and the Issues," in *The American Elections of 1984,* Austin Ranney, ed. (Washington, DC: American Enterprise Institute, 1985), p. 129; Schneider, "The November 6 Vote for President," p. 214.

80. Schneider, "The November 6 Vote for President," p. 243.

81. Nelson W. Polsby, "The Democratic Nomination and the Evolution of the Party System," in *The American Elections of 1984,* Austin Ranney, ed. (Washington, DC: American Enterprise Institute, 1985), pp. 37–39.

82. William Galston, interview by author, College Park, MD, 12 September 1995.

83. Gillon, *Democrats' Dilemma,* p. 358. According to David Broder, Hart's economic policy "drew heavily" on *Renewing America's Promise.* See David S. Broder, "Zigzagging in Search of Identity: The Democratic Convention," *WP,* 15 July 1984, sec. A, p. 1.

84. Henry A. Plotkin, "Issues in the Campaign," in *The Election of 1984: Reports and Interpretations,* Gerald M. Pomper et al. (Chatham, NJ: Chatham House Publishers, 1985), p. 46.

85. Ibid., pp. 40–41.

86. *NES Guide to Public Opinion and Electoral Behavior,* http://www.umich.edu/~nes/resources/nesguide/toptables/tab4e_1/htm.

87. Schneider, "The November 6 Vote for President," pp. 219–20.

88. Plotkin, "Issues," p. 45.

89. Mann, "Elected Officials," p. 114; Hale, "The Making of the New Democrats," p. 211.

90. Plotkin, "Issues," pp. 53, 55.

91. Gillon, *Democrats' Dilemma,* p. 72.

92. Gary R. Orren, "The Nominating Process: Vicissitudes of Candidate Selection," in *The Elections of 1984,* Michael Nelson, ed. (Washington, DC: CQ Press, 1985), pp. 34–35.

93. Ibid.

94. Mann, "Elected Officials," p. 108.

95. To elaborate on the dissonance between the attitudes of convention delegates and those of the rank and file, note that 4 percent of delegates labeled themselves conservative, while 25 percent of all Democrats did the same. See Mann, "Elected Officials," p. 116.

The idea of mainstream-candidate-as-marginal came from observations shared with me by Stanley B. Greenberg, interview by author, Washington, DC, 17 April 1996.

96. Memorandum from Al From to Gillis Long, "Subject: Politics," 26 April 1984, AFPP, pp. 1–2, 5.

97. Ibid., pp. 3, 8.

98. Elizabeth Drew, *Campaign Journal: The Political Events of 1983–1984* (New York: Macmillan, 1985), p. 521.

99. David McCurdy, interview by author, McLean, VA, 11 September 1995.

100. David McCloud, interview by author, Reston, VA, 13 September 1995.

101. Marshall interview.

102. Hale, "The Making of the New Democrats," p. 214.

103. Charles S. Robb, interview by author, Washington, DC, 12 September 1995. The meeting did not take place until early the next year, since, according to Robb,

Senate Minority Leader Robert Byrd thought the group was conspiring against him and put pressure on the group not to meet.

104. Memorandum from Al From to Gillis Long, "Subject: Tonight's Dinner," 28 November 1984, AFPP, pp. 1–4.

105. Ibid.

106. Ibid.

107. From interview.

108. Howell Raines, "Conservative Shift Is Sought as Democrats Meet to Pick Chief," *NYT*, 30 January 1985, sec. B, p. 12; Peter R. Rosenblatt, "Centrism Is Crucial," *NYT*, 19 November 1984, sec. A, p. 23.

109. *RAP*, p. vi.

110. Raines, "Conservative Shift"; Letter from Paul G. Kirk, Jr., to Governor Scott Matheson (D-UT), 10 December 1984, AFPP, p. 2.

111. Kirk to Matheson, 10 December 1984, p. 2.

112. From to Long, "Subject: Tonight's Dinner," 28 November 1984, p. 4.

113. Ibid., p. 5.

114. Kirk to Matheson, 10 December 1984, p. 2.

115. Klinkner, *Losing Parties*, p. 181; Robb interview.

116. From interview.

117. Memorandum from Al From to Governor Charles Robb, "Subject: Strategy for Kansas City," 14 December 1984, AFPP, p. 1.

118. Klinkner, *Losing Parties*, p. 181.

119. From to Robb, "Subject: Strategy for Kansas City," 14 December 1984, pp. 1, 3.

Chapter 3: "Saving the Democratic Party," 1985–1986

1. Al From, interview by author, Washington, DC, 5 March 1999.

2. Sam Attlesey, "Both National Parties Focusing on Texas," *Dallas Morning News*, 30 June 1985, sec. A, p. 52, DLCPB, vol. 1.

3. Richard Pearson, "Rep. Gillis Long, 61, Influential Democrat," *WP*, 22 January 1985, sec. D, p. 4.

4. Memorandum from Al From, "Subject: Saving the Democratic Party," 2 January 1985, AFPP, p. 1.

5. Statement by Rep. Richard Gephardt, Chairman, Democratic Leadership Council, 28 February 1985, DNCP, General Files, Box 88-60, p. 1.

6. Will Marshall, interview by author, Washington, DC, 19 September 1995.

7. Robb's election was in 1981. The DLC's membership list has always been very fluid, especially during this early period. However, these calculations are based on "Members of the Democratic Leadership Council," *Middlesex Report* 3, no. 19 (18 March 1985), DLCPB, vol. 1.; and Congressional Quarterly, *Guide to US Elections*, 3rd. ed. (Washington, DC: CQ, 1994).

8. Memo from From, "Subject: Saving the Democratic Party," 2 January 1985, p. 1.

9. Memorandum from Al From to Governors Babbitt and Robb, Senators Chiles and Nunn, and Representative Gephardt, "Subject: The DLC and the Democratic Party," 24 February 1985, AFPP, p. 1.

10. Paul G. Kirk, Jr., interview by author, Washington, DC, 10 September 1996.

11. Philip A. Klinkner, *The Losing Parties: Out-Party National Committees 1956–1993* (New Haven, CT: Yale University Press, 1994), p. 186.

12. Transcript of Democratic National Committee Meeting, 1 February 1985, DNCP, DNC Microfilming Project—Transcripts, Box 8, Folder: DNC Meeting, February 1, 1985, p. 7.

13. From to Governors Babbitt and Robb, Senators Chiles and Nunn, and Representative Gephardt, "Subject: The DLC and the Democratic Party," 24 February 1985, p. 1.

14. Ibid., p. 3.

15. Stanley B. Greenberg, "Forging Democratic Ideas," 4 February 1985, DNCP, Democratic Policy Commission Files, Box 2, Folder #69: Stan Greenberg, Forging Democratic Ideas, pp. 1–2.

16. Stanley B. Greenberg, interview by author, Washington, DC, 17 April 1996.

17. Greenberg, "Forging Democratic Ideas," pp. 7, 10, 12.

18. Memo from From, "Subject: Saving the Democratic Party," 2 January 1985, p. 2.

19. Charles S. Robb, interview by author, Washington, DC, 12 September 1995.

20. Memo from From, "Subject: Saving the Democratic Party," 2 January 1985, p. 2; emphasis his.

21. Ibid., p. 8.

22. Tom Sherwood and James R. Dickinson, "Robb Trying to Form New Party Policy Group; Would Project More Moderate Image," *WP*, 16 February 1985, sec. 1, p. 9.

23. Dan Balz, "Southern and Western Democrats Launch New Leadership Council; Party Faction Challenges Power of DNC Chief," *WP*, 1 March 1985, sec. 1, p. 2; John Herbers, "Democratic Chiefs Divided on Ways to Rebuild Party," *NYT*, 1 April 1985, sec. A, p. 1; Kirk interview.

24. Richard Rose and Thomas T. Mackie, "Do Parties Persist or Fail? The Big Trade-Off Facing Organizations," in *When Parties Fail: Emerging Alternative Organizations*, Kay Lawson and Peter H. Merkl, eds. (Princeton, NJ: Princeton University Press, 1988), p. 540.

25. Kirk interview.

26. Greenberg interview.

27. Rose and Mackie, "Do Parties Persist or Fail?" p. 540.

28. David E. Price, *Bringing Back the Parties* (Washington, DC: CQ Press, 1984), p. 291. They were the Center for National Policy, the National Policy Exchange, the Democracy Project, and the Roosevelt Center for American Policy Studies.

29. Al From, interview by author, Washington, DC, 7 September 1995.

30. Jon F. Hale, "The Making of the New Democrats," *Political Science Quarterly* 110, no. 2 (1995), p. 232; Marshall interview.

31. Hale, "The Making of the New Democrats," p. 215.

32. From interview, 7 September 1995.

33. Marshall interview.

34. Robb interview; Memorandum from Al From to Bob Strauss, "Subject: The Future," 18 September 1984, AFPP, p. 1.

35. Michael J. Malbin, *Unelected Representatives: Congressional Staff and the Future of Representative Government* (New York: Basic Books, 1980), p. 4. It is interesting to note that From was used as a case study in two works on political

entrepreneurship: Malbin's book and Bernard Asbell, *The Senate Nobody Knows* (Garden City, NY: Doubleday, 1978).

36. Memorandum from Al From to Dick Gephardt, "Fundraising for the DLC" [ca. 1985], AFPP, p. 1.

37. Memorandum from Al From, "DLC Update and Next Steps," 12 March 1985, AFPP, p. 1.

38. Memorandum from Al From to DLC Governing Board, "DLC Strategy," 5 September 1985, AFPP, p. 1.

39. Julie Norris, "Graham, Chiles Push for Middle Ground at Democrats' Leadership Fundraiser," *Morning Journal* (Daytona Beach, FL), 7 September 1985, DLCPB, vol. 1.

40. "Spreading Out," *New York Post*, 25 June 1986, DLCPB, vol. 2.

41. Sam Hopkins, "Democrats Optimistic on Georgia Trip," *Atlanta Journal-Constitution*, 10 November 1985, DLCPB, vol. 1.

42. Robert Strauss, interview by author, Washington, DC, 26 June 1996.

43. See Melissa Moss Silver, interview by author, Washington, DC, 27 September 1995; David McCloud, interview by author, Reston, VA, 29 August 1995.

44. Kent Jenkins, Jr., "Tribute to Robb Shows Off Skills of Council Organizers," *Virginia-Pilot* (Richmond, VA), 18 June 1986, DLCPB, vol. 2; Silver interview.

45. Representative Richard Gephardt, Senator Sam Nunn, Governor Charles Robb, Senator Lawton Chiles, Representative James Jones to Harry A. Jacobs, Jr., 20 December 1985, DNCP, General Files, Box 88-60, Folder: DDC/Democratic Leadership Council/General, p. 1.

46. Memorandum from Al From to DLC Governing Board, "Fundraising," 29 October 1985, AFPP, p. 2.

47. Phil Gailey, "Dissidents Defy Top Democrats; Council Formed," *NYT*, 1 March 1985, sec. A, p. 1.

48. Dan Balz and David S. Broder, "Rival Democratic Councils Forming," *WP*, 27 February 1985, sec. 1, p. 7.

49. George J. Church, "Moving toward the Middle," *Time*, 18 March 1985, p. 25, DLCPB, vol. 1.

50. Gailey, "Dissidents Defy."

51. For an explicit statement of this fear by a friend of From's and former fellow member of Senator Edmund Muskie's staff, see Leon G. Billings to Al From, 8 March 1985, AFPP.

52. Memorandum from Al From to Governor Charles Robb, "Subject: DLC Strategy," 23 March 1986, AFPP, p. 2.

53. Memorandum from Al From and Will Marshall, "Subject: The Florida Message—Defining the DLC," 13 May 1985, AFPP, p. 1; Kevin Merida and Sam Attlesey, "Democratic Team Blitzes Texas in Campaign to Polish Image," *Dallas Morning News*, 2 July 1985, DLCPB, vol. 1.

54. Jon Margolis, "Political Defections No Quick Fix," *Chicago Tribune*, 18 April 1986, sec. 1, p. 1.

55. Memorandum from Al From to DLC Governing Group, "Subject: The DLC Game Plan," 15 April 1985, AFPP, p. 4.

56. Attlesey, "Both National Parties Focusing on Texas."

57. Memo from From and Marshall, "The Florida Message," 13 May 1985, p. 1; "DLC Talking Points" [ca. 1985], AFPP, p. 2.

58. "DLC's 'National Issues Blitz' Helps Focus Midterm Debate," *DLC Newsgram* 1, no. 1 (November 1986), p. 2.

59. Ibid.; Thomas D. Brandt, "Even the Liberal Democrats Find DLC Plans on the Level," *Washington Times*, 21 October 1986, sec. A, p. 1; Memorandum from Al From to DLC Governing Board, "Subject: Meeting with Paul Kirk," 15 April 1986, AFPP.

60. Brandt, "Even the Liberal Democrats Find DLC Plans on the Level"; Robb interview.

61. Memorandum from Al From to DLC Governing Group, "Subject: The Future of the DLC," 7 November 1986, AFPP.

62. "DLC Members Gain in Senate Victory," *DLC Newsgram* 1, no. 1 (November 1986), p. 4; Richard Fly, "How the Democrats' Young Turks Are Seizing Power," *Business Week*, 15 December 1986, p. 29, DLCPB, vol. 3.

63. Memorandum from Will Marshall to Governor Robb, "Re: Tomorrow's New Democratic Forum Breakfast," 29 July 1986, AFPP, p. 2; Marshall interview.

64. Phil Gailey, "Operation Patch and Mend," *NYT*, 20 November 1985, sec. B, p. 6; Merida and Attlesey, "Democratic Team Blitzes Texas."

65. "DLC Talking Points" [ca. 1985], p. 2.

66. Al From to DLC Members, 5 April 1985, AFPP, p. 1; Memorandum from Elaine Kamarck to Al From, "Re: Democratic Leadership Council Quarterly," 19 November 1985. The three task forces established were Economic Growth and Competitiveness, which was chaired by Senator Lloyd Bentsen (TX), Governor James Blanchard (MI), and Rep. Leon Panetta (CA); National Defense Strategy, chaired by Nunn, Babbitt, and Rep. Les Aspin (WI); and Party Renewal, chaired by Chiles, Robb, and Rep. Martin Frost (TX). See DLC General Membership Meeting, 15 July 1985, DNCP, General Files, Box 88-60.

67. Phil Gailey, "Democrats Call Trade Top Issue," *NYT*, 3 October 1985, sec. D, p. 15; Peter Behr, "Democrats Air Analysis Showing U.S. Losing to Trade Competition," *WP*, 3 October 1985, sec. E, p. 4; Nicol Rae, *Southern Democrats* (Oxford: Oxford University Press, 1994), p. 22.

68. Memorandum from Al From to Governor Robb, "Subject: Proposed Strategy," 12 August 1986, AFPP, p. 1.

69. Ibid.

70. Ibid., p. 2. On Robb's three speeches, see Governor Charles S. Robb, Chairman, DLC, "Remarks to the National Press Club," 3 April 1986, in *1985–1995: Moving beyond the Left-Right Debate—A Collection of the Greatest New Democrat Speeches*; Peter Hardin, "Robb Unveils Ambitious Plan to Combat Welfare Dependency," *Richmond (VA) News Leader*, 12 April 1986, DLCPB, vol. 2; "For the Record," *WP*, 1 October 1986, sec. A, p. 18; and Phil Gailey, "Robb Recommends 'Tough Diplomacy,'" *NYT*, 7 May 1986, sec. A, p. 26.

71. Dale Eisman, "Democratic Panel Stakes Out Policies," *Richmond (VA) Times-Dispatch*, 12 December 1986, DLCPB, vol. 3.

72. Memorandum, "Subject: National Committee Media Strategy/Marketing," 19 February 1986, DNCP, Democratic Policy Commission Files, Box 5, pp. 1–4.

73. Phil Gailey, "From Biden to Babbitt to Nunn," *NYT*, 18 May 1986, sec. 6, p. 70.

74. Kirk interview.

75. Memo, "Subject: National Committee Media Strategy/Marketing," 19 February 1986, pp. 6–7.

76. E. J. Dionne, Jr., "Democrats Fashion Centrist Image in New Statement of Party Policy," *NYT,* 21 September 1986, sec. A, p. 1.

77. Peter T. Kilborn, "US Competitiveness Is Key Economic Issue," *NYT,* 15 December 1986, sec. B, p. 18.

78. Gailey, "From Biden to Babbitt," p. 70.

79. Dionne, "Democrats Fashion Centrist Image," p. 1.

80. Memorandum from Al From to Governor Robb, "Subject: DLC Strategy—Confidential," 10 October 1986, AFPP, p. 1.

81. Klinkner, *Losing Parties,* p. 186.

82. Memorandum from Al From to Directors and Co-Chairs, "Subject: DLC Operational Plan," 4 March 1985, AFPP, p. 2; see Paul Taylor, "Sure, the Democrats Agree, But on What?" *WP,* 11 May 1986, sec. D, p. 1.

83. Arthur Schlesinger, Jr., "For Democrats, Me-Too Reaganism Will Spell Disaster," *NYT,* 6 July 1986, sec. 6, p. 13.

84. Richard Stengel, "Rising Stars from the Sunbelt," *Time,* 31 March 1986, p. 30, DLCPB, vol. 2.

85. Paul Taylor, "Democrats' New Centrists Preen for '88," *WP,* 10 November 1985, sec. A, p. 1.

86. John Dillon, "Democrats, Left and Right, Searching for a Comeback Formula," *Christian Science Monitor,* 2 May 1986, DLCPB, vol. 2.

87. Paul Taylor, "Jackson Says Democrats Are Pushing Blacks Out," *WP,* 7 December 1985, sec. A, p. 15.

88. R. H. Melton, "While Trying to Close Rift, Wilder Repeats Criticisms; He Scores Robb's Letters and Calls Group 'Demeaning,'" *WP,* 5 December 1986, sec. B, p. 3. Wilder's comments are an accurate reflection of the type of criticism leveled against the DLC, but they need to be understood in light of his ongoing feud with Robb. In fact, upon his election as Virginia's governor, Wilder embraced and was embraced by the DLC.

89. Warren E. Miller and the National Election Studies, *NES Guide to Public Opinion and Electoral Behavior, 1952–1994* (Ann Arbor: University of Michigan, Center for Political Studies, 1994), http://www.umich.edu/~nes/resources/nesguide/2ndtables/tab2a_2_1.htm.

90. Edward G. Carmines and James A. Stimson, *Issue Evolution: Race and the Transformation of American Politics* (Princeton, NJ: Princeton University Press, 1989).

91. Robb interview; see From interview, 7 September 1995.

92. Memorandum from Al From to Dick Gephardt, "DLC Update," 29 April 1985, AFPP, p. 5.

93. Robb interview.

94. Memo from Marshall to Robb, "Re: Tomorrow's New Democratic Forum Breakfast," 29 July 1986, p. 2.

95. Robb interview.

96. From interview, 7 September 1995.

97. Interview not for attribution.

98. From interview, 7 September 1995.

99. Memo from From to DLC Governing Board, "DLC Strategy," 5 September 1985, p. 1.

100. From interview, 7 September 1995.

101. Al From, "Worthy Heirs of the Democratic Legacy," *NYT*, 20 July 1986, sec. 4, p. 22.

102. Memorandum from Will Marshall to Governor Robb, "Re: Drawing Distinctions," 2 June 1986, AFPP, p. 1.

103. Memo from From to Robb, "Subject: DLC Strategy—Confidential," 10 October 1986, p. 7.

104. "DLC Talking Points" [ca. 1985], p. 2; Memo from From to Robb, "Subject: DLC Strategy—Confidential," 10 October 1986, p. 1; also see Lawton Chiles's comments in Norma Wagner, "Chiles Tells Polk County Democrats to Whip Party Back in Shape," *Lakeland (FL) Ledger*, 13 April 1985, DLCPB, vol. 1.

105. Memorandum from Al From to Senator Chiles, "Subject: Your Meeting with Don Fowler," 9 October 1985, AFPP, p. 3.

106. Memorandum from Al From to Lawton Chiles, "Attendees to DLC Party Renewal Task Force Meeting, Wednesday, June 26 at 10:30 AM," 25 June 1985, AFPP; Senator Lawton Chiles and Representative Martin Frost to Paul G. Kirk, Jr., DNC Chairman, 17 October 1985, AFPP, p. 2; see Representative Martin Frost's testimony to the Fairness Commission as reported in Paul Taylor, "Jackson Seeks New Delegate Rules," *WP*, 24 August 1985, sec. A, p. 21; "Statement of Principles on Presidential Nominating Procedures—Draft," 22 July 1985, AFPP; Senator Lawton Chiles and Representative Martin Frost to Paul G. Kirk, Jr., DNC Chairman, 17 October 1985, AFPP, p. 2.

107. Klinkner, *Losing Parties*, pp. 184–85; see James R. Dickinson, "DNC Chief Urges End to Party Factionalism; Leadership Groups' Size Causes Concern," *WP*, 17 May 1985, sec. A, p. 5.

108. Klinkner, *Losing Parties*, pp. 184–85.

109. Ibid.; Taylor, "Jackson Seeks New Delegate Rules."

110. Klinkner, *Losing Parties*, pp. 184–85; Memorandum from Al From to Governor Robb, "Subject: DLC Update," 31 October 1985, AFPP, p. 1.

111. Al From to Paul G. Kirk, Jr., 19 October 1985, DNCP, General Files, Box 88-60, Folder: DDC/Democratic Leadership Council/General.

112. Memo from From to Robb, "Subject: DLC Update," 31 October 1985, pp. 1, 10.

113. Kirk interview.

114. Klinkner, *Losing Parties*, pp. 183–84.

115. Memo from From to Robb, "Subject: DLC Update," 31 October 1985, p. 2.

116. Kirk interview.

117. For example, From advised Babbitt to tell the Democratic Governors Association meeting that there was no tension between the DNC and DLC. See Memorandum from Al From to Governor Babbitt, "The NGA and DGA Meetings," 1 August 1985, AFPP.

118. Memo from From to Robb, "Subject: DLC Update," 31 October 1985, p. 2; Memo from From to DLC Governing Board, "Subject: Meeting with Paul Kirk," 15 April 1986, p. 1.

119. Memorandum from Wally Chalmers to Paul G. Kirk, Jr., "Re: DLC STEP Program," 26 April 1987, DNCP, General Files, Box 88-60, Folder: DDC/Democratic Leadership Council/General, p. 1.

120. Klinkner, *Losing Parties,* p. 186.

121. Robb interview; Memo from Chalmers to Kirk, "Re: DLC STEP Program," 26 April 1987, p. 2.

122. See Memorandum from Don Sweitzer to Paul Kirk and Vic Raiser, 29 June 1986, DNCP, General Files, Box 88-60, Folder: DDC/Democratic Leadership Council/General.

123. "DLC Williamsburg Conference, 10 Dec–12 Dec 1986, Tentative Schedule as of November 19, 1986," DNCP, General Files, Box 88-60, Folder: DDC/Democratic Leadership Council.

124. See Harry A. Jacobs, Jr., to Paul G. Kirk, Jr., 24 December 1985, DNCP, General Files, Box 88-60, Folder: DDC/Democratic Leadership Council/General. This leading Democratic supporter voiced this concern to Kirk.

125. See assorted documents, DNCP, General Files, Box 88-60, Folder: DDC/Democratic Leadership Council/General.

126. Memo from Don Sweitzer to Paul Kirk and Vic Raiser, 29 June 1986.

127. Ibid.

128. Memorandum from Jean B. Dunn to Paul G. Kirk, Jr., confidential, 29 July 1986, DNCP, General Files, Box 88-60, Folder: DDC/Democratic Leadership Council/General, p. 1.

129. Representative Buddy MacKay to Paul G. Kirk, Jr., 26 November 1985, DNCP, General Files, Box 88-60, Folder: DDC/Democratic Leadership Council/General, p. 1.

130. Memo from From to Robb, "Subject: DLC Update," 31 October 1985, p. 2; see Jack W. Germond and Jules Witcover, "Kirk Shows Up Soreheads," *Baltimore Sun,* 23 September 1985, DLCPB, vol. 1.

131. Memorandum, "Subject: National Committee Media Strategy/Marketing," 19 February 1986, DNCP, Democratic Policy Commission Files, Box 5, unmarked folder, p. 5; see "DPC Progress Report #6," 19 October 1985, DNCP, Democratic Policy Commission Files, Box 8, Folder: Early Progress Reports, p. 5; Transcript of the DNC Executive Meeting, Orlando, FL, 22 November 1985, DNCP, DNC Microfilming Project—Transcripts, Box 9, Folder: Executive Committee—November 22, 1985, p. 59; Memorandum from Joe Rothstein and Co., Inc., "Subject: Delivery Systems for Coordinated Democratic Message," 19 February 1986, DNCP, Democratic Policy Commission Files, unmarked folder.

132. Memorandum to Al From from Phil Burgess, "Subj.: Policy Commission Draft Report," 30 June 1986, Democratic Leadership Council Papers (hereafter cited as DLCP), Box 1, Correspondence File III.

133. Paul G. Kirk, Jr., to Representative Buddy MacKay, 20 December 1985, DNCP, General Files, Box 88-60, Folder: DDC/Democratic Leadership Council/General.

134. Memo from From to Robb, "Subject: DLC Update," 31 October 1985, p. 2; Memo from From to DLC Governing Board, "Subject: Meeting with Paul Kirk," 15 April 1986, p. 1.

135. Memo from From to DLC Governing Board, "Subject: The Future of the DLC," 7 November 1986, p. 2.

136. Memo from From to Robb, "Subject: DLC Update," 31 October 1985, p. 2; Memo from From to DLC Governing Board, "Subject: Meeting with Paul Kirk," 15 April 1986, p. 1.

137. Jon Margolis, "'Progressive Democrats Becoming Norm," *Chicago Tribune,* 14 December 1986, DLCPB, vol. 3.

138. Phil Gailey, "Democratic Panel Is Formed to Lure Voters Back to Party," *NYT,* 16 May 1985, sec. A, p. 26.

Chapter 4: Selling Super Tuesday, 1987–1988

1. Memorandum from Al From to Governor Robb, "Subject: Where Now," 26 June 1987, AFPP, Washington, DC, p. 2.

2. Stanley B. Greenberg, "The National Security Debate Survey: The Southern Swing Voters," 14 October 1987, DNCP, 1988 Democratic Platform Committee Files, Box 88-10, Folder: Democratic Leadership Council, p. 6.

3. E. J. Dionne, Jr., "Study Sees Tough Battle for Swing Vote in South," *NYT,* 16 October 1987, sec. A, p. 14.

4. Greenberg, "The National Security Debate Survey," p. 27.

5. "DLC Presidential Debates Set Stage for Super Tuesday," *DLC Newsgram* 1, no. 5 (December 1987), p. 3.

6. See Arthur T. Hadley, *The Invisible Primary* (Englewood Cliffs, NJ: Prentice-Hall, 1976); Emmett H. Buell, Jr., "The Invisible Primary," in *In Pursuit of the White House: How We Choose Our Presidential Nominees,* William G. Mayer, ed. (Chatham, NJ: Chatham House Publishers, 1996), pp. 1–43.

7. Memorandum from Al From to Governor Robb, "Subject: A Nunn Candidacy," 11 January 1987, AFPP, p. 1.

8. Memorandum from Al From to Governor Robb, "Subject: Six-Month DLC Strategy—Confidential," 10 January 1987, AFPP, p. 4.

9. Michael Kelly, "Gore, Robb Are at Odds on Strategy," *Memphis (TN) Commercial Appeal,* 22 June 1987, DLCPB, vol. 3.

10. Memorandum from Al From to Senator Nunn, "Subject: Should You or Shouldn't You?—Confidential," 7 August 1987, AFPP, p. 3.

11. Memorandum from Al From and Will Marshall to Senator Al Gore, "Subject: A Strategic Political Message," 31 December 1987, AFPP. See also a memo that they sent to Gore in the thick of the 1988 campaign: Memorandum from Al From and Will Marshall to Senator Gore, "Re: Theme and Message," 21 March 1988, AFPP.

12. Memorandum from Al From to Governor Robb, "Re: Ideas for Tomorrow's Seminar," 19 March 1987, AFPP, pp. 1–2; Democratic Leadership Council, "New Directions, Enduring Values," 1987, Communications Director's Files (hereafter cited as CDF), p. 1; Memo from From to Robb, "Re: Ideas for Tomorrow's Seminar," 19 March 1987, p. 1; Ralph Z. Hallow, "Democrats Too Far Out, Party Analysts Declare," *Washington Times,* 4 September 1987, DLCPB, vol. 4.

13. DLC, "New Directions, Enduring Values," p. 2.

14. Ibid., p. 1.

15. Memorandum from Al From and Will Marshall to Senator Nunn, "Re: Beyond Super Tuesday," 2 March 1988, AFPP, p. 1.

16. See, for example, Ann Lewis's comments in Margie Fisher, "Democratic Council Gets New Image," *Roanoke (VA) Times and World News,* 5 July 1987, DLCPB, vol. 4.

17. Memo from From to Robb, "Subject: Six-Month DLC Strategy—Confidential," 10 January 1987; Bob Evans, "Debate: Forum in Action," *Daily Press* (VA), 29 February 1988, DLCPB, vol. 5.

18. Memo from From to Robb, "Subject: Where Now," 26 June 1987, p. 7.

19. Memo from From to Robb and Nunn, "Subject: Next Steps for the DLC—Confidential," 27 November 1987, p. 1.

20. Ibid., p. 13.

21. Memo from From to Robb, "Subject: Six-Month DLC Strategy," 10 January 1987, p. 10.

22. Memorandum from Al From to Bob Strauss, "Subject: Coordinating the Democratic Message," 14 January 1987, AFPP.

23. Barbara Norrander, *Super Tuesday: Regional Politics and Presidential Primaries* (Lexington: University Press of Kentucky, 1992), p. 25; Harold W. Stanley and Charles D. Hadley, "The Southern Presidential Primary: Regional Intentions with National Implications," *Publius: The Journal of Federalism* 17, no. 3 (summer 1987), p. 85.

24. Stanley and Hadley, "Southern Presidential Primary," p. 86.

25. Norrander, *Super Tuesday*, pp. 87–88.

26. Ibid., p. 27; Stanley and Hadley, "Southern Presidential Primary," p. 88.

27. Stanley and Hadley, "Southern Presidential Primary," p. 87.

28. Charles S. Bullock III, "The Nomination Process and Super Tuesday," in *The 1988 Presidential Election in the South: Continuity Amidst Change in Southern Party Politics*, Lawrence W. Morehead, Robert P. Steed, and Tod A. Baker, eds. (New York: Praeger, 1991), p. 4.

29. Philip A. Klinkner, *The Losing Parties: Out-Party National Committees, 1956–1993* (New Haven, CT: Yale University Press, 1994), p. 185.

30. Paul R. Abramson, John H. Aldrich, and David W. Rohde, eds., *Change and Continuity in the 1988 Elections*, rev. ed. (Washington, DC: CQ Press, 1991), p. 18.

31. See Byron E. Shafer, *Bifurcated Politics: Evolution and Reform in the National Party Convention* (Cambridge, MA: Harvard University Press, 1988), chaps. 3 and 4.

32. John Kessel, *Presidential Campaign Politics*, 4th ed. (Pacific Grove, CA: Brooks/Cole, 1992), pp. 91, 92, table 3-5. Interestingly, only 48 percent of Democratic activists called themselves "liberal," although over two-thirds of them scored as such on Kessel's index. I agree with Kessel that this phenomenon reflects more the unpopularity of the term in 1988 than a change in ideological belief. See p. 116.

33. Ibid., p. 116.

34. Memo from From to Robb, "Subject: Six-Month DLC Strategy," 10 January 1987, p. 4.

35. "The Iowa 'Veto,'" *WP*, 16 November 1987, sec. A, p. 12.

36. Mark Z. Barabak, "Iowa's Weighty Role in Presidential Race," *San Francisco Chronicle*, 24 November 1987, DLCPB, vol. 5.

37. Memo from From to Robb, "Subject: Where Now," 26 June 1987, p. 2; Paul Taylor, "Robb Warns against Catering to Interests; Democrats Discuss Avoiding a 'Bidding War,'" *NYT*, 23 June 1987, sec. A, p. 9.

38. Memorandum from Al From to Senator Graham and Senator Breaux, 19 March 1987, AFPP, p. 2.

39. Ibid.

40. Al From to Paul G. Kirk, Jr., 24 April 1987, DNCP, General Files, Box 88-60, Folder: DDC/Democratic Leadership Council/General, p. 1; Kevin Sack, "Nunn to Step on DLC Stage," *Atlanta Journal-Constitution*, 21 June 1987, DLCPB, vol. 3; "The DLC Super Tuesday Education Project: STEP Fact Sheet," DNCP, General Files, Box 88-60, Folder: DDC/Democratic Leadership Council/General, p. 1; Memo from From to Graham and Breaux, 19 March 1987, p. 2; Carl Irving, "Democrats Pondering the South," *San Francisco Examiner*, 22 June 1987, DLCPB, vol. 3; Robin Toner, "Reporter's Notebook: Mending Democratic Coalition in South," *NYT*, 24 June 1987, sec. A, p. 25.

41. Sack, "Nunn to Step on DLC Stage."

42. "The DLC Super Tuesday Education Project: STEP Fact Sheet," p. 1; "DLC Sets Sights on Super Tuesday," *DLC Newsgram* 1, no. 3 (April 1987), p. 1.

43. "DLC Presidential Debates Set Stage for Super Tuesday," *DLC Newsgram* 1, no. 3 (April 1987), p. 4.

44. Norrander, *Super Tuesday*, appendix, pp. 202, 206, tables A.1, A.5. These calculations are based on the fourteen primaries held in southern states on Super Tuesday 1988. Candidate delegate totals do not reflect delegates won only in states where they won a plurality of the popular vote, but reflect total delegates won in the fourteen contests.

45. Memo from From and Marshall to Gore, "Subject: A Strategic Political Message," 31 December 1987; Thomas B. Edsall, "Gore Gambling on Primary Victories in March; Presidential Campaign Strategy Envisions Turnaround on 'Super Tuesday' in the South," *WP*, 18 October 1987, sec. A, p. 4.

46. Barabak, "Iowa's Weighty Role."

47. "A Conversation with Albert Gore," in *Candidates '88*, Marvin Kalb and Hendrik Hertzberg, eds. (Dover, MA: Auburn House, 1988), p. 76.

48. Bullock, "The Nomination Process and Super Tuesday," p. 11.

49. Ibid., p. 10.

50. Ibid., p. 14.

51. Compare their 1986 ADA ratings: Gore's was at 70 and Nunn's was at 30. See Alan Ehrenhalt, ed., *Politics in America: The 100th Congress* (Washington, DC: CQ Press, 1987), pp. 353, 1404.

52. Bullock, "The Nomination Process and Super Tuesday," p. 5.

53. Charles D. Hadley and Harold W. Stanley, "Super Tuesday 1988: Regional Results and National Implications," *Publius: The Journal of Federalism* 19, no. 3 (summer 1989), p. 26.

54. Bullock, "The Nomination Process and Super Tuesday," p. 14.

55. Hadley and Stanley, "Super Tuesday 1988," p. 23.

56. Paul G. Kirk, Jr., interview by author, Washington, DC, 10 September 1996.

57. Ibid. Also see Norrander, *Super Tuesday*, p. 92; Abramson et al., *1988 Elections*, p. 25.

58. Hadley and Stanley, "Super Tuesday 1988," p. 27; on attention given to and money spent on the southern primaries, see Norrander, *Super Tuesday*, pp. 93–100.

59. Richard Ben Cramer, *What It Takes: The Way to the White House* (New York: Random House, 1992), pp. 276–99.

60. Ehrenhalt, *Politics in America*; David S. Broder, "Gephardt's 'Greening': An Eye on the Center; Courting of Liberals Could Backfire in the South," *WP*, 31 August 1987, sec. A, p. 7.

61. Ibid.

62. Ehrenhalt, *Politics in America*, p. 854.

63. David McCurdy, interview by author, McLean, VA, 11 September 1995.

64. "A Conversation with Richard Gephardt," in *Candidates '88*, Marvin Kalb and Hendrik Hertzberg, eds. (Dover, MA: Auburn House, 1988), p. 76. For a description of these efforts, see Cramer, *What It Takes*.

65. Memorandum to Dick Gephardt, "Subject: Your Announcement—Confidential," 7 February 1987, AFPP.

66. Ibid., p. 1.

67. Durwood McAlister, "Gephardt Wastes Opportunity Provided by DLC," *Atlanta Journal*, 26 February 1987, DLCPB, vol. 3.

68. Leslie Phillips, "'Super Vote' Architect: It's a Start," *USA Today*, 29 February 1988, DLCPB, vol. 5.

69. Sidney Blumenthal, "Richard Gephardt: The Insider as Populist; the Economic Battle Cry that Revived a Presidential Campaign," *WP*, 13 February 1988, sec. B, p. 1.

70. Memo from From to Gephardt, "Subject: Your Opportunity—Confidential," 15 July 1985, p. 4.

71. Fred Barnes, "Ladies and Gentleman, The Next Vice President . . . ," *Washingtonian*, September 1986, DLCPB, vol. 2, p. 202.

72. Broder, "Gephardt's Greening," p. 7.

73. Ibid.

74. Al From, interview by author, Washington, DC, 7 September 1995.

75. Memorandum from Al From to Governor Robb and Senator Nunn, "Subject: Next Steps for the DLC—Confidential," 27 November 1987, AFPP, p. 4.

76. Robert Kuttner, "Red-faced White Boys," *New Republic*, 21 March 1988, p. 10, DLCPB, vol. 6.

77. Heather Booth, telephone interview by author, Washington, DC, 9 January 1996.

78. Frank LoMonte, "Jury Still Undecided about Super Tuesday," *Savannah (GA) Morning News*, 13 March 1988, DLCPB, vol. 6; see Charles S. Robb, "Super Tuesday Worked," *WP*, 13 March 1988, sec. C, p. 7.

79. David McCloud, interview by author, Reston, VA, 29 August 1995.

80. Bullock, "The Nomination Process and Super Tuesday," p. 4; Memorandum from Melissa Moss to Al From, "Super Tuesday GOTV," 1 December 1987, AFPP, p. 1.

81. Memorandum from Al From and Will Marshall to Senator Nunn, "Re: The Vice Presidency," 29 June 1988, DLCP, Box: Dolo (Al) 1, Folder: Nunn Memo, p. 1.

82. Peter Hardin, "Dukakis 'Very Interested' in National Service Idea," *Richmond (VA) News-Leader*, 11 May 1988, DLCPB, vol. 6.

83. Randall Rothenberg, *The Neoliberals: Creating the New American Politics* (New York: Simon and Schuster, 1984), pp. 209–10.

84. David Johnson, "Youth Brigades of Another Kind Are Gaining Favor," *NYT*, 22 November 1987, sec. 4, p. 5.

85. "The Citizens Corps—Questions and Answers," *DLC Newsgram* 2, no. 2 (June 1988), p. 3.

86. Al From, "Inside the DLC," *DLC Newsgram* 2, no. 2 (June 1988).

87. On the emergence of the concept of the "undeserving poor," see Michael B. Katz, *The Undeserving Poor: From the War on Poverty to the War on Welfare* (New York: Pantheon Books, 1989).

88. Steven Waldman, *The Bill: How Legislation Really Becomes Law: A Case Study of the National Service Bill*, rev. ed. (New York: Penguin Books, 1996), p. 4.

89. "The Citizens Corps—Questions and Answers," p. 3.

90. Memorandum from Al From and Will Marshall to Senator Gore, "Re: Theme and Message," 21 March 1988, AFPP, p. 5.

91. Memorandum from Al From to Senator Nunn, "Subject: The Next 120 Days," 28 March 1988, AFPP, p. 4.

92. Waldman, *The Bill*, p. 5. And on labor's views on the DLC plan, see James J. Kennedy, Jr., to Al From, 6 April 1987, DLCP, Dolo (Al) Box 1, Corr. File 4, p. 3. Kennedy was the executive assistant to the secretary-treasurer of the AFL-CIO.

93. Johnson, "Youth Brigades."

94. "DLC Launches 'National Service '88,'" *DLC Newsgram* 2, no. 3 (November 1988), p. 1.

95. Ibid.

96. Memo to Senators Graham and Breaux, 19 March 1987, p. 2; and Memo from From to Robb, "Subject: Where Now," 26 June 1987, p. 6.

97. "Rules Committee Members as Provided by the DNC Secretary's Office" [ca. 1988], DNCP, Rules Committee Files, Box 88-105; "Appointments to the Platform Committee" [ca. 1988], DNCP, Political Director's Files, Box 88-115, Folder: 1988 Platform.

98. Kirk interview.

99. Memorandum from DNC Press Office to State Party Chairs and DNC Members, "Re: The 1988 Platform," 7 June 1988, DNCP, Political Director's Convention Files, Box 88-115, Folder: 1988 Platform.

100. Gerald M. Pomper, "The Presidential Nominations," in *The Election of 1988: Reports and Interpretations*, Gerald M. Pomper et al. (Chatham, NJ: Chatham House Publishers, 1989), p. 53; also see Congressional Quarterly, *Guide to US Elections*, 3rd ed. (Washington, DC: CQ, 1994), p. 166.

101. See DNCP, 1988 Democratic Platform Committee Files, Box 88-10, Folder: Democratic Leadership Council; Memo from From to Nunn, "Subject: The Next 120 Days," 28 March 1988, p. 4.

102. Pomper, "The Presidential Nominations," p. 53.

103. Larry David Smith, "The Party Platforms as Institutional Discourse: The Democrats and Republicans of 1988," *Presidential Studies Quarterly* 22, no. 3 (summer 1992), p. 534.

104. "Five Possible Rules Changes—A Discussion" [ca. 1988], DNCP, Rules Committee Files, Box 88-105, p. 1; see Memo from From to Nunn, "Subject: The Next 120 Days," 28 March 1988, p. 4.

105. Ibid.

106. "Five Possible Rules Changes," p. 2.

107. Wally Chalmers to Scott Long/Kathy Vick, 11 May 1988, DNCP, Rules Committee Files, Box 88-105.

108. "Chairman Kirk Issues 8 'Resolves' to Keep 1988 Nominating Process Focused on Victory in November," DNC News Release, 11 March 1987, DNCP, General Files, Box 88-62, Folder: General/Resolves '88.

109. Paul G. Kirk, Jr., to Senator Sam Nunn, 22 June 1988, DLCP, Box: Dolo (Al) 4, Folder: Platform.

110. Kuttner, "Red-faced White Boys."

111. Fisher, "Democratic Council Gets New Image."

Chapter 5: Folding the Big Tent, 1988–1990

1. Paul R. Abramson, John H. Aldrich, and David W. Rohde, *Change and Continuity in the 1988 Elections*, rev. ed. (Washington, DC: CQ Press, 1991), p. 43.

2. Peter Jennings, the ABC News anchor, used this phrase in a question to Dukakis in the first presidential debate, but the observation had been made throughout the race. Hence, the Jennings question. See "The First Bush-Dukakis Debate: September 25, 1988," transcript, http://www.politicsnow.com/news/debates/pndebate092588.

3. Abramson et al., *1988 Elections*, pp. 2, 44–46.

4. Ibid., pp. 49–50.

5. Ibid., pp. 57, 60.

6. Ibid., p. 123; Gerald M. Pomper, "The Presidential Election," in *The Election of 1988: Reports and Interpretations*, Gerald M. Pomper et al. (Chatham, NJ: Chatham House Publishers, 1989), p. 135.

7. Abramson et al., *1988 Elections*, pp. 57, 60.

8. Pomper, "The Presidential Election," p. 134, table 5.2.

9. Barbara G. Farah and Ethel Klein, "Public Opinion Trends," in *The Election of 1988: Reports and Interpretations*, Gerald M. Pomper et al. (Chatham, NJ: Chatham House Publishers, 1989), p. 108, table 4.1; William Schneider, "A Loud Vote for Change," *NJ*, 24, no. 45 (7 November 1992), p. 2543, table. Schneider's data are from the CNN–*Los Angeles Times* exit polls.

10. Abramson et al., *1988 Elections*, p. 3.

11. Frances E. Rourke and John T. Tierney, "The Setting: Changing Patterns of Presidential Politics, 1960 and 1988," in *The Elections of 1988*, Michael Nelson, ed. (Washington, DC: CQ Press, 1989), p. 20; Harold W. Stanley, "The Reagan Legacy and Party Politics in the South," in *The 1988 Presidential Election in the South: Continuity Amidst Change in Southern Party Politics*, Lawrence W. Morehead, Robert P. Steed, and Tod A. Baker, eds. (New York: Praeger, 1991), p. 24.

12. Walter Dean Burnham, "The Reagan Heritage," in *The Election of 1988: Reports and Interpretations*, Gerald M. Pomper et al. (Chatham, NJ: Chatham House Publishers, 1989), p. 27.

13. Pomper, "The Presidential Election," pp. 31–32; Abramson et al., *1988 Elections*, pp. 174, 195. Also see Martin P. Wattenberg, *The Rise of Candidate-Centered Politics: Presidential Elections of the 1980's* (Cambridge, MA: Harvard University Press, 1991).

14. Pomper, "The Presidential Election," pp. 31–32.

15. Ibid., p. 136. The argument that low turnout hurt the Democratic Party disproportionately was often made by liberals. For example, see Frances Fox Piven and Richard A. Cloward, *Why Americans Don't Vote* (New York: Pantheon Books, 1988).

16. Ibid.; Abramson et al., *1988 Elections*, pp. 108–9.

17. The latter opinion was shared by Robert Shapiro, who crafted Dukakis's economic policy. Robert Shapiro, interview by author, Washington, DC, 18 September 1995.

18. William Galston, interview by author, College Park, MD, 12 September 1995.

19. Transcript of DNC Executive Meeting, Washington, DC, 8 February 1989, DNCP, DNC Microfilming Project Transcripts, Box 9, Folder: Executive Committee—Feb 8, 1989, pp. 20–21.

20. Pomper, "The Presidential Election," p. 148.

21. Farah and Klein, "Public Opinion Trends," pp. 111, 113, 115.

22. Ibid., p. 103. Also see Rourke and Tierney, "The Setting," p. 19.

23. Farah and Klein, "Public Opinion Trends," p. 111, table 4.3.

24. Ibid., pp. 115, 116, table 4.6.

25. Jean Bethke Elshtain, "Issues and Themes in the 1988 Campaign," in The Elections of 1988, Michael Nelson, ed. (Washington, DC: CQ Press, 1989), p. 120.

26. Jeff Faux, "The Myth of the New Democrats," American Prospect (fall 1993), pp. 20–29; Jeff Faux, interview by author, Washington, DC, 19 July 1996; Richard M. Vallely, "Vanishing Voters," in The American Prospect Reader in American Politics, Walter Dean Burnham, ed. (Chatham, NJ: Chatham House Publishers, 1995), pp. 145–46.

27. Quoted in David S. Broder and Paul Taylor, "Bush Names James Baker Secretary of State; Once Again Democrats Debate Why They Lost," WP, 10 November 1988, sec. A, p. 1.

28. John Baker to Paul G. Kirk, Jr., 4 October 1988, DNCP, General Files, Box 88-64, Folder: General/Polls '88, p. 1.

29. Transcript, 8 February 1989, DNCP, DNC Microfilming Project Transcripts, p. 20.

30. Joseph A. Califano, Jr., "Tough Talk for Democrats," NYT, 8 January 1989, sec. 6, p. 28; see Wilson Carey McWilliams, "The Meaning of the Election," in The Election of 1988: Reports and Interpretations, Gerald M. Pomper et al. (Chatham, NJ: Chatham House Publishers, 1989), p. 198.

31. Pomper, "The Presidential Election," p. 148; McWilliams, "The Meaning of the Election," p. 199; William G. Mayer, The Changing American Mind: How and Why American Public Opinion Changed between 1960 and 1988 (Ann Arbor: University of Michigan Press, 1992), p. 339; E. J. Dionne, Jr., Why Americans Hate Politics (New York: Simon and Schuster, 1992), p. 314.

32. Abramson et al., 1988 Elections, p. 204; Martin P. Wattenberg, The Decline of American Political Parties: 1952–1988, enlarged ed. (Cambridge, MA: Harvard University Press, 1990), p. 140, table 9-1.
The National Election Studies calculated Democratic Party identification at a postwar low of 47 percent and Republican Party identification at a postwar high of 41 percent, if one included those leaning toward one party or another. See Warren J. Miller and the National Election Studies, NES Guide to Public Opinion and Electoral Behavior, 1952–1994 (Ann Arbor: Inter-University Consortium for Political and Social Research, 1994), http://www.umich.edu/~nes/resources/nesguide/toptables/tab2a_2.htm.

33. Abramson et al., 1988 Elections, pp. 206–8; Miller and NES, NES Guide to Public Opinion and Electoral Behavior, http://www.umich.edu/~nes/resources/nesguide/2ndtables/t2a_2_1.htm.

34. Memorandum from Al From to Governor Robb, "Subject: Six-Month DLC Strategy—Confidential," 10 January 1987, AFPP, pp. 5, 10.

35. Memo from From to Nunn, "Subject: Monday's DLC Mini-Retreat," 9 July 1988, p. 3; Memo from From and Marshall to Nunn, "Re: Today's Meeting with Governor Dukakis," 29 June 1988.

36. Memo from From to Nunn, "Subject: Monday's DLC Mini-Retreat," 9 July 1988, p. 5; Bernard Weinraub, "Campaign Trail; Democrats Line Up for Party Fight," *NYT*, 27 October 1988, sec. B, p. 14.

37. Quoted in Carla Hall, "Ron Brown and the Party's Acid Test; the New Democratic Chairman, Reaching Out," *WP*, 14 March 1989, sec. E, p. 1.

38. Ibid.; "Field of Democrats Narrows," *NYT*, 27 January 1989, sec. A, p. 12; "Brown's Path Clear for Leader of Party as Contender Quits," *NYT*, 31 January 1989, sec. A, p. 17; Thomas B. Edsall, "White Southerners Pledge Loyalty to Brown," *WP*, 10 February 1989, sec. A, p. 10.

39. Hall, "Ron Brown and the Party's Acid Test"; Donald Lambro, "Party Chairman Urges Democratic Tilt toward Middle," *Washington Times*, 31 October 1989, DLCPB, vol. 8.

40. Hall, "Ron Brown and the Party's Acid Test."

41. Elaine Kamarck, interview by author, Washington, DC, 11 January 1996.

42. William Galston and Elaine Ciulla Kamarck, "The Politics of Evasion: Democrats and the Presidency" (Washington, DC: Progressive Policy Institute, September 1989), p. 1.

43. For an example of this turnout theory, see Piven and Cloward, *Why Americans Don't Vote*.

44. Galston and Kamarck, "The Politics of Evasion," p. 8.

45. Ibid., pp. 7–10.

46. See Faux, "The Myth of the New Democrats."

47. Galston and Kamarck, "The Politics of Evasion," pp. 2–3.

48. Ibid., p. 1.

49. Ibid., p. 11.

50. Ibid., p. 13; for the nationalization of American politics, see William M. Lunch, *The Nationalization of American Politics* (Berkeley: University of California Press, 1987).

51. Galston and Kamarck, "The Politics of Evasion," pp. 15–18.

52. Galston interview.

53. Quoted in Thomas B. Edsall, "Jackson, Robb Tussle over Democratic Strategy," *WP*, 11 March 1989, sec. A, p. 4; see E. J. Dionne, "Party Told to Win Middle-Class Vote," *NYT*, 12 March 1989, sec. 1, p. 32.

54. Edsall, "Jackson, Robb Tussle."

55. See ibid.; Dionne, "Party Told to Win"; Howard Fineman, "The Democrats: A War Within," *Newsweek*, 21 November 1988, DLCPB, vol. 7.

56. Robin Toner, "Jackson Urges Support for 'Special Interests,'" *NYT*, 23 June 1987, sec. B, p. 8.

57. Memorandum from Al From to Senator Nunn, "Subject: Tomorrow's DLC Governing Board Meeting," 23 February 1989, DLCP, Box: Network and BOA Meetings: 1989–1990, Folder: DLC Board Mtg., 2/23/89, p. 1.

58. Memorandum from Al From to Senators Nunn, Robb, Breaux and Governor

Clinton, "Subject: DLC Strategy through 1990—Confidential," 3 November 1989, AFPP, p. 6.

59. Memorandum from Al From to Senator Nunn, "Subject: The DLC Movement: An Overall Strategy," 1 May 1989, AFPP, p. 2.

60. Ibid., p. 4.

61. James A. Barnes, "The DLC Wants a Cornerstone for 1992," *NJ* 21, no. 12 (25 March 1989), p. 749.

62. Memorandum from Al From and Will Marshall to Interested Parties, "Re: The New Progressive Institute," 20 May 1988, AFPP, p. 2; emphasis theirs.

63. David M. Ricci, *The Transformation of American Politics: The New Washington and the Rise of Think Tanks* (New Haven, CT: Yale University Press, 1993), pp. 23, 162; Jerome L. Himmelstein, *To the Right: The Transformation of American Conservatism* (Berkeley: University of California Press, 1990), p. 29. See Himmelstein, p. 82, for a more complete list of conservative organizations, and James Allen Smith, *The Idea Brokers: Think Tanks and the Rise of the New Policy Elite* (New York: Free Press, 1991), p. 203.

64. R. Kent Weaver, "The Changing World of Think Tanks," *PS: Political Science and Politics* 22, no. 3 (September 1989), p. 564. Alice Rivlin, a longtime Brookings economist, confirms Weaver's assessment in "Policy Analysis at the Brookings Institution," in *Organizations for Policy Analysis: Helping Government Think,* Carol H. Weiss, ed. (Newbury Park, CA: Sage Publications, 1992), pp. 22–23. For more on the rise of think tanks in American politics, see Carol H. Weiss, "Helping Government Think: Functions and Consequences of Policy Analysis Organizations," in ibid., pp. 4–8.

65. Weaver, "Changing World," p. 567. For example, the Heritage Foundation—perhaps the quintessential advocacy think tank—spends between 35 and 40 percent of its budget on public relations. See Smith, *The Idea Brokers*, p. 201.

66. Quoted in Smith, *The Idea Brokers*, p. 201; "The Jefferson-Jackson Institute: A Proposal by Al From and Will Marshall," October 1988, AFPP, p. 1; Dan Balz, "Moderates, Conservative Democrats Buck 'Constraints,' Form Think Tank," *WP,* 30 June 1989, sec. A, p. 21.

67. Al From, interview by author, Washington, DC, 7 September 1995.

68. E. J. Dionne, "The New Think Tank on the Block," *NYT,* 28 June 1989, sec. A, p. 20.

69. Memo from From and Marshall to Interested Parties, "Re: The New Progressive Institute," 20 May 1988, pp. 10–11; see Memorandum from Al From and Will Marshall, "The Progressive Institute," 7 September 1988, AFPP.

70. Carol Matlack, "Marketing Ideas," *NJ,* 22 June 1991, DLCPB, vol. 14, p. 1554.

71. John F. Hale, "The Making of the New Democrats," *Political Science Quarterly* 110, no. 2 (1995), p. 214.

72. Memorandum from Al From to the DLC Governing Board, "Subject: The Future of the DLC," 7 November 1986, AFPP.

73. Memorandum from Al From to Governor Robb and Senator Nunn, "Subject: Next Steps for the DLC—Confidential," 27 November 1987, AFPP, pp. 6–7.

74. Will Marshall, interview by author, Washington, DC, 19 September 1995.

75. Memo from From to Nunn, Robb, Breaux and Clinton, "Subject: DLC Strategy Through 1990—Confidential," 3 November 1989, p. 6; Memo from From to DLC Governing Board, "Subject: Thursday's Meeting," 22 February 1989, p. 3.

76. Balz, "Moderates, Conservative Democrats Buck 'Constraints.'"

77. Memorandum from Al From to DLC Governing Board, "Subject: Thursday's Meeting," 22 February 1989, DLCP, Box: Network and BOA Meetings, 1989–90, Folder: DLC Board Meeting 23 February 1989. I have counted at least six alternative names for the Progressive Policy Institute: Foundation for National Progress, the Progressive Institute, Jefferson-Jackson Institute, the Truman Center, Institute for National Progress, and the New Progressive Institute.

78. Deb Smulyan, interview by author, Alexandria, VA, 21 September 1995.

79. Memo from From and Marshall to Interested Parties, "Re: The New Progressive Institute," 20 May 1988, p. 14; Al From, "The NPI and the DLC," undated, AFPP, p. 1.

80. Michael Steinhardt, interview by author, New York, NY, 4 September 1996; Memorandum from Al From to Michael Steinhardt, "Subject: Agenda for Friday's Meeting" [ca. 1988], AFPP, p. 3. In the end, Steinhardt donated $250,000 annually for three years.

81. From, "The NPI and the DLC," p. 1; Memo from From to Nunn, "Subject: Monday's DLC Mini-Retreat," 9 July 1988, p. 3.

82. Memorandum from Al From to Senator Nunn, "Subject: The Think Tank and the DLC," 12 September 1988, AFPP, p. 1; Memo from From and Marshall to Interested Parties, "Re: The New Progressive Institute," 20 May 1988, p. 2.

83. Memo from From to Nunn, "Subject: Monday's DLC Mini-Retreat," 9 July 1988, p. 4.

84. From, "The NPI and the DLC," p. 1.

85. Memorandum from Al From to PPI Board of Trustees, "Subject: The PPI and the DLC," 11 January 1989, DLCP, Box: Dolo (Al) #2, Folder: PPI Board Meeting—1/90, pp. 1–2; Untitled Memorandum [prospectus for the Institute for National Progress], 26 August 1988, AFPP, p. 4.

86. "Strategic Plan: Progressive Policy Institute, Confidential," September 1989, DLCP, Box: Dolo (A1) #2, unmarked folder, pp. 8–9; Memorandum from Al From and Will Marshall to the Board of Trustees, "Re: The Next 90 Days and Beyond," 11 January 1989, DLCP, Box: Dolo (Al) #2, Folder: PPI Board Meeting—1 /90, pp. 1–3.

87. Memo from From and Marshall to Board of Trustees, "Next 90 Days," 11 January 1989, AFPP, pp. 2–3; [Elaine Kamarck], "Progressive Policy Institute—Planning Memorandum," 7 February 1989, DLCP, Box: Dolo (Al) #2, Folder: Memo-Planning PPI, p. 2; Shapiro interview.

88. Smith, *The Idea Brokers*, p. 200.

89. "Strategic Plan," September 1989, p. 9.

90. Ibid., pp. 10–11; [Kamarck], "Progressive Policy Institute," 7 February 1989, pp. 1–2. The proposed name for the journal was *The Progressive Review*. See "PPI Projects," 1 August 1989, DLCP, Box: Dolo (Al) #2, Folder: Proposal General, p. 6.

91. Dionne, "New Think Tank"; Jonathan Rauch, "Paycheck Politics," *NJ*, 8 July 1989, DLCPB, vol. 8.

92. *Mainstream Democrat* 1, no. 1 (September–October 1989).

93. Bruce Reed, interview by author, Washington, DC, 20 September 1995.

94. Thomas B. Edsall and Maralee Schwartz, "For Democrat Brown, Warmth Turns to Chills," *WP*, 12 March 1989, sec. A, p. 18; E. J. Dionne, Jr., "Again, Democrats Agonize over the Rules," *NYT*, 21 May 1989, sec. 4, p. 5.

95. Dionne, "Again, Democrats"; Thomas B. Edsall, "No New Selection Rules, DNC Chairman Vows," *WP,* 13 April 1989, sec. A, p. 22; see Nelson W. Polsby, "The Democratic Nomination and the Evolution of the Party System," in *The American Elections of 1984,* Austin Ranney, ed. (Washington, DC: American Enterprise Institute, 1985), p. 53.

96. "Interview/Robert Beckel; 'Dukakis-Jackson Deal Handicaps Democrats,'" *Mainstream Democrat* 1, no. 1 (September–October 1989), pp. 14–15.

97. Dionne, "Again, Democrats"; Edsall, "No New Selection Rules."

98. Memorandum from Al From to Senator Nunn, "Subject: Talking Points for Tomorrow's DLC Session," 7 December 1989, AFPP, p. 2. Attendees of this meeting included Robb, McCurdy, Nunn, From, Marshall, Kamarck, Galston, and a group of large donors.

Chapter 6: Pursuing the Presidency, 1990–1992

1. "Strategic Plan: Progressive Policy Institute, Confidential," September 1989, DLCP, Box: Dolo (Al) #2, unmarked folder, p. 3.

2. Memorandum from Al From to Senator Sam Nunn, "Talking Points for Tomorrow's DLC Session," 7 December 1989, AFPP, p. 3.

3. Memorandum from Al From to DLC Staff, "Subject: This Afternoon's Staff Meeting," 8 August 1990, AFPP, p. 2; Al From, interview by author, Washington, DC, 7 September 1995. Although this memo was written a year after the movement strategy was well under way, I use it here since it so clearly reflects From's thinking.

4. Memorandum from Al From to DLC Governing Board, "Subject: Thursday's Meeting," 22 February 1989, DLCP, Box: Network and BOA Meetings: 1989–1990, Folder: DLC Board Meeting, 2/23/89, p. 3.

5. See Morley Winograd, "Draft: DLC Marketing Plan" [ca. 1990], DLCP, Box: DAB Events, 1991 Clev, 1992 N. Orleans, 1992 Demo Conv., Folder: Strategy/Message, p. 1; Memorandum from Al From to Bill Clinton, "Subject: 1990 DLC Strategy—Confidential," 15 April 1990, AFPP, p. 4; Memorandum from Linda Moore to Al From, "Re: DLC and the Field Program," 22 May 1991, AFPP; Memorandum from Bruce Reed to DLC Strategists, "Re: 1990 Media Plan," 3 April 1990, DLCP, Dolo (Al) #1, Folder: Bruce Reed, p. 2.

6. Memorandum from Al From to Bill Clinton, "Subject: Strategy for the Mainstream Movement—Confidential," 5 September 1990, DLCP, Box: Network and BOA Meetings: 1989–90, no folder, p. 1.

7. Memorandum from Al From to Governor Robb, "Subject: Six-Month DLC Strategy," 10 January 1987, AFPP, p. 7.

8. From interview, 7 September 1995.

9. Michael Steinhardt, interview by author, New York, NY, 4 September 1996.

10. Memorandum from Al From to Bill Clinton, "Subject: The DLC Chairmanship—Personal and Confidential," 23 February 1990, AFPP, p. 2.

11. Ibid.; emphasis his.

12. Ibid., p. 3.

13. Ibid.

14. Arthur T. Hadley, *The Invisible Primary* (Englewood Cliffs, NJ: Prentice-Hall, 1976), pp. 14–20.

15. Memo from From to Clinton, "Subject: 1990 DLC Strategy—Confidential," 15 April 1990, p. 1.

16. Memorandum from Bruce Reed to Al From, "Re: DLC Strategy, 1990–1," 30 August 1990, DLCP, Dolo (Al) #1, Folder: Bruce Reed, p. 1.

17. Ibid., p. 2.

18. Ibid., pp. 2–3; Memo from Reed to DLC Strategists, "Re: 1990 Media Plan," 3 April 1990, p. 4.

19. Memorandum from Al From to Sam Nunn, "Subject: DLC Strategy—Confidential," 6 July 1989, AFPP, pp. 1–2.

20. See Sam Nunn, "Goals for America," keynote address in *1990 Annual Conference of the Democratic Leadership Council,* 23–24 March 1990, Fairmont Hotel, New Orleans, LA (Washington, DC: Democratic Leadership Council, 1990), p. 37.

21. Memorandum from Will Marshall to PPI Trustees, "Re: Progressive Principles," 5 September 1990, DLCP, Dolo (Al) #2, Folder: PPI, p. 1.

22. Ibid., p. 2; "Progressive Policy Institute: Annual Report" [1990], DLCP, Dolo (Al) #2, Folder: PPI, p. 1.

23. "Progressive Policy Institute: Annual Report" [1990], p. 1.

24. Jean Bethke Elshtain, "Issues and Themes in the 1988 Campaign," in *The Elections of 1988,* Michael Nelson, ed. (Washington, DC: CQ Press, 1989), p. 122.

25. Judith Colp, "James Pinkerton: Paradigm's Prophet," *Washington Times,* 18 July 1991, sec. E, p. 1.

26. Mickey Kaus, "Paradigm's Loss: Jim Pinkerton and Bill Clinton," *New Republic* 207, no. 5 (27 July 1992), p. 16.

27. Ibid.; Morton Kondracke, "Neo-politics: The Left-Right Smooch-in," *New Republic* 205, no. 22 (25 November 1991), p. 18.

28. "The New Orleans Declaration: A Democratic Agenda for the 1990s" (Washington, DC: Democratic Leadership Council, March 1990), p. 2.

29. Ibid., p. ii.

30. Ibid., p. 2; see Memo from From to Clinton, "Subject: The DLC Chairmanship—Personal and Confidential," 23 February 1990, p. 4.

31. Ibid.

32. "New Orleans Declaration," p. 11.

33. Ibid.; Susan F. Rasky, "Mitchell Draws Line in Budget Talks," *NYT,* 12 July 1990, sec. B, p. 6; Memorandum from Dave Eisenstadt and Bruce Reed to Bill Clinton, "Re: Time Editorial Board," 20 November 1990, DLCP, Dolo (Al) #3, Folder: New York—Clinton—11/20/90, p. 3.

34. Senator Sam Nunn, "Beyond Right and Left: A Choice for the New American Economy," speech, Boston, 1991, in *1985–1995: Moving beyond the Left-Right Debate—A Collection of the Greatest New Democrat Speeches* (Washington, DC: Democratic Leadership Council, n.d.); see Clinton, DLC New Orleans Convention Closing Remarks.

35. Doug Ross, speech, in *1990 Annual Conference of the Democratic Leadership Council,* 23–24 March 1990, Fairmont Hotel, New Orleans, LA (Washington, DC: Democratic Leadership Council, 1990), pp. 241–42.

36. Memo from Marshall to PPI Trustees, "Re: Progressive Principles," 5 September 1990, p. 3.

37. "New Orleans Declaration," p. 8.

38. See ibid.

39. Ibid., p. 10.

40. Ibid., p. 9.

41. Memo from Marshall to PPI Trustees, "Re: Progressive Principles," 5 September 1990, pp. 2, 4; Minutes of PPI Board of Trustees Meeting, 10 September 1990, DLCP, Dolo (Al) #2, no folder, p. 5.

42. "New Orleans Declaration," p. 3; see Will Marshall and Bert Brandenburg, "Ending the Deadlock: A Progressive Solution to the Civil Rights Stalemate," *PPI Backgrounder,* 18 February 1991, p. 1.

43. Memo from Marshall to PPI Trustees, "Re: Progressive Principles," 5 September 1990, p. 5; see nearly identical language in "New Orleans Declaration," p. 3.

44. Nunn, "Beyond Right and Left."

45. DLC Advertisement, *Washington Post Weekly Edition,* DLCPB, vol. 10, 26 March–1 April 1990.

46. "New Orleans Declaration," p. 8.

47. Quote from "New Orleans Declaration," p. 10. Memo from Marshall to PPI Trustees, "Re: Progressive Principles," 5 September 1990, p. 2; Lloyd Bentsen, "DLC New Orleans Convention Keynote Address," New Orleans, LA [23–24 March 1990], in *1985–1995: Moving beyond the Left-Right Debate—A Collection of the Greatest New Democrat Speeches* (Washington, DC: Democratic Leadership Council, n.d.).

48. "New Orleans Declaration," p. 11. In fact, it was mentioned in a section on balancing the budget.

49. Ibid., p. 3.

50. See "Suggested DLC Themes and Legislative Proposals," 27 November 1990, DLCP, Box: Network and BOA Meetings, 1989–1990, no folder; Memorandum from Al From to Dave McCurdy, "Subject: Congressional Reform," 14 November 1990, AFPP; "Congressional Reform—Discussion Draft," 3 December 1990, DLCP, Box: Network and BOA Meetings, 1989–1990, no folder.

51. Memorandum from Al From, Will Marshall, Bruce Reed, and Doug Ross, "Re: Launching the Mainstream Movement," AFPP, p. 2; "The Road to Cleveland," *DLC Newsbrief,* CDF, winter 1991, p. 1; "DLC Domestic Policy Forums, Spring 1991," DLCP, Box: Network and BOA Meetings, 1989–1990, Folder: 2/4/91 Bd. Meeting.

52. Memorandum from Will Marshall to PPI Trustees, "Re: PPI 1991 Agenda," 25 January 1991, DLCP, Dolo (Al) #2, no folder, p. 1.

53. Ibid.; "Progressive Policy Institute Annual Report" [1990], p. 6.

54. Al From, interview by author, Washington, DC, 10 November 1997.

55. Memo from Marshall to PPI Trustees, "Re: PPI 1991 Agenda," 25 January 1991, p. 1.

56. Steve Patterson, interview by author, Washington, DC, 11 July 1996. Patterson was McCurdy's chief of staff.

57. "House Democrats Form Group to Counter Conservatives," *DLC Newsbrief,* CDF, summer 1990, p. 3; McCurdy interview.

58. Susan B. Glasser, "Moderate Democrats Form Caucus, To Use Gingrich's TV Tactics," *Roll Call,* DLCPB, vol. 10, 9 July 1990.

59. Memorandum from Al From to Bill Clinton, "Subject: DLC Strategy—Now until Cleveland, Confidential," 4 December 1990, AFPP, p. 1.

60. Bill McMahon, "Breaux Promoting State Demo Council," *Sunday Advocate* (Baton Rouge, LA), 5 April 1987, DLCPB, vol. 3; Randolph Pendleton, "Democratic Leadership Group Opens Florida Chapter This Week," *Tallahassee (FL) Democrat,* 8 March 1986, DLCPB, vol. 1.

61. Memo from Al From to Senator Robb and Senator Nunn, "Subject: Next Steps for the DLC—Confidential," AFPP, 27 November 1987, p. 9; Memo from Al From to Senator Robb, "Subject: Where Now," 26 June 1987, AFPP, p. 7; "DLC Launches Nationwide Network," *DLC Newsgram* 2, no. 3, (November 1988), p. 3.

62. See Rob Gurwitt, "Go Past the Beltway and Turn Right," *Governing,* DLCPB, vol. 13, April 1991, p. 21; Smulyan interview.

63. Memo from From to DLC Staff, "Subject: This Afternoon's Staff Meeting," 8 August 1990, pp. 3–4.

64. Memo from Reed to DLC Strategists, "Re: 1990 Media Plan," 3 April 1990, p. 2.

65. Memorandum from Al From to Bill Clinton, "Subject: Post-Session and Pre-Cleveland—Confidential," 11 February 1991, AFPP, p. 2.

66. "Mainstream Movement Pushes Democrats in New Directions," and "South Carolina, Mass., So. California, and Minnesota Start Chapters," *DLC Newsbrief,* CDF, summer 1990, pp. 1–2.

67. Memorandum from Linda Moore to Nancy Hernreich, Al From, Craig Smith, and Deb Smulyan, "Re: Summer Travel Schedule," 20 April 1990, DLCP, Box: Network and BOA Meetings, 1989–1990, Folder: Trip Schedules, p. 1. Indiana voted for the Republican presidential candidate in every presidential election from 1968 to 1992; Wisconsin actually was won by Dukakis in 1988.

68. Memo from Eisenstadt and Reed to Clinton, "Re: Time Editorial Board," 20 November 1990.

69. "Road to Cleveland," *DLC Newsbrief;* Memo from From to Clinton, "Subject: DLC Strategy—Now until Cleveland, Confidential," 4 December 1990, p. 1.

70. See "Democrats to Hear Nunn at Formation of Council," *News Times* (CT), DLCPB, vol. 12, 4 March 1991; Adam Nagourney, "Group Hopes to Steer Democrats Right," *USA Today,* DLCPB, vol. 13, 23 April 1991; "Oregon Democrats Join New Drive to Beat GOP," *Salem (OR) Statesman-Journal,* DLCPB, vol. 13, 12 April 1991; Jim Underwood, "Arkansas Governor Promotes Council," *Cleveland Plain-Dealer,* DLCPB, vol. 13, 24 April 1991; Peter Blake, "'Moderate' Dems Pitch Their Own Tent," *Rocky Mountain News* (CO), DLCPB, vol. 12, 18 March 1991.

71. Based on my own calculations and numbers from Ross K. Baker, "Sorting Out and Suiting Up: The Presidential Nominations," in *The Election of 1992,* Gerald Pomper et al. (Chatham, NJ: Chatham House Publishers, 1993), p. 53, table 2.4.

72. Elaine Kamarck, interview by author, Washington, DC, 11 January 1996.

73. "The Democratic Party's Civil War Comes to Minnesota," *Minnesota's Journal of Law and Politics,* DLCPB, vol. 10, June 1990.

74. Hugh McDiarmid, "Democratic Group, State Labor at Odds," *Detroit Free Press,* DLCPB, vol. 12, 12 March 1991.

75. Quoted in ibid.

76. Peter Howe, "Bozzotto Miffed with Democrats," *Boston Globe,* DLCPB, vol. 12, 17 March 1991.

77. John Distabo, "Democratic Forum's Plans Prompt Warning," *Union Leader* (NH), DLCPB, vol. 12, 26 March 1991.

78. Memo from From to Clinton, "Subject: DLC Strategy—Now until Cleveland, Confidential," 4 December 1990, p. 4; Memo from From to Clinton, "Subject: 1990 DLC Strategy—Confidential," 15 April 1990, p. 4; Memo from Linda Moore to From, "Re: DLC and the Field Program," 22 May 1991, p. 2; Memorandum from Deb Smulyan to Governor Clinton, "Re: Meeting with Bob Kogod," 6 December 1990, DLCP, Box: Network and BOA Meetings: 1989–1990, no folder; "Prospectus: Building the Mainstream Movement through a DLC Direct Mail Campaign" [ca . 1990], DLCP, Box: Network and BOA Meetings: 1989–1990, no folder, p. 1.

79. See DLC Advertisement, *Washington Post Weekly Edition*, DLCPB, vol. 10, 26 March–1 April 1990; "New Product for Agency: Democrats," *NYT*, 26 March 1990, sec. D, p. 13.

80. Linda Moore, interview by author, Washington, DC, 7 September 1995.

81. Memo from From to Clinton, "Subject: Strategy for the Mainstream Movement—Confidential," 5 September 1990, p. 5; "DLC 1991 National Convention, Cleveland, Ohio, May 5–7, 1991, Confidential Draft Plan" [February 1991], DLCP, Box: Network and BOA Meetings: 1989–1990, Folder: 2/4/91 Bd. Meeting, p. 2.

82. Robin Toner, "Democrat Session Preview '92 Race," *NYT*, 8 May 1991, sec. A, p. 18.

83. Steven Nider, interview by author, Washington, DC, 20 September 1995; Robin Toner, "Adding up Concern for Bush and Doubts about Quayle, the Democrats Get Zero," *NYT*, 12 May 1991, sec. 4, p. 1.

84. As Kiki Moore put it, Clinton got "the spotlight dance." Kiki Moore, interview by author, Washington, DC, 30 August 1995. She is no relation to Linda Moore.

85. David Maraniss, *First in His Class: The Biography of Bill Clinton* (New York: Simon and Schuster, 1995), p. 459.

86. William Galston, interview by author, College Park, MD, 12 September 1995.

87. Kiki Moore interview; Will Marshall, interview by author, Washington, DC, 19 September 1995; see the comments of Barrie Wigmore, PPI trustee, in Paul Starobin, "An Affair to Remember," *NJ* 25, no. 3 (16 January 1993), p. 120. Wigmore, a key benefactor of the Clinton run, said that this speech sold him on Clinton as a presidential candidate.

88. See the account in Maraniss, *First in His Class.*

89. Bill Clinton, Keynote Address, DLC National Convention, Cleveland, OH, 1991, in *1985–1995: Moving beyond the Left-Right Debate—A Collection of the Greatest New Democrat Speeches* (Washington, DC: Democratic Leadership Council, n.d.).

90. Dave McCurdy, speech, in *Official Transcript; Proceedings before the Democratic Leadership Council: 1991 National Convention— "The New Choice in American Politics,"* Cleveland, OH, 6–7 May 1991 (Washington, DC: Democratic Leadership Council, 1991), p. 106.

91. Clinton, Keynote Address, DLC National Convention, Cleveland, OH, 1991.

92. "The New American Choice: Opportunity, Responsibility, Community" (Washington, DC: Democratic Leadership Council, May 1991), pp. 8, 9.

93. Ibid., pp. 15, 16.

94. Ibid., p. 22.

95. Ibid., pp. 34–35.

96. Ibid., pp. 43–44.

97. Ibid., p. 24.

98. Ibid., p. 18.

99. *Official Transcript; Proceedings before the Democratic Leadership Council,* p. 240.

100. "New American Choice," p. 11.

101. Ibid., p. 26.

102. E. J. Dionne, Jr., *Why Americans Hate Politics* (New York: Simon and Schuster, 1992), p. 112.

103. "New American Choice," p. 20.

104. Clinton, Keynote Address, DLC National Convention, Cleveland, OH, 1991.

105. "New American Choice," pp. 38–39.

106. Ibid., p. 42.

107. Ibid., p. 8.

108. *Official Transcript; Proceedings before the Democratic Leadership Council,* pp. 122–42.

109. See Will Marshall and Bert Brandenberg, "Affirmative Inaction," *Mainstream Democrat,* March 1991, p. 14; "Business as Usual," *New Republic* 205 (11 November 1991), p. 8.

110. *Official Transcript; Proceedings before the Democratic Leadership Council,* p. 127.

111. Morley Winograd and Dudley Buffa, *Taking Control: Politics in the Information Age* (New York: Henry Holt and Company, 1996), p. 170. Winograd, a former chairman of the Michigan State Democratic Party, was an active participant in DLC affairs.

112. See the comments of one of Jackson's closest aides: Frank Watkins, interview by author, Washington, DC, 20 December 1996.

113. Jesse Jackson, remarks in *1990 Annual Conference of the Democratic Leadership Council,* 23–24 March 1990, Fairmont Hotel, New Orleans, LA (Washington, DC: Democratic Leadership Council, 1990), pp. 281–89.

114. Robin Toner, "Eyes to the Left, Democrats Edge toward the Center," *NYT,* 25 March 1990, sec. 1, p. 26.

115. *1990 Annual Conference of the Democratic Leadership Council,* p. 297.

116. From interview, 7 September 1995; From interview, 10 November 1997.

117. David S. Broder, "Hill Liberals Launch Democratic Coalition; US Doesn't Need 2 GOP's, Manifesto Says," *WP,* 14 May 1990, sec. A, p. 20; Howard M. Metzenbaum, telephone interview by author, Fort Lauderdale, FL, 17 January 1997.

118. Metzenbaum interview; Broder, "Hill Liberals."

119. Thomas B. Edsall, "Liberal Democrats Fragmented by Politics of War; Disputes over Gulf Distract Coalition from Focus on Strategy Meeting on Domestic Issues," *WP,* 27 January 1991, sec. A, p. 5.

120. Basil Talbott, "Jackson, McGovern Get Brush-off," *Chicago Sun-Times,* 14 April 1991, DLCPB, vol. 13.

121. Donald M. Rothberg, "Jackson Slams Democratic Group for 'Personal Attacks,'" *Associated Press,* 24 April 1991, DLCPB, vol. 13.

122. A. L. May, "Snub of Jackson Draws Irate Response from Democratic Leaders," *Atlanta Journal-Constitution,* 18 April 1991, DLCPB, vol. 13; Michael K. Frisby, "Jackson Counters Slight with Challenge," *Boston Globe,* 17 April 1991, DLCPB, vol. 13.

123. *Associated Press*, 29 April 1991, DLCPB, vol. 13; "Dem Round-up," *Hotline*, DLCPB, vol. 13, p. 4.

124. From interview, 7 September 1995.

125. Frisby, "Jackson Counters Slight."

126. "DLC 'Racked with Divisions' on Convention Eve," *Hotline* [4 May 1991], DLCPB, vol. 14.

127. Frisby, "Jackson Counters Slight."

128. Interview not for attribution.

129. Adam Nagourney, "Offshoot Group Stirs Dem Dissent," *USA Today*, 3 May 1991, sec. A, p. 11, DLCPB, vol. 14.

130. "DLC 'Racked with Divisions.'"

131. Kiki Moore interview.

132. Ibid.

133. Bill Gray, speech, in *Official Transcript; Proceedings before the Democratic Leadership Council: 1991 National Convention— "The New Choice in American Politics,"* Cleveland, OH, 6–7 May 1991 (Washington, DC: Democratic Leadership Council, 1991), p. 287.

134. Gwen Ifill, "Democratic Group Argues over Goals," *NYT*, 7 May 1991, sec. A, p. 21; "The White Men in Suits Move In," *Economist*, 11–17 May 1991, DLCPB, vol. 14; Dan Balz, "Democrats Face Minority Skepticism; Blacks Ask Whether Moderates' Strategy Abandons Civil Rights," *WP*, 8 May 1991, sec. A, p. 7.

135. Jim Underwood, "Jackson, White Keep a Distance as Democrats Meet in Cleveland," *Cleveland Plain-Dealer*, 7 May 1991, DLCPB, vol. 14.

136. Bill Whalen, "Fast Track May Derail Democrats," *Insight*, 3 June 1991, DLCPB, vol. 15, p. 24.

137. Meredith L. Oakley, *On the Make: The Rise of Bill Clinton* (Washington, DC: Regnery Publishing, 1994), p. 451.

138. Jeff Hagen, "Taking the Mainstream to Cleveland," *Cleveland Edition*, 13 December 1990, DLCPB, vol. 11.

139. David S. Broder, "The DLC at Six; It's Gone about as Far as It Can Go," *WP*, 12 May 1991, sec. C, p. 7; Ifill, "Democratic Group Argues."

140. Jesse L. Jackson, "For the Democrats, a Strategy of Inclusion," *WP*, 22 May 1991, sec. A, p. 21.

141. Toner, "Adding up Concern"; "Scuffling," *Wall Street Journal*, 14 June 1991, DLCPB, vol. 15. See Jackson, "For the Democrats"; Lawrence J. Haas, "An Economist with a Fiscal Mission," *NJ*, 16 February 1991, DLCPB, vol. 11, p. 402.

142. Curtis Wilkie, "N.H. Democratic Leader Cool to Group Led by Gov. Clinton," *Boston Globe*, 18 June 1991, DLCPB, vol. 15.

143. See a letter to the editor by the president of the Michigan AFL-CIO: Frank Garrison, "Democrats Can Win by Being Democrats," *Detroit Free Press*, 26 March 1991, DLCPB, vol. 12. On the DLC's attempt to mend fences with labor, see Memorandum from Deb Smulyan to Governor Clinton, "Re: Labor Lunch," 6 December 1990, DLCP, Box: Network and BOA Meetings: 1989–1990, no folder.

144. "Political Slights," *USA Today*, 7 June 1991, DLCPB, vol. 15.

145. Interview not for attribution; Smulyan interview; From interview, 7 September 1995; David S. Broder, "'Mainstream' Democratic Group Stakes Claim on Party's Future," *WP*, 3 May 1991, sec. A, p. 15.

146. Memorandum from Al From to Bill Clinton, "The Next 100 Days," 29 May 1991, AFPP, p. 4.

147. Ibid.

148. Edsall, "Liberal Democrats Fragmented."

149. Broder, "Hill Liberals."

150. Memorandum from Al From to the DLC Governing Board, "Subject: Tomorrow's Governing Board Meeting," 7 November 1991, AFPP, p. 9; Ed Kilgore, interview by author, Washington, DC, 8 September 1995; Kiki Moore interview.

151. "What Is to Be Done?" *New Republic*, 20 May 1991, DLCPB, vol. 14, pp. 28, 29; see James MacGregor Burns, William Crotty, Lois Lovelace Duke, and Lawrence D. Longley, eds., *The Democrats Must Lead: The Case for a Progressive Democratic Party* (Boulder, CO: Westview Press, 1992).

152. Memorandum from Bruce Reed to DLC Senior Staff, "Re: DLC, 1991–2," 22 May 1991, DLCP, Box: DAB Events, 1991 Clev, 1992 N. Orleans, 1992 Demo Conv., Folder: Strategy/Message, p. 1.

153. Ibid., p. 2.

154. Ibid.

155. Memorandum from Al From to Bill Clinton, "Subject: The Next 100 Days," 29 May 1991, AFPP, p. 1; Starobin, "An Affair to Remember," p. 120.

156. Memorandum from Kiki Moore to Al From, "Re: Media Strategy Outline," 21 May 1991, DLCP, Box: DAB Events, 1991 Clev, 1992 N. Orleans, 1992 Demo Conv., Folder: Strategy/Message, p. 1.

157. Oakley, *On the Make*, p. 453.

158. Ron Fournier, "Clinton's Presidential Decision Time Is Approaching," *Associated Press*, 11 August 1991, DLCPB, vol. 16. Also see Felice Belman, "Clinton Addresses Democrats," *Concord (NH) Monitor*, 5 August 1991, DLCPB, vol. 16; "August 4–5, 1991; New Hampshire," in DLCP, Box: Network and BOA Meetings: 1989–90, Folder: New Hampshire Trip, August 1991.

159. Maraniss, *First in His Class*, p. 460.

160. Ibid., p. 461.

161. Bill Clinton, Announcement of Presidential Bid, 3 October 1991, Little Rock, AR, in *1985–1995: Moving beyond the Left-Right Debate—A Collection of the Greatest New Democrat Speeches* (Washington, DC: Democratic Leadership Council, n.d.). See "New American Choice," p. 5.

162. Quoted in Rhodes Cook, "Arkansan Travels Well Nationally as Campaign Heads for Test," *Congressional Quarterly Weekly Report* (hereafter referred to as *CQWR*), 11 January 1992, DLCPB, vol. 19, p. 58.

163. James W. Davis, *President as Party Leader* (Westport, CT: Greenwood Press, 1992), pp. 19–21.

164. Ibid., p. 15.

Chapter 7: Counting on Clinton, 1992–1994

1. Rhodes Cook, "Harkin, Wilder Join the Race; Several Rivals in the Wings," *CQWR* 49, no. 37 (14 September 1991), p. 2641. On 16 December 1991, the ADA endorsed Harkin.

2. Wilson Carey McWilliams, "The Meaning of the Election," in *The Election of 1992: Reports and Interpretations,* Gerald Pomper et al. (Chatham, NJ: Chatham House Publishers, 1993), p. 202; Rhodes Cook, "'Super' Kick Propels Front-Runners onto Fast Track to Nomination," *CQWR* 50, no. 11 (14 March 1992), p. 632. Wilder entered the race briefly, but withdrew on 8 January 1992.

3. Paul R. Abramson, John H. Aldrich, and David W. Rohde, *Change and Continuity in the 1992 Elections,* rev. ed. (Washington, DC: CQ Press, 1995), p. 24.

4. Betsey Wright, interview by author, Washington, DC, 28 June 1996. See Elaine Kamarck, interview by author, Washington, DC, 11 January 1998; Meredith L. Oakley, *On the Make: The Rise of Bill Clinton* (Washington, DC: Regnery Publishing, 1994), p. 442.

5. Abramson et al., *1992 Elections,* p. 31; James A. Barnes, "The Hard-Charger," *NJ* 24, no. 3 (18 January 1992), p. 131.

6. Paul Starobin, "An Affair to Remember," *NJ* 25, no. 3 (16 January 1993), p. 120.

7. Ibid., p. 123.

8. Rhodes Cook, "Cuomo Says 'No' to Candidacy at Last Possible Moment," *CQWR* 49, no. 49 (21 December 1991), p. 3736.

9. Ross K. Baker, "Sorting Out and Suiting Up: The Presidential Nominations," in *The Election of 1992: Reports and Interpretations,* Gerald Pomper et al. (Chatham, NJ: Chatham House Publishers, 1993), p. 69.

10. Rhodes Cook, "Super Tuesday Tone to Be Set in Early Southern Face-offs," *CQWR* 50, no. 9 (29 February 1992), p. 485. DLC Senate calculations by the author; congressional numbers from Jon F. Hale, "The Making of the New Democrats," *Political Science Quarterly* 110, no. 2 (1995), p. 226.

11. Ronald D. Elving, "McCurdy Bows Out of Race; Cuomo Teases Again," *CQWR* 49, no 42 (19 October 1991), p. 3041; Steve Patterson, interview by author, Washington, DC, 11 July 1996.

12. Abramson et al., *1992 Elections,* p. 32.

13. Rhodes Cook and Ronald D. Elving, "Pennsylvania Primary Signals Breakthrough for Clinton," *CQWR* 50, no. 18 (2 May 1992), p. 1186.

14. Baker, "Sorting Out," p. 52.

15. Ibid., p. 61, table 2.61, p. 69.

16. Ibid., p. 62; see Rhodes Cook, "Clinton, Brown Taste First Wins; Bush-Buchanan Duel Rolls On," *CQWR* 50, no. 10 (7 March 1992), p. 559.

17. Sidney Blumenthal, "The Anointed," *New Republic,* 3 February 1992, DLCPB, vol. 19, p. 26.

18. Bob Kuttner, "A Democrat with Appeal to Conservatives and Liberals," *Boston Globe,* 5 January 1992, DLCPB, vol. 19.

19. Robin Toner, "Democrats Review Presidential Bids, Vowing to Avoid Losers' Mistakes," *NYT,* 23 September 1991, sec. B, p. 8.

20. Barnes, "Hard-Charger," p. 130; Donald Lambro, "Insurgent DLC Sees Victory within Grasp," *Washington Times,* 2 May 1992, DLCPB, vol. 20.

21. Memorandum from Al From to Bill Clinton, "Subject: DLC Strategy and Detroit—Personal and Confidential," 9 March 1991, AFPP; Memorandum from Al From to Bill Clinton, "Subject: Post-Session and Pre-Cleveland—Confidential," 11 February 1991, AFPP.

22. For an account of the early beliefs of Clinton, see David Maraniss, *First in His Class: The Biography of Bill Clinton* (New York: Simon and Schuster, 1995)

pp. 29–30, 453; Steven Waldman, *The Bill: How Legislation Really Becomes Law: A Case Study of the National Service Bill,* rev. ed. (New York: Penguin Books, 1995), pp. 4, 11; Bill Clinton to Al From, 8 December 1987, DLCP, Box: Dolo (Al) #1, Correspondence File 5; Bill Clinton to Al From, 17 March 1987, DLCP, Box: Dolo (Al) #1, Correspondence File 4; David Stoesz, *Small Change: Domestic Policy under the Clinton Presidency* (White Plains, NY: Longman Publishers, 1996), p. 69; Clinton's 1987 congressional testimony on welfare reform as documented by Gareth Davies, *From Opportunity to Entitlement: The Transformation and Decline of Great Society Liberalism* (Lawrence, KS: University Press of Kansas, 1996), pp. 1–2.

23. Bruce Reed, interview by author, Washington, DC, 20 September 1995.

24. Barnes, "Hard-Charger," p. 129.

25. James A. Barnes, "Clinton's Inaugural Economic Address . . . The Making of a Candidate's Speech," *NJ* 24, no. 3 (18 January 1992), pp. 130–31.

26. Bill Clinton, Speech at Georgetown University, Washington, DC, 23 October 1991, in *1985–1995: Moving beyond the Left-Right Debate—A Collection of the Greatest New Democrat Speeches* (Washington, DC: Democratic Leadership Council, n.d.).

27. Barnes, "Hard-Charger," p. 129.

28. Bill Clinton, Speech at Georgetown University, Washington, DC, 23 October 1991.

29. Bill Clinton, Speech at Georgetown University, Washington, DC, 12 December 1991, in *1985–1995: Moving beyond the Left-Right Debate—A Collection of the Greatest New Democrat Speeches* (Washington, DC: Democratic Leadership Council, n.d.).

30. Bill Clinton, Announcement of Presidential Bid, Little Rock, AR, 3 October 1991, in ibid.

31. Bill Clinton, Speech at Georgetown University, Washington, DC, 20 November 1991, in *1985–1995: Moving beyond the Left-Right Debate—A Collection of the Greatest New Democrat Speeches* (Washington, DC: Democratic Leadership Council, n.d.). Rob Shapiro, PPI vice-president, coordinated the economic policy content of this speech. For an example of a liberal agenda for 1992, see Samuel Bowles, David M. Gordon, and Thomas Weisskopf, "A Democratic Economic Policy," in *The Democrats Must Lead: The Case for a Progressive Democratic Party,* James MacGregor Burns, William Crotty, Lois Lovelace Duke, and Lawrence D. Longley, eds. (Boulder, CO: Westview Press, 1992), pp. 187–97.

32. Baker, "Sorting Out," pp. 62.

33. Ibid., pp. 58, 63; Richard E. Cohen, "Keeping Their Distance," *NJ* 24, no. 15 (11 April 1992), p. 868.

34. Memorandum from Al From to Senator Breaux, "Subject: 1992 DNC Convention," 15 November 1991, DLCP, Box: DAB Events, 1991 Clev, 1992 N. Orleans, 1992 Demo Conv., Folder: DNC Convention, p. 2.

35. Robin Toner, "1992 Ticket Puts Council of Moderates to Stiff Test," *NYT,* 15 July 1992, sec. A, p. 7; Lloyd Grove, "Al From, the Life of the Party," *WP,* 24 July 1992, sec. D, p. 1.

36. Al From to John Breaux, 15 January 1992, DLCP, Box: DAB Events, 1991 Clev, 1992 N. Orleans, 1992 Demo Conv., Folder: 1992 DNC Convention; Wright interview.

37. Anthony Corrado, "The Politics of Cohesion: The Role of the National Party Committees in the 1992 Election," in *The State of the Parties: The Changing Role of Contemporary American Parties*, 2nd ed., John C. Green and David M. Shea, eds. (Lanham, MD: Rowan and Littlefield, 1996), pp. 70–71; L. Sandy Maisel, "The Platform Writing Process: Candidate-Centered Platforms in 1992," in ibid., p. 294.

38. Corrado, "Politics of Cohesion," p. 75.

39. Maisel, "Platform Writing Process," p. 291. Romer was an active DLC member and eventually became its vice-chairman. Because of her involvement in the House Bank scandal, Oakar was quietly replaced by Representative Nancy Pelosi (CA).

40. Ibid., p. 293.

41. Ibid., p. 294; Al From, interview by author, Washington, DC, 10 November 1997.

42. Maisel, "Platform Writing Process," p. 295.

43. Ibid., p. 296.

44. Mary Frances Berry, interview by author, Washington, DC, 15 December 1995.

45. Maisel, "Platform Writing Process," p. 310.

46. Ibid., pp. 289–90; Baker, "Sorting Out," p. 63; Ryan J. Barilleux and Randall E. Adkins, "The Nominations: Process and Patterns," in *The Elections of 1992*, Michael Nelson, ed. (Washington, DC: CQ Press, 1993), p. 53.

47. John Benedetto, "Ticket Clings to Centrist Roots," *USA Today*, 14 July 1992, sec. A, p. 5. Also see the accompanying table, "Moderate Influence on Party Platform."

48. Hale, "The Making of the New Democrats," p. 227.

49. David E. Rosenbaum, "Democratic Platform Shows Shift in Party's Focus," *NYT*, 14 July 1992, sec. A, p. 9.

50. Louis Menand, "After Elvis," *New Yorker*, 26 October and 2 November 1998, p. 164.

51. It should be noted that the sign also read: "Change versus more of the same. And don't forget about healthcare."

52. E. J. Dionne, Jr., *They Only Look Dead: Why Progressives Will Dominate the Next Political Era* (New York: Simon and Schuster, 1996), pp. 93–95.

53. Walter Dean Burnham, "The Legacy of George Bush: Travails of an Understudy," in *The Election of 1992: Reports and Interpretations*, Gerald Pomper et al. (Chatham, NJ: Chatham House Publishers, 1993), p. 30. On Democratic fundraising, see F. Christopher Arterton, "Campaign '92: Strategies and Tactics of the Candidates," in ibid., pp. 83–95.

54. Arterton, "Campaign '92," pp. 76, 80.

55. Ibid., pp. 82, 102.

56. Ibid., p. 99.

57. Ibid.; Paul J. Quirk and Jon K. Dalager, "The Election: A 'New Democrat' and a New Kind of Presidential Campaign," in *The Elections of 1992*, Michael Nelson, ed. (Washington, DC: CQ Press, 1993), p. 62.

58. James A. Barnes, "Tainted Triumph?" *NJ* 24, no. 45 (7 November 1992), p. 2540.

59. Rhodes Cook, "Clinton Picks the GOP Lock on the Electoral College," *CQWR* 50, no. 44 (7 November 1992), p. 3548.

60. Barnes, "Tainted Triumph?" p. 2540.

61. Rhodes Cook, "House Republicans Scored a Quiet Victory," *CQWR* 51, no. 16 (17 April 1993), p. 965; see Dave Kaplan and Charles Mathesian, "Elections Wave of Diversity Spares Many Incumbents," *CQWR* 50, no 44 (7 November 1992), p. 3576.

62. Richard E. Cohen, "No Honeymoon Cruise," *NJ* 24, no. 45 (7 November 1992), p. 2553.

63. Cook, "Clinton Picks," p. 3548; William Schneider, "A Loud Vote for Change," *NJ* 24, no. 45 (7 November 1992), p. 2543, table.

64. Cook, "Clinton Picks," pp. 3550, 3551; Barnes, "Tainted Triumph?" p. 2540.

65. See Gerald Pomper, "The Presidential Election," in *The Election of 1992: Reports and Interpretations*, Gerald Pomper et al. (Chatham, NJ: Chatham House Publishers, 1993), p. 139, table 5.2. Data from the *New York Times*/CBS News poll. Of the two-party vote, Clinton won 54 percent of it.

66. Rhodes Cook, "Clinton Struggles to Meld a Governing Coalition," *CQWR* 51, no. 32 (7 August 1993), p. 2178.

67. Arterton, "Campaign '92," p. 102; Cook, "Clinton Picks," pp. 3550, 3551.

68. See Walter Dean Burnham, "Bill Clinton: Riding the Tiger," in *The Election of 1996: Reports and Interpretations*, Gerald Pomper et al. (Chatham, NJ: Chatham House Publishers, 1997), p. 2; Ronald Radosh, *Divided They Fell: The Demise of the Democratic Party, 1964–1996* (New York: Free Press, 1996), pp. 151–54.

69. Schneider, "A Loud Vote," pp. 2542, 2544; Quirk and Dalager, "The Election," p. 62; Cook, "Clinton Picks," p. 3549.

70. Schneider, "A Loud Vote," p. 2542; Neil Brown, "Voters Looking for Change Run to New Generation," *CQWR* 50, no. 44 (7 November 1992), p. 3547.

71. See Scott Leigh, "Jackson Disputes Centrist Strategy as Clinching Clinton Win," *Boston Globe*, 2 December 1992, DLCPB, vol. 24.

72. Bill Clinton and Al Gore, *Putting People First: How We Can All Change America* (New York: Random House, 1992).

73. Baker, "Sorting Out," p. 63; and James A. Barnes, "Clinton's Moment," *NJ* 24, no. 28 (11 July 1992), p. 1619.

74. Schneider, "A Loud Vote," pp. 2542, 2544.

75. Warren J. Miller and the National Election Studies, *NES Guide to Public Opinion and Electoral Behavior* (Ann Arbor, MI: Inter-University Consortium for Political and Social Research, 1994), http://www.umich.edu/~nes/resources/nesguide/toptables/tab4e_5.htm.

76. Burnham, "The Legacy of George Bush," p. 21; Schneider, "A Loud Vote," p. 2544, table.

77. Schneider, "A Loud Vote," p. 2544, table.

78. Stephan M. Nichols and Paul Allen Beck, "Reversing the Decline: Voter Turnout in the 1992 Election," in *Democracy's Feast: Elections in America*, Herbert F. Weisberg, ed. (Chatham, NJ: Chatham House Publishers, 1995), pp. 29–30; Herbert F. Weisberg and David C. Kimball, "Attitudinal Correlates of the 1992 Presidential Vote: Party Identification and Beyond," in ibid., p. 80; Herb Asher, "The Perot Campaign," in ibid., p. 164; Miller and NES, *NES Guide to Public Opinion and Electoral Behavior*, http://www.umich.edu/~nes/resources/nesguide/toptables/tab5a_1.htm.

79. Harold W. Stanley and Richard G. Niemi, "The Demise of the New Deal Coalition: Partisanship and Group Support, 1952–1992," in *Democracy's Feast:*

Elections in America, Herbert F. Weisberg, ed. (Chatham, NJ: Chatham House Publishers, 1995), p. 223.

80. Pomper, "The Presidential Election," p. 150.

81. Everett Carll Ladd, "The 1992 Vote for President Clinton: Another Brittle Mandate?" *Political Science Quarterly* 108, no. 1 (1993), pp. 1–2.

82. John S. Jackson III and Nancy L. Clapton, "Leaders and Followers: Major Party Elites, Identifiers, and Issues: 1980–92," in *The State of the Parties: The Changing Role of Contemporary American Parties,* 2nd ed., John C. Green and Daniel M. Shea, eds. (Lanham, MD: Rowman and Littlefield, 1996), p. 332, table 20.1a. Their elite data are from the Party Elite Study conducted by Southern Illinois University at Carbondale; the mass data are from the NES. Also see James A. McCann, "Presidential Nomination Activists and Political Representation: A View from the Active Minority Studies," in *In Pursuit of the White House: How We Choose Our Presidential Nominees,* William G. Mayer, ed. (Chatham, NJ: Chatham House Publishers, 1996), p. 79, table 3.3.

83. Jackson and Clapton, "Leaders and Followers," pp. 332–38.

84. Barnes, "Clinton's Moment," p. 1619.

85. Paul J. Quirk and Joseph L. Hinchliffe, "Domestic Policy: The Trials of a Centrist Democrat," in *The Clinton Presidency: Early Appraisals,* Colin Campbell and Bert A. Rockman, eds. (Chatham, NJ: Chatham House Publishers, 1996), p. 262.

86. Jack W. Germond and Jules Witcover, "Due Bills," *NJ* 24, no. 45 (7 November 1992), p. 2550.

87. Al From and Will Marshall, "The Road to Realignment: Democrats and Perot Voters," in *The Road to Realignment: The Democrats and Perot Voters,* Stanley B. Greenberg, Al From, and Will Marshall (Washington, DC: Democratic Leadership Council, July 1993), p. I-1.

88. Ibid., pp. I-1, I-4; see Kevin P. Phillips, *The Emerging Republican Majority* (Garden City, NY: Doubleday, 1969).

89. From and Marshall, "Road to Realignment," pp. I-1, I-2; Dan Balz, "How Clinton Might Win Perot's Voters; DLC Study Dissects the 'Radical Middle,'" *WP,* 8 July 1993, sec. A, p. 1.

90. Stanley B. Greenberg, "The Perot Voters and American Politics: Here to Stay?" in *The Road to Realignment: The Democrats and Perot Voters,* Stanley B. Greenberg, Al From, and Will Marshall (Washington, DC: Democratic Leadership Council, July 1993), pp. II-2, II-3. Seventy-eight percent of Perot voters believed that the poor got something for nothing.

91. Will Marshall and Martin Schram, eds., *Mandate for Change* (New York: Berkley Books, 1993).

92. Greenberg et al., *The Road to Realignment,* inside cover.

93. On how this dynamic worked with respect to national service, see Waldman, *Bill,* p. 199.

94. Elizabeth Drew, *On the Edge: The Clinton Presidency* (New York: Simon and Schuster, 1994), p. 42.

95. Ibid., p. 48.

96. John B. Judis, "The Old Democrat," *New Republic,* 22 February 1993, DLCPB, vol. 25, p. 19.

97. Joe Klein, "The Center Does Not Hold," *Newsweek,* 31 May 1993, DLCPB, vol. 25, p. 24.

98. For the DLC's view, see Al From, "Guinier Had to Go, Now," *NYT,* 5 June 1993, sec. 1, p. 21.

99. Byron E. Shafer, "'We Are All Southern Democrats Now?' The Shape of American Politics in the Very Late Twentieth Century," in *Present Discontents: American Politics in the Very Late Twentieth Century,* Byron E. Shafer, ed. (Chatham, NJ: Chatham House Publishers, 1997), p. 164.

100. Chuck Alston, "The President's Position on Taxes: Reversal or 'Healthy Evolution'?" *CQWR* 51, no. 8 (20 February 1993), p. 384.

101. Clifford Krauss, "Leading Conservative Democrat Criticizes Clinton," *NYT,* 18 May 1993, sec. A, p. 15.

102. See Jeff Faux, "The Myth of the New Democrats," *American Prospect* (fall 1993), p. 29; Jeff Faux, "Industrial Policy," *Dissent* (fall 1993), p. 469; Harold Meyerson, "Conflicted President, Undefined Presidency," *Dissent* (fall 1993), pp. 439, 446.

103. Dionne, *They Only Look Dead,* p. 131.

104. "Address of the President to the Joint Session of Congress," 22 September 1993, in *Health Security: The President's Report to the American People* (Washington, DC: White House Domestic Policy Council, 1993), p. 90.

105. "The Prescription Is Competition," *New Democrat* 5, no. 5 (December 1993), p. 5; Robin Toner, "3 Schools of Thought on Clinton's '3rd Way,'" *NYT,* 14 December 1993, sec. A, p. 22; see Rob Shapiro's comment in Morton M. Kondracke, "Go Slow Warns Ex-Clinton Aide about Health Reform," *Roll Call,* 12 August 1993, DLCPB, vol. 26.

106. Will Marshall, "Under Indictment: Americans Want to Change, but Not Demolish, the Welfare System," *New Democrat* 5, no. 5 (December 1993), p. 6. See Mickey Kaus, "They Blew It," *New Republic,* 5 December 1994, front cover.

107. Michael Kelly, "'New Democrats' Say Clinton Has Veered and Left Them," *NYT,* 23 May 1993, sec. A, p. 20.

108. Joel D. Aberbach, "The Federal Executive under Clinton," in *The Clinton Presidency: Early Appraisals,* Colin Campbell and Bert A. Rockman, eds. (Chatham, NJ: Chatham House Publishers, 1996), p. 177.

109. Cook, "Clinton Struggles," p. 2178.

110. Drew, *On the Edge,* pp. 128–29; Gerald F. Seib, "New Democrat: An Old Concept Worth Revisiting," *Wall Street Journal,* 24 August 1994, DLCPB, vol. 28.

111. Jason DeParle, "The Difficult Math of Welfare Reform," *NYT,* 5 December 1993, sec. A, p. 30.

112. David Masci, "$30 Billion Anti-Crime Bill Heads to Clinton's Desk," *CQWR* 52, no. 39 (27 August 1994), p. 2488.

113. Ibid., p. 2493.

114. Holly Idelson, "An Era Comes to a Close," *CQWR* 53, no. 50 (23 December 1995), pp. 3871–73.

115. Barbara Sinclair, "Trying to Govern Positively in a Negative Era: Clinton and the 103rd Congress," in *The Clinton Presidency: Early Appraisals,* Colin Campbell and Bert A. Rockman, eds. (Chatham, NJ: Chatham House Publishers, 1996), p. 109; Charles O. Jones, "Campaigning to Govern: The Clinton Style," in ibid., p. 37.

116. "NAFTArmath: The Victory Was Clinton's Finest Hour," *New Democrat* 5, no. 5 (December 1993), p. 5.

117. Dennis Farney, "Way Ahead in Connecticut Race, Sen. Lieberman Preaches

Virtues of Moderation to Democrats," *Wall Street Journal*, 28 October 1994, DLCPB, vol. 28.

118. Fred Siegel, "Coasts to Clinton: Don't Tread on Us," *Wall Street Journal*, 19 September 1994, DLCPB, vol. 28; Robert Andrews, interview by author, Washington, DC, 14 September 1995.

119. See the analysis in Albert R. Hunt, "The DLC's Phony Liberal Scare," *Wall Street Journal*, 23 December 1993, DLCPB, vol. 27.

120. David M. O'Brien, "Clinton's Legal Policy and the Courts: Rising from Disarray or Thinking Around and Around?" in *The Clinton Presidency: Early Appraisals*, Colin Campbell and Bert A. Rockman, eds. (Chatham, NJ: Chatham House Publishers, 1996), p. 131; Quirk and Hinchliffe, "Domestic Policy," p. 264; Jeffrey H. Birnbaum, "Centrist Reed and Liberal Sperling Represent the Contradictory Blend of Clinton's Ideology," *Wall Street Journal*, 10 December 1993, DLCPB, vol. 27.

121. Ruy A. Teixera, "Intellectual Challenges Facing the Democratic Party," in *The Politics of Ideas: Intellectual Challenges to the Party after 1992*, John K. White and John C. Green, eds. (Lanham, MD: Rowman and Littlefield, 1995), p. 53.

122. Drew, *On the Edge*, p. 421; Aberbach, "Federal Executive," p. 166; Bert A. Rockman, "Leadership Style and the Clinton Presidency," in *The Clinton Presidency: Early Appraisals*, Colin Campbell and Bert A. Rockman, eds. (Chatham, NJ: Chatham House Publishers, 1996), p. 357. And see Faux, "Myth of the New Democrats," p. 21.

123. Rockman, "Leadership Style," p. 331.

124. Ibid., p. 338.

125. Data from Barnes, "Tainted Triumph?" p. 2539, table; "Senate Results; Democrats Pick up a Seat," *NJ* 24, no. 45 (7 November 1992), p. 2570; "The House in the 103rd Congress . . . Unofficial Results of the 435 Races," *NJ* 24, no. 45 (7 November 1992), pp. 2572–74, table. Every congressional and senatorial winner ran ahead of Clinton's national percentage. Only two Republican representatives ran behind him in their state (Arkansas), and two ran even with him.

126. Robin Toner, "Health Care Reform: A Case Study," in *Back to Gridlock: Governance in the Clinton Years*, James L. Sundquist, ed. (Washington, DC: Brookings Institution, 1995), p. 31; Jason DeParle, "Clinton Social Policy Camps: Bill's vs. Hillary's," *NYT*, 20 December 1992, sec. A, p. 1.

127. Interview not for attribution; Craig Smith, interview by author, Washington, DC, 11 September 1995. Elements of this attitude are apparent in some of the DLC's publications. See William A. Galston and Elaine Ciulla Kamarck, "The Transition: Reasserting Presidential Leadership," in *Mandate for Change*, Will Marshall and Martin Schram, eds. (New York: Berkley Books, 1993), p. 328.

128. Smith interview. Smith was White House political director through 1997 and 1998.

129. Dan Balz, "Clinton, Centrist Democrats Avoid Rift on Overhaul of Health Care," *WP*, 4 December 1993, sec. A, p. 10; Thomas L. Friedman, "Clinton Reassures Centrist Council," *NYT*, 4 December 1993, sec. A, p. 10.

130. Galston and Kamarck, "The Transition," p. 322.

131. David Von Drehle, "Wild Cards and Sure Things Talking about a Transition," *WP*, 7 October 1992, DLCPB, vol. 23; "Picking out Plans," *WP*, 1 October 1992, DLCPB, vol. 23.

132. Jeffrey H. Birnbaum, "Bid by Moderates, Liberals to Influence Clinton Could Pose Sensitive Conflict in His Presidency," *Wall Street Journal*, 2 December 1992,

DLCPB, vol. 24; Adam Nagourney, "Democratic Council to Play Key Role in Administration," *USA Today,* 4 December 1992, DLCPB, vol. 24.

133. See "Facts about the Dem. Leadership Council " [ca. 1993], CDF, Folder: Development Lit., p. 1.

134. Author's calculations.

135. Patterson interview. Patterson was McCurdy's chief of staff for twelve years.

136. Al Kamen, "Justice Department Civil Division Slot for an In-Law of the Vice-President?" *WP,* 18 March 1993, sec. A, p. 25.

137. Michael Steinhardt, interview by author, New York, NY, 4 September 1996; John M. Goshko, "Neoconservative Democrats Complain of Big Chill; Clinton Allies Decry Appointments Tally," *WP,* 15 March 1993, sec. A, p. 17.

138. David S. Broder, "Diversity Was Paramount in Building the Cabinet," *WP,* 25 December 1992, sec. A, p. 1.

139. Reed interview. Also see David McCurdy, interview by author, McLean, VA, 11 September 1995; Stoesz, *Small Change,* p. 216.

140. Quirk and Hinchliffe, "Domestic Policy," p. 285.

141. Clifford D. May, "Clinton, Like Us, Is Outnumbered," *Rocky Mountain News* (CO), 25 May 1994, DLCPB, vol. 28. Also see Al From, "Happy Days Are Here . . . And Gone," *New Democrat* 6, no. 5 (November 1994), pp. 31–32; Al From, interview by author, Washington, DC, 7 September 1995; Will Marshall, interview by author, Washington, DC, 19 September 1995.

142. George Stephanopoulos, *All Too Human: A Political Education* (Boston: Little, Brown, 1999), p. 140.

143. Jeffrey H. Birnbaum and Michael K. Frisby, "Clinton's Hiring of Gergen Suggests Appeal to Moderates, But Doubts Linger," *Wall Street Journal,* 1 June 1993, DLCPB, vol. 26; Fred Barnes, "The Turning," *New Republic,* 28 June 1993, DLCPB, vol. 26, p. 10; Drew, *On the Edge,* p. 187.

144. See the comments by Gerald McEntee, president of AFSCME, in James A. Barnes, "Good Soldiers," *NJ* 25, no. 31 (31 July 1993), p. 1913.

145. Sinclair, "Trying to Govern," p. 90.

146. Pamela Fessler, "Clinton Plans for Smooth Start with Focus on the Economy," *CQWR* 50, no. 44 (7 November 1992), p. 3554.

147. Rockman, "Leadership Style," p. 330; Thomas E. Mann, "President Clinton and the Democratic Congress," in *Back to Gridlock: Governance in the Clinton Years,* James L. Sundquist, ed. (Washington, DC: Brookings Institution, 1995), p. 12.

148. Sinclair, "Trying to Govern," p. 93.

149. Quirk and Hinchliffe, "Domestic Policy," pp. 265, 283; McCurdy interview.

150. Robert D. Reischauer, "Budget Policy under United Government: A Case Study," in *Back to Gridlock? Governance in the Clinton Years,* James L. Sundquist, ed. (Washington, DC: Brookings Institution, 1995), pp. 20–29.

151. Sinclair, "Trying to Govern," pp. 96–99; see the comments of Howard Paster, Clinton's first congressional liaison, in James L. Sundquist, ed., *Beyond Gridlock? Prospects for Governance in the Clinton Years—and After* (Washington, DC: Brookings Institution, 1993), p. 16.

152. Bruce Reed believed that this was the case. See Reed interview; Peter J. Berger, "Gore's Dilemma," *New Yorker,* 12 November 1994, DLCPB, vol. 29, p. 107.

153. Galston and Kamarck, "The Transition," p. 322.

154. Ibid.; see, for example, Rob Shapiro, interview by author, Washington, DC,

18 September 1995; William Galston, interview by author, College Park, MD, 12 September 1995; From interview, 7 September 1995; McCurdy interview; Marshall interview; Al From, "On a Roll: Clinton Cannot Afford to Squander His Momentum from 1993," *New Democrat* 6, no. 1 (February 1994), p. 20.

155. Drew, *On the Edge*, pp. 20–21.

156. McCurdy interview.

157. Ibid.

158. Charles O. Jones, "Separating to Govern: The American Way," in *Present Discontents: American Politics in the Very Late Twentieth Century*, Byron E. Shafer, ed. (Chatham, NJ: Chatham House Publishers, 1997), p. 65.

159. Reed interview.

150. Stephanopoulos, *All Too Human*, p. 277.

161. Lloyd Grove, "Lobbyists' Thermidor: Clinton Sups with Special Interests at Democratic Leadership Council Fete," *WP*, 9 December 1992, sec. C, p. 1; Winston McGregor, interview by author, Washington, DC, 13 September 1995; "Financial Information" (Washington, DC: Democratic Leadership Council, 1995).

162. McGregor interview.

163. See McCurdy's comments in Ronald Brownstein, "Now It's Moderate Democrats Facing Heat," *Los Angeles Times*, 17 October 1994, DLCPB, vol. 28.

164. McGregor interview; Linda Moore, interview by author, Washington, DC, 7 September 1995; and Deb Smulyan, interview by author, Alexandria, VA, 21 September 1995.

165. Richard L. Berke, "Centrists Are Wary of Clinton Tilting," *NYT*, 3 December 1993, sec. A, p. 24.

166. Dan Balz, "'New Democrats' Promise New Pressure on Clinton; DLC Chairman Warns President Not to Let Party Liberals 'Water Down' Centrist Agenda," *WP*, 5 December 1993, sec. A, p. 4.

167. Ibid.; McCurdy interview. For another version of this stance, see Memorandum from Chuck Alston to Deb Smulyan, "'Fighting for Change': DLC Annual Conference Talking Points," 11 October 1993, Communication Director's Files.

168. James A. Barnes, "Will DLC Be a Lobbying Heavyweight?" *NJ*, 23 October 1993, DLCPB, vol. 26, p. 2542.

169. Joe Klein, "Assault on the Center," *Newsweek*, 31 October 1994, DLCPB, vol. 28, p. 33.

170. Galston interview; Eliza Newlin Carney, "Party Pooper?" *NJ* 28, no. 14 (6 April 1996), pp. 770–71.

171. See From's comments in Donald Lambro, "'New Democrats' Eye Big Changes in Party, Federal Government," *Washington Times*, 20 November 1993, DLCPB, vol. 27.

Chapter 8: Rising from the Ashes, 1994–1996

1. Robert Dreyfuss, "Political Snipers," *American Prospect* no. 23 (fall 1995), pp. 28–36, http://epn.org/prospect/23/23drey.html; Chris Casteel, "McCurdy vs. Inhofe: Records of Contrast," *Sunday Oklahoman*, 9 October 1994, p. 1; J. E. McReynolds, "'Tis the Season to Get Muddy; Politicians Go on the Attack," *Sunday Oklahoman*, 16 October 1994, p. 16.

2. David McCurdy, interview by author, McLean, VA, 11 September 1995.

3. Franco Mattei, "Eight More in '94: The Republican Takeover of the Senate," in *Midterm: The Elections of 1994 in Context,* Philip A. Klinkner, ed. (Boulder, CO: Westview Press, 1996), p. 21.

4. Harold W. Stanley, "The Parties, the President, and the 1994 Midterm Elections," in *The Clinton Presidency: Early Appraisals,* Colin Campbell and Bert A. Rockman, eds. (Chatham, NJ: Chatham House Publishers, 1996), p. 192.

5. Rhodes Cook, "Losses in Swing Districts Doomed Democrats," *CQWR* 52, no. 45 (19 November 1994), p. 3354.

6. Rhodes Cook, "Dixie Voters Look Away; South Shifts to the GOP," *CQWR* 52, no. 44 (12 November 1994), p. 3231.

7. Stanley B. Greenberg, *Middle-Class Dreams: The Politics and Power of the New American Majority* (New York: Random House, 1995), p. 18; "Portrait of the Electorate: Who Voted for Whom in the House," *NYT,* 13 November 1994, sec. A, p. 24. These data are from the 1992 exit polls conducted by Voter Research and Surveys and the 1994 exit polls done by Mitofsky International.

8. Alan L. Abramowitz, "The End of the Democratic Era? 1994 and the Future of Congressional Election Research," *Political Research Quarterly* 48, no. 4 (December 1995), p. 879; Warren E. Miller and National Election Studies, *NES Guide to Public Opinion and Electoral Behavior, 1952–1994* (Ann Arbor: University of Michigan, Center for Political Studies, 1994), http://www.umich.edu/~nes/resources/nesguide/toptables/tab2a_2.htm and http://www.umich.edu/~nes/resources/nesguide/2ndtables/t2a_2_1.htm.

9. Gary C. Jacobson, "The 1994 House Elections in Perspective," in *Midterm: The Elections of 1994 in Context,* Philip A. Klinkner, ed. (Boulder, CO: Westview Press, 1996), p. 5. Clinton's approval rating was 51 percent in the Northeast and 45 percent in the rest of the country.

10. Jeff Shear, "The Santa Clauses," *NJ* 26, no. 43 (22 October 1994), p. 2453; William Schneider, "Clinton: The Reason Why," *NJ* 26, no. 46 (12 November 1994), p. 2632.

11. Ceci Connolly, "GOP Accentuates the Positive; Hopefuls to Sign Compact," *CQWR* 52, no. 37 (24 September 1994), p. 3712; Harold E. Bruno, Jr., "A Political Observer's View," in *Back to Gridlock: Governance in the Clinton Years,* James Sundquist, ed. (Washington, DC: Brookings Institution, 1995), p. 17.

12. Miller and NES, *NES Guide to Public Opinion and Electoral Behavior,* http://www.umich.edu/~nes/resources/nesguide/toptables/tab4e_1.htm; Schneider, "Clinton: The Reason Why," p. 2632.

13. See Becky Cain, "The Voters' Perspective," in *Back to Gridlock: Governance in the Clinton Years,* James L. Sundquist, ed. (Washington, DC: Brookings Institution, 1995), p. 41.

14. Jeff Faux, "A New Conversation: How to Rebuild the Democratic Party," *American Prospect* (spring 1995), p. 37; also see Bob Herbert, "No GOP Imitations, Please," *NYT,* 20 November 1994, sec. 4, p. 15; Adolph Reed, "Why They Won: The Democrats Lost Faith," *Village Voice* (New York, NY), 28 November 1994, DLCPB, vol. 29, p. 19.

15. Daniel Cantor and Juliet Schor, "Democrats Arise! (Which Way Is Up?); A Populist Manifesto," *NYT,* 5 December 1994, sec. A, p. 19.

16. Stanley, "The Parties, the President," p. 193; see Robert W. Merry, "Voters'

Demand for Change Puts Clinton on Defensive," *CQWR* 52, no. 44 (12 November 1994), p. 3207.

17. Burt Solomon, "Color Gore a New Democrat Who May Yet Turn His Boss into One," *NJ* 24, no. 47 (19 November 1994), p. 2741.

18. Mark Penn and Douglas Schoen, "A Contract with the Middle Class," in *Back from the Dead: How Clinton Survived the Republican Revolution*, Evan Thomas et al. (New York: Atlantic Monthly Press, 1997), p. 220.

19. James A. Barnes and Richard E. Cohen, "Seeking the Center," *NJ* 26, no. 46 (12 November 1994), p. 2624.

20. Richard L. Berke, "Moderate Democrats' Poll Sends the President a Warning," *NYT,* 18 November 1994, sec. A, p. 30.

21. Michael Tomasky, "Why They Won: The Left Lost Touch," *Village Voice* (New York, NY), 22 November 1994, DLCPB, vol. 29, p. 19; Walter Dean Burnham, "Bill Clinton: Riding the Tiger," in *The Election of 1996: Reports and Interpretations*, Gerald Pomper et al. (Chatham, NJ: Chatham House Publishers, 1997), p. 13.

22. Vin Weber, "The Capitol Hill Perspective: A Republican View," in *Back to Gridlock: Governance in the Clinton Years*, James L. Sundquist, ed. (Washington, DC: Brookings Institution, 1995), p. 50.

23. See Cantor and Schor, "Democrats Arise!"; Reed, "Why They Won"; Faux, "A New Conversation."

24. Al From, "Can Clinton Recover? Or Will GOP Prevail?" *USA Today*, 10 November 1994, DLCPB, vol. 29; Peter J. Berger, "Gore's Dilemma," *New Yorker*, 12 November 1994, DLCPB, vol. 29, p. 108; Solomon, "Color Gore," p. 2741; Dick Morris, *Behind the Oval Office: Winning the Presidency in the Nineties* (New York: Random House, 1997), p. 116.

25. Will Marshall, "Clinton and Congress—Democrats, Arise! (Which Way Is Up?); A Mainstream Contract," *NYT,* 5 December 1994, sec. A, p. 19.

26. David Osborne, "Can This President Be Saved?" *Washington Post Magazine*, 8 January 1995, DLCPB, vol. 29, p. 14.

27. Ibid., pp. 15, 31.

28. Al From, interview by author, Washington, DC, 5 March 1999.

29. Will Marshall, et al., *The New Progressive Declaration: A Political Philosophy for the Information Age* (Washington, DC: Progressive Foundation, July 1996).

30. See Fred Siegel and Will Marshall, "Liberalism's Lost Tradition," *New Democrat* 7, no. 5 (September/October 1995), pp. 11–12.

31. "Time to Move On," *New Democrat* 7 (September/October 1995), p. 2; Douglas Ross, interview by author, Washington, DC, 21 September 1995.

32. David Osborne, "A New Federal Compact: Sorting out Washington's Proper Role," in *Mandate for Change*, Will Marshall and Martin Schram, eds. (New York: Berkley Books, 1993), p. 242.

33. Marshall et al., *New Progressive Declaration*, p. 17.

34. John B. Judis, "Beyond the Clinton Presidency," *New Republic*, 16 and 23 September 1996, pp. 24–25.

35. Siegel and Marshall, "Liberalism's Lost Tradition," p. 8.

36. Ibid., p. 11.

37. Marshall et al., *New Progressive Declaration*, p. 21.

38. Will Marshall, "A New Fighting Faith," *New Democrat* 8, no. 5 (September/October 1996), p. 17; Marshall et al., *New Progressive Declaration*, pp. 3–4, 19.

39. "AFL-CIO Struggle Questions Labor, Democrat Identities," *Associated Press*, 25 June 1995, http://www.nando.net:8000/newsroom/ap/ntn/politics/politics570_5.html.

40. "Clinton Reaches out to GOP, Assesses Voters' Message," *CQWR* 52, no. 44 (12 November 1994), p. 3293; Solomon, "Color Gore," p. 2741.

41. Elizabeth Drew, *Showdown: The Struggle between the Gingrich Congress and the Clinton White House* (New York: Simon and Schuster, 1996), p. 20.

42. Ibid.

43. Ibid., p.26.

44. E. J. Dionne, Jr., *They Only Look Dead: Why Progressives Will Dominate the Next Political Era* (New York: Simon and Schuster, 1996), pp. 76, 192.

45. George Hager, "Can GOP Count on Its Own to Back Ambitious Plan?" *CQWR* 52, no. 38 (1 October 1994), p. 2765.

46. Drew, *Showdown*, pp. 45, 265.

47. Morris, *Behind the Oval Office*, p. 80.

48. Drew, *Showdown*, p. 63; Morris, *Behind the Oval Office*, p. 100.

49. Morris, *Behind the Oval Office*, p. 38; Charles O. Jones, "Separating to Govern: The American Way," in *Present Discontents: American Politics in the Very Late Twentieth Century*, Byron E. Shafer, ed. (Chatham, NJ: Chatham House Publishers, 1997), pp. 68–69. This description is from accounts by Morris of what the White House planned it to be, and by Jones of what it appeared to be. It is a testament to Jones's skill as an observer that they are virtually identical.

50. From interview, 5 March 1999; see the account in Drew, *Showdown*, p. 67.

51. Bill Clinton, "Remarks by the President in State of Union Address," 24 January 1995, http://www.allpolitics.com/resources/sotu/full.texts/1995.html.

52. Bill Clinton to Al From, 26 January 1995, AFPP.

53. Drew, *Showdown*, pp. 208–9.

54. Ibid., p. 257.

55. Ibid., p. 265.

56. Ibid., pp. 234–35.

57. Garry Wills, "Does He Believe Anything? (Actually, Yes)," *NYT*, 19 January 1997, sec. 6, p. 35.

58. Joe Klein, foreword to *Back from the Dead: How Clinton Survived the Republican Revolution*, Evan Thomas et al. (New York: Atlantic Monthly Press, 1997), p. xi.

59. Marjorie Random Hershey, "The Congressional Elections," in *The Election of 1996: Reports and Interpretations*, Gerald Pomper et al. (Chatham, NJ: Chatham House Publishers, 1997), p. 213.

60. Anthony Corrado, "Financing the 1996 Elections," in *The Election of 1996: Reports and Interpretations*, Gerald Pomper et al. (Chatham, NJ: Chatham House Publishers, 1997), p. 147. By 1 January 1996, the Democrats had spent $18 million on television advertising in 42 percent of the nation's media markets.

61. Scott Keeter, "Public Opinion and the Election," in *The Election of 1996: Reports and Interpretations*, Gerald Pomper et al. (Chatham, NJ: Chatham House Publishers, 1997), p. 117.

62. "The End of the Beginning," *New Democrat* 8, no. 5 (September/October 1996), p. 11; "Welfare Reform: A Bipartisan Consensus," *New Dem News* 1.16 (19 September 1995).

63. George Stephanopoulos, *All Too Human: A Political Education* (Boston: Little, Brown, 1999), p. 420.

64. Ibid.

65. New York Times News Service, "Prepared Text for President's State of Union Message," 24 January 1996, http://www.nando.net/newsroom/ntn/top/012496/topstory_13598_S1.html.

66. "President Clinton's State of the Union: A New Course for the Democrats," *New Dem News* 2.04 (30 January 1996).

67. "Senate Results: The Winners and Losers," *NJ* 26, no. 46 (12 November 1994), p. 2646; Mary Jacoby, "Aftershocks," *Roll Call,* 9 January 1995, DLCPB, vol. 29, p. 3.

68. Stephen Barr and Ann Devroy, "Clinton Vows Commitment to Centrism," *WP,* 7 December 1994, sec. A, p. 1; Douglas Jehl, "Clinton Accused of Forsaking the Center," *NYT,* 7 December 1994, sec. B, p. 10.

69. McCurdy interview.

70. Jacob Weisberg, "New Democrat Diaspora," *New York,* 12 December 1994, DLCPB, vol. 29, p. 32.

71. Stephanopoulos, *All Too Human,* p. 326; Morton M. Kondracke, "Clinton's Oval Office Tussle with McCurdy," *Roll Call,* 12 December 1994, DLCPB, vol. 29, p. 6; David Remnick, "Curious George," *New Yorker,* 21 and 28 October 1996, p. 166; Barr and Devroy, "Clinton Vows."

72. Jehl, "Clinton Accused."

73. Kondracke, "Clinton's Oval Office Tussle"; Barr and Devroy, "Clinton Vows"; Ann Devroy, "Clinton Revs up, Steers to the Center; DLC Speech Reveals New Attempt to Reach out to Middle Class," *NYT,* 8 December 1994, sec. A, p. 1.

74. Al From, interview by author, Washington, DC, 7 September 1995. Also see Chuck Alston, interview by author, Washington, DC, 1 September, 1995.

75. Will Marshall, interview by author, Washington, DC, 19 September 1995.

76. See Elaine Kamarck's comments in Michael Kramer, "Clinton's Troops Turn Away," *Time,* 10 July 1995, p. 31.

77. Joel Kotkin, "New Democrats Need to Sever Ties to Clinton," *Wall Street Journal,* 7 December 1994, DLCPB, vol. 29; also see Joel Kotkin, "The Third-Wave Party," *WP,* 29 January 1995, sec. C, pp. 1, 4; Joel Kotkin, telephone interview by author, Los Angeles, CA, 22 August 1997.

78. Michael Steinhardt, interview by author, New York, NY, 4 September 1996.

79. Ibid. Other DLC funders supporting the third-party option were Barry Diller and Mitch Hart. See Kramer, "Clinton's Troops," p. 31.

80. Eliza Newlin Carney, "Party Pooper?" *NJ* 28, no. 14 (6 April 1996), p. 770; Ross interview; William Galston, interview by author, College Park, MD, 12 September 1995.

81. Marshall et al., *New Progressive Declaration,* p. 25.

82. Ross interview.

83. Al From and Jack Kemp, "A GI Bill for Workers' Empowerment," *Los Angeles Times,* 20 June 1995, DLCPB, vol. 30; "What Comes Next," *New Dem News* 1.7 (26 September 1995).

84. Evan Thomas et al., *Back from the Dead: How Clinton Survived the Republican Revolution* (New York: Atlantic Monthly Press, 1997), p. 23.

85. Bill Andreson, interview by author, Washington, DC, 28 September 1995.

Andreson is the chief of staff to Senator Joe Lieberman and his main liaison to the DLC.

86. For more on this last view, see Steinhardt interview; Joel Kotkin, "The New Democrat Sellout," *Investor's Business Daily*, 2 May 1996; Kotkin interview.

87. Alston interview.

88. Simon Rosenberg, interview by author, Washington, DC, 1 September 1995.

89. Ibid.

90. Rosenberg interview; Memorandum from Chuck Alston to Interested Parties, "Summary of Annual Event Content, marketing ideas; draft #2," CDF, 11 July 1995, p. 1.

91. Carney, "Party Pooper?" p. 770; "PPI's Efforts to Combat Teen Pregnancy Take Hold in the States," *DLC Update* 2.07 (21 February 1996); "PPI Welfare Policy Model for Reform in the States," *New Dem News* 2.05 (6 February 1996). The DLC changed the name of its e-mail news service from the *New Dem News* to the *DLC Update*.

92. "1995 DLC Annual Conference: Building a New Generation of Democratic Leaders," *New Dem News* 1.9 (11 October 1995).

93. "1995 DLC Annual Conference Wrap-up," *New Dem News* 1.15 (21 November 1995).

94. "The DLC Difference," 8 August 1995, http://www.dlcppi.org/differen.htm; "Elected Officials—Members," 23 August 1995, DLC Database.

95. Mike Tobin, "Dooley Trying to Woo Recruits to His New Democrat Coalition," *States News Service*, 21 November 1996.

96. Jacoby, "Aftershocks"; Eliza Newlin Carney, "A New Coalition for New Democrats," *NJ* 28, no. 48 (30 November 1996), p. 2605.

97. "A PAC of Its Own," *New Democrat* 8, no. 5 (September/October 1996), p. 9; "New Democrats Endorse 20 Candidates for the US Senate and House 'Poised to Lead American into the 21st Century,'" New Democrat Network press release, 25 September 1996.

98. Interview not for attribution.

99. Paul R. Abramson, John H. Aldrich, and David W. Rohde, *Change and Continuity in the 1996 Elections* (Washington, DC: CQ Press, 1998), p. 10.

100. Ibid., p. 154, table 7-5.

101. Ibid., p. 34.

102. Ibid., p. 33.

103. Rhodes Cook, "Clinton's Easy Second-Term Win Riddles GOP Electoral Map," *CQWR* 54, no. 45 (9 November 1996), pp. 3191, 3193.

104. Ibid.; James A. Barnes, "Planting the Seeds," *NJ* 28, no. 45 (9 November 1996), p. 2403; Schneider, "Clinton: The Reason Why," p. 2407, table. Forty-nine percent of moderates backed Clinton in 1992, and 42 percent voted for Dukakis in 1988. See William Schneider, "A Loud Vote for Change," *NJ* 24, no. 45 (7 November 1992), p. 2543, table.

105. Gerald Pomper, "The Presidential Election," in Gerald Pomper et al., *The Election of 1996: Reports and Interpretations* (Chatham, NJ: Chatham House Publishers, 1997), pp. 180–81, table 5.2; Rhodes Cook, "Suburbia: Land of Varied Faces and a Growing Political Force," *CQWR* 55, no. 21 (24 May 1997), p. 1216, table.

106. Abramson et al., *1996 Elections*, p. 124, table 6-3.

107. Ibid., p. 33; Nicholas Lemann, "The New American Consensus," *NYT*, 1 November 1998, sec. 6, p. 42.

108. Mark J. Penn, *Rebuilding the Vital Center: 1996 Post-Election Voter Survey* (Washington, DC: Democratic Leadership Council, 1996), p. 3.

109. Pomper, "The Presidential Election," pp. 182–83.

110. Voters News Service, Presidential Election 1996: National Exit Poll, http://www.allpolitics.com/election/natl.exit.poll/index1.html.

111. "Text of Sunday's Presidential Debate in Hartford," *Associated Press*, 7 October 1996, http://www.nando.net/newsroom/nt/1007debtex.html.

112. Abramson et al., *1996 Elections*, p. 33.

113. Ibid., p. 35.

114. Ruth Marcus, "Democrats Avoiding Dissent over Platform," *WP*, 11 July 1996, sec. A, p. 7.

115. "1996 Democratic National Platform," adopted 27 August 1996, http://www. democrats.org/party/ convention/convplt.html.

116. Ibid.

117. Jeff Faux, interview by author, Washington, DC, 19 July 1996; Robert L. Borosage and Stanley B. Greenberg, "Controversy: Why Did Clinton Win?" *American Prospect* no. 31 (March–April 1997), pp. 17–21.

118. Al From, foreword to *Rebuilding the Vital Center: 1996 Post-Election Voter Survey*, Mark J. Penn (Washington, DC: Democratic Leadership Council, 1996), p. I.

119. See the comments of Amy Isaacs, national director of the ADA, in "Moderate Democrats Say Party Needs to Move to the Center," *NYT News Service*, 21 November 1996, http://www.nando.net/newsroom/politics/112196/politics 5_3963.html.

120. Paul Starobin, "Can the Center Hold?" *NJ* 28, no. 45 (9 November 1996), p. 2392; Corrado, "Financing the 1996 Elections," p. 159.

121. Hershey, "Congressional Elections," p. 227; Richard E. Cohen, "Guessing Game," *NJ* 28, no. 45 (9 November 1996), p. 2421.

122. Hershey, "Congressional Elections," p. 225.

123. "A Second Term for Bill Clinton," *NYT News Service*, 27 October 1996, http://www.nando.net/newsroom/ntn/politics/102796/politics17_205_S1.html; "Why We're for Clinton-Gore," *New Republic*, 11 November 1996, p. 4. See Dionne, *They Only Look Dead*, p. 15; Barnes, "Planting the Seeds," p. 2404.

124. Richard N. Goodwin, "Has Anybody Seen the Democratic Party," *NYT*, 25 August 1996, p. 36; Thomas Goetz, "Passing on the Right: As the Liberal Wing Remains Silent, the Democratic Leadership Council Rises Again," *Village Voice* (NY), 10 September 1996, p. 28; Robert Kuttner, "A Liberal Dunkirk?" *American Prospect* no. 29 (November–December 1996), pp. 6–10.

125. "Many Disillusioned Liberals See No Alternative to Clinton," *NYT News Service*, 27 May 1996, http://www.nando.net/newsroom/ntn/politics/052696/politics4_4491.html.

126. Jerry Hagstrom, "NEA 'Mad and Mobilized,' Official Says," *NJ* 28, no. 35 (31 August 1996), p. 1849.

127. John F. Harris, "Clinton at the Center of Another Cliffhanger," *WP*, 10 November 1997, sec. A, p. 1.

128. Thomas B. Edsall, "Organized Labor Flexes Muscle with Democrats: Unions' Strength on 'Fast Track' Brings Mixed Reactions on Their Alliance with the Party,"

WP, 16 November 1997, sec. A, p. 10. Also see James A. Barnes and Richard E. Cohen, "Divided Democrats," *NJ* 29, no. 46 (15 November 1997), pp. 2304–7.

129. "About NDN," http://www.newdem.org; "Membership List," http://www.newdem.org; Mike Tobin, "Dooley Trying to Woo Recruits to His New Democrat Coalition," *States News Service*, 21 November 1996.

130. "Election '96: A Call for a Third Way," *DLC Update* 2.52 (8 November 1996).

131. John F. Harris, "Clinton Choice for Commerce Post Reflects Renewed Ties with Centrist DLC," *WP*, 19 August 1997, sec. A, p. 11.

132. Dan Balz, "Gore, Gephardt in Duel to Frame Democratic Party's Economic Vision," *WP*, 1 June 1997, sec. A, p. 10.

133. Richard A. Gephardt, "What Unites Us: Our Core Democratic Values," address to the Kennedy School of Government/ARCO Forum, Cambridge, MA, 2 December 1997.

134. Thomas B. Edsall and John E. Yang, "Clinton Loss Illuminates Struggle within Party," *WP*, 11 November 1997, sec. A, p. 1.

135. Al From, "Remarks at the 1997 DLC Annual Conference," Washington, DC, 27 October 1997.

136. "An Appeal to Congress from the States: Give President Clinton the Authority to Negotiate Tough, Fair Trade Agreements," Democratic Leadership Council, ca. July 1997; Edward G. Rendell to Mayor, 28 August 1997, DLCP; Susan Hammer to Fellow Mayor, 28 August 1997, DLCP; Governor Lawton Chiles to Governor Howard Dean, 9 July 1997, DLCP.

137. Barnes and Cohen, "Divided Democrats," p. 2306.

138. Edsall and Yang, "Clinton Loss Illuminates Struggle," sec, A, p. 1.

139. Ibid., sec. A, p. 6. Also see Robert L. Borosage, "The Presidency Vanishes into the Fuzzy 'Center,'" *Los Angeles Times*, 18 December 1996; "Founders: Campaign for America's Future," pamphlet, Campaign for America's Future, Washington, DC, 1996.

Conclusion: Securing a Legacy

1. Jacob Weisberg, "The Governor-President Bill Clinton," *NYT*, 17 January 1999, sec. 6, p. 33.

2. Bill Nichols, "From Moderate Democrats, Liberal Praise for Clinton," *USA Today*, 12 December 1996, sec. A, p. 4.

3. See "No to Impeachment," *DLC Update*, 14 December 1998.

4. Al From, "The Next Politics," speech to the DLC annual conference, Washington, DC, 2 December 1998, http://www.dlcppi.org/speeches/alfrom/98conf_from.htm; Ross K. Baker, "Presidential Legacy Can't Survive Failure of the President," *Los Angeles Times*, 11 September 1998, sec. B, p. 11; David Shribman, "Past Clinton, on Middle Road," *Boston Globe*, 22 September 1998, sec. A, p. 3.

5. Bill Clinton, "Remarks by the President at Democratic Leadership Council Dinner," speech to the DLC annual conference, Washington, DC, 2 December 1998, http://www.dlcppi.org/speeches/98conf_clinton.htm.

6. Ceci Connolly, "New Democrat Dinner Is Record Fundraiser," *WP*, 14 February 1999, sec. A, p. 6.

7. William A. Galston and Elaine C. Kamarck, "Five Realities that Will Shape 21st Century Politics," *Blueprint: Ideas for a New Century* 1 (fall 1998), p. 10.

8. Ibid., pp. 12–19.

9. Al From and Will Marshall, "Building the Next Democratic Majority," *Blueprint: Ideas for a New Century* 1 (fall 1998), pp. 66–70; Al From, "Politics of the 21st Century," speech to the Democratic Party Legislative Ball, Salt Lake City, UT, 13 January 1999, http://www.dlcppi.org/speeches/alfrom/99saltlak.htm; From, "The Next Politics."

10. Al From, "Understanding the Third Way," *New Democrat* 10, no. 5 (September–October 1998), p. 28.

11. Tony Blair, "Money for Modernization: The Comprehensive Spending Review," 14 July 1998, http://www.number-10.gov.uk. Also see Tony Blair, "New Politics for a New Century," *Independent* (UK), 21 September 1998, sec. "Comment," p. 4.

12. Democratic National Committee, "The Democratic Party Platform 1992" (Washington, DC: Democratic National Committee, 1992), p. 3.

13. Thomas B. Edsall, "Clinton and Blair Envision a 'Third Way' International Movement," *WP,* 28 June 1998, sec. A, p. 24.

14. Richard L. Berke, "Clintons Seek to Repair Rifts for Democrats," *NYT,* 19 July 1998, sec. 1, p. 1; James Bennet, "With Nation Glued to Television, Clinton Sticks with His Peers," *NYT,* 22 September 1998, sec. A, p. 17.

15. Tony Judt, "The 'Third Way' Is No Route to Paradise," *NYT,* 27 September 1998, sec. 4, p. 15.

16. William Claiborne, "Democrats Gain Seats in State Legislatures," *WP,* 5 November 1998, sec. A, p. 46; Dan Balz and David S. Broder, "Shaken Republicans Count Losses, Debate Blame," *WP,* 5 November 1998, sec. A, p. 1.

17. "Exit Poll around the Nation," *WP,* 5 November 1998, sec. A, p. 33; "A Look at Voting Patterns of 115 Demographic Groups in House Races," *NYT,* 9 November 1998, sec. A, p. 20.

18. William Schneider, "To the 'New Rich,' Bill's OK," *NJ* 30, no. 46 (14 November 1998), p. 2746.

19. John Maggs, "Wrestling with Failure," *NJ* 30, no. 45 (7 November 1998), p. 2616.

20. "National Exit Poll," *WP,* 4 November 1998, sec. A, p. 32, table.

21. Connolly, "New Democrat Dinner"; "The Center Holds," *DLC Update,* 9 November 1998.

22. William Schneider, "No Modesty, Please, We're the DLC," *NJ* 30, no. 50 (12 December 1998), p. 2962.

23. Balz and Broder, "Shaken Republicans."

24. "Center Holds."

25. John Kerry, "Education Reform," speech to the DLC annual conference, Washington, DC, 2 December 1998, http://www.dlcppi.org/speeches/98conf_jkerry.htm.

26. Bob Kerrey, "Retirement Security," speech to the DLC annual conference, Washington, DC, 2 December 1998, http://www.dlcppi.org/speeches/98conf_bkerrey.htm.

27. Katharine Q. Seelye, "Gore Tries a 2000 Theme: 'Practical Idealism,'" *NYT,* 3 December 1998, sec. A, p. 26; Dan Balz, "The Hum of Democratic Hopefuls,"

WP, 6 December 1998, sec. A, p. 4; Ronald Brownstein, "Four Democrats Offer Their Looks at Life after Clinton-Gore," *Los Angeles Times*, sec. A, p. 5.

28. Carl M. Cannon, "What Hath Bill Wrought?" *NJ* 30, no. 45 (7 November 1998), p. 2622.

29. Weisberg, "The Governor-President Clinton," pp. 32, 34.

30. Schneider, "No Modesty Please."

31. Frank Watkins, interview by author, Washington, DC, 20 December 1996.

32. Al Cross, "National Post Awaits Indiana Democrat," *Courier-Journal* (Louisville, KY), 12 February 1999, sec. A, p. 1.

33. Even harsh critics of the Democrats have noticed this. See Matthew Rees, "The Mini-Clintons," *Weekly Standard* 2, no. 5 (14 October 1996), p. 8. For an example of this phenomenon, see Joe Frolik, "Boyle, Hyatt Take Leaf from Clinton's Book," *Cleveland Plain-Dealer*, 1 May 1994, DLCPB, vol. 28.

34. Richard Morin and David S. Broder, "Poll Shows GOP Leads on Foreign Policy," *WP*, 17 March 1999, sec. A, p. 1.

35. Peter H. Stone, "For Incumbents, a Fistful of Dollars," *NJ* 30, no. 45 (7 November 1998), p. 2680; Balz and Broder, "Shaken Republicans."

36. Connolly, "New Democrat Dinner."

37. Frank Swoboda, "AFL-CIO Plots a Push for Democratic House," *WP*, 18 February 1999, sec. A, p. 1.

38. "Now Appearing in a Station Near You (Maybe)," *NJ* 31, no. 4 (23 January 1999), p. 153; Jackie Calmes, "Clinton's Best Allies Now Are the Liberals He Spurned in the Past," *Wall Street Journal*, 19 October 1998, sec. A, p. 1.

39. Ronald Brownstein, "Clinton's Reversion to Old Tactics Doesn't Bode Well for Democrats," *Los Angeles Times*, 22 March 1999, http://www.latimes.com/HOME/NEWS/ASECTION/t000025585.html; "State of Shame," *Wall Street Journal*, 21 January 1999, sec. A, p. 18; Paul A. Gigot, "Bill Gets on Hillary's Good Side," *Wall Street Journal*, 22 January 1999, sec. A, p. 20.

40. "Convention Delegates: Who They Are and How They Compare on the Issues," *NYT*, 26 August 1996, sec. A, p. 12, table.

41. James Bennet, "In Poll, Ardor for President, Faults and All," *NYT*, 26 August 1996, sec. A, p. 12.

42. Dick Morris, *Behind the Oval Office: Winning the Presidency in the Nineties* (New York: Random House, 1997), p. 319.

43. Steven Waldman, *The Bill: How Legislation Really Becomes Law: A Case Study of the National Service Bill*, rev. ed. (New York: Penguin Books, 1996), p. 117.

44. Amitai Etzioni, "Is Bill Clinton a Communitarian?" *National Civic Review* 82, no. 3 (summer 1993), p. 223.

45. On these different strategies, see Samuel P. Huntingdon, "The Visions of the Democratic Party," *Public Interest* 79 (spring 1985), pp. 69–72.

46. Paul R. Abramson, John H. Ardrich, and David W. Rohde, *Change and Continuity in the 1992 Elections*, rev. ed. (Washington, DC: CQ Press, 1995), pp. 23–24.

47. Office of the Press Secretary, "The Economy under President Clinton" (Washington, DC: White House, 5 March 1999), p. 1.

48. This finding is from a Gallup–*USA Today* poll taken in January 1999. See "Poll Readings," *NJ* 31, no. 4 (23 January 1999), p. 229.

49. David Byrd, "Down, but Not Out," *NJ* 31, no. 3 (16 January 1999), p.116;

"What a Difference Six Years Makes," *NJ* 31, no. 3 (16 January 1999), p. 123, table.

50. See Walter J. Stone, Ronald B. Rapoport, and Alan I. Abramowitz, "The Reagan Revolution and Party Polarization in the 1980s," in *The Parties Respond: Changes in the American Party System*, L. Sandy Maisel, ed. (Boulder, CO: Westview Press, 1990), p. 68.

51. See William Schneider quoted in Frolik, "Boyle, Hyatt Take Leaf from Clinton's Book."

52. Kevin Sack, "GOP Moderates Meet to Frown before an Unflattering Mirror," *NYT*, 15 February 1999, sec. A, p. 1; John Harwood, "GOP's New Campaign Themes Copied from Clinton Playboook," *Pittsburgh Post-Gazette*, 18 October 1998, sec. A, p. 8; E. J. Dionne, Jr., "A Fourth Way," *WP*, 30 March 1999, sec. A, p. 17.

Bibliography

Interviews

Alston, Chuck. Washington, DC, 1 September 1995.
Andreson, Bill. Washington, DC, 28 September 1995.
Andrews, Robert A. Washington, DC, 14 September 1995.
Berry, Mary Frances. Washington, DC, 15 December 1995.
Booth, Heather. Washington, DC, 9 January 1996 (telephone).
Bowser, Alan. Fairfax, VA, 6 September 1995.
Breaux, John. Washington, DC, 11 January 1996.
Dooley, Calvin. Washington, DC, 16 April 1997.
Faux, Jeff. Washington, DC, 19 July 1996.
From, Al. Washington, DC, 7 September 1995, 10 November 1997, and 5 March 1999.
Galston, William. College Park, MD, 12 September 1995.
Greenberg, Stanley B. Washington, DC, 17 April 1996.
Kamarck, Elaine Ciulla. Washington, DC, 11 January 1996.
Kilgore, Ed. Washington, DC, 8 September 1995.
Kirk, Paul G., Jr. Washington, DC, 10 September 1996.
Kiss, James. New York, NY, 21 December 1995.
Kotkin, Joel. Los Angeles, CA, 22 August 1997 (telephone).
Manilow, Lewis. Chicago, IL, 9 January 1996 (telephone).
Marshall, Will. Washington, DC, 19 September 1995.
McCloud, David. Reston, VA, 29 August 1995.
McCurdy, David. McLean, VA, 11 September 1995.
McGregor, Winston. Washington, DC, 13 September 1995.
Metzenbaum, Howard M. Fort Lauderdale, FL, 17 January 1997 (telephone).
Moore, Catherine A. (Kiki). Washington, DC, 30 August 1995.
Moore, Linda. Washington, DC, 7 September 1995 and 22 March 1999 (telephone).
Nider, Steven. Washington, DC, 20 September 1995.
Patterson, Steve. Washington, DC, 11 July 1996.
Reed, Bruce. Washington, DC, 20 September 1995.
Robb, Charles S. Washington, DC, 12 September 1995.
Rosenberg, Simon. Washington, DC, 1 September 1995.

Ross, Douglas. Washington, DC, 21 September 1995.
Shapiro, Robert. Washington, DC, 18 September 1995.
Siegel, Fred. Brooklyn, NY, 29 December 1995.
Silver, Melissa Moss. Washington, DC, 27 September 1995.
Smith, Craig. Washington, DC, 11 September 1995.
Smulyan, Deb. Alexandria, VA, 21 September 1995.
Steinhardt, Michael. New York, NY, 4 September 1996.
Strauss, Robert. Washington, DC, 26 June 1996.
Watkins, Frank. Washington, DC, 20 December 1996.
Wigmore, Barrie. New York, NY, 21 December 1995.
Wright, Betsey. Washington, DC, 28 June 1996.

Archival Sources

Alston, Chuck. Communications Director's Files. Democratic Leadership Council Headquarters, Washington, DC (CDF).
Democratic Leadership Council. *1985–1995: Moving beyond the Left-Right Debate—A Collection of the Greatest New Democrat Speeches.* Democratic Leadership Council, Washington, DC.
———. *1990 Annual Conference of the Democratic Leadership Council: March 23–24, 1990; The Fairmont Hotel, New Orleans, LA.* Democratic Leadership Council, Washington, DC. Transcript.
———. *Official Transcript; Proceedings before the Democratic Leadership Council: 1991 National Convention: "The New Choice in American Politics," May 6–7, 1991.* Democratic Leadership Council, Washington, DC, 1991.
Democratic Leadership Council Papers. Democratic Leadership Council, Washington, DC (DLCP).
Democratic Leadership Council Press Books, vols. 1–30. Democratic Leadership Council, Washington, DC (DLCPB).
Democratic National Committee Papers. National Archives, Washington, DC (DNCP).
From, Al. Personal Papers. Democratic Leadership Council, Washington, DC (AFPP).

Newspapers and Periodicals

American Prospect, 1990–1997
Congressional Quarterly Weekly Report, various years
Mainstream Democrat, 1989–1991
National Journal, various years.
New Democrat, 1991–1999
New Republic, various years

New York Times, 1985–1999
Washington Post, 1985–1999

Books and Articles

Abramowitz, Alan L. "The End of the Democratic Era? 1994 and the Future of Congressional Election Research." *Political Research Quarterly* 48, no. 4 (December 1995), pp. 873–79.

Abramson, Paul R., John H. Aldrich, and David W. Rohde. *Change and Continuity in the 1980 Elections.* Rev. ed. Washington, DC: CQ Press, 1983.

———. *Change and Continuity in the 1988 Elections.* Rev. ed. Washington, DC: CQ Press, 1991.

———. *Change and Continuity in the 1992 Elections.* Rev. ed. Washington, DC: CQ Press, 1995.

———. *Change and Continuity in the 1996 Elections.* Washington, DC: CQ Press, 1998.

Asbell, Bernard. *The Senate Nobody Knows.* Garden City, NY: Doubleday, 1978.

Barone, Michael, and Grant Ujifusa. *The Almanac of American Politics, 1988.* Washington, DC: National Journal, 1988.

Birnbaum, Jeffrey H. *Madhouse: The Private Turmoil of Working for the President.* New York: Random House, 1996.

Blumenthal, Sidney. *The Rise of the Counter-Establishment: From Conservative Ideology to Political Power.* New York: Times Books, 1986.

Brinkley, Alan. *The End of Reform: New Deal Liberalism in Recession and War.* New York: Random House, 1995.

Brock, Clifton. *Americans for Democratic Action: Its Role in National Politics.* Washington, DC: Public Affairs Press, 1962.

Brown, Peter. *Minority Party: Why Democrats Face Defeat in 1992 and Beyond.* Washington, DC: Regnery Gateway, 1991.

Burnham, Walter Dean. *The Current Crisis in American Politics.* New York: Oxford University Press, 1982.

———, ed. *The American Prospect Reader in American Politics.* Chatham, NJ: Chatham House Publishers, 1995.

Burns, James MacGregor. *The Deadlock of Democracy: Four-Party Politics in America.* Englewood Cliffs, NJ: Prentice-Hall, 1963.

Burns, James MacGregor, William Crotty, Lois Lovelace Duke, and Lawrence D. Longley, eds. *The Democrats Must Lead: The Case for a Progressive Democratic Party.* Boulder, CO: Westview Press, 1992.

Campbell, Colin, and Bert A. Rockman, eds. *The Clinton Presidency: Early Appraisals.* Chatham, NJ: Chatham House Publishers, 1996.

Carmines, Edward G., and James A. Stimson. *Issue Evolution: Race and the Transformation of American Politics.* Princeton, NJ: Princeton University Press, 1989.

Carter, Dan T. *The Politics of Rage: George Wallace, the Origins of the New Conservatism, and the Transformation of American Politics.* New York: Simon and Schuster, 1995.

Clark, Peter B., and James Q. Wilson. "Incentive Systems: A Theory of Organizations." *Administrative Science Quarterly* 6 (September 1961), pp. 129–66.

Clinton, Bill, and Al Gore. *Putting People First: How We Can All Change America.* New York: Random House, 1992.

Congressional Quarterly. *Guide to US Elections.* 3rd ed. Washington, DC: CQ, 1994.

Cramer, Richard Ben. *What It Takes: The Way to the White House.* New York: Random House, 1992.

Dalton, Russell J., Scott C. Flanagan, and Paul Allen Beck, eds. *Electoral Change in Advanced Industrial Democracies: Realignment or Dealignment?* Princeton, NJ: Princeton University Press, 1984.

Davies, Gareth. *From Opportunity to Entitlement: The Transformation and Decline of Great Society Liberalism.* Lawrence, KS: University Press of Kansas, 1996.

Davis, James W. *President as Party Leader.* Westport, CT: Greenwood Press, 1992.

Davis, Lanny J. *The Emerging Democratic Majority: Lessons and Legacies from the New Politics.* New York: Stein and Day, 1974.

Dionne, E. J., Jr. *They Only Look Dead: Why Progressives Will Dominate the Next Political Era.* New York: Simon and Schuster, 1996.

———. *Why Americans Hate Politics.* New York: Simon and Schuster, 1992.

Dolbeare, Kenneth M., and Linda J. Metcalf. *American Ideologies Today: Shaping the New Politics of the 1990s.* 2nd ed. New York: McGraw-Hill, 1993.

Dow, Robert M., Jr. "Senator Henry M. Jackson and US-Soviet Detente." D.Phil. diss., University of Oxford, 1995.

Drew, Elizabeth. *Campaign Journal: The Political Events of 1983–1984.* New York: Macmillan, 1985.

———. *On the Edge: The Clinton Presidency.* New York: Simon and Schuster, 1994.

———. *Showdown: The Struggle between the Gingrich Congress and the Clinton White House.* New York: Simon and Schuster, 1996.

Dutton, Frederick G. *Changing Sources of Power: American Politics in the 1970's.* New York: McGraw-Hill, 1971.

Edsall, Thomas Byrne, with Mary D. Edsall. *Chain Reaction: The Impact of Race, Rights, and Taxes on American Politics.* New York: W. W. Norton, 1991.

Ehrenhalt, Alan, ed. *Politics in America: The 100th Congress.* Washington, DC: CQ Press, 1987.

———. *The United States of Ambition: Politicians, Power, and the Pursuit of Office.* New York: Random House, 1991.

Ehrman, John. *The Rise of Neoconservatism: Intellectuals and Foreign Affairs 1945–1994.* New Haven, CT: Yale University Press, 1995.

Epstein, Leon D. *Political Parties in the American Mold.* Madison: University of Wisconsin Press, 1986.

Etzioni, Amitai. "Is Bill Clinton a Communitarian?" *National Civic Review* 82, no. 3 (summer 1993), pp. 221–25.

Faux, Jeff. "Industrial Policy." *Dissent* (fall 1993), pp. 467–74.

———. *The Party's Not Over: A New Vision for the Democrats.* New York: Basic Books, 1996.

Freeman, Jo. "The Political Culture of the Democratic and Republican Parties." *Political Science Quarterly* 101, no. 3 (1986), pp. 327–56.

Galston, William, and Elaine Ciulla Kamarck. "The Politics of Evasion: Democrats and the Presidency." Washington, DC: Progressive Policy Institute, September 1989.

Genovese, Eugene D. *The Southern Tradition: The Achievement and Limitations of an American Conservatism.* Cambridge, MA: Harvard University Press, 1994.

Gillon, Steven M. *The Democrats' Dilemma: Walter F. Mondale and the Liberal Legacy.* New York: Columbia University Press, 1992.

Goldman, Peter, and Tony Fuller. *The Quest for the Presidency, 1984.* New York: Bantam Books, 1985.

Green, John C., and Daniel M. Shea, eds. *The State of the Parties: The Changing Role of Contemporary American Politics.* 2nd ed. Lanham, MD: Rowan and Littlefield, 1996.

Greenberg, Stanley B. *Middle Class Dreams: The Politics and Power of the New American Majority.* New York: Random House, 1995.

Greenberg, Stanley B., Al From, and Will Marshall. *The Road to Realignment: The Democrats and the Perot Voters.* Washington, DC: Democratic Leadership Council, July 1993.

Hadley, Arthur T. *The Invisible Primary.* Englewood Cliffs, NJ: Prentice-Hall, 1976.

Hadley, Charles D., and Harold W. Stanley. "Super Tuesday 1988: Regional Results and National Implications." *Publius: The Journal of Federalism* 19, no. 3 (summer 1989), pp. 19–37.

Hale, Jon F. "A Different Kind of Democrat: Bill Clinton, the DLC, and the Construction of a New Party Identity." Paper presented at the annual meeting of the American Political Science Association, Washington, DC, September 1993.

———. "The Making of the New Democrats." *Political Science Quarterly* 110, no. 2 (1995), pp. 207–32.

Hamby, Alonzo L. *Liberalism and Its Challengers: From FDR to Bush.* 2nd ed. Oxford: Oxford University Press, 1992.

Heclo, Hugh. "General Welfare and Two American Political Traditions." *Political Science Quarterly* 101, no. 2 (1986), pp. 179–96.

Himmelstein, Jerome L. *To the Right: The Transformation of American Conservatism.* Berkeley: University of California Press, 1990.

Hodgson, Godfrey. *The World Turned Right Side Up: A History of the Conservative Ascendancy in America.* Boston: Houghton Mifflin, 1996.

Hunter, James Davison, and Os Guiness, eds. *Articles of Faith, Articles of Peace: The Religious Liberty Clauses and the American Public Philosophy.* Washington, DC: Brookings Institution, 1990.

Huntingdon, Samuel P. "The Visions of the Democratic Party." *Public Interest* 79 (spring 1985), pp. 63–78.

Inglehart, Ronald. *The Silent Revolution: Changing Values and Political Styles among Western Publics.* Princeton, NJ: Princeton University Press, 1977.

Jacobson, Gary C. *The Electoral Origins of Divided Government: Competition in US House Elections, 1946–1988.* Boulder, CO: Westview Press, 1990.

Kalb, Marvin, and Hendrik Hertzberg, eds. *Candidates '88.* Dover, MA: Auburn House, 1988.

Kamarck, Elaine Ciulla, ed. "The Future of the Republican Presidential Coalition: A Symposium." Washington, DC: Progressive Policy Institute, February 1990.

Katz, Michael B. *The Undeserving Poor: From the War on Poverty to the War on Welfare.* New York: Pantheon Books, 1989.

Kessel, John. *Presidential Campaign Politics.* 4th ed. Pacific Grove, CA: Brooks/Cole, 1992.

Key, V. O., Jr., "A Theory of Critical Elections." *Journal of Politics* 17 (February 1955), pp. 3–18.

King, Anthony S., ed. *The New American Political System.* 1st ed. Washington, DC: American Enterprise Institute for Public Policy Research, 1978.

Kingdon, John W. *Agendas, Alternatives, and Public Policies.* Boston: Little, Brown, 1984.

Kleppner, Paul, et al., eds. *The Evolution of American Electoral Systems.* Westport, CT: Greenwood Press, 1981.

Klinkner, Philip A. *The Losing Parties: Out-Party National Committees 1956–1993.* New Haven, CT: Yale University Press, 1994.

———. *Midterm: The Elections of 1994 in Context.* Boulder, CO: Westview Press, 1996.

Kuttner, Robert. *The Life of the Party: Democratic Prospects in 1988 and Beyond.* New York: Viking, 1987.

Ladd, Everett Carll, Jr. "The 1992 Vote for President Clinton: Another Brittle Mandate?" *Political Science Quarterly* 108, no. 1 (1993), pp. 1–28.

Ladd, Everett Carll, Jr., with Charles D. Hadley. *Transformations of the American Party System: Political Coalitions from the New Deal to the 1970's.* 2nd ed. New York: W. W. Norton, 1978.

Lawrence, David G. "Ideological Extremity, Issue Distance, and Voter Defection." *Political Research Quarterly* 47, no. 2 (June 1994), pp. 397–422.

Lawson, Kay, ed. *How Political Parties Work: Perspectives from Within.* Westport, CT: Praeger, 1994.

Lawson, Kay, and Peter H. Merkl, eds. *When Parties Fail: Emerging Alternative Organizations.* Princeton, NJ: Princeton University Press, 1988.

Lipset, Seymour Martin. *American Exceptionalism: A Double-Edged Sword.* New York: W. W. Norton, 1996.

———, ed. *Party Coalitions in the 1980's.* San Francisco: Institute for Contemporary Studies, 1981.

———. "Political Renewal on the Left: A Comparative Perspective." Washington, DC: Progressive Policy Institute, January 1990. Pamphlet.

Lowi, Theodore. "Toward Functionalism in Political Science: The Case of Innovation in Party Systems." *American Political Science Review* 57 (September 1963), pp. 570–83.

Lubell, Samuel. *The Future of American Politics.* New York: Harper and Brothers, 1951.

Lunch, William M. *The Nationalization of American Politics.* Berkeley: University of California Press, 1987.

Maclean, Douglas, and Claudia Mills, eds. *Liberalism Reconsidered.* Totowa, NJ: Rowman and Allanheld, 1983.

Maisel, L. Sandy, ed. *The Parties Respond: Changes in the American Party System.* Boulder, CO: Westview Press, 1990.

Malbin, Michael J. *Unelected Representatives: Congressional Staff and the Future of Representative Government.* New York: Basic Books, 1980.

Maraniss, David. *First in His Class: The Biography of Bill Clinton.* New York: Simon and Schuster, 1995.

Marshall, Will, and Martin Schram, eds. *Mandate for Change.* New York: Berkley Books, 1993.

Marshall, Will, et al. *The New Progressive Declaration: A Political Philosophy for the Information Age.* Washington, DC: Progressive Foundation, July 1996.

Mayer, William G. *The Changing American Mind: How and Why American Public Opinion Changed between 1960 and 1988.* Ann Arbor: University of Michigan Press, 1992.

———. *The Divided Democrats: Ideological Unity, Party Reform, and Presidential Elections.* Boulder, CO: Westview Press, 1996.

———, ed. *In Pursuit of the White House: How We Choose Our Presidential Nominees.* Chatham, NJ: Chatham House Publishers, 1996.

McKay, David. *Domestic Policy and Ideology: Presidents and the American State, 1964–1987.* Cambridge: Cambridge University Press, 1989.

Meyerson, Harold. "Conflicted President, Undefined Presidency." *Dissent* (fall 1993), pp. 439–46.

Miller, James. *Democracy Is in the Streets: From Port Huron to the Siege of Chicago.* New York: Simon and Schuster, 1987.

Miller, Warren E., and M. Kent Jennings. *Parties in Transition: A Longitudinal Study of Party Elites and Party Supporters.* New York: Russell Sage Foundation, 1986.

Miller, Warren E., and National Election Studies. *NES Guide to Public Opinion and Electoral Behavior, 1952–1994.* Ann Arbor: University of Michigan, Center for Political Studies, 1994. http://www.umich.edu/~nes/resources/nesguide.

Miller, Warren E., and Santa A. Traugott. *American National Election Studies Data Sourcebook, 1952–1986.* Cambridge, MA: Harvard University Press, 1989.

Moore, Jonathan, ed. *The Campaign for President: 1980 in Retrospect.* Cambridge, MA: Ballinger, 1981.

Morehead, Laurence W., Robert P. Steed, and Tod A. Baker, eds. *The 1988 Presidential Election in the South: Continuity amidst Change in Southern Party Politics.* New York: Praeger, 1991.

Morris, Dick. *Behind the Oval Office: Winning the Presidency in the Nineties.* New York: Random House, 1997.

Moynihan, Daniel P. "The Politics of Stability." *New Leader* 20 (9 October 1967), pp. 6–10.

National House Democratic Caucus. *Renewing America's Promise: A Democratic Blueprint for Our Nation's Future.* Washington, DC: 1984.

Nelson, Michael, ed. *The Elections of 1984.* Washington, DC: CQ Press, 1985.

———. *The Elections of 1988.* Washington, DC: CQ Press, 1989.

———. *The Elections of 1992.* Washington, DC: CQ Press, 1993.

———. *The Elections of 1996.* Washington, DC: CQ Press, 1997.

———. *Historic Documents on Presidential Elections, 1787–1988.* Washington, DC: Congressional Quarterly, 1991.

Norrander, Barbara. *Super Tuesday: Regional Politics and Presidential Primaries.* Lexington: University Press of Kentucky, 1992.

Oakley, Meredith L. *On the Make: The Rise of Bill Clinton.* Washington, DC: Regnery Publishing, 1994.

Peele, Gillian. *Revival and Reaction: The Right in Contemporary America.* Oxford: Clarendon Press, 1984.

Penn, Mark J. *Rebuilding the Vital Center: 1996 Post-Election Survey.* Washington, DC: Democratic Leadership Council, 1996.

Phillips, Kevin P. *The Emerging Republican Majority.* Garden City, NY: Doubleday, 1969.

———. *Post-Conservative America: People, Politics and Ideology in a Time of Crisis.* New York: Random House, 1982.

Piven, Frances Fox, and Richard A. Cloward. *Why Americans Don't Vote.* New York: Pantheon Books, 1988.

Polsby, Nelson W. *Political Innovation in America: The Politics of Policy Initiation.* New Haven, CT: Yale University Press, 1984.

Pomper, Gerald M., et al. *The Election of 1980: Reports and Interpretations.* Chatham, NJ: Chatham House Publishers, 1981.

———. *The Election of 1984: Reports and Interpretations.* Chatham, NJ: Chatham House Publishers, 1985.

———. *The Election of 1988: Reports and Interpretations.* Chatham, NJ: Chatham House Publishers, 1989.

———. *The Election of 1992: Reports and Interpretations.* Chatham, NJ: Chatham House Publishers, 1993.

———. *The Election of 1996: Reports and Interpretations.* Chatham, NJ: Chatham House Publishers, 1997.

Price, David E. *Bringing Back the Parties.* Washington, DC: CQ Press, 1984.

Radosh, Ronald. *Divided They Fell: The Demise of the Democratic Party, 1964–1996.* New York: Free Press, 1996.

Rae, Nicol C. *The Decline and Fall of the Liberal Republicans: From 1952 to the Present.* Oxford: Oxford University Press, 1989.

———. *Southern Democrats.* Oxford: Oxford University Press, 1994.

Ranney, Austin, ed. *The American Elections of 1980.* Washington, DC: American Enterprise Institute, 1981.

———. *The American Elections of 1984.* Washington, DC: American Enterprise Institute, 1985.

Reich, Robert B., ed. *The Power of Public Ideas.* Cambridge, MA: Harvard University Press, 1990.

Ricci, David M. *The Transformation of American Politics: The New Washington and the Rise of Think Tanks.* New Haven, CT: Yale University Press, 1993.

Robinson, Edgar Eugene. *They Voted for Roosevelt: The Presidential Vote, 1932–1944.* New York: Octagon Books, 1970.

Rothenberg, Randall. "The Neoliberal Club." *Esquire* (February 1982), pp. 37–46.

———. *The Neoliberals: Creating the New American Politics.* New York: Simon and Schuster, 1984.

Runkel, David R., ed. *Campaign for President: The Managers Look at 1988.* Dover, MA: Auburn House, 1989.

Salamon, Lester M., and Michael S. Lund, eds. *The Reagan Presidency and the Governing of America.* Washington, DC: Urban Institute Press, 1984.

Salmore, Barbara G., and Stephen A. Salmore. *Candidates, Parties, and Campaigns: Electoral Politics in America.* 2nd ed. Washington, DC: CQ Press, 1989.

Sandel, Michael J. *Democracy's Discontent: America in Search of a Public Philosophy.* Cambridge, MA: Harvard University Press, 1996.

Scammon, Richard M., and Alice V. McGillivray. *America Votes 14: A Handbook of Contemporary American Election Statistics.* Washington, DC: Congressional Quarterly, 1981.

———. *America Votes 15: A Handbook of Contemporary American Election Statistics.* Washington, DC: Congressional Quarterly, 1983.

Scammon, Richard M., and Ben J. Wattenberg. *The Real Majority.* New York: Coward-McCann, 1970.

Schlesinger, Arthur M., Jr. *The Vital Center: The Politics of Freedom.* London: Andre Deutsch, Limited, 1970.

Schlesinger, Arthur M., Jr., and Fred Israel, eds. *History of American Presidential Elections, 1789–1968.* Vol. 4. New York: McGraw-Hill, 1971.

Schneider, William. "A Consumer's Guide to Democrats in '88." *Atlantic* (April 1987), pp. 37–59.

———. "JFK's Children: The Class of '74." *Atlantic* (March 1989), pp. 35–58.

———. "The Suburban Century Begins." *Atlantic* (July 1992), pp. 33–44.

Shafer, Byron E. "Anti-Party Politics." *Public Interest* 63 (spring 1981), pp. 95–111.

———. *Bifurcated Politics: Evolution and Reform in the National Party Convention.* Cambridge, MA: Harvard University Press, 1988.

———. *Quiet Revolution: The Struggle for the Democratic Party and the Shaping of Post-Reform Politics.* New York: Russell Sage Foundation, 1983.

————, ed. *Present Discontents: American Politics in the Very Late Twenti-eth Century*. Chatham, NJ: Chatham House Publishers, 1997.

————. "Republicans and Democrats as Social Types: Or, Notes toward an Ethnography of the Political Parties." *Journal of American Studies* 20, no. 3 (1986), pp. 341–54.

Shafer, Byron E., and William J. M. Claggett. *The Two Majorities: The Issue Context of American Politics*. Baltimore: Johns Hopkins University Press, 1995.

Siegel, Fred. *The Future Once Happened Here: New York, DC, LA, and the Fate of America's Big Cities*. New York: Free Press, 1997.

Silbey, Joel H. *The American Political Nation, 1838–1893*. Stanford, CA: Stanford University Press, 1991.

Smith, James Allen. *The Idea Brokers: Think Tanks and the Rise of the New Policy Elite*. New York: Free Press, 1991.

Smith, Larry David. "The Party Platforms as Institutional Discourse: The Democrats and Republicans of 1988." *Presidential Studies Quarterly* 22, no. 3 (summer 1992), pp. 531–41.

Sorauf, Frank J. *Money in American Elections*. Glenview, IL: Scott, Foresman and Company, 1988.

Stanley, Harold W., and Charles D. Hadley. "The Southern Presidential Primary: Regional Intentions with National Implications." *Publius: The Journal of Federalism* 17, no. 3 (summer 1987), pp. 83–100.

Steinfels, Peter. *The Neoconservatives: The Men Who Are Changing America's Politics*. New York: Simon and Schuster, 1979.

Stephanopoulos, George. *All Too Human: A Political Education*. Boston: Little, Brown, 1999.

Stoesz, David. *Small Change: Domestic Policy under the Clinton Presidency*. White Plains, NY: Longman Publishers, 1996.

Sundquist, James L., ed. *Beyond Gridlock? Prospects for Governance in the Clinton Years—and After*. Washington, DC: Brookings Institution, 1993.

————. *Back to Gridlock: Governance in the Clinton Years*. Washington, DC: Brookings Institution, 1995.

————. *Dynamics of the Party System: Alignment and Realignment of Political Parties in the United States*. Rev. ed. Washington, DC: Brookings Institution, 1983.

Thomas, Evan, et al. *Back from the Dead: How Clinton Survived the Republican Revolution*. New York: Atlantic Monthly Press, 1997.

Thompson, Kenneth W. *The President and the Public Philosophy*. Baton Rouge: Louisiana State University Press, 1981.

U.S. House Democratic Caucus. Caucus Committee on Party Effectiveness. *Rebuilding the Road to Opportunity: A Democratic Direction for the 1980s*. 93rd Cong., 2nd sess., 1982.

Waldman, Steven. *The Bill: How Legislation Really Becomes Law: A Case Study of the National Service Bill*. Rev. ed. New York: Penguin Books, 1995.

Ware, Alan. *The Breakdown of Democratic Party Organization, 1940–1980.* Oxford: Clarendon Press, 1985.

———. *Political Parties and Party Systems.* Oxford: Oxford University Press, 1996.

Wattenberg, Martin P. *The Decline of American Political Parties: 1952–1988.* Enlarged ed. Cambridge, MA: Harvard University Press, 1990.

———. *The Rise of Candidate-Centered Politics: Presidential Elections of the 1980's.* Cambridge, MA: Harvard University Press, 1991.

Weaver, R. Kent. "The Changing World of Think Tanks." *PS: Political Science and Politics* 22, no. 3 (September 1989), pp. 563–78.

Weisberg, Herbert, ed. *Democracy's Feast: Elections in America.* Chatham, NJ: Chatham House Publishers, 1995.

Weisberg, Jacob. *In Defense of Government: The Fall and Rise of Public Trust.* New York: Scribner, 1996.

Weiss, Carol H., ed. *Organizations for Policy Analysis: Helping Government Think.* Newbury Park, CA: Sage Publications, 1992.

White, John K., and John C. Green, eds. *The Politics of Ideas: Intellectual Challenges to the Party after 1992.* Lanham, MD: Rowman and Littlefield, 1995.

Wildavsky, Aaron. "At Once Too Strong and Too Weak: President Clinton and the Dilemma of Egalitarian Leadership." *Presidential Studies Quarterly* 23, no. 3 (summer 1993), pp. 437–44.

Wilson, James Q. *The Amateur Democrat: Club Politics in Three Cities.* Chicago: University of Chicago Press, 1962.

———. "American Politics Then and Now." *Commentary* 67, no. 2 (February 1979), pp. 39–46.

———. *The 1980 Election.* Lexington, MA: D. C. Heath and Company, 1981.

Winograd, Morley, and Dudley Buffa. *Taking Control: Politics in the Information Age.* New York: Henry Holt and Company, 1996.

Woodward, Bob. *The Agenda: Inside the Clinton White House.* New York: Simon and Schuster, 1994.

Index